The TRUE
ADVENTURES of the
ROLLING STONES

October 21, 1969

Mr. Stanley Booth
745 Hawthorne Street
Memphis, Tennessee

Dear Stanley:

This letter assures you of the Rolling Stones' full and exclusive
cooperation in putting together a book about the Stones for publication.

Yours faithfully,

Mick Jagger

Keith Richard

Charlie Watts

Bill Wyman

Mick Taylor

The TRUE
ADVENTURES of the
ROLLING
STONES

ANNIVERSARY 30th EDITION

Stanley Booth

CHICAGO
REVIEW
PRESS

An A Cappella Book

The Library of Congress has cataloged the previous edition as follows:
Booth, Stanley, 1942–
   The true adventures of the Rolling Stones / Stanley Booth.
      p. cm.
   Originally published: 1st Vintage books ed. New York : Vintage Books, 1985, c1984.
   ISBN 1-55652-400-5
      1. Rolling Stones. 2. Rock musicians—Biography. I. Title.

ML421.R64 B66 2000
782.42166'092'2—dc21
[B]
                              99-048688

Thanks to the Colonel Bobby Ray Watson Archives for the words of Joe Callicott, to Stanley Kesler and Roland Janes for deciphering the conversation at Sun Recording Studio, and to David Maysles for his technical assistance.

Cover design: Matthew Simmons
Cover photo: Photograph by Ethan Russell. Copyright © Ethan Russell. All rights reserved.

This edition of The True Adventures of the Rolling Stones is an unabridged republication, with minor emendations, a new foreword, and a new afterword, of the edition published as Dance with the Devil in New York in 1984. It is published by arrangement with the author.

FOR

ALL THE

CHILDREN

We want the heats of the orgy and not its murder, the warmth of pleasure without the grip of pain, and so the future threatens a nightmare, and we continue to waste ourselves . . . we are the cowards who must defend courage, sex, consciousness, the beauty of the body, the search for love, and the capture of what may be, after all, an heroic destiny.

NORMAN MAILER: *Advertisements for Myself*

FOREWORD

by Greil Marcus

At the end of this book, in an afterword written sixteen years after *The True Adventures of the Rolling Stones* was first published, which was fifteen years after the events that the book—an insider's journal of the Rolling Stones' American tour in the fall of 1969, interlaced with alternating chapters re-creating the band's history from the start to the death of founding member Brian Jones just months before the tour began—recounts, Stanley Booth names his "stylistic heroes." First there's Jack Kerouac, then Vladimir Nabokov, Evelyn Waugh, "and—most of all—Raymond Chandler. I tried," Booth writes, "to make every sentence one that could be spoken by Chandler's detective narrator Philip Marlowe."

He comes close enough. "He was the only person I had ever seen who could make falling asleep pretentious" is a line Chandler would have copied in his notebook for further use. Sometimes, as when following a typically gooey first-acid-trip description with perhaps the only truly uncanny acid-trip description in print—uncanny because it is just a hair away from ordinary life—Booth steps back in literary time from Chandler, and forward from him, so that you hear echoes of both Dashiell Hammett and Ross Macdonald. Booth and a friend have found their way to an all-night café, and at the café "there was a cop, all dark blue, black leather, and menacing devices. He was sitting at a table with a cup of coffee, talking to someone on a walkie-talkie. There had been a burglary at a warehouse in a black neighborhood. The burglar was a black teenage girl. The cop said he'd be right there, his tone loaded with sex and sadism. The only way he could be intimate with a black girl was to punish her. After he left, the place still reeked with his lust, if you had taken acid."

Booth gets closest to Chandler when you can't feel him trying to, when he seems completely caught up in his story, as in a passage about the Rolling Stones' manager in 1969, the late Allen Klein, "who scared Phil Spector, a man with so many bodyguards and fences and so much bullet-proof glass that he ridiculed the Stones for getting arrested; even Spector seemed afraid of this pudgy glum-faced accountant in his bulging yellow T-shirt. But what scared me most was the knowledge that whatever they were up to, I had to know about it. No matter if Klein took my book, took my money, had me killed, I had to stick around and see what happened." *Down these mean streets a man must go who is not himself mean*, though Booth can be mean enough.

There's more to the connection than style—or maybe the question of what constitutes a style, what goes into it, what stands behind it, encompasses more than we tend to think it does. In one of most damning, tough-minded moments in *The True Adventures of the Rolling Stones*, again from the afterword, Booth draws down on the weight of social history that hangs in the air over each show chronicled—from the first night of the tour in Fort Collins, Colorado, on November 7 to the last day at Altamont on December 6—over each song playing on the radio and then in Booth's pages. This is the kind of history that lets Booth write that "in 1969, few people at Madison Square Garden on Thanksgiving Day thought that what the Rolling Stones were doing was a performance. . . . [They] had, most of them, lived through a time of cold war, hot war, race riots, student riots, police riots, assassinations, rapes, murders, trials, waking nightmares. But Keith, Mick, Charlie, Bill, and the new guitar player were impersonating the Rolling Stones, and the audience were impersonating their audience. . . . Dancing under the circumstances . . . seemed to have a transcendent value. Many people thought then that dancing and music could have a major role in changing the structure of society. They may have been naive, but they were much more interesting than the sensible people who came along later." It's a sentiment Booth translates in 2000, in his afterword, as "children starve, governments kill prisoners, wars continue to rage, trillions of dollars are wasted on insane self-endangering weapons. Do I think music can stop these things? No. Do I think it should try? Perhaps not directly. But consider this line that I used to hear Furry Lewis sing: 'My ole mistress promised me, when she died, she'd set me free; she lived so long till her head got bald, and God had to kill her with a white oak maul.' Can't you hear the protest in that? . . . There is at the heart of this music a deep strain of mysterious insurrection, and the music dies without it." Booth's damning words are these: "In the sixties we believed in a myth—that music had the power to change people's lives. Today we believe in a myth—that music is just entertainment"—or that style is just style or that detective stories are just detective stories.

In 2011, eleven years after Booth honored Raymond Chandler in his afterword to this book, the British novelist Jenny Diski, writing of the time when she, too, believed in the myth Booth once believed in, described Philip Marlowe and Hammett's Sam Spade as figures of a later era, regardless of their provenance in the Twenties or Thirties or Forties: "the hard men with soft, democratic centers, American Romantics tinged with the Founding Fathers and Melville's melancholic sense of humanity." They were men "dragged, flinching with distaste, into the dirty underworld by good and bad men and women, and by their doomed vocation to set the world to rights. Private eyes, but really public defenders. . . . Men who behaved as if there was a point in trying to right wrongs, even if they knew the world better than that." Looking back on nights in theaters watching Humphrey Bogart in John Huston's film of Hammett's *The Maltese Falcon* or in Howard Hawks's film of Chandler's *The Big Sleep*, to Diski the legacy of style was clear enough: "And maybe, later on, it was Marlowe and Spade who gave us the courage and foolheadedness to take to the streets." They were, she said, "part of the equation."

It's a notion that, for me anyway, might have seemed far-fetched, even contrived, without Booth's affirmation that every time he stood on the stage behind one of Keith Richards's amps as the Rolling Stones played "Gimme Shelter" or "Street Fighting Man," Philip Marlowe was standing behind him. What Diski reveals is how big, and how deep, Booth's ambitions really were when he said he didn't want a sentence in his book that Marlowe couldn't speak: not only sentences like "He was the only person I had ever seen who could make falling asleep pretentious," but sentences like "There is at the heart of this music a deep strain of mysterious insurrection, and the music dies without it."

Fervor drives *The True Adventures of the Rolling Stones*, the fervor of, among other things, trying to locate the heart of that insurrection—what Albert Camus, in *The Rebel*, describing a prisoner in Soviet Siberia who had constructed a silent piano with wooden keys, called "that harmonious insurrection"—to locate it, name it, describe it, before it slips away. "You had to be there," Booth writes of a show at the L.A. Forum in Los Angeles. He doesn't mean that he can't call up what went on that night; he can. He means that if you were alive on that night, or even if you weren't born yet, if you had had the choice to go, you couldn't, as a serious, thinking, breathing person, pass it up. "You had to be there"—and because you weren't, Booth is saying, it's my obligation to put you there, onstage, backstage, in the crowd, in the sound as it happened.

Thanks to long, seamlessly integrated stories told by Keith Richards, Charlie Watts, the late Ian Stewart (an original Rolling Stone, excluded because of his looks, who became the band's roadie and offstage piano player), and Shirley Arnold (the fan who became the manager of the fan club), the sense of Booth's having been present is almost as strong as in the chapters from the fall of 1969, when he was. "I'll never forget Bo's face when Brian played some of those Elmore James things," Stewart tells Booth of a backstage palaver in the United Kingdom in 1963. Booth instantly steps into Stewart's shoes: "If the Stones were astonished to be playing with Bo Diddley, how must Bo Diddley . . . have felt, seeing a blond English cherub with a bruised and swollen eye, playing guitar just like Elmore James, who had learned from Robert Johnson, who had learned at the crossroads from the Devil himself." But Booth's presence, which is to say your presence, is so strong for certain nights in 1969 that you almost don't want to be there, for fear that the music as Booth renders it won't live up to the hopes invested in it—invested in it by the musicians, the audience, the writer, and, catching the fever, the reader. And there are the incidents from Altamont, the disastrous free concert that ended both the band's tour and the decade the tour summed up, that are so vivid, so poetically horrible—"a tall white boy with a black cloud of electric hair was dancing, shaking, infuriating the Angels by having too good a time. . . . [An] Angel pushed him and another Angel started laying into the crowd with a pool cue and then a number of Angels were grabbing people, hitting and kicking, the crowd falling back from the fury with fantastic speed, the dancer running away from the stage . . . the Angels catching him from behind, the heavy end of a pool cue in one long arc crashing into the side of his head, felling him like a sapling so that he lay straight and didn't move and I thought, My God, they've killed him"— that truly make you wish you weren't there. I was, as it happened, and as I read Booth's pages again, now forty-two years after the fact, I felt every terror, every horror, every repeating shock, as if it wasn't over yet.

It isn't; that's the burden of Booth writing of the time that has passed between a phone call in 1969 and the present day, "We said goodbye, a thunderhead of music, drugs, money and anguish starting to gather out in the future, as Thanksgiving continued in Great Neck"; of writing "how ready was any of us to live in the real world, a world that would each year become more like Altamont?" Those retrospective prophecies say why it took him fifteen years to write his book and why, today, it can still take you for a walk down the street, make you laugh, fill you with delight, and, as you step off the curb, turn your knees to water.

ACKNOWLEDGMENTS

Without the love and sustenance of my mother and father and the inspiration of my daughter, this book would not exist. The efforts of Robert Green also made it possible. Any good qualities of the writing are due in great measure to my teachers, Walter Smith and Helen White. During the years of work on this book I was assisted in various ways by Paul Bomarito, Gerald Wexler, Arthur Kretchmer, Jann Wenner, Aubrey Guy, Edward Blaine, Charles Baker, James Allison, Lucius Burch, Irvin Salky, Saul Belz, George Nichopoulos, Joseph Battaile, the late John Dwyer, the late Colonel Thomas Thrash, and the late George Campbell. Peter Guralnick and Gary Fisketjon have given me help beyond the call of sanity. Keith Richards, Bill Wyman, Ian Stewart, James Dickinson, Helen Spittall, Shirley Arnold, Georgia Bergman, the late Alexis Horner, and the late Leslie Perrin have the writer's permanent appreciation. Many people encouraged the writing of this book, and a few tried to stop it, making it inevitable. For the book's contents, only the writer is to blame.

CONTENTS

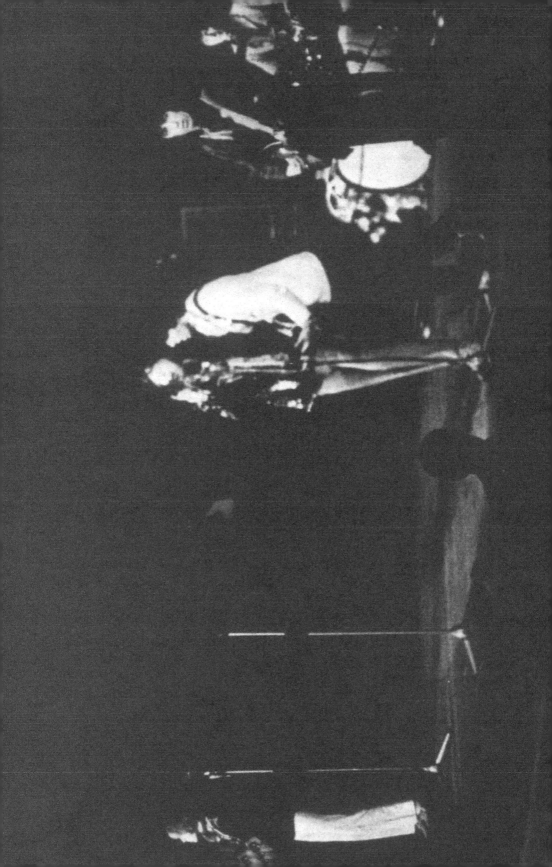

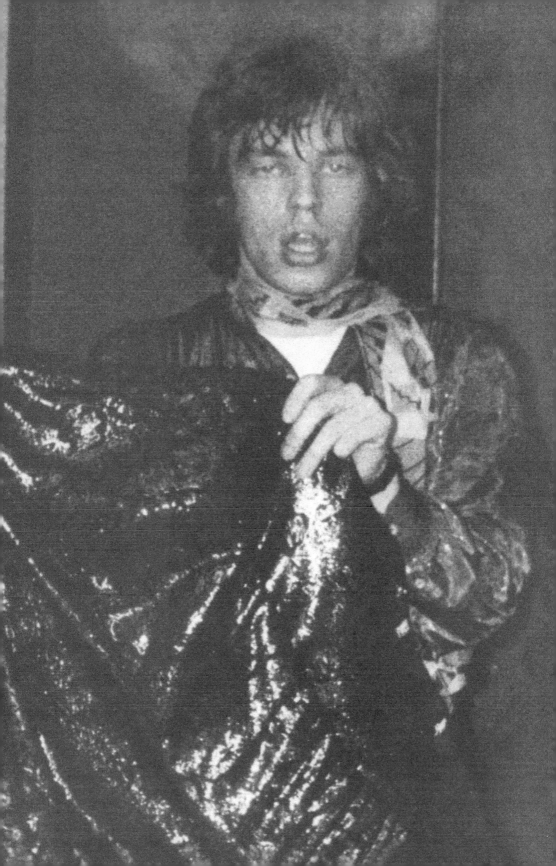

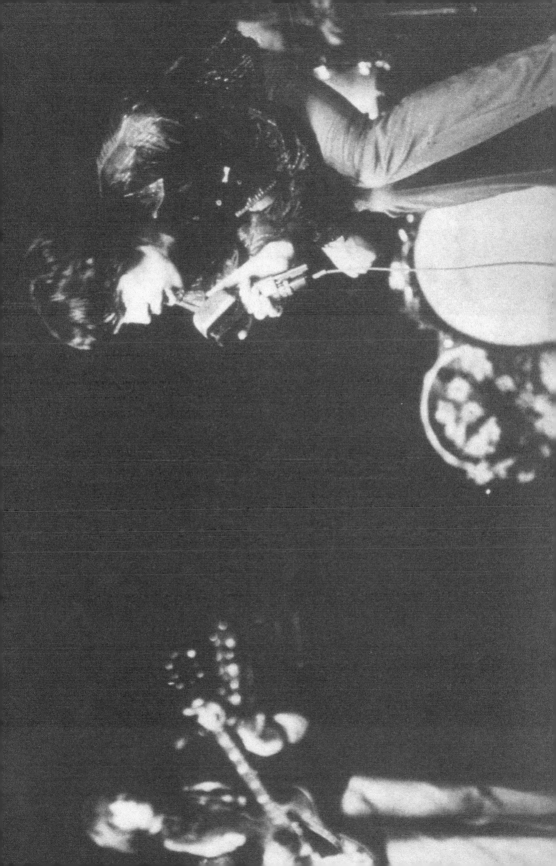

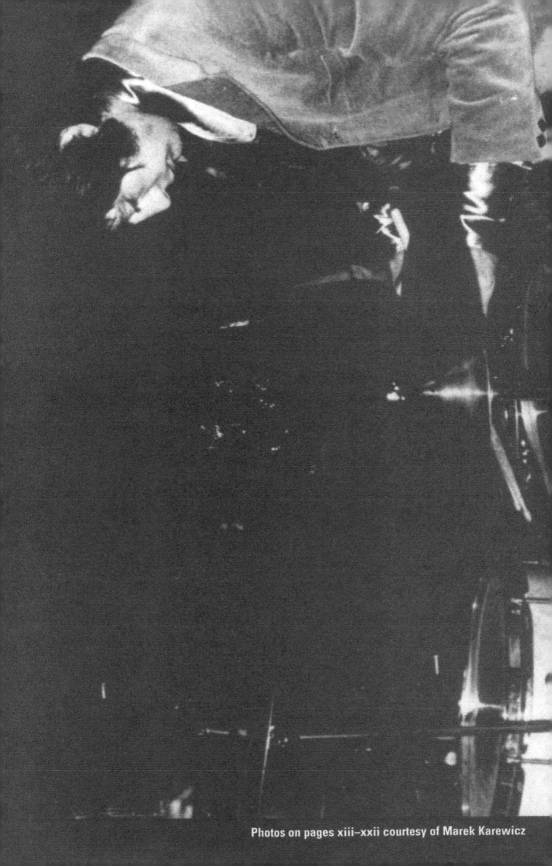

THE

KILLING

GROUND

It is late. All the little snakes are asleep. The world is black outside the car windows, just the dusty clay road in the headlights. Far from the city, past the last crossroads (where they used to bury suicides in England, with wooden stakes driven through their hearts), we are looking for a strange California hillside where we may see him, may even dance with him in his torn, bloody skins, come and play.

A train overpass opens in the sky before us; as we come out of it there is an unmarked fork in the road. The Crystals are singing "He's a Rebel." The driver looks left, right, left again. "He don't know where he's going," Keith says. "Do you—are you sure this is the way?" Mick asks. Turning left, the driver does not answer. The radio is quite loud. "Maybe he didn't hear you." Mick closes his eyes. Certain we are lost, but so tired, with no sleep for the past forty hours, less able each moment to protest, to change direction, we proceed in a black Cadillac limousine into the vastness of space.

"Something up ahead here," the driver says. Parked by the road is a Volkswagen van, a German police dog tied by a rope to the back door handle. The dog barks as we pass. Farther on there are more cars and vans, some with people in them, but most of the people are in the road, walking in small groups, carrying sleeping bags, canvas knapsacks, babies, leading more big ugly dogs. "Let's get

See the way he walks down the
   street
Watch the way he shuffles his feet
Oh, how he holds his head up high
When he goes walkin' by
He's my guy
When he holds my hand I'm so
   proud
'Cause he's not just one of the
   crowd
My baby's always the one
To try the things they've never done
And just because of that they say
He's a rebel
And he'll never ever be
Any good
He's a rebel
'Cause he never ever does
What he should

out," Keith says. "Don't lose us," Mick tells the driver, who says, "Where are you going?" but we are already gone, the five of us, Ron the Bag Man, Tony the Spade Heavy, the Okefenokee Kid, and of course Mick and Keith, Rolling Stones. The other members of the band are asleep back in San Francisco at the Huntington Hotel, except Brian, who is dead and, some say, never sleeps.

The road descends between rolling dry-grass shoulders, the kind of bare landscape where in 1950s science fiction movies the teenager and his busty girlfriend, parked in his hot rod, receive unearthly visitors, but it is crowded now with young people, most with long hair, dressed in heavy clothes, blue jeans, army fatigue jackets. against the December night air that revives us as we walk. Mick is wearing a long burgundy overcoat, and Keith has on a Nazi leather greatcoat, green with mold, that he will leave behind tomorrow or more accurately today, about sixteen hours from now, in the mad blind panic to get away from the place we are lightly swaggering toward. Mick and Keith are smiling, it is their little joke, to have the power to create this gathering by simply wishing for it aloud and the freedom to walk like anybody else along the busy barren path. There are laughter and low talking within groups, but little cross-conversation, though it seems none of us is a stranger; each wears the signs, the insignia, of the campaigns that have brought us, long before most of us have reached the age of thirty, to this desolate spot on the western slope of the New World.

"Tony, score us a joint," Keith says, and before we have been another twenty steps giant black Tony has dropped back and fallen into stride with a boy who's smoking and hands Tony the joint, saying "Keep it." So we smoke and follow the trail down to a basin where the shoulders stretch into low hills already covered with thousands of people around campfires, some sleeping, some playing guitars, some passing smokes and great red jugs of wine. For a moment it stops us; it has the dream-like quality of one's deepest wishes, to have all the good people, all one's family, all the lovers, together in some private country of night. It is as familiar as our earliest dreams and yet so grand and final, camp-fires flickering like distant stars as far as our eyes can see, that it is awesome, and as we start up the hillside to our left, walking on sleeping bags and blankets, trying not to step on anyone's head, Keith is saying it's like Morocco, outside the gates of Marrakech, hear the pipes . . .

The people are camped right up to a cyclone fence topped with barbed wire, and we are trying to find the gate, while from behind us the Maysles film brothers approach across sleeping bodies with blinding blue-white quartz lamps. Mick yells to turn off the lights, but they *pretend to be deaf and keep coming. The kids who have been looking up as we pass, saying Hi, Mick, now begin to join us; there is a caravan of young girls and boys strung out in the spotlights when we reach the gate which is, naturally, locked. Inside we can see the Altamont Speedway clubhouse and some people we know standing outside it. Mick calls, "Could we get in, please?" and one of them comes over, sees who we are, and sets out to find someone who can open the gate. It takes a while, and the boys and girls all want autographs and to go inside with us. Mick tells them we can't get in ourselves yet, and no one has a pen except me, and I have learned not to let go of mine because they get the signatures and go spinning away in a frenzy of bliss and exhilaration, taking my trade with them. So we stand on one foot and then the other, swearing in the cold, and no one comes to let us in, and the gate, which is leaning, rattles when I shake it, and I say we could push it down pretty easy, and Keith says, "The first act of violence."*

J. P. ALLEY: *Hambone's Meditations*

1

Something about the curious wanderings of these griots through the yellow desert northward into the Maghreb country, often a solitary wandering; their performances at Arab camps on the long journey, when the black slaves came out to listen and weep; then the hazardous voyage into Constantinople, where they play old Congo airs for the great black population of Stamboul, whom no laws or force can keep within doors when the sound of griot music is heard in the street. Then I would speak of how the blacks carry their music with them to Persia and even to mysterious Hadramaut, where their voices are held in high esteem by Arab masters. Then I would touch upon the transplantation of Negro melody to the Antilles and the two Americas, where its strangest black flowers are gathered by the alchemists of musical science and the perfume thereof extracted by magicians. . . . (How is that for a beginning?)

LAFCADIO HEARN:
in a letter to Henry E. Krehbiel

SHE WAS SITTING on a cream-colored couch, pale blond head bent over a red-jacketed book, legs crossed, one heel resting on the marble coffee table. Behind her in the picture window there was a thick green hedge and then, far away below, the City of the Angels, bone-white buildings reaching out to where, this being a fairly clear day, the Pacific Ocean could be seen, glinting in the sunlight through the poison mist that the land and sky became at the horizon. There were other people on the matching couches of the room, the lobby of that motel-like mansion, and more coming in now, but she did not look up, not even when I said "Excuse me" and stepped over her extended leg to sit down next to her husband, Charlie Watts, one of the Rolling Stones.

"Do you remember him, Shirley?" he asked.

A fast glance. "No."

"A writer. You remember."

"I hope he's not like one who came to our house," she said. Then she looked at me again and something happened in her green eyes. "*You're* the one." She closed the book. "You wrote about me in the kitchen."

"Somebody else," I said. "You're reading Priestley? *Prince of Pleasure.* Do you know Nancy Mitford's books?"

"You said I was *washing dishes.* I have never been so insulted."

"But Shirley, you *were* washing dishes. What else could I say?"

"You should have made something up."

"Where was this?" asked Bill Wyman, another Rolling Stone, sitting with his girlfriend, Astrid Lindstrom, the Swedish Ice Princess, far away from me at the end of the couch. "Great bass sound, ennit?" A portable phonograph in a corner of the room was playing 1930s records by the Kansas City Six.

"Yeah, Walter Page, really good," Charlie said. "An American magazine. They had it at the office."

"Was it about all of us? We never *saw* it," Astrid said. Wyman kept scrapbooks.

"I shouldn't want to, if I were you," Shirley said.

"Never get a sound like that with an electric bass," said Wyman, a bass player whose hands were too small to play the acoustic bass.

"The electric bass is more flexible," I said, trying to help divert the conversation. "You can do more things with it."

"You can't do *that,*" Wyman said. "Can you, Charlie?"

"Never," Charlie said as Page's bass and Jo Jones' brushes blended with Freddie Green's guitar, their rhythm steady as a healthy heartbeat.

"Sorry," I said.

"We've had you on the defensive since you got here," Charlie said. "Did you happen to bring the paper with Ralph Gleason's column? We haven't seen it."

"I read it on the way in."

"Was it bad?"

"It could have been worse, but not much." Once I asked Charlie how he felt about the many press attacks on the Stones, and he said, "I never think they're talking about me." And Shirley had said, "Charlie and Bill aren't really Stones, are they? Mick, Keith, and Brian, they're the big bad Rolling Stones."

Charlie smiled, pulling down the corners of his mouth. "I always liked Gleason's jazz pieces. I know him, actually. I mean I met him, the last time we played San Francisco. I'd like to ask him why he's become so set against us."

A man with receding black curly hair and bushy scimitar sideburns was coming into the room from the open doorway at the far end, wearing white shorts, carrying two tennis rackets and a towel. "Tennis, anyone?" he asked in a voice it would hurt to shave with.

I had never seen him, but I knew his voice from suffering it on the telephone. He was Ronnie Schneider, nephew of Allen Klein, the Rolling Stones' business manager. Almost before I knew it I was standing between him and the door. "Did you get my agent's letter?" I asked after telling him who I was.

"Yeah, I got it," he said. "There are some things we have to change. Tell your agent to call me."

"He says he's been trying to get you. There's not much time."

"I *know*," Ronnie said, his voice a fiend's imitation of girlish delight. He gave me a bright smile, as if I had just swallowed the hook. "Doesn't anybody here want to play tennis?"

"I'll play," Wyman said.

"Here, this one's warped." Ronnie handed him a racket shaped like a shoehorn, and they went out across the patio and the juicy Saint Augustine grass to the tennis court. I watched them through the glass door as they walked; then I noticed that my hat was in my hand, and I decided to sit down and try to relax.

Serafina, the Watts' eighteen-month-old daughter, came in with her nanny, and Shirley took her out to the kitchen for something to eat. Astrid went along, possibly to chill the orange juice. The Kansas City Six were playing "Pagin' the Devil."

"What did Gleason say, exactly?" Charlie asked me.

"He said the tickets cost too much, the seating is bad, the supporting acts aren't being paid enough, and all this proves that the Rolling Stones despise their audience. I may have left something out. Right. He also said, 'They put on a good show.' "

The back door opened and in walked a gang of men. Tall and lean and long-haired, they stood for a moment in the center of the room as if posing for a faded sepia photograph of the kind that used to end up on posters nailed to trees. The Stones Gang: Wanted Dead or Alive, though only Mick Jagger, standing like a model, his knife-blade ass thrust to one side, was currently awaiting trial. Beside him was Keith Richards, who was even thinner and looked not like a model but an insane advertisement for a dangerous carefree Death—black ragged hair, dead-green skin, a cougar tooth hanging from his right earlobe, his lips snarled back from the marijuana cigaret between his rotting fangs, his gums blue, the world's only bluegum white man, poisonous as a rattle-snake.

From his photographs I recognized Brian Jones' replacement, Mick Taylor. He was pink and blond, pretty as a Dresden doll beside Jagger and Richards, who had aged more than a year in the year since I'd seen them. One of the others, with dark hair frosted pale gold and a classic country and western outfit from Nudie the Rodeo Tailor, I remembered seeing on television and record covers—he was Gram Parsons, and he came, so I'd heard, from my hometown, Waycross, Georgia, on the edge of the Okefenokee Swamp. We had not met, but I had reviewed his band the Flying Burrito Brothers' new album, *The Gilded Palace of Sin*. I had no idea he knew the Stones. Seeing him here, finding another boy from Waycross at this altitude, I sensed a pattern, some design I couldn't make out, and I got up to speak to Gram Parsons, as if he were a prophet and I were a pilgrim seeking revelation.

But as I stepped around the table Jagger turned, and for the first time since he came into the room we were facing, too close, his eyes like a deer's, large, shadowed, startled. I remembered reading on the plane out here a *Time* magazine report of a study showing that when two people look at each other, the one who looks away first is likely to dominate the situation. So I gave Mick a friendly smile, and he looked away, just like the dominant people in *Time*. I had the feeling I'd lost a game I was trying not to play, but then I was past Mick, saying to Gram, "Good to see you."

"Yeah," Gram said reasonably, "but who are you?"

I told him, and he said, "I dug what you wrote about our band."

"I'm from Waycross," I said. He peered at me for a second, then handed me the joint he'd been smoking. We walked out onto the narrow front lawn (as we went out, Keith was saying to Charlie, "Did you see what your friend Gleason said?"), sat on the grass beside the hedge, and talked about people and places in Georgia. Gram said he had no intention of going back. I remembered my mother telling me that after Gram's mother and father had divorced, his father, a man called "Coon Dog" Connor, had killed himself, and Gram's mother married a New Orleans man named Parsons. I wouldn't know until later, when people started writing articles and books giving Gram belated credit for creating a new form of music, that his mother, whose father had owned Cypress Gardens and most of the oranges in central Florida, had died of alcoholic malnutrition the day before Gram graduated from high school. Even the house in Waycross where Gram lived had been sold and moved off beside the main southbound highway.

From where we were sitting, high in the sky over Sunset Boulevard,

it seemed that by facing the east we could see, except for the smog, all
the way back to Georgia. But if the smog had gone, what could we have
seen except the people who make the smog? Gram inhaled deeply on
the joint, an Indian silver swastika bracelet hanging on his wrist, his
eyes opaque pale green, like bird's eggs. "Look at it, man," he said, as
if he had heard my thoughts. "They call it America, and they call it
civilization, and they call it television, and they believe in it and salute
it and sing songs to it and eat and sleep and die still believing in it,
and—and—I don't know," he said, taking another drag, "then sometimes the Mets come along and win the World Series—"

With all the revelation I could handle for the moment, I spun back
through the house to the patio, where most of the people who were
here already and some new ones who had arrived were breaking up a
powwow, leaving Jagger talking upward to a very tall young man with
a Buffalo Bill mane and red side whiskers. "Now, Chip," Mick was
saying (so I knew he was real, this man who called himself Chip
Monck), "we can't *do* audience-participation things. I mean, I appreciate
your suggestion, and we do want to get them involved, but we can't
play 'With a Little Help from My Friends,' and—what do they *know*?
You can't expect people to sing along on 'Paint It Black.' Rock and
roll has become very cool now, but the Rolling Stones are not a cool
sort of thing, it's a much more old-fashioned thing we do, it's not as if
the Rolling Stones were, y'know, five *dedicated musicians*—I mean,
I'd much rather go on stage in a gold Cadillac or wearing a gold suit
or summink like that—"

Suddenly but gently, calmly, Chip put his hands on Mick's shoulders
and said, in the mellow baritone that soothed the dope-freaked, mud-
soaked thousands two months ago at the Woodstock Pop Festival, "I
just want you to know how pleased I am to be working with you guys."

Mick laughed. When Chip had touched him, Mick's hands had come
up to hold Chip at arm's length by the collarbone. Not certain whether
Mick was laughing at him, Chip also laughed. They stood, knees slightly
bent, in the classic starting position of wrestlers, grinning at each other.

Inside, someone was playing the piano. I looked, saw that it was Keith,
joined him on the bench and asked, "What about this book?" I trusted
Keith, at least to tell the truth; a bluegum man don't have to lie.

"What about it?" he asked, playing no recognizable melody.

"I need a letter."

"I thought Jo sent you a letter."

"Many letters, but not what I need. She says I need Allen Klein's
approval."

"You don't need anybody's approval. All you need is us. Jo! Hey, Jo!"

From the depths of this serpentine house Georgia Bergman emerged.
She was the Stones' secretary, an Anglo-American girl in her middle

twenties, with black kinky hair done in the current electric fashion, sticking out all around like a fright wig.

"What about this letter?" Keith asked. He was still playing, nothing you could recognize.

"We sent it," Jo said, "but it wasn't right, it didn't work, it umm—"

"I'll talk to Mick about it," Keith said, no certain comfort to me, but I said "Fine," and Jo took me for a walk on the grounds of this place, rented at great expense from some of the Du Ponts. We strolled out the back, toward the far corner of the property, where there were a child's playhouse, slide, and swings. I walked with my head down, groping toward thought.

Just over a year earlier, in September 1968, thinking that with one more story I could publish a collection of pieces about music, I went to England to visit the Rolling Stones. For almost three years, since Mick, Keith, and Brian had been arrested for possession of drugs, the Stones had stayed out of sight, performing in public only once. I saw the Stones, attended Brian Jones' trial, and wrote a story, but I had only glimpsed—in Brian's eyes as he glanced up from the dock—the mystery of the Rolling Stones. In the spring, after the story was published, I asked the Stones' cooperation in writing a book about them. It was June, and I was still waiting for an answer, when Brian, who had started the band, left it because, he said, of "musical differences" with the other Stones. Less than a month later, Jo Bergman called me in the middle of the night to say that Brian had been found dead, drowned in his swimming pool.

After some weeks Jo sent me a letter for the Stones, offering their cooperation subject to agreements between the Stones, the publishers, and me, but you can't do good work that way. You have to write the best you can and share control of nothing, neither the manuscript nor the money. Any other arrangement produces not writing but publicity. Finally Jo turned the book matter over to Ronnie Schneider for Allen Klein, widely considered the most powerful agent in show business. In self-defense, I hired an agent, Klein's literary equivalent. He sent Schneider a letter to sign for the Stones. But Keith said I didn't need Klein. Then why did Jo tell Klein, or his nephew Schneider, about my book?

Jo sat in a swing and swung slowly back and forth. It was, as I would learn, typical of the Stones' manner of doing business that I didn't know exactly what Jo did for them, and neither did she, and neither did they. She had consulted an astrologer in London who had told her that I would write this book, but that it would cost me everything except my life. She did not know the details—that while writing it I would be assaulted by Confederate soldiers and Hell's Angels, would go to jail, be run over by a lumber truck on the Memphis-Arkansas bridge, fall off a Georgia waterfall and break my back, have epileptic seizures while withdrawing from drugs—but if she had known, she would not have told me. She didn't tell me about the astrologer until much later, when there was no way to turn back. Now, eager, I climbed a swing chain with my hands—climbed it easily, for months I'd done nothing but write Basic English letters to the Stones and lift weights. As I reached the top and started down, my scarf fluttered up, my left hand clutched it around the chain, the silk was like oil, and I crashed to the ground, searing my hand, mangling the little finger, shocking it blue-white, with great crimson drops welling up where the flesh was torn away from the nail, dropping in the dust. "I thought you'd do that," Jo said, and I thought, Where am I, what is happening to me? I was in California, being punished for wearing a scarf.

I walked away from the playground with a kind of psychic limp. Al Steckler, a promotion man from the Klein office in New York, was arriving at the back gate, carrying an attaché case. We'd met in London. I told him hello and went inside to sit on the couch and suck my little finger. The next thing I knew, Jagger was sitting beside me, asking, "What about this book?"

"What about it?" I looked around the room. Steckler and a few other people were there, Jo sitting on the floor with a Polaroid camera, taking a picture of Mick and me.

"Those books are never any good," Mick said.

"That's true," I said, assuming that he meant books like *My Story* by Zsa Zsa Gabor, as told to Gerold Frank. "But I'm not going to write one of those books."

"What would your book be about?"

"About?"

"You know, what would be in it?"

"What will be in your next song?"

"A girl in a barroom, man, I don't know. It's much easier to write a song than a book."

"I am hip," I said. "I am fucking cognizant, Bucky." He laughed so pleasantly that I said, "Well, maybe I can give you some idea." I gazed into the gloom, frowning, and Mick said, "You don't have to tell me now, you can give it some thought if you like—"

"Naw, if I think about it too long I'll get bored."

Mick laughed again. The others were quiet, watching us. Jo was waiting for the photograph to develop.

"Maybe I can make a comparison," I said, and I told Mick that I had written a story about a blues singer who had swept the streets in Memphis for more than forty years, but he's more than just a street sweeper, because he's never stopped playing, if you see what I mean. I didn't look at Mick to find out whether he saw. You write, I told him,

about things that move your heart, and in the story about the old blues
singer I wrote about where he lives and the songs he sings and just lists
of the things he swept up in the streets, and I can't explain to him,
Furry Lewis, what it is about him that moves my heart, and I can't tell
you what I would write about the Rolling Stones, and so, well, I guess I
can't answer your question. No, he said, you answered it, and for the
first time since I thought, long months ago, of writing this book, I felt
almost good about it. That should have warned me.

Jo showed us the photograph. It was too dark, Mick and I were dark
isolate heads, like Mount Rushmore as a ruin. Steckler opened his case
to submit for Mick's approval the cover for the Stones' concert program,
featuring a girl wearing an Empire hairdo, a cloudy cape blown back
to reveal her zaftig figure, and a surprised expression. Mick approved.
Keith and Gram came in from the tennis court (none of the Stones
could play tennis, and they lost balls, can after can of balls, day after
day; you'd come up Doheny toward this place, on Oriole Drive, and
tennis balls would pass you, headed toward Sunset) and sat down
at the piano. Mick sang along with them. The afternoon lengthened. It
was one of those Scott Fitzgerald Sunday afternoons in Hollywood that
go on and on.

> Just a kid actin' smart
> I went and broke my darlin's heart
> I guess I was too young to know

The force of romantic poetry, its details cribbed by Coleridge and
Wordsworth from the writings of William Bartram on the country and
the legends around the Okefenokee Swamp, had landed Mick and Keith
(whose dog Okefenokee I would later meet), the two English rhythm
& blues boys, at the piano with a Georgia country cracker singing Hank
Williams songs. Mick didn't look sure he liked it.

Steckler was saying to the telephone, "A week from now is no good.
We must have extra lines in by tomorrow . . . Would it help if I called
the governor? . . . I'm quite serious, dear."

> I'll never see that gal of mine
> Lord, I'm in Georgia doin' time
> I heard that long, lonesome whistle blow

Just off the living room in the office (I told you this place was like a
motel), yet another promo man, David Sandison from England, was
pounding out a press release that, as I read it over his shoulder, said
nothing about Brian Jones, only noted that this tour "marks the American debut with the Stones of Mick Taylor." It condemned, without
naming him, Ralph Gleason's attack on the Stones, assuring the press
that "everyone will get to see and hear the group to best advantage."

The release also said the tour "will take in 13 cities" and then listed
fourteen cities where the Stones would play. I was glad to see that I
was not the only one who didn't quite know what was going on.

In an alcove of the office there were a bar and a refrigerator. "Want
a beer?" Sandison asked, fetching one for himself.

"No, thanks," I said. The office was not bad as offices go, with
bookshelves around the walls and a large desk cluttered with papers.

"At first they were going to play three days each in three cities,"
Sandison said, opening the green Heineken bottle and filling a glass.
"Then there were seven cities." He took a long drink and I saw, there on
the desk, partly covered by other papers, the letter I'd heard about but
not seen, from my agent to "Mr. Ronny Schneider."

"Now there are—how many? Fifteen?" Sandison asked.

"Dear Mr. Schneider," I read. *"This letter will confirm . . . your
willingness and that of the Stones to cooperate . . . we will seek and
obtain the approval of the Stones . . . through your office before entering . . . agreement with publishing house . . . Rolling Stones will share
in the proceeds. . . ."*

"Or is it thirteen?" Sandison asked.

*". . . we further agree that the final text will be cleared with the Stones
and their management. . . ."*

"Doesn't matter, it'll probably change again tomorrow," Sandison
said, coming back from the bar as I slipped the letter into my shirt.

"I wouldn't be surprised at anything," I said, going out into the hall,
where I came face to face with Schneider.

"I've been looking for you," he said. "We need to talk about our
deal. First of all, I think the boys should get half."

"Talk to my agent," I said, planning to tell my agent not to talk to
him. "I don't know nothing about that stuff."

Earlier this afternoon I had driven out of Memphis, Tennessee, where
I lived, along the wide, tree-lined streets, oaks arching over the road out
of town, the old town center within the Parkways, on the way to the
airport. Farther out along the road there was a wide strip of land that
had been, ten years ago when I first came to Memphis, a row of three or
four farms, with a mule in the field, an unpainted cabin or one wrapped
with imitation redbrick tarpaper, an old Ford disintegrating in the front
yard, an old black man in overalls sitting on the front porch smoking a
pipe, all of it laced over with poverty and honeysuckle, all of it now
gone; as I passed there was only a flat expanse of mud, little puddles
standing in it, a television picture tube sunk like a fossil in the timeless
ooze. I had to pass the mud-colored office building where Christopher,
who if she wants can be one person after another, who—allow me to
show you this blue-eyed watercolor unicorn—was teaching our cat

Hodge the alphabet, had for the last four years taken reservations for Omega Airlines. She had a sweet disposition, and her manners were just as nice. "Rats and mice," she would say when she wanted to curse. But the work at Omega was hard on her, and so on us. For the last three years, since Christopher and I had entered what passed for married life, I had taken flights at family rates to research the stories I wrote so slowly that no one could imagine how desperate I was for the money.

Later twenty of us, the Stones and company, lazed around a sunken, white-clothed table at the Yamato-E, a Japanese restaurant in the Century Plaza Hotel, waiting for dinner. It took a long time, and some-one—Phil Kaufman—passed around a handful of joints. Kaufman, from Los Angeles, a dwarfy German type with a yellow mustache, hung out with Gram and had been hired to help take care of the Stones while they were in town. He had done time on a dope charge at Terminal Island Correctional Institute, San Pedro, California, with someone named Charlie Manson. The rest of us had not heard of Manson yet, although we soon would, but it would be several years—four—before Kaufman made the news by stealing Gram's dead body from a baggage ramp at the L.A. airport and burning it in the Mojave Desert. (The subject of funeral arrangements had come up during a conversation be-tween Gram and Phil some months before the night—in September 1973—when Gram overdosed on morphine and alcohol.) As I started to light one of the joints, I noticed that the others were putting theirs away. Chip Monck, who had been flying around for the last few days, checking light and sound conditions at the concert locations, and who was now sitting across the table from me asleep, his head lolling to one side, woke up, saw me holding a joint and a burning match, said that there would be no dope on this tour, and if you got arrested with any, you'd be on your own. Then he fell asleep again. I thought he sounded silly, but I put the joint in my pocket.

As Keith was coming back from the toilet, a man and woman passed behind him, and the woman, seeing his ragged black mane, said in a loud, drunken voice, "You'd be cute if you put a rinse on your hair."

Keith turned, smiling, showing his fangs. "You'd be cute," he said, "if you put a rinse on your cunt."

Some of the group, led by Jo Bergman, were singing "Happy Birth-day." Ronnie Schneider was twenty-six today. I was twenty-seven. I did not sing. Neither did the Stones.

After dinner we went in a fleet of Cadillacs to the Ash Grove, a small club where the old blues singer Big Boy Crudup was sharing the bill with the young blues singer Taj Mahal. The place was too crowded to see if you were sitting, so some of us were standing in the aisle when a tall redheaded cowboy kid with freckles came up and told us he was

Taj's road manager, and he was happy the Stones were in L.A. because
he remembered how good the Stones were to them when they were in
London. We got grass, coke, Scotch, wine, anything you want backstage.

We were in the aisle again, Crudup was singing "That's All Right,
Mama," with Taj's band, two black men, two white men, and one Indian
playing together, and I was feeling each vibration of the music with
every spidery tracing of my nervous system when the road manager
said to me, "You know, it's hard, workin' for niggers."

I didn't know what to say to that. He nodded at the rest of the band:
"And that bass player and guitar player and drummer may look like,
uh, Caucasians, but in they hearts they niggers."

I didn't know what to say to that either. Then he completed the
thought: "But you know, you can have more fun with niggers than
anybody else in the world."

2

Music's music. Talkin' 'bout puttin' on a show in New York, I'm gone be like the monkey, I ain't gwine. There's so much shootin' and killin' and goin' on now. These places, all the folks be all crowded, you don't know what's gone happen. Ain't I'm right? You can't tell how these guys *is*, fella. Pshaw, man, they's snipers everywhere. I don't mean hidin'. I can recall three or four fellas was killed dead for playin' music. Me and you partners—I got you wid me—we playin'—you see what I'm talkin' 'bout. Well, we *over* dem. I ain't gone call 'em, dey dead now. Poisoned one and kilt the other. They done it 'cause he could play better than they could. I'm tellin' you what I know, now. I wouldn't kill nobody 'cause he could beat me doin' anything. That's right. Ain't I'm right? Anybody gone kill me, 'cause you and me can do a little better than they can. They callin' on us all the time. Ain't callin' on them. Me and you goin', say we goin', let's go. We play over there, jump up an' mess you up. Mess you up, boy. Another thing, you be around these places, don't do much drinkin'. Drop a spool on you. Don't drink much whiskey. Keep on playin'. They drop a button on you, boy, 'fore you can be sure. They got a gang, now. You try it. Mess you up, boy. Buck Hobbs—some friends I ain't gone call they names—he could play, they couldn't play like him. The same song I play 'bout Frankie and Albert, all them old

songs, "John Henry," he could play. Others couldn't beat
him. One hit him 'cross the head one night with a guitar,
'cause they couldn't beat him. It didn't make him no
difference. He just rock right on. Got down and stopped
playin', he got hold of a drink, he was dead. Buck Hobbs.
They kilt him. I think about all that. I don't want to leave
here. House full. Fightin'. Over in our home where I was
born, up in Pleasant Hill, that's where they done it. Just
near Pleasant Hill. In the grove.

MISSISSIPPI JOE CALLICOTT

THE 11:45 A.M. TRAIN from Paddington Station (£3 2s 5d
return and Who is the third that walks beside you?) rolled west from
the drab blocks of flats at the outskirts of London to the May-green
fields around Reading and Didcot, with trees, hedges, pink pigs, black
and white cattle, tractors, thatch-roofed barns and houses under heavy
white clouds.

I sat facing forward, trying to read the biography of Hemingway that
William Burroughs recommended during one of our talks about Brian
Jones, earlier in the spring, when my life, as Brian's had, was beginning to come apart. I was reading to find out how Hemingway kept
going after he lost Hadley. For the first time in almost ten years—it was
1970—I was a single man; that is to say, alone.

Past Kemble, after the Swindon change, there were hills, horses on
hillside fields in the sun. To the left of the track the land dropped away,
green treetops down in the valley reminded me of the foothills of middle
Georgia. Outside Stroud, as we were crossing a stream moving quickly
through young willows, I saw ducks rising together and schoolchildren
on a narrow dirt path leading under a small brick bridge, one boy
waving a Union Jack at the train. Two seats ahead of me, a woman was
telling her little boy and girl to stop singing "Yellow Submarine."

After Gloucester, where the land is flat again, the train heads north
to come to Cheltenham. The official guidebook still called it Cheltenham
Spa, though the "healing medicinal waters" that attracted "the elite of
many generations" went bad some years ago. Exactly how many years
ago the guidebook didn't say. It didn't matter. I didn't come here to
take a bath.

Taxis were parked outside the redbrick train station, but because I
always do things the hard way, I let them leave with other passengers

and started walking, with a black nylon flight bag—too small to hold clothes, a tape recorder, and the book about Hemingway—slung on a strap from my shoulder, the book like a circuit rider's Bible in my hand. There are back streets in Cheltenham that look like back streets in Queens, New York, or Birmingham, Alabama, Depression-era apartment buildings and houses with lawns where no grass grows. The book and the bag were both getting heavy by the time I reached the center of town. Cheltenham was built mostly during the Regency, and the stately columns of the Municipal Center regard, across the broad Promenade and its tree-darkened sidewalks, the Imperial Gardens, bright with red, mauve, and yellow tulips planted in neat curves and rectangles, sparrows dancing about, pigeons whirling and coursing overhead.

I walked on to a side street, found a phone kiosk, and from its picture in the yellow pages chose the Majestic Hotel on Park Place. It looked like the hotel where W. C. Fields would stay when he was in town. It was also between where I was and Hatherley Road, where Brian Jones grew up.

I had walked far enough to welcome, if I had any sense, a ride in a taxi, but I was not ready for that. I wanted to walk past the fine shops of the Promenade and the neat houses under the manicured trees. Cheltenham was designed to be a nice place, and it is a nice place, up to the point where they decide you are not so nice. Some of Cheltenham's nicest people had not spoken to Brian Jones' mother and father in years, while others stopped speaking to them only when Brian was buried in consecrated ground, his final outrage. You can listen close and hear the clippers clipping the hedges of Cheltenham.

The Majestic Hotel loomed like a faded ghost among apartment buildings going to seed. The desk clerk was in a little glass case like a ticket booth. The bartender leaned on his elbows in the empty cocktail bar, wrinkling the sleeves of his starched white jacket. The elevator smelled as if it had been closed since the 1920s. Slowly it took me to the third floor, to my single with a sink. The room was loaded, as are all single hotel rooms, with intimations of loneliness and death, of killing the night in loneliness. I lay down on the salmon-colored bedspread.

My feet rested for a few minutes, but my mind didn't. No book is any help against loneliness, and no drug can touch it. After she left him, Brian must have kept on thinking about Anita Pallenberg as, alone, I kept on thinking. Anita thought that Marlon, the son she had with Keith last year after Brian died, would be Brian reborn. He wasn't, but she did not stop thinking about Brian. "I'll see him again. We promised to meet again. It was life or death," Anita said. "One of us had to go." A tough decision. I swung my tired feet off the bed. Thinking was getting me nowhere.

The elevator was just as slow going down. The bartender was still leaning on the bar, not a customer in sight.

I walked back to the Imperial Gardens and sat on a green park bench to smoke some marijuana and observe the end of Wednesday afternoon. Maids were clearing the red, blue, and green tables under the orange-and-yellow-striped umbrellas that said *Tuborg,* where a few people were still eating snacks among the flowers. The inscription on the gardens' sundial read: "I only count your sunny hours/Let others tell of storms and showers." Now just one boy and girl were lying on the grass, not moving, as if they intended to spend the night here.

Looking out over the tulips and trees and softly humming motors of twilit Cheltenham, I thought of Brian saying, on a visit home near the end of his life, "If only I'd never left here." I fieldstripped the cigaret end, tearing the short paper, rolling it into a tiny pill that would vanish, with the smoking material, into the wind. Then I crossed the Promenade, passing the third military monument I'd seen in this town. The two others were for Africa 1899–1902 and World War I. This one's plaque read, "This memorial was originally surmounted by a gun taken at Sevastopol. During the war of 1939–1945 the gun was handed to the government to provide the metal for armaments." Though it was smaller, Cheltenham reminded me of Macon, Georgia, where I went to high school wearing an army uniform, carrying a rifle: the last place where I felt constrained to fieldstrip cigarets, not because of smoking marijuana, but to keep the area well-policed. Both are pretty towns with many trees.

It was 6:44, and I just had time for a sandwich. Down the street was a café that looked as deserted as the bar at the Majestic, just an East Indian girl in a white uniform behind the counter. She was putting things away, getting ready to close, but she asked if I wanted to eat.

I bought a watery orange drink and a cheese sandwich, because there aren't many ways to ruin a cheese sandwich. A woman came in, took the money from the cash register, let the girl out the back door and locked it. As the girl left I realized that she had the only dark skin I had seen in this town.

Back at the hotel, I was so cool and relaxed that my tape recorder was still packed away when the desk clerk called to say that a taxi was waiting. I loaded the recorder with tape and then decided to leave it.

Before I could look over my notes the taxi pulled into the parking lane to let me out. The mustard-colored semi-detached houses with tiny squares of glass behind brick fences, perched uneasily on the rim of the middle class, looked so small and regular that I thought I must be at the wrong place. But I entered at the gate and went up to the front door, where a glowing plastic bell-ringer bore the name L. B. Jones. I rang the bell and waited, trying to smile. It was night now, and I was standing in a pool of yellow light under the porch lantern, cars racing past on the dark road, flashing in each other's headlights.

The little man who opened the door had receding grey hair and a rather broad but sharp-nosed face, red under the pale, lined skin. As I began talking, I couldn't stop thinking that he was the same size as Brian, that they must have identical skeletons. He had Brian's, or Brian had his, way of walking almost on tiptoe, holding his hands back beside his hips. He had the same short arms and small, strong hands, and though Mr. Jones' eyes, behind glasses framed with gilt metal and grey plastic, did not have the quality Brian's eyes had of being lit from within, he had Brian's funny one-eyed way of looking at things. He stood before me, one foot forward, hands down by his pockets almost in fists, peering with one eye.

I said who I was, Mr. Jones said he was glad to see me and led me into the living room, where I sat on a couch, my back to the front wall, and he sat in a stuffed chair printed with ugly flowers before the unlit electric fireplace. He told me that I was the fourth of my countrymen who had come to discuss writing about Brian. "People come with letters from publishers, then they go away and one hears nothing more. I don't know what to make of it. I think they're pulling my leg," he said, again turning one eye on me.

I started to answer him, getting as far as, "Er, ah," when Brian's mother came in. I struggled to my feet and said hello. She looked gentler than Mr. Jones. She called him Lewis and he called her Louie, short for Louisa. Her eyes were a normal, pretty blue. Her hair was as yellow as Brian's, a shade that appeared to age well if given the chance.

We all sat down, Mrs. Jones in a chair at one end of the room, me at the other end, Mr. Jones in the middle, gazing at the cold fireplace. I tried to explain what I was doing, but the room was capturing all my mind. It contained, besides us and an orange tomcat, typically turgid English furnishings, an old Heathkit record player, an older radio, a black and white television set, a flowering bonsai tree under a glass dome, an American Indian figurine given to each of the Stones in 1964 by the German teen magazine *Bravo,* and on the mantle over the fireplace, a little rubber doll with bright red trousers and a white mane of spun nylon hair, the most vulgar possible caricature of Brian, and yet it seemed a totem to him, the central object in this tiny grotesque room. The orange cat curled in Mrs. Jones' lap. I asked his name, and she said "Jinx."

"Such a shame," Brian's father was saying. "Brian could have been a brilliant journalist, he could always play better chess than anyone else at school, so much talent wasted." He put his back teeth together and grimaced as if a horrible transformation was taking place.

Mrs. Jones asked, "Did you have a good supper tonight, love?"

I thought of the supper I had tonight and other suppers missed and other things than suppers missed and some of the things not missed, all because of what I had seen in her son's eyes. "Fine, thanks," I said. Then I started asking questions.

Mr. and Mrs. Jones met in South Wales, where they were living with their parents. Mr. Jones' parents were schoolteachers. His father sang in opera societies and led the choir at church. Mrs. Jones' father was for over fifty years a master builder and church organist near Cardiff. Mrs. Jones' mother was sickly and so didn't train for anything and was now quite well at eighty-three. Her parents were living, his were dead.

Mr. Jones studied engineering at Leeds University, then married and started working for Rolls-Royce. In 1939, with the war under way, he was transferred to Cheltenham, where he and Mrs. Jones had lived ever since, he working as an aeronautical engineer, she giving piano lessons.

Brian was born on the last day of February 1942. The Joneses' second child, a daughter, died at about the age of two.

"How did she die?" I asked as gently as possible.

"She died, and that's all I'll say about it," Mr. Jones said. I tried to explain again why I was asking questions, but Mr. Jones had been hurt too many times by lies and by the truth in print, and he was nowhere near ready to trust a writer. He told me that their youngest child, Barbara, born in 1946, now a physical education teacher, wanted no part of anything to do with Brian, and he asked me to leave her alone. He ground his teeth again. But he couldn't stop himself from talking and bringing out family photograph albums.

One photograph showed Brian about five years old, playing with a grey tabby cat.

"One day when both Brian and the cat were very young, Brian announced that the cat's name was Rolobur," said Mrs. Jones. " 'That's Rolobur,' he said. Don't know whether he was trying to say something else and it came out Rolobur, or what. He painted it blue once."

"The cat?"

"With no idea to hurt it," Mr. Jones said. "Which he didn't, he used food coloring that soon came off, and the cat lived with us for about sixteen years."

"Brian was a strange child," his mother said.

She started giving Brian piano lessons when he was six, and he studied it until he was fourteen. "But he wasn't terribly interested," she said. "Then he started playing the clarinet."

"Which didn't help his asthma any," Mr. Jones said. "Brian had croup when he was four, and it left him with asthma. He had terrible asthma attacks. It was always bad when he went to the beach on holiday, and he'd been having bad attacks down at Cotchford, very bad attacks down there just before his death."

Cotchford Farm was once the home of A. A. Milne; Pooh Bear lived in its Hefalump Wood. It seemed right that Brian should have the place, where he died so soon, less than a year after he bought it. Many things had hurt him by then, and Mr. Jones could not stop going over them, trying to find where things went wrong, where to place the blame. "I was down there with him, in a sort of junk room there at Cotchford, not long before he died. He came across a photograph of Anita and just stood for a moment looking at it. He said, 'Anita,' almost as if he were talking to himself, as if he'd forgotten I was there. Then he put the photograph down and we went on talking, doing what we'd been doing. The loss of Anita upset him terribly. Nothing was the same for Brian after that. Then the drug charges, all that trouble. I didn't know how to help him. We were close when he was young, but later we had . . . differences of opinion."

So much promise . . . a choirboy . . . first-chair clarinet . . . now old friends were saying, Well, it's about time you retired, isn't it? He stared at the cold fire, clenching his teeth, then went on talking.

"Brian rejected all discipline. He was suspended from school twice. Once when he was in the sixth form he and some of the other lads used their mortarboards as boomerangs, sailing them up in the air. Brian's came apart, and he refused to wear it. They suspended him. 'A most salutary experience' for Brian, a week's suspension, according to that twit of a headmaster. Brian spent the whole week down at the Cheltenham Lido, swimming, and came back a hero to all the other boys. I hardly knew how to deal with him. The headmaster would complain about him, and I'd become very serious and sit Brian down for a talk. 'Why is the headmaster always writing us with complaints? Why do you disobey them?' And Brian would say, 'Look, Dad, they're only teachers. They've never done anything. You want me to do the things you did, but I can't be like you. I have to live my own life.' He was terribly logical about it all. I could hardly get anywhere trying to argue with him.

"Brian simply loathed school, the exams, the discipline, all that. He made his O levels and A levels in spite of himself. At eighteen he left school. He wouldn't consider going to university. He had a dread of going to university and couldn't face years of study before he could be self-supporting. He hated the idea of being twenty-five or twenty-six before he could start earning his own living. For a while he was keen on dentistry, but after he left school, he decided to go to work in London for an ophthalmic firm. There was an ophthalmic college affiliated with the firm, and Brian studied there for a while, at the same time he was working. The firm had a branch in Newport, but Brian wanted to go to London. He wanted the London nightlife, the jazz clubs, all that. He loved jazz, Stan Kenton, that sort of thing.

"I took him to London for an interview with the ophthalmic firm. He put on quite a good show, and we left, and I said, 'Well, what train shall we take home, the five o'clock?' And he said, 'No, Dad, I want to go to some jazz clubs before we go home, would you like to come along?' I told him, 'No, no, I don't want to go.' Brian said, 'I'll come home on a later train.' He'd been to London more often than I'd known, hitch-hiking, going to these clubs. I came on home and Brian stayed in London. He came home about six A.M. He bought me a hamburger that night in London. I don't know why I should remember that. I suppose it was the first time he ever bought me a meal.

"Brian was obsessed with music. He used to play these, what are they, Modern Jazz Quartet records—"

"The reverberations used to drive me crazy," Mrs. Jones said.

"These records were playing morning, noon, and night," Mr. Jones said. "I saw it as a positive evil in his life, undermining a quite good career. Maybe music was his eventual downfall, but at the time I saw it as an evil because he was so obsessed. Music had driven out all thoughts of a conventional career. His involvement with music and London life, the life of the nightclubs, all that, ruined his career at the ophthalmic firm and school. He threw school and his job over and came back home. He had odd jobs, played with a band, worked in a music shop in Cheltenham, selling sheet music, records. He was becoming totally absorbed in a musical atmosphere. I knew Brian had musical ability, but I was very chary that he could achieve success. To me the most important thing was his security. I was unsatisfied to see him just drifting, and I saw no security or success likely to come from jazz. But to him—a religion it was, he was a fanatic. He went back to London for good when he was about twenty."

At about the same time, two other young men were coming to London, where they would meet Brian, and none of them would ever be the same.

"Brian's fall wasn't my fault or because of drugs," Anita said. "It was Mick and Keith."

3

Why is the jass music, and therefore, the jass band? Jass was a manifestation of a low streak in man's tastes that has not yet come out in civilisation's wash. Indeed one might go farther and say that jass music is the indecent story syncopated and counter-pointed. Like the improper anecdote, also, in its youth, it was listened to blushingly behind closed doors and drawn curtains, but, like all vice, it grew bolder until it dared decent surroundings, and there was tolerated because of this oddity . . . on certain natures sound loud and meaningless has an exciting, almost an intoxicating effect, like crude colours and strong perfumes, the sight of flesh or the sadic pleasure in blood. To such as these the jass music is a delight. . . .

New Orleans Times-Picayune, 1918

I WOKE UP under a Wizard of Oz bedspread, magenta and turquoise, with Dorothy and the Scarecrow and all the rest of them in a balloon. There were a pair of single beds in the room, where rich little Du Ponts used to sleep. David Sandison spent the night in the other bed, but he was already up. I showered and dressed looking out over Los Angeles, invisible under a dense elephant-colored cloud. Then I strolled the length of the house to the kitchen and looked in the refrigerator. It was odd to wake up in a big characterless house on a sunny morning when you couldn't see the rest of the world around you for the noxious vapors and to open the fridge and find bottles of raw milk and whole-grain bread. California. It was ten o'clock, and I was sitting at the circular breakfast bar eating an orange and whole-wheat bread with blackberry preserves, recording things in my midget legal notebook.

Jo Bergman told me as I passed the office, where she and Sandison were working on the publicity kits for this morning's press conference, that Ronnie Schneider had gone back to New York for a few days. I figured that should make him easier to avoid.

Jo, David, and I left early for the Beverly Wilshire Hotel, where the press conference would take place, in one of the limousines that were on duty around the clock at all three of the Stones' L.A. abodes—our place with the Watts family on Oriole Drive, the Laurel Canyon house where Keith and the two Micks were staying, and the Beverly Wilshire, where Bill Wyman and Astrid would be until Jo could "get them a house together." This did not imply any question of her getting them separate houses; it simply meant until Jo got them, rented for them, a house. "Together" was Californian, or Hip, as obscenity used to be Army. There were certain words and phrases used by people who liked to think themselves hip, *au courant,* and the hip people in London or Los Angeles or Katmandu, the farthest spot in the world from Coral Gables, Florida, all used them, but you heard them used most, and regular English used least, in California. Out here whole neighborhoods had been talking for weeks, since they learned the Stones were coming, without resorting to even the most basic English: "Far-out dudes, man." "Heavy." "What a trip." All of which might mean nothing or might be code for some mysterious poetic message, like Catullus speaking from the grave about Mick's sullen grace, Keith's cold killer beauty.

Jo, born in Oakland, California, reared in the United States and England, had spent most of her adult life working for celebrities, and spoke a mixture of Hip and an even more esoteric language, Celebrity Code: "Did I tell Mick the telegram—? She'll kill me— A baby, that's really far out!" she would say, all in a kind of intense breathless Lady Macbeth rush of pleasure and excitement, even genuine wholehearted concern, speaking this tongue in which words, phrases, entire paragraphs were omitted, leaving anyone who didn't know the code, or the private affairs of the celebrity being talked about, leaning forward listening with a game smile to the fervent delivery, the smile becoming more glazed as the gaps widened. Celebrity Code is a great and ancient language, difficult to learn, and I never heard anybody speak it better than Jo Bergman.

The conference was to be in the San Souci (sic) Room at the Wilshire; we entered it through a labyrinth of bars and luncheon rooms.

The Los Angelesization of Los Angeles had not yet reached the Beverly Wilshire, where the San Souci Room glowed softly in the gentle radiance of its crystal light fixtures, the harsh Southern California sun shut out by damask and organdy drapes, but it seemed near: outside the window an air hammer was making a racket that threatened to become mayhem, as if at any moment the bit might come through the wall. "What's that god-awful noise?" Jo asked the hotel's man, whose blue pin-striped suit we were following into the room.

"Ah, what time's your meeting?"

"Eleven-thirty."

"They'll be stopping at eleven."

Fifty or sixty folding chairs had been arranged in semicircles before a long table; to the right were a bar and another table with tea and coffee services and fruit salad and little cakes, big bouquets on the tables. I wandered around the room making notes, the air hammer stopped, Steckler showed up, and the press began to arrive. They all appeared to be in their early twenties, most of them carrying notebooks, cameras, and tape recorders, all dressed in the current style, achieved by spending large sums of money to look poor and bedraggled, like a new race of middle-class gypsies. They ate like gypsies, snatching up the cakes and fruit and drinks.

Close to eleven-thirty, three television crews arrived, their dress running more to business suits and ties. With one of them was Rona Barrett, the televised Hollywood gossip, a small woman whose large blonded hairdo was frozen within a layer of spray shellac. She perched on a folding chair, a cultured pearl among the suede and denim.

At noon the Stones stumbled into the room in single file like drunken Indians and arranged themselves at the long table. Flashbulbs popped. Television cameras hissed. The Stones sat and scratched their heads.

With the Stones, sitting next to Keith, was another young Englishman, wearing a burgundy-colored leather jacket, dark glasses, and piratical dark greasy locks. He was Sam Cutler, a recent addition to the Stones' entourage whose function, other than to carry whatever Keith would not want to be caught carrying, was unclear.

Finally the flashes stopped and for a long moment there were no questions, no one could think what to ask, the confrontation was enough: three years ago when the Stones last toured the United States, most of the people now here to interview them were teenagers screaming in darkened arenas their adoration of the Stones, who were going in the interim to be arrested, to swap women, to break up, to die, and yet here they are, elbows on the table.

The younger reporters, most of whom if the place had been raided would probably have gone down for possession of dope, did not look like any the Stones had seen before at an American press conference.

But this generation, like every other, contained mostly dull-normal people who needed others to live their lives for them. Luckily there are always a few people who can and do live other people's lives for them. They are the stars of the time, and at this time no public figure was so loved and hated as Mick Jagger, what a name, a name to open sardine tins with. Jagger sat smiling in lime-colored trousers, an open-throated black silk shirt with green and white flecks, some kind of large animal tooth hanging on a chain below his strong but delicately fashioned—like a silver necklace—collarbone.

If the questions here were like most of the ones I had been asked about the Stones, they would be short and direct: Are you queer? What kind of dope do you take? Did you kill Brian? But the first questions, fielded by Jagger, revealed only that the Stones' new album, *Let It Bleed,* would be finished and released in about three weeks, and that the Stones had no real plans for a record label of their own. "That's about all we'll get, the label," Mick said. "Unless you hire a fleet of lorries and sell the records for half price there's no point in it."

The meeting, it appeared, would be friendly and dull, without the conflict that once characterized the Stones' encounters with the press. So the great feeling of unity with the Stones this crowd would have had three years ago watching them meet the press on television was missing, and a reporter was moved to ask for a reply to the statement in Ralph Gleason's column of the day before that "the price of tickets for your concerts was too high and that a lot of people who would like to see you can't really afford it."

Without seeming to defer in the slightest degree to the prattling of a middle-aged jazz columnist, Mick generously said, "Maybe we can fix something up for those people."

"A free concert?" someone asked, but Mick said he didn't know and evaded the issue with aristocratic ease: "We can't set the price of tickets. I don't know how much people can afford. I mean, I've no idea."

Someone else asked whether the U.S. State Department gave the Stones any trouble or asked them to sign anti-drug statements before allowing them to enter the country. Mick said, "Of course not, we've never done anything wrong," and through the laughter and applause Rona Barrett asked, "Do you consider yourself an anti-establishment group, or are you just putting us on?"

"We're just putting you on," Mick said.

"Taking you for a ride," Keith murmured, reptile eyelids drooping.

Rona presses on: "How did you enjoy eating at the Yamato last night?"

"She was under the table," Keith explained, but it didn't stop her.

Mick told a questioner that the Stones hoped to hire Ike and Tina Turner, Terry Reid, B. B. King, and Chuck Berry as supporting acts for the tour, and the question of a free concert returned. These young reporters seemed to suggest even more strongly than had Ralph Gleason that the Stones had an obligation to a new community, formed largely in the Stones' image. It seemed the sort of thing that the Stones in their independence had never flirted with, and Mick avoided the subject again: "If we feel that's what's got to be done, then we'll do it. I'm leaving that very fluid, you notice, I'm not committing meself."

"And how is Marianne Faithfull?" Rona Barrett asked Mick. If you didn't know better, you would have thought she was the only reporter interested in the Stones' personal lives.

Three days after Brian Jones died, Marianne Faithfull, Jagger's *régulière* for the past two years, in Australia with Mick to appear in a movie, looked into a mirror and saw not her face but Brian's. Then she took an overdose of sleeping pills. Only luck and prompt medical attention saved her life. After recuperating in Australia and Switzerland, she returned to Mick's house in London, where she was now, feeling neglected.

"She's all right," Mick said to Rona. "How are you?"

Rona, undaunted, wanted to know of any plans Mick had to run for public office: "I'm not feeling very messianic," he said, laughing.

Other people asked more questions about festivals and free concerts. The subject would not go away; this year the popular imagination had been outraged or delighted, captured anyway, by the pop festivals, mammoth exhibitions of drugs, sex, and music. Last year's spectacle was the police violence in Chicago during the Democratic Party's nominating convention; the year before that, we had the discovery by the mass media of the widespread use among the young of psychedelic drugs; this year there had been giant music festivals at such places as Woodstock, Hyde Park, Atlanta, Denver, the Isle of Wight, Dallas, where people came without paying, whether or not tickets were sold, went naked, had sex and took drugs openly with almost no arrests because there was no way short of war to arrest hundreds of thousands of people. It seemed that the World War II babies had grown into a force traditional society might be unable to restrain. There should be, Keith said about the festivals, "ten times more of them."

But, someone still wanted to know, what about the prices of the tickets to the Stones' concerts?

Mick, Keith, and Sam Cutler began talking at once, stopped together, and Sam said, "Could I just say this: The prickets—" And Keith kissed him on the cheek.

They were still, after all, the Rolling Stones. Mick made a little speech, the questions trailed off, and Mick said, "Thank you very much, people," sounding like the late Merriman Smith ending a presidential press conference.

The Stones left the room. There at the end Mick had said: "We aren't doing this tour for money but because we wanted to play in America and have a lot of fun. We're really not into that sort of economic scene. I mean, either you're gonna sing and all that crap or you're gonna be a fucking economist. We're sorry people can't afford to come. We don't know that this tour is more expensive. You'll have to tell us." It seemed, since the Stones had always avoided having other people tell them what to do, a serious step.

Steckler, Sandison, Jo, and I met the Stones in Bill Wyman's suite, where the serious question in the sitting room was whether the Stones would release a single record from their new album before the tour started. Steckler suggested they release the album's country version of "Honky Tonk Women," their latest single, thus becoming the first musical group to release the same song twice in a row.

Jagger suggested releasing the title track, "Let It Bleed," as a single "if anybody would play it on the radio."

"Not with those lyrics," Jo said.

"Well, they're not just dirty, I mean they're double entendre," Mick said.

" 'If you want someone to cream on, you can cream on me,' is pretty single entendre," Jo said.

"We also have to decide which press you'll talk to," Steckler said, and named several periodicals that had requested interviews.

"*Saturday Review,* what's that like?" Mick asked.

"Dullest magazine in America," I said. "Duller than the *Saturday Evening Post.* Duller than *Grit.*"

"That's all right, then."

The meeting was short; nothing was settled, except to try living for a few more days. No blueprint, no master plan.

After lunch of ham sandwiches and beer back at the Oriole house, Steckler, Sandison, and I visited the Laurel Canyon place. A pudgy young man named Bill Belmont, part of Chip Monck's stage production crew, came along in the limousine with us and pointed out the sights like a tour guide who dreams of being a press agent: "That cabin there, that's Frank Zappa's house, used to belong to Tom Mix. This house we're going to, where the Stones are, used to be Carmen Miranda's house and Wally Cox's house and then it belonged to Peter Tork of the Monkees and now it belongs to Steve Stills. David Crosby lived there for a while. I can tell you everything. You see that story in *Rolling Stone* about the Doors? I did that. I told the guy the whole article. He just wrote down what I said."

At a dirt road on the valley side of Laurel Canyon there was a gate, but it was open and we drove up, the dark green valley walls around us. The house was stone, with a swimming pool and big paved drive where two limousines and two rented sedans were parked. From the far end of the house across the pool came muffled sounds of electric guitars and a harmonica.

A lemon tree was growing by the drive, and the clowns I was with amused themselves by tearing off and throwing lemons. I threw one or two myself, just to be sociable, but I come from a place where the people are proud but poor, and I can't really enjoy throwing food unless I'm trying to hit someone with it.

After a while we went into the house, a wood-leather-and-stone robber's roost with stone floors, a big stone fireplace, no softening touches. The kitchen had a refrigerator big as one in a commissary at a turpentine camp, but it was stocked with beer instead of pigfeet and Big Oranges. We drank Heinekens and waited for the rehearsal to end. Belmont, Steckler, and Sandison were lounging in chairs around the living room. I didn't know why any of them was here. I had come to speak to Keith and Mick about the letter I needed to get a publisher, to go on living, to write a book. I lay down on a leather couch, gazed out the window, and saw, coming down the valley-side, a small brown fawn.

Soon the music at the back of the house stopped and the Stones came out. I followed Keith into the kitchen. He opened a 35-millimeter film can and with a tiny spoon lifted out a mound of white crystals, and didn't see me until he had the spoon halfway home. His hand stopped, I said, "Caught you," and he shrugged, raised the spoon and sniffed. Then I said, "Um, Keith, what about the, ah, book?"

"I'll talk to Mick about it."

Time passed, nothing happened. In the living room the people were still slouching about. Keith stood with one hand loose on forward-slung hips, the other shoving a beer into his mouth, looking like a baby with its bottle. I found Mick sitting at a piano just outside the door of the rehearsal room. "What about the book?" I asked.

"I've got to talk to Keith about it."

Then I went back to Keith and said, "Have you talked to Mick yet? We got to go."

"Hey," Keith said to Mick, who happened to be walking past, "what about this book?"

"What about it?"

They strolled into the kitchen as daylight faded. Finally we really were leaving, and I said to Keith, "So?"

"You write the letter," he said, "and we'll sign it."

So far so good, I thought, back at the Oriole house eating bouillabaisse. I had never eaten bouillabaisse before, and though I enjoyed it, I was still wondering what to do next. Write the letter and they'll sign it. Then what? Will they leave me alone to make a contract and write a book?

I tried to digest bouillabaisse and these questions while sitting after dinner with Jo, Sandison, Steckler, and the Watts family. The night was cool, and in the fireplace four gas jets were blasting a stack of wood logs to blazes. A couple of people stopped by, one with a large vial of cocaine, so after everybody else had gone to bed, Sandison, Steckler, and I were up talking. Steckler had no coke but was excited to be away from home. He was in his late thirties, in this crowd an older man, and he worked for Allen Klein, who as the manager of the world's two most popular acts, the Beatles and the Rolling Stones, may have been the most powerful man in show business; but Steckler, so close to all that power and money, seemed naive, too earnest about the poetry and truth of rock music. He had a neat brown haircut, a baby-pink face, and sincere eyes that would do many unpleasant things but would never lie to you.

"Who's Schneider?" I asked him when the logs were white powder, the fire four blue jets of flame.

"Klein's nephew."

"Besides that."

"He worked for Klein until a few weeks ago. They had a disagreement and Ronnie formed Rolling Stones Promotions to do this tour."

"What besides this tour does he do for the Rolling Stones?"

"Not a thing," Steckler said.

After everyone else had gone to bed, I carried a typewriter from the office to the kitchen, closed all the connecting doors, and wrote a letter to myself from the Rolling Stones, assuring me of their cooperation, with their names typed below, spaced to leave room for their signatures. Then I took the typewriter back and tiptoed to bed.

4

One night this guy comes into the bar with his cap on
sideways, you know. And this is Elmore.

WARREN GEORGE HARDING LEE JACKSON: *Living Blues*

V A L E N T I N O , a scarred grey tabby cat who once belonged to
Brian Jones, yawned and stretched on the terrace. Keith and I were
sitting on a Moroccan carpet in the side yard, nine-month-old Marlon,
born last year, 1969, crawling naked in the grass, little yellow baby-
turds shooting out his ass. His mother, the flashing-eyed Anita, was still
upstairs in the tapestry-bedecked bedroom where she and Keith slept,
on the dresser in a silver frame a small photograph of Brian. Inside the
lid of the downstairs toilet was a collage of Rolling Stones photographs.
These people didn't try to hide things. The first night I spent at Keith's
house, Anita tossed a blanket beside me on the cushion where I was
lying. "You don't need sheets, do you," she asked.

"No, I'll be fine," I said.

"Mick has to have sheets," she said. "Put it in the book."

Redlands, a thatch-roofed house in West Witterling, near Chichester
in West Sussex, had been Keith Richards' country home since 1965. In
1967, along with Mick Jagger, he was arrested here. This morning the place seemed, in the pale spring sunlight, like a veterans'
hospital, and Keith and I like two old soldiers, taking frequent medica-
tions and talking about the past.

"My great-grandfather's family came up to London from Wales in the nineteenth century," Keith said, "and so my grandfather, my father's father, was a Londoner. His wife, my grandmother, was mayoress of Walthamstow, a borough of London, during the war. It was the height of fame for the family. They were very puritan, very straight people. Both dead now.

"But then you come to Gus: my mother's father, Theodore Augustus Dupree. He was a complete freak. He used to have a dance band in the thirties, played sax, fiddle, and guitar. The funkiest old coot you could ever meet.

"That side of the family came to England from the Channel Islands. They were Huguenots, French Protestants who were driven out of France in the seventeenth century. And in the mid-nineteenth century Gus' father came to Wales, to Monmouth.

"Gus was so funny. He had seven daughters, and they used to bring their boyfriends home, and they'd be sitting round all prim and proper, and he'd be upstairs dangling contraceptives out the window. There's so many stories about him that I don't remember even one solid story. In the fifties, the *late* fifties, he was playing fiddle in a country and western band round the U.S. air force bases in England. Real double-string stuff and everything. He's a friend of Yehudi Menuhin. Gus admired him, got to know him. He's one of these cats that can always con what he wants. I should imagine he's a bit like Furry Lewis. And from living with all these women, he has such a sense of humor, because you either go crazy or laugh at it, with eight women in the house. It was his guitar I used to turn on to when I was a kid.

"My grandmother used to play piano with my grandfather until I think one day she caught him playin' around with some other chick, and she never forgave him, and she refused ever to touch the piano again. And she's never played it to this day, since the thirties or forties or whatever. I think she's even refused to fuck him since then. Very strange.

"My mother and father were together for a long time before they got married. I think they met in '34, maybe even '33, got married in '36. They separated in '63. This is the strange part of the story, far as I'm concerned. They separated right after I left home, virtually within months. Mainly because my old man, I guess, I should imagine, for a woman, he'd be incredibly boring to live with. He worked, still does, I believe, at an electronics factory, as a supervisor or something, he's worked his way, been there since he was twenty-one or so. Always very straitlaced, prudish—never got drunk, very controlled, very hung up. I should say he was very hung up. And the bastard—what's really weird about it, because I like him still, I find certain things about him rather endearing—he's refused to acknowledge me since he split with my mother, because, I think, I was still on friendly terms with my mother after she split. So he immediately gets all uptight, I guess, and thinks— I dunno, I've written to him a couple of times. I wrote to him when I got busted, 'cause I wanted to explain that thing to him, I didn't want him to just get it all out of the newspapers. But I didn't get an answer, which rather pissed me off. Haven't heard from him since '63. Seven years."

"Were you very close to him as a kid?"

"No, it wasn't possible to be that close to him, he didn't know how to open himself up. He was always good to me."

"Was he strict on things like your going out as you got older?"

"He tried to be, but he kind of gave up, you know? I think because of my mother, who had this tendency to give in to me, especially as I got older. And also because—I think he just gave up on me. I've disappointed him incredibly."

"You turned out to be a Dupree instead of a Richards—"

"Exactly. I really didn't turn out to be anything like he wanted."

"Where does he live?"

"As far as I know, he still lives in, where we all used to live, this fucking horrible council house in Dartford. It's eighteen miles to the east on the edge of London, just outside the suburbs where the country starts creeping in. He really had no sense of taking a gamble on anything. Fucking soul-destroying council estate. A mixture of terrible apartment blocks and horrible new streets full of semi-detached houses, all in a row, all new, a real concrete jungle, a really disgusting place. And because he wouldn't take a chance on anything, he wouldn't try to get us out of there, which is what I think eventually did my mother in as far as he was concerned. I'm gonna have to go and see him one day, just because I'm not gonna be as stubborn as him. One day I'm just gonna get hold of him and try to make contact, whether he likes it or not."

"He hasn't married again?"

"Far as I know, no. I can't even imagine him gettin' himself together to find another woman. He'd just rather stay bitter and feel sorry for himself. It's a shame. As far as I'm concerned, I'd like to have him down here. He's a gardener, he could look after the place, and he'd love to do it if he was really honest with himself. And I'd really dig it if he'd just live here and look after this place."

(Ten years later, Keith would make his father part of the family again, but with no false feeling on either side. When, in 1983, Bert Richards answered the phone at Keith's house in Jamaica, the friend calling said, "You must be so proud of him." "Well . . ." Keith's father said, refusing to commit himself.)

"How did you feel about school?"

"I wanted to get the fuck out of there. The older I got, the more I wanted to get out. I just knew I wasn't gonna make it. In primary school you didn't do that much, but later, when I went to that fucking technical school in Dartford, the indoctrination was blatantly apparent. I went to primary school, which in England is called, or was then, infant school, from five to seven. When I started going to school, just after the war, they taught you the basics, but mainly it was indoctrination in the way schools were run, who's to say yes to who and how to find your place in class. It's what you've let yourself in for for the next ten years.

"When you're seven you go to junior school. They had just started building a few new schools by the time we'd finished the first one, so we went to a new one nearer where we lived. That's where I met Mick, 'cause that's where he went too, Wentworth County Primary School. He happened to live near by me, I used to see him around . . . on our tricycles.

"In junior school they start grading you each school year, each section of kids into three sections, fast, average, and slow. When you're eleven you take an examination called the eleven plus, which is the big trauma, because this virtually dictates the rest of your life as far as the system goes. It probably includes more psychology now, but then they were just trying to see how much you knew and how quick you learned it and whether you could write it down. That decided whether you went to grammar school, which is where you receive a sort of semiclassical education for the masses, or to what they call a technical school, which I ended up in, which is actually for kids that are usually pretty bright but that just won't accept discipline very well. The school for kids that don't stand much of a chance of doing anything except unskilled or semiskilled labor is called secondary modern. For those who had the bread there were plenty of public schools, but this was the system for state education.

"After eleven I lost touch with Mick because he went to a grammar school and I went to this technical school. I lost touch with Mick for— it seemed a long time, actually it was about six years."

Keith Richards, the youngest of the original Rolling Stones, was born on December 18, 1943. Michael Philip Jagger was born in the same year and the same town, Dartford, on July 26. When she was four years old, Mick's mother had come to Dartford from Australia, where six generations of her family had lived. "The women in my family went to Australia to get away from the men," she said. She married Joseph Jagger, a physical education teacher who came to Dartford from a family of strict nondrinking Baptists in the north of England. Their son Michael was from an early age interested in athletics and in earning money.

"When I was twelve years old," Mick said, "I worked on an American army base near Dartford, giving other kids physical instruction—because I was good at it. I had to learn their games, so I learned football and baseball, all the American games. There was a black cat there named José, a cook, who played R&B records for me. That was the first time I heard black music. In fact that was my first encounter with American thought. They buried a flag, a piece of cloth, with full military honors. I thought it was ridiculous, and said so. They said, 'How would you feel if we said something about the Queen?' I said, 'I wouldn't mind, you wouldn't be talking about me. She might mind, but I wouldn't.' "

We talked in many places—movie sets, motel rooms, airplanes, at Mick's house on Cheyne Walk, with Marsha Hunt, the Afro-American actress, pregnant with Mick's first child, wearing her 'bosom Scotch-taped into a hippie-Indian dress.

One night at Keith's London house, a few doors up from Mick's, Keith, Mick, Anita, and I were talking, and Anita mentioned that Mrs. Jagger often speaks of how Mick used to enjoy camping and the outdoor life. In a high-pitched, proper voice, imitating Mrs. Jagger, I said, "As a child, Mick was very butch."

"Yeah, I was butch," Mick said. "But she was always butcher."

"Technical school was completely the wrong thing for me," Keith said. "Working with the hands, metalwork. I can't even measure an inch properly, so they're forcing me to make a set of drills or something, to a thousandth-of-an-inch accuracy. I did my best to get thrown out of that place. Took me four years, but I made it."

"You tried to get yourself thrown out how? By not showing up?"

"Not so much that, because they do too many things to you for doing that. It makes life difficult for you. I was trying to make it easier for me.

"At this time rock and roll had just hit the scene. That also played a very heavy part in my decision. The first record that really turned me on out of the rock and roll thing was 'Heartbreak Hotel.' "

"Did you see *Blackboard Jungle* over here?"

"Yeah, that was the first ripping-the-seats-up, Teddy Boys type of scene here. I was very young at that time. I did the first school year, I did the second year, I did the third year, and at the end of the third year I'd fucked up so much that they made me do the third-year course again, which was really to humiliate me. It meant you had to stay down with the younger kids and couldn't take the G.C.E. examinations, which in this country are very important in getting a job. I didn't take the fucking things at all. I did the third year again, and I did the fourth year, and at the end of the fourth year—remember, everybody else was at the end of the fifth year—I made things so bad—culminating in a spate of truancy which they wouldn't take from me—they kicked me out.

"The particular thing was splitting constantly very early in the day, and just generally turning out contrary to their demands, and millions of things, like I used to wear two pairs of pants to school, a very tight pair and a very baggy pair which I would put on as soon as I got near the school, because they would just send you home if you had tight pants on. That's another thing about English schools, you had to wear the school uniform . . . the cap, very strange contraption, like a skull-cap with a peak on it, school badge on the front. And a dark blazer with a badge on the breast pocket, a tie, and gray flannel trousers. I refused to go to and from school with those fucking clothes on.

"But in kicking me out, they as a final show of benevolence fixed up this place for me in art school. Actually that was the best thing they could have done for me, because the art schools in England are very freaky. Half the staff anyway are in advertising agencies, and to keep up the art bit and make a bit of extra bread they teach school like one day a week. Freaks, drunks, potheads. Also there's a lot of kids. I was fifteen and there are kids there nineteen, in their last year. A lot of music goes on at art schools. That's where I got hung up on guitar, because there were a lot of guitar players around then, playing anything from Big Bill Broonzy to Woody Guthrie. I also got hung up on Chuck Berry, though what I was playing was the art school stuff, the Guthrie sound and blues. Not really blues, mostly ballads and Jesse Fuller stuff. In art school I met Dick Taylor, a guitar player. He was the first cat I played with. We were playing a bit of blues, Chuck Berry stuff on acoustic guitars, and I think I'd just about now got an amplifier like a little beat-up radio. There was another cat at art school called Michael Ross. He decided to form a country and western band—this is *real* amateur—Sanford Clark songs and a few Johnny Cash songs, 'Blue Moon of Kentucky.' The first time I got onstage and played was with this C&W band. One gig I remember was a sports dance at Eltham, which is near Sidcup, where the art school I went to was.

"I left technical school when I was fifteen. I did three years of art school. I was just starting the last year when Mick and I happened to meet up on the train at Dartford Station. Between the ages of eleven and seventeen you go through a lot of changes. So I didn't know what he was like. It was like seeing an old friend, but it was also like meeting a new person. He'd left grammar school and he was going to the London School of Economics, very heavily into a university student number. He had some records with him, and I said Wotcha got? Turned out to be Chuck Berry, *Rocking at the Hop*.

"He was into singin' in the bath sort of stuff, he had been singin' with a rock group a few years previous, couple of years. Buddy Holly stuff and 'Sweet Little Sixteen,' Eddie Cochran stuff, at youth clubs and things in Dartford, but he hadn't done that for a while when I met him.

I told him I was messin' around with Dick Taylor. It turned out that Mick knew Dick Taylor because they'd been to grammar school together, so, fine, why don't we all get together? I think one night we all went round to Dick's place and had a rehearsal, just a jam. That was the first time we got into playing. Just back-room stuff, just for ourselves. So we started gettin' it together in front rooms and back rooms, at Dick Taylor's home particularly. We started doing things like Billy Boy Arnold stuff, 'Ride an Eldorado Cadillac,' Eddie Taylor, Jimmy Reed, didn't attempt any Muddy Waters yet, or Bo Diddley, I don't think, in that period. Mick laid a lot of sounds on me that I hadn't heard. He'd imported records from Ernie's Record Mart.

"At this time the big music among the kids was traditional jazz, some of it very funky, some of it very wet, most of it very, *very* wet. Rock and roll had already drifted into pop like it has already done again here because the mass media have to cater to everybody. They don't have it broken down into segments so that kids can listen to one station. It's all put together, so eventually it boils down to what the average person wants to hear, which is average rubbish. Anyway, that was the scene then, no good music coming out of the radio, no good music coming out of the so-called rock and roll stars. No good nothing.

"Just about the time Mick and I are getting the scene together with Dick Taylor, trying to find out what it's all about, who's playing what and how they're playing it, Alexis Korner starts a band at a club in the west of London, in Ealing, with a harmonica player called Cyril Davies, a car-panel beater at a junkyard and body shop. Cyril had been to Chicago and sat in with Muddy at Smitty's Corner and was therefore a very big deal. He was a good harp player and a good night man; he used to drink bourbon like a fucking fish. Alexis and Cyril got this band together and who happens to be on drums, none other than Charlie Watts. We went down about the second week it opened. It was the only club in England where they were playing anything funky, as far as anybody knew. The first person we see sitting in—Alexis gets up and says, 'And now, folks, a very fine bottleneck guitar player who has come all the way from Cheltenham to play here tonight'—and suddenly there's fucking Elmore James up there, 'Dust My Broom,' beautifully played, and it's Brian."

5

If the fool would persist in his folly, he would become wise.
—WILLIAM BLAKE: *Proverbs of Hell*

IT WAS AFTER ELEVEN in the morning when I clawed my
way down the hall toward the fresh fruit salad in the refrigerator,
hoping it would cure the headache left me as a souvenir of last night's
cocaine. David Sandison, coming out of the office, loomed before me,
his face mournful as a basset hound's. He asked if I'd just got up and
I said brusquely, "That's right," wanting the thick apple juice, cold
strawberries, pineapple and orange slices—they might try to steal
from you, but they'd never starve you—and he said, "Then you
haven't heard about Kerouac."

"What about him?"

"He's dead."

"Where'd you hear that?" I asked, because you never want to believe
these things.

"It's been on the radio this morning. He died last night. He was
living in Florida. Did you know that?"

I didn't answer because in my mind I was riding on a Trailways bus
from Waycross to Macon, Georgia, Lumber City just ahead, reading
a story in a book I had borrowed from the Okefenokee Regional Library,
since Waycross did not have a bookstore, if you discounted a place
where they sold Bibles. In the story a Mexican girl was singing to a
young American man a Piano Red song we used to play on the jukebox

at the lake where my high school friends and I danced and drag-raced and made love in cars. I had never read a story like this one. The people in it drove fast and made love in cars, and that made my life seem more like something you might read about, or as the song said, "If you can't boogie, you know I'll show you how." Then I remembered that the only work I had an actual contract to do was a story for *Esquire* about Kerouac. Waiting to hear from the Stones, I had postponed going to Florida for an interview. The thought jolted me back to the present, sitting on a couch in the living room, still hungry. My mood had changed, and I made a ham sandwich and drank a beer.

Mick, Mick, and Keith had arrived, Jagger in the office with the door closed, Keith playing tennis with Mick Taylor, then displaying in the pool what he called "the form perfected over six years lounging on the beaches of the world." Only six years a Rolling Stone, and he looked a hundred. How old had Kerouac looked? Sandison grimly watched Keith swimming. Before going into the publicity racket Sandison was a reporter for a small-town English newspaper. Both his body and his prematurely balding head were pear-shaped; Kerouac had lived the vagabond life unknown to the pear-shaped. Sandison really felt as if something had been taken away from him. He told Keith about Kerouac, and though Keith had never read him, he sort of swam more seriously for a few strokes.

When Keith had dressed again and we were heading back to the house, I remembered to tell him that I had written the letter. "Yeah," he said, "I'll speak to Mick about it," plunging me again into gloom, things seemed never to get past this point, but I went to my Oz room and got the famous letter. A minute later, when I got back, Keith was gone. Jagger was in the living room on a couch with Jo Bergman, talking business, frowning. I looked in the backyard and saw nobody, then went out front and found Mick Taylor alone. I did not say, Where the hell is Keith? but airily remarked, "Insane business, people running about." It was the first sentence I could remember saying to Mick Taylor. He smiled simply and said, "I don't mind the business part as long as I don't have to do it." *Then* I said, "Where the hell is Keith?"

"He and Charlie just left for the studio."

I went inside thinking, To hell with it.

Then as I passed, Jagger looked up and said, "Isn't there a letter or summink somebody wants me to sign?" Now we both were frowning. I produced the letter and he signed it, Jo behind the couch not even thinking about not reading over our heads.

I had typed the Stones' names in the order—Jagger, Richards, Watts, Wyman, Taylor—that I wanted to collect them, because I knew that once Jagger and Keith had signed the others would; so I rode with the two Micks past the Whisky-à-Go-Go and Hollywood High School to

Sunset Sound Studios, where they were finishing their new album. I asked Keith, slumped on a couch in front of the recording console, to sign the letter and he did, in the wrong place. "Doesn't matter," I said, and though Mick Taylor was at the bottom of the list he was sitting next to Keith, so I passed him the paper and pen, and he signed. Charlie signed leaning over the console. That made four out of five. I went to an office and called Wyman at the Beverly Wilshire, where he and Astrid were still living and were not happy about it. He said he was not coming to the studio, but he'd be over to the Oriole house for dinner about seven-thirty and he'd sign it then. "That'll be all right, won't it," he asked, and I said sure. But I wanted to get the letter out tonight. The tour was starting soon, I expected big expenses, and I knew in my bones that it would take forever to get a publishing contract and even longer to get paid.

When I went back to the control room Charlie and Mick Taylor were leaving, and I rode with them back to the Oriole house. Wyman and Astrid were coming over for dinner because they were bored with eating out, and we were going out because we were bored with eating at home. I had nothing to worry about except that we might leave before Wyman arrived, so I worried about that. But they came in and sat down to dinner just as we were leaving. I laid the letter beside Wyman's plate and asked him to sign it. He perused it, taking his time. I had already waited longer than I wanted to. "Right there," I said, handing him a pen. Wyman picked up the letter and asked, "You don't mind if I read it, do you?" I said sure, go ahead, it's just one sentence, no big deal. "Still got you on the defensive," Charlie said, but Bill signed, I put the letter in my notebook, and out we went.

The next step was to make copies of the letter and mail the original to my agent, but I wouldn't be able to do that till tomorrow. Still, I had the letter, the letter was signed, it was in my notebook, my notebook was in my hand. We were rolling in a limousine past expensive houses on streets named after birds.

Dinner at a trendy, surly restaurant was not much fun, but afterwards we met the other Stones at the Whisky-à-Go-Go to hear Chuck Berry.

On the Strip, on the corner, past the tense, remote loungers at the entrance, into the darkness, the land of dreams, where it was hot and smoky and crowded, a big barn with a small elevated dance floor, the bandstand high in a corner, unfamous people looking for famous people, famous people looking for each other, the Rolling Stones sitting at tables in the corner not looking for anybody. I sat with Jagger, Keith, and Wyman, an odd combination. Young girls, two or three or seven together, kept walking by our tables, passing maybe six times before they got up the nerve to ask for the Stones' autographs. The waitresses hovered around us, dollar bills folded lengthways between their fingers.

Onstage were four white musicians, loud and incompetent. A light show was playing on two walls, one covered with Jello-colored liquid globs and swirls, the other showing salmon leaping up a small waterfall, one clip repeating over and over, intercut between scenes from a Japanese movie featuring a giant beast come from the sky to devour the world. The eating of Tokyo blended perfectly with the rest of the action in the room, where people who had grown up surrounded by crazy images—like the girl on the dance floor dressed in black leather, looking mean in her boots and wrist guards—tried to be as real as Batman or Wonder Woman or Zontar, the Thing from Venus, shuddering there on the wall.

But then a lean, high-cheekboned, brooding-eyed black man came onstage, wearing his guitar low as a gunfighter's gun, stroking it with obscene expertise, and even Keith's image—the worst image in the room, Indian, pirate, witch, the image that grins at Death—reverted to what he was when he first heard Chuck Berry, a little English schoolboy in his uniform and cap. A few years passed before Keith could see Chuck Berry in person, because Berry was in the federal penitentiary at Terre Haute for taking a fourteen-year-old Indian whore across a state line for the wrong reasons, but Keith and Jagger both learned Berry's trademark duck walk from the film *Jazz on a Summer's Day*, which Keith saw fourteen times. Later, when Chuck Berry was out of prison and Mick and Keith were Rolling Stones, they met him, and unlike many of their musical idols, he snubbed them repeatedly, so that they respected him all the more and were trying to hire him for the present tour.

And now as Berry played "Sweet Little Sixteen," playing sloppily with this punk band, not even playing the right changes, still from time to time in the breaks there was a flash of the magic of his guitar, and Keith, once more the schoolboy who wore tight pants under his baggy ones, leaned across the table to Wyman, because Wyman used to go to dances in two pairs of pants, a baggy pair over tight ones, they wouldn't let you in the door wearing tight ones (it is possible that the single most powerful unifying social element for this generation has been that we all, girls too, grew up wearing pants that clearly showed our sexual organs, straining right there against the denim), and to Wyman, a tiny man with the face of a funny gargoyle, who started a groupie empire, in fact, *the* groupie empire ("It originated with Bill," Keith said. "He screwed thousands. He marked it all down in his diary." Actually he stopped counting after, I think, 278), Keith said, "He's not doin' much, that band's so bad, but every once in a while, wow—"

Wyman, watching Berry, who had let nothing, not even prison, stop him from singing about sixteen-year-old pussy, smiled and said, "Yeah,'e's great, inne—"

When Berry's set ended we left the Whisky (our leaving, like all our arrivals and departures, swift and dramatic, everyone staring at the Stones as we swept out into limousines at the curb) and rolled, four carloads of us, down the superhighway toward the Corral, a night-club in Topanga Canyon, to hear Gram Parsons and the Flying Burrito Brothers.

Along the miles and miles of highway, we (the Wattses, Bill and Astrid, two or three others) were talking about music—Shirley who loves old-time rock and roll very elated about seeing Chuck Berry—when for the first time on this tour we encountered Wyman's Weakness. Bill told the driver to stop at a gas station, got to go to the loo, and we rolled on and no place was open, and Bill again said, Hey, you gotta stop somewhere, gotta go to the loo, and the driver said, Doesn't seem to be any place open. Well, stop at one that isn't open, Bill said, just let me out of the car, and Charlie reminded him that "It was you got us in trouble like that the time before, Bill."

It was March 18, 1965, the last night of the Rolling Stones' fifth tour of England. The tour had lasted two weeks, fourteen consecutive nights of playing movie houses, two shows nightly. It had not been especially eventful. Three shows had been recorded for a concert album. In Manchester, at the Palace, a girl fell fifteen feet from the upper circle of seats into the stalls. The fall went almost unnoticed as 150 screaming girls stormed the stage when Mick sang "Pain in My Heart." The girl ran away from attendants attempting to take her to an ambulance and was later seen outside the stage door, still screaming, "Mick, Mick." At Sunderland, where the Stones played the Odeon, fans wanted to buy the water the Stones had used to wash their hair, and someone sold their fag ends, cigaret butts, for a penny each. At Sheffield, a grown man seeking an autograph pulled Charlie off his stool while he was playing. At the Leicester Trocadero, another girl fell out of the upper circle, losing her front teeth. "We were scared," Mick said later. "You know how these things catch on. We could easily end up with an outbreak of people swan-diving from their balconies and somebody killed."

At the Rochester Odeon, which they would remember as one of the worst theaters in England, the stage door watchman wouldn't believe, because of the way they looked, that the Stones were the Show, and refused to let them in. Keith shoved him down and they went in anyway. At the Sunderland Odeon, while Charlie was announcing the song "Little Red Rooster," a girl leapt onto Mick's back. He calmly carried her to the edge of the stage and set her down.

On the last night of the tour, March 18, after two shows at the ABC Theater at Romford, the Stones headed for London in Mick's Daimler. Before he reached home, Wyman needed to urinate. As their road manager Ian Stewart described the situation, "Really, if you sit in a dressing room all night, drinking Coca-Cola, go onstage for about thirty minutes, leap about like idiots, drop your guitar to run out into a car in the bloody cold weather, you're just about ready for a quick tiddle."

Mick turned the big, black car into a Francis service station in Romford Road, Forest Gate, east London. It was about eleven-thirty. According to the station attendant, forty-one-year-old Charles Keeley, "a shaggy-haired monster wearing dark glasses" got out of the car and asked, "Where can we have a piss here?" Keeley told Wyman that the public toilets were closed for reconditioning, which was a lie, and then denied him access to the staff toilet. Wyman's behavior, according to Keeley, "did not seem natural or normal." He was "running up and down the forecourt, taking off his dark glasses and dancing." Then "eight or nine youths and girls got out of the car." Mr. Keeley, "sensing trouble," told the driver of the car, Mick Jagger, to get them off the forecourt. Jagger pushed him aside and said, "We'll piss anywhere, man." This phrase was taken up by the others, who repeated it in "a gentle chant." One danced to the phrase. Then Wyman went to the road and urinated against a garage. Mick Jagger and Brian Jones followed suit farther down the road. According to Mr. Keeley, "Some people did not seem offended. They even went up and asked for autographs." One customer, however, told the Stones their behavior was "disgusting." At this the Stones "started shouting and screaming." The incident ended with the Daimler driving away, its occupants making "a well-known gesture with two fingers."

Mr. Keeley took down the license number. The customer who had spoken out against the Stones was one Eric Lavender, aged twenty-two, secretary-warden of a Forest Gate community youth center. "If the police do not prosecute, I will press a private prosecution," said the indignantly alliterative Lavender.

At the police prosecution of the affair, the Stones told a different, and much shorter, story. Wyman testified that he had said nothing more to Mr. Keeley than " 'May I use the toilet?' I never swear." Being refused, they got back in the car and drove off. Mick also denied any insulting behavior and said that he had never sworn at school, university, or since. Brian said he was not the type of person to insult anyone—"I am easily embarrassed." The court sided with Messrs. Keeley and Lavender, and the Stones were ordered to pay fifteen guineas costs, in spite of Wyman's plaintive statement: "I happen to suffer from a weak bladder."

But as he told the story now, while we rolled down the California coast on this pleasurable night, this pleasure-seeking night, before a tour that would be stranger than any of the Stones' previous ones, Bill's memory lifted the story to heroic proportions: ". . . so I go behind this place, see, and I've got me chopper out, when here comes this bloke waving a bloody electric torch, cryin, 'Ere, 'Ere—"

"He probably had to have a torch to see it," Shirley said.

We found a gas station and while waiting for Bill we lost the other limousines. None of us knew where the Corral was, least of all the driver, and we raced along the highway looking for spoor. Somebody thought it was down that turning to the right, is that it, nah, that place is closed, and then there it was on the left, a little roadhouse, capacity about two hundred, tables and a small dance floor, crowded with rednecks and members of Los Angeles rock and roll society. Bruce Johnston of the Beach Boys was present, and so were the young ladies Miss Christine and Miss Mercy, members of the Bizarre Records act called the G.T.O.'s, meaning Girls Together Outrageously or Orally or anything else starting with O. Miss Mercy was dark and heavy, a fortune-teller with kohl-rimmed eyes, many bracelets, rings, and scarves. Miss Christine, willowy and blond, in a long red dress with virginal lace at the bosom, was a California-bred magnolia blossom. Dancing together, they glided before us like one person, red yellow and blue jukebox lights washing over the room as Gram sang "I made her the image of me."

We sat at a long table, the Stones Gang and their friends and women, drinking pitchers and pitchers of beer, whooping and hollering while the Burritos played "Lucille" and old Boudleaux Bryant songs, a real rock and roll hocdown. It had been nearly six years since the Stones played in English clubs where sweat condensed on the walls and people swung from the rafters. They were glad when they stopped working in clubs and went on to bigger places, but later they missed them, as they had come, over nearly three years, since their drug arrests, to miss playing itself.

Now, getting ready to go back on the road, it was good to be at the Corral and see all these different types, motorcycle boots, eagle tattoos, lesbian romancers, white English niggers, Beach Boys, Georgia boys, brought together by the music. The night seemed to pass like a dream, one minute all of us were singing along and the next minute it was closing time and we were going out. We dozed on the way home, and when we got there I drank a glass of raw milk and went to bed, with my notebook, the letter inside, under my pillow. I was nearly unconscious, but I always read something before I go to sleep. I had been rereading Kerouac, preparing to visit him, and I opened the book I was reading to the place where I had stopped:

Never dreaming, was I, poor Jack Duluoz, that the soul is dead. That from Heaven grace descends, the ministers thereof. . . . No Doctor Pisspot Poorpail to tell me; no example inside my first and only skin. That love is the heritage, and cousin to death. That the only love can only be the first love, the only death the last, the only life within, and the only word . . . choked forever.

6

One evening there, hot and astonished in the Empire, we discovered ragtime, brought to us by three young Americans: Hedges Brothers and Jacobsen, they called themselves. It was as if we had been still living in the nineteenth century and then suddenly found the twentieth glaring and screaming at us. We were yanked into our own age, fascinating, jungle-haunted, monstrous. We were used to being sung at in music halls in a robust and zestful fashion, but the syncopated frenzy of these three young Americans was something quite different; shining with sweat, they almost hung over the footlights, defying us to resist the rhythm, gradually hypnotising us, chanting and drumming us into another kind of life in which anything might happen.

J. B. PRIESTLEY: *The Edwardians*

"So WE START TALKING to Brian," Keith said, "and he's moving up to London with his chick and his baby. His second baby, his first one belongs to some other chick. He's left her and he's really cuttin' up in Cheltenham. He can't stay there any longer, he's got shotguns coming out of the hills after him, so he's moving up to town."

"He used to come up on the weekends and I'd say, 'Look, man, stick it out till you've got a bit of bread together, and *then* come to

London,' " Alexis Korner said. Korner, who sang and played guitar, was one of the first Europeans to perform the music of American country blues artists. Brian, after changing from clarinet to alto saxophone and playing in a Cheltenham band called the Ramrods, had become interested in the blues and had begun playing guitar.

"I'd met Brian," Korner said, "because while I was working with the Chris Barber band doing odd concerts we played one in Cheltenham and Brian came up to me after the concert and asked if he could speak to me. That's how we got together. He used to show up at the Ealing club on Thursdays and weekends and occasionally play a bit.

"Brian couldn't stand Cheltenham. He simply loathed Cheltenham. He couldn't stand the restrictions of Cheltenham. He couldn't stand the restrictions imposed by his family on his thinking and his general behavior. That's why he came to London, just bang! like that. Every weekend I'd be saying, 'For God's sake, Brian, hold on a bit longer, don't suddenly arrive in London. It's a very hard place.' And then in the end one of my weekend chats didn't do anything and he arrived in London and that was that. One day he said, 'I'm leaving Cheltenham and coming to London, can you put me up?' So he arrived, so we put him up. He slept on the floor for a few nights and then he found a place of his own and went to work at Whiteley's, a store in Queensway.

"Mick sent me a tape of some stuff he and Keith had got down, odds and ends of Bo Diddley and Chuck Berry numbers. I either answered the letter or we got together by phone, and he came over to my place. Mick was into the club at Ealing almost from the beginning, sort of standing around waiting to sing his three songs every night. If we made any bread, Mick got thirty bob to get back to Dartford on, if not, not. Keith was a very quiet guitar player who used to come up occasionally with Mick from Dartford. He didn't make every gig but he'd come up most times, and sometimes he'd play and sometimes he wouldn't. It was a very loose arrangement.

"In general terms Mick wasn't a good singer then, just as he isn't a good singer now, in general terms. But it was the personal thing with Mick, he had a feel of belting a song even if he wasn't. He had this tremendous personal—which is what the blues is about, more than technique; he's always had that. I've got a very early photo of Mick with a zip-up cardigan and a collar and tie and baggy trousers—Mick always had that, and he had this absolute certainty that he was right.

"Mick was very edgy, because he was having a lot of arguments with his family. I remember his mother ringing me up one night and saying 'We've always felt that Mick was the least talented member of the family, do you really think he has any career in music?' I told her that I didn't think he could possibly fail. She didn't believe me—she didn't see how I could make a statement of that sort. I don't suppose she can to this day. Don't suppose she'll ever understand why he is what he is. You know that about someone or you don't know it, and blood relationship has nothing to do with it. I never met any of Mick's family. I spoke to his father on the odd occasion, but I find it very difficult to speak to gym instructors. He was a basketball player, I saw him on television once or twice refereeing basketball games. Mick used to come out from Dartford with a sigh of relief as he left and got into the area where he could say what he wanted, which he felt he couldn't do at home."

On May 19, 1962, a news item appeared in the music paper *Disc*, titled "Singer Joins Korner":

> A nineteen-year-old Dartford rhythm-and-blues singer, Mick Jagger, has joined Alexis Korner's group, Blues Inc., and will sing with them regularly on their Saturday night dates at Ealing and Thursday sessions at the Marquee Jazz Club, London.
>
> Jagger, at present completing a course at the London School of Economics, also plays harmonica.

"In the early summer," Keith said, "Brian decided to get a band together. So I went round to this rehearsal in a pub called the White Bear, just off Leicester Square by the tube station. Got up there and there's Stu, this is where Stu comes in."

Stu—Ian Stewart, a boogie-woogie piano player—comes from a Scottish town just north of England, Pittenweem, Fife. "I'd always wanted to play this style of piano," Stu said, " 'cause I'd always been potty on Albert Ammons. The BBC used to have jazz programs every night, and one night many years ago my ears were opened. I'd thought boogie was a piano solo stuff, and they had this program called 'Chicago Blues.' I don't remember any of the records, all I can remember is that they had this style of piano playing with guitars, harmonicas, and a guy singing. So when a little advert appeared in *Jazz News*—a character called Brian Jones wanted to form an R&B group—I went along and saw him. I'll never forget, he had this Howlin' Wolf album goin', I'd never heard anything like it. I thought, Right, this is it. He said, 'We're gonna have a rehearsal.' "

"We have one rehearsal which is a bummer," Keith said, "with Stu, Brian, a guitar player called Geoff somebody, oh garn what was his name, and a singer and harp player called—we used to call him 'Walk On,' that was the only song he knew. He was a real throwback, greasy ginger hair. These two cats don't like me 'cause they think I'm playing rock and roll. Which I am, but they don't like it. Stu loves it 'cause it swings, and Brian digs it. Brian doesn't know what to do, whether to kick me out and keep it together with these cats or kick

those two out and have only half a band again. Nobody is even thinking yet of actually playing for the audience. Everybody's still very
much into rehearsing together and playing together just to try to get
it together and find out whether you'll ever get anywhere near it.
Brian was working. He had a job in a record store. After being thrown
out of another for nicking something or other. He decides to get rid
of these two cats, which is all right with me, and meanwhile I persuaded Mick to come to rehearsal, which is now going to consist of
Stu, me, Mick, Brian, and Dick Taylor on bass, no drummer. Piano,
two guitars, harmonica, and bass. Mick starts learning to play harmonica. We get this other pub for rehearsals, the Bricklayers' Arms in
Berwick Street. We had a rehearsal up there and it was great, really
dug it. It was probably terrible. But it swung and we had a good time.
Most of the pubs round the West End have a room upstairs or in
the back which they rent off to anybody for five bob an hour or
fifteen bob a night. Just a room, might have a piano in it, but nothing
else, bare floorboards and a piano. Cardboard boxes full of empty
bottles. That was virtually home for the rest of the summer. We'd
rehearse twice a week, no gigs. The first fans if I remember appeared
on the scene at this point. I left art school during this period. I did
try for one job with my little portfolio, and I was promptly turned
down by the cat who designed the cover for *Let It Bleed*. Mick meanwhile still singing with Korner, to make a little bread and 'cause he
dug it. Brian was living right in the middle of where all the spades live
here, in a basement, very decrepit place with mushrooms and fungus
growing out of the walls, with Pat and his kid. Now sometime this
summer something really weird happens. One night Mick, who'd been
playin' a gig with Korner, went round to see Brian, if I remember
rightly, and Brian wasn't there but his old lady was. Mick was very
drunk, and he screwed her. . . . This caused a whole trauma, at
first Brian was terribly offended, the chick split, but what it really did
was put Mick and Brian very tight together, because it put them through
a whole emotional scene and they really got into each other, and they
became very close . . . so that kind of knitted things together. Mick
was still very strongly into school, music was just a sort of absorbing
hobby, nobody was taking it seriously except Brian, who was really
deadly serious about it."

After Brian's death, Alexis Korner's wife went into Whiteley's, Brian's
first employer in London, "and suggested," Korner said, "they erect
a plaque. They were absolutely shocked. She said, 'On houses where
famous men have lived they put up plaques saying Charles Dickens
1860, or whatever, I don't see why you shouldn't put up a plaque in
the electrical department saying Brian Jones worked here in 1962,
I can't see any reason why you shouldn't.' "

7

During the entire trip my dreams stubbornly followed the tactic of ignoring Africa. They drew exclusively upon scenes from home, and thus seemed to say that they considered—if it is permissible to personify the unconscious processes to this extent—the African journey not as something real, but rather as a symptomatic or symbolic act. Even the most impressive events of the trip were rigorously excluded from my dreams. Only once during the entire expedition did I dream of a Negro. His face appeared curiously familiar to me, but I had to reflect a long time before I could determine where I had met him before. Finally it came to me: he had been my barber in Chattanooga, Tennessee! An American Negro. In the dream he was holding a tremendous, red-hot curling iron to my head, intending to make my hair kinky—that is, to give me Negro hair. I could already feel the painful heat, and awoke with a sense of terror.

—C. G. JUNG: *Memories, Dreams, Reflections*

INSTEAD OF SNEAKING past the office door as usual, I went in this morning to tell Jo Bergman that I needed to use one of the numerous limousines or rented cars. She asked where I was going and I said, playing it close to the vest, Got to run some errands. Jo said she had to look at a house for Bill Wyman on Beverly Boulevard,

and I could use a car while she was there if I would take her (Jo
didn't drive) and come back for her. So I cruised in an Oldsmobile
down Santa Monica and up Beverly, dropped Jo off, doubled back to
a Xerox copy shop on Santa Monica and waited, jingling the car keys,
probably making even slower the bovine matron who operated as deliberately as the giant machine that hummed and flashed and finally
spat out grey speckled copies of the Stones' letter. I paid the b.m. a
dollar fifty for them, drove to the post office, sent the original air
mail special to the literary agency and one copy home to Memphis. I
went out past the blind man's cigaret stand to the Olds and headed
down Sunset Strip, looking for a telephone booth. I didn't see one on
the street, so I stopped across from the Playboy Club, ran inside like a
man in a spy story and asked the bunny lady who greeted me if I might
use the phone. It was only about 11:00 A.M., no other customers yet,
but she was all decked out—a young blond, God knows what she really
looked like—in the sadomasochist high heels, blue satin up the crack,
pushed-up bosom (as if her breasts were two poisonous fruits, delicious but untouchable, offered on a tray to tantalize), and bunny ears.
I'm working on a story for *Playboy* magazine, I told her, and I need
to call my agency. It sounded convincing, the last time I was in Hollywood I had been working for *Playboy*, and she called someone upstairs
in the Byzantine hierarchy to see if it was permitted to let a writer use
the phone, then gave me the receiver and walked discreetly a few steps
away, her fluffy white bunny-tail bouncing.

I sat on her little greeting stool, called the agency, and told the
number-one assistant agent that the fabled letter was on its way, that
Schneider should be avoided like a school of sharks, and that the
book contract should be sent to the Oriole house in a plain wrapper.
Then back up to the house on Beverly Boulevard, whose red bricks,
shrubbery, and oriental carpets Jo thought would do for Bill and Astrid.
Something about it seemed sinister to me, but that could have been
just a negative reaction to Jo, talking on the way back to Oriole about
her nervous rash and her herb doctor while she chain-smoked cigarets.

At Oriole I ate white cheddar sandwiches and drank beer for breakfast. Charlie was going to Sunset Sound, and Sandison was coming
along, something about seeing a writer from the *Saturday Review*. I
joined them. A limousine took us there, and we went down the little
alley and through the many gates and doors, locking each one behind
us, to the control room, a carpeted capsule containing a large console
with hundreds of lights, buttons, switches, levers, a vast dark window
before us, giant speakers mounted on the wall over the window, tilted
toward our heads, exploding with sound.

Keith, sitting at the console, was wearing a fringed leather jacket
of the kind then popular. But Keith, true to form, was wearing the

worst-looking one I had ever seen, the leather faded yellow, cracked and dry, the lining ripped out. His ear-tooth was dangling, a big yellow joint was in his left hand, in his right hand the red knob that boosted the intensity of his guitar track. The tracks were stacked eight deep on the wide plastic tape wheeling through the recording machine, a sound engineer watching seven of the tracks, Keith watching his own. Jagger stood behind them, dressed in tight blue slacks, blue open-throated pullover, left hand on hip, right elbow tight to side, right hand palm up holding a joint the size of the average Negro basketball player's putz, which he was smoking not like Joan Crawford or even Bette Davis but like Theda Bara, eyes closed, lips pursed, then mouth slightly open, smoke hanging luxuriantly in thick open lips, soft sucking inhale.

Keith was grinning, showing bad teeth, making deep wrinkles around his eyes as his guitar lick came around and he turned the knob to make it scream, boosting the pain each time like men drunk in bars at the turn of the century twisting the knobs of an electric shock machine, five cents a shock—except that Keith was doing it to get your attention, just giving you a little high voltage to bring your mind around to what was being said: *Did you hear about the Midnight Rambler?*—Jagger's harmonica and Keith's guitar whining and bending, swooping together, just about to jump the garden wall— *Says every-body's got to go*

We were locked up in the studio not because of the dope but because the Stones, lacking work permits, were not supposed to use American recording studios. What they were doing was illegal, and they were enjoying it very much. In the middle of the song, *the one you never seen before*, two men came into the control room, one in a silk suit that changed from blue to green like automobile enamel, a cigar in his leaden jaw, glossy machined-looking black hair, Pete Bennett: "I'm the best guy in the world to have pushin' ya record fa ya." With him in Hush Puppies and a yellow T-shirt, looking, though only in his thirties, old and grey and sort of like Jack Ruby with cancer, was the legendary Allen Klein, who I realized had failed to squash my plans for a book like a bug under his Hush Puppies only because, so far, he hadn't got around to it. I was frightened that he would notice me and step on me, and I scooted around to the front of the console, sat on a couch, and buried my face in a magazine. It contained an interview with Phil Spector, who when he was twenty-one became famous as rock and roll music's first teenaged millionaire. In the course of the interview Spector ridiculed almost everyone in the music business, including the Mafia, but of Allen Klein he would say only, "I don't think he's a very good cat." I huddled lower on the leatherette. The song was building to some insane climax, message of fear riding on waves of harmonica and guitar—faster and faster, breathless, frantic, and I wondered what the hell I was doing with these mad English owl-hoots, and what were they doing that they needed Allen Klein, who scared Phil Spector, a man with so many bodyguards and fences and so much bullet-proof glass that he ridiculed the Stones for getting arrested; even Spector seemed afraid of this pudgy glum-faced accountant in his bulging yellow T-shirt. But what scared me most was the knowledge that whatever they were up to, I had to know about it. No matter if Klein took my book, took my money, had me killed, I had to try to stick around and see what happened. I had to do it—to do something—for Christopher, but I had liked Brian and wanted to know him better. Also, I had the feeling something was going to happen, something I shouldn't miss. The song had slowed down now to excruciating little bird calls between harp and guitar, Mick and Keith exploring the poetry of the last breathless moments as the blade rides, and Mick groaned in the voice of someone who told you he was not the Boston Strangler.

As I sat on that Naugahyde couch, in crazy sixties-end Los Angeles, roaring from the speakers were such sounds, such low-down human groans and cries not new, old as time, almost, but never on a record had they seemed so threatening. I had heard such sounds before, heard them as a little boy lying in bed in the wiregrass country of south Georgia, heard the sounds of animals crying far off in the woods, heard the sounds the black woods hands made having what they called church, far off in the woods, the all-night drums, like the heartbeat of the dark swampy woods, *boom*dada *boom*dada, and heard the sounds that I could not identify—the really frightening ones. I had not been so frightened since I was a boy lying slender and white and frail in the dark bed, finding a sound in the night, losing it, waiting for it again, a soft sighing sound that might have been the wind easing through the tops of the long-needle pines, or might have been cattle lowing a long way off, but always came back to sounding most like a simple human exhalation right outside the rusty screen of my bedroom window, the quietly released breath of a man standing quietly, just watching, waiting. I loved the woods but for years I lay awake at night fearing that sound. When I was old enough to have a rifle I would sometimes hear the sound, the wind, the distant animal call, the careful breathing in the dark, and I would lie there as long as I could stand it and then take my rifle and slip out of the dark house, not waking anyone, and look around outside, crouching low, breathing with my mouth open to keep from making the fearful telltale sound. It was the same feeling I had now, as the sounds, the awful wails of guitar and mouth harp, pitched and blended together. The feeling came partly from the music and partly from the presence behind my back of this man Klein, a full-blood Jew they would call him in the

Swamp, a man of great power, to me almost incalculable power, a man who did not know me, who cared nothing for me. I did not know yet how good or evil the Stones were, but of Klein I was simply afraid, because even though I had a letter from the Stones, a magic piece of paper, there was still the tour, this gauntlet I had to run, and a man like Klein could, I sensed, stop me any time he wanted to take the trouble. But when I was twelve, standing in the dark outside my grandfather's house, frightened nearly to death, I was still, in some part of my mind that is a gift from my father who got it from his father who got it from God knows where, calm and ready, I think, to do what had to be done. If there had suddenly appeared before me one of the men my grandfather worked with and whom I loved so much, loved their voices and their looks, their yellow eyeballs and smooth bulging black muscles, transformed by poison whiskey (it had happened; my grandfather was nearly stabbed with a sharpened three-corner file) into a mad death-wielding animal, I could have stayed calm enough and steady enough in my terror to shoot him. So I stayed calm and steady in my terror, sensing the craziness of the Stones, of mad Keith, and knowing that what the Stones had already done had killed one of them.

Sandison came in—I hadn't noticed that he'd left—with a girl, and they sat beside me on the couch. She was wearing blue jeans and carrying a notebook. The song track was so loud as to preclude introductions. I spoke into her ear: "You must be from the *Saturday Review*."

"Yes," she shouted back. I read her lips. "Who are you?"

This was giving me something to do besides get scared. "Jann Wenner," I said.

She looked at me as if I were crazy, which I had just been thinking about becoming. Then she turned to Sandison and in a second he answered her, speaking my name so loudly that I heard it. If I heard it, could Klein hear it? If he heard it, would he recognize it? If I had known more about Klein, I would be even more worried. But he had not heard; when I looked around, he was going out the door with Mick. They went into the studio, leaving the door open, light from the hall falling into the big high-ceilinged room, dimly illuminating Mick at the piano bench, Klein sitting backwards around a folding chair. Mick was erasing with the back of his hand something Klein had said. Big as Klein was, this skinny foppish young Englishman could stand him off, deny him the tour and get away with it. It was almost enough to make you afraid of Mick, of the Stones.

When they finished talking Klein left, Pete Bennett with him, and Jagger came back into the control room. For the moment the tapes were still, and Sandison introduced the *Saturday Review*'s girl reporter to Mick. She looked sleepy, hypnotized by Mick's presence like a chicken by a snake. Then she remembered something. "Oh!" She picked up her carpetbag and took out a bunch of marijuana plant-tops. "I brought you some flowers."

"Oh, thank you," Mick said, taking the boughs and throwing them on the couch. "That's very nice."

Sandison was speaking to Mick, who emitted a tiny guffaw apropos of nothing Sandison was saying and threw a slow-motion pitch toward the girl's left tit. She slowly managed to react; as his hand barely missed her breast she threw the same sort of punch back at him, but its aim was uncertain, she couldn't very well hit him in the balls and it was pointless to strike his flat chest. Also, in the midst of the act, the sense of it seemed to come to her—she was returning a playful punch Mick Jagger had made at her tit, her tit had become more popular than she ever expected—and this was not stupid, he really was a star, his potency existed in the room, her hand stopped in mid-air, opened, fluttered like a shot bird to her side.

Mick took her up to a chair beside the control board and told her to ask him some questions. She began to ask tiny *Saturday Review* questions, and he gave brief, smiling replies. Al Steckler arrived with the pictures for the concert programs, showed them to Mick and asked, What about text? I don't know, Mick said, Keith, what about a text? Yeah, Keith said, something short, just— Maybe we can get Sam to do something. Hey, Mick said, looking at me. Ah, Keith said. *You're* a writer, Mick said.

"What— what— all right, what do you want?"

"Something for the program," Mick said. "Not very long. Something lighthearted."

"How long, Al?"

"A hundred and eighty words."

"A what? How do you know?"

Al shrugged. "That's long enough."

"You know," Mick said. "Something lighthearted."

"I need it as soon as I can get it," Al said.

I figured I'd better go home and start writing. Sandison was leaving, so we went together. There were no cars at the studio, but we expected to get a cab on Sunset. Once we got out, the doors locked behind us, there were of course no cabs, this was Los Angeles. We walked along, thinking we'd find a cab in each block. Two with fares passed and then none, but I didn't mind, it was a pleasure to walk toward the sunset on Sunset. There were all sorts of signs around, a machine that took your fifty cents and dropped into your hot hand a map to the homes of Hollywood stars, and just a step away another machine selling the *L.A. Times*, whose headline read I WANT HELP, SAYS ZODIAC

KILLER. We passed Ralph's Pioneer House, the Vienna Hofbrau, Father Payton's Crusade for Family Prayer, and a man who was walking along reading the newspaper. (I want help!) On his back he was wearing a battery-powered machine with a mask that fit over his mouth and nose, allowing him to breathe the polluted air. Across the street was the Apocalypse, a store specializing in pornographic books and notions. Sandison had "never been in one in America," so I went in with him. Kama Sutra Oil, plastic vibrating dildoes, inflatable vaginas, posters of men, boys, women, girls, and various animals, separately and in combinations. The books were equally various: *Hot Snatch*, *Pedophilia*, *The Story of O*, all manner of porn for all persuasions. By the time we left the store the books had become in my mind one giant volume called *The Return of the Son of the Curse of the Vengeance of the Giant Vaginas*.

Night fell, the lights came on, cars buzzed around us, the mist filled our lungs. We found a taxi in the deadly romantic murk and made it back up to Oriole.

While I was wandering around the house trying to get high enough to write 180 words, Steckler gripped my biceps, gave me the high beam from his baby blues and said "Please." I told him if he wanted his fucking text to leave me the hell alone. Bowery Boys Routine #87, the Artist. I went back to the bedroom and tried to write. A few minutes ago I had been in the office with Sandison and his friend Sharon, from United Press International, who told me that Kerouac's wake had been going on since two o'clock that afternoon. He would be buried tomorrow. Sandison had read aloud selections from the pornography he'd bought, and now as I sat on the Wizard of Oz bedspread I could think only of phrases like "Keith's proud nipples stiffened." There was an idea at the back of my mind, certain words kept flashing: *Stones*, *Apocalypse*, *I want help*, but it was too heavy, not lighthearted. Finally I told Steckler that there was nothing new to be said about the Stones in 180 words.

"That's all right," he said. "I never thought it needed words."

8

At the present time Buddy Bolden is made out to be an epochal figure, his importance in the history of jazz seems to be overwhelming, and legends are woven about his person: he was somewhat of a scoundrel and sot, he never paid his musicians, he delighted in regaling or shocking his audience by singing obscene couplets, his instrumental talents and his powers of improvisation earned him the soubriquet of "King" Bolden; he used to place himself near the open window and blow his horn like a maniac, he could be heard miles away across the river, and all within range, attracted as if by a magnet by this clarion call, would flock around the great cornetist. We are witnessing the birth of an epic of our own times.

ROBERT GOFFIN: *Jazz*

"BECAUSE the chick has split, and Brian's very upset, and because he gets thrown out of his pad, Mick takes it on himself to find Brian a nice pad where he can live," Keith said. "Mick finds him a pad in Beckenham, halfway between London and Dartford. Weird little pad in a suburban street full of houses. Brian had one big room built onto this house. It was quite groovy, until he invites some chicks down to cook for him one day, and they burn half of it down, but he's still got to live there, so there's a hole in the ceiling, piece of canvas above it, tryna hide it from the landlord. When I left home I went to live with Brian in this place. We used to lay around, listen to sounds and play all day and always read *Billboard*, just to see what was goin' on and keep in touch with some kind of reality. Used to read every page, even jukebox profits, used to know everything about what was happening in the charts, absolutely everything."

"We were still rehearsing," Stu said. "We didn't have a name or anything. In those days it was the thing to do, to open your own club. You'd find a room that you thought would be a good place and you'd have a club. Korner had started a very successful club up in London —the Marquee Club on Thursday nights—and he was packin' the place. Thursday night was the BBC live jazz broadcast. They said to Alexis, Do you want to do this? which meant that he had to go to BBC studios. So he said to us, Do you want to fill in for me one night? We said Yeah—had to think of a name, so in desperation it became the Rolling Stones. The Marquee was our first job.

"At the start, nobody in England played this kind of music. But nobody. Mick and Keith and Brian were about the only people in the country that knew the music and were trying to play it. Everybody else were jazz musicians trying to play the blues, that hadn't really heard them. And having seen the Stones once at the Marquee, the people who were running the scene in those days were one hundred percent against us, and it was one bloody fight to get anywhere. They thought R&B was a jazz thing and there should be three saxophones. They said, What, two guitars and a bass guitar, that's rock and roll, we don't want to know about it, we'll try and put it down.

"We tried to open in Ealing on a Tuesday night and for two weeks we got not a soul, not one person would come to Ealing to see the Rolling Stones. We tried Tuesday night at the Flamingo, and it was the same thing. That lasted only two or three weeks. I'll never forget the first time we went down to the Flamingo. We did an audition on a Sunday afternoon, and the Flamingo was a pretty smart place. It was *the* modern jazz club in town, and everybody was going down there in their zoot suits, white shirts, and all that. I'll never forget sayin' to Keith, 'You're not going to the Flamingo lookin' like that, are you?' He said, 'What ho, Stu, I've only got one pair of fuckin' jeans.' "

"Winter of '62 was the tough one," Keith said. "It's down to cello-taping your pants up, Scotch tape across the rips. We're going through the weirdest period, completely broke, and this guy arrives, this strange little guy who lived in the next town to Brian, used to go to school with him. He was about five feet three, very fat, wore thick spectacles. He belonged to the Territorial Army, sort of a civil defense thing. They all live in tents and get soaking wet and get a cold and learn how to shoot a rifle and at the end they get eighty quid cash. This cat arrives in London fresh from the hills, from his tent. And he wants to have a good time with Brian, and Brian took him for every penny. The guy would do anything for Brian. Brian would say, 'Give me your overcoat.' Freezing cold, it's the worst winter, and he gave Brian this army overcoat. 'Give Keith the sweater.' So I put the sweater on. 'Now, you walk twenty yards behind us.' And off we'd walk to the local hamburger place. 'Ah, stay there. No, you can't come in. Give us two quid.' This cat would stand outside the hamburger joint, freezing cold, giving Brian the money to pay for our hamburgers.

"Brian gets him to buy a new guitar, a new Harmony electric. He pays for everything, and so in two weeks we've spent all the money and we say, 'See ya, man,' and put him on a train and send him home. He's incredibly hurt, but all the same, we've taken him around with us to all these clubs, and although he regrets very much being fleeced, he still comes up to London again later with even more bread, and we fleece him again. Terrible sadistic scenes we were pulling on him, Brian and I were really evil to this guy. It ended up with us stripping him off and trying to electrocute him.

"That was the night he disappeared. It was snowing outside. We came back to the pad and he was in Brian's bed. Brian for some reason got very annoyed that he was in his bed asleep. We had all these cables lyin' around and Brian pulled out this wire: 'This end is plugged in, baby, and I'm comin' after you.' Brian would run after him with this long piece of wire cable that's attached to an amplifier, electric sparks, chasing around the room, and he ran screaming down the stairs out into the street with nothing on, screaming, 'Don't go up there, they're mad, they're trying to electrocute me.' Somebody brought him in an hour later and he was blue.

"The next day the cat split. Brian had a new guitar, and his amp fixed, a whole new set of harmonicas. This was down at Edith Grove. The second time the guy came we were at Edith Grove in this pad Mick found. I'm not in on it 'cause I haven't got any bread, can't afford rent. Brian can afford it 'cause he's working, Mick can afford it 'cause he's got a scholarship grant from the university. It's Brian, Mick, and these two cats from the LSE. One's a Norwegian and one's a cat that comes from the Midlands. The straightest people you've ever seen in your life. Underneath are three old tarts, and on top are student teachers. It's a three-story house, with the second floor Mick and Brian and those two guys, and immediately I start in with the immortal phrase, Can I crash at your pad? So as not to have to go home. So virtually I leave home. Because I'm staying there all the time these cats are always kicking up a fuss, they won't pay the rent and they'll kick Brian out for letting me stay there. We're always very brought down when they arrive, and they're sittin' in the corner of the room lookin' very out of it, 'cause there are three or four musicians in another corner trying to get their thing together, and these guys are trying to study.

"Absolutely no bread at this point, Brian's in and out of work more frequently than ever. Got caught stealing again and very luckily was let off. He was always very good, Brian, at getting out of things. He'd always chat up the manager and they'd say, Yeah, we understand, your wife's left you (wasn't his wife but he'd always tell them it was), and your grandmother died and anything else he could think of. Brian was the one who kept us all together then. Mick was still going to school. I was sort of halfway looking for a job. I went out one morning and came back in the evening and Brian was blowing harp. He's standing at the top of the stairs saying, 'Listen to this: Whoooo. Whooooo.' All these blue notes comin' out. 'I've learned how to do it. I've figured it out.' One day.

"We were rehearsing two or three times a week, no gigging, we didn't dare. Dick Taylor's still with us, he's on bass by now. We were looking for drums. Charlie was gigging with Alexis Korner. We couldn't afford him. We picked up a drummer called Tony Chapman. Terrible drummer, always comin' in on the onbeat. Then Dick Taylor decided, I think, that he was gonna go on to another art school in London. Stu drifted with us for some reason.

"Brian's just about making enough to keep us from being chucked out of this place, and it's winter, it's like the worst winter ever. Brian and me sitting around this gas fire, wondering where to get the next shilling to put in it to keep the fire going. Collecting beer bottles and selling them back to the pubs, getting like three shillings, and going to pads where we knew there'd been parties on, walkin' in sayin' Hello, how nice, we'll help you clean up, and we'd steal the bottles and whatever food we could find lying around the kitchen and run for it. It's gettin' really sick, down to pickin' people's pockets, in fact that's why these two LSE cats leave. They split, and we get this other cat in who's worth a brief mention 'cause he was as horrifyingly disgusting as Brian and myself at the time and also 'cause he used to call himself Phelge, which was just a nickname, but he insisted on being called Phelge.

"Nanker Phelge"—listed as the writer of the Stones' original songs on their first records—"was a creation of Brian's. This guy who called himself Phelge was going through this incredible scene at the time— everybody went through it in a way, Mick went through his first camp period, he started wandering round in a blue linen housecoat, wavin' his hands everywhere—'Oh! Don't!' A real King's Road queen for about six months, and Brian and I used to take the piss out of him. Mick was on that kick, and this guy that we lived with, Phelge, was into being the most disgusting person—he was going through being the most disgusting thing ever. Literally. You would walk into this pad, and he would be standing at the top of the stairs, completely nude except for his underpants, which would be *filthy*, on top of his head, and he'd be spitting at you. It wasn't a thing to get mad about, you'd just collapse laughing. Covered in spit, you'd collapse laughing.

"And this pad is getting so screwed up, for like six months we used the kitchen to play in, just rehearse in, because it was cold, and slowly the place got filthy and started to smell, so we bolted the doors and locked them all up, and the kitchen was condemned. I was at that time into making tapes, I had a tape recorder, reels and reels of tape in the bedroom. See, it was interesting, the place was built like if that was the bedroom, the stairs would be coming up here, and turn round and then come along here, and the kitchen would be off here, and the bog would be here. I used to have a bed here, and the window there, and the window to the bog would be there. All this was outside a courtyard in the garden. I had the microphone through the window in the cistern of the bog, and the tape recorder at the foot of the bed. And I had reels and reels of tapes of people goin' to the bog. Chains pullin'. On cheap tape recorders, if you record the flushing of a john, it sounds like people applauding, so it would be like some incredible show Brian and I would make up, like with the chick from downstairs: 'And now, folks, Miss Judy Whatever.' Every time somebody would come into the bog, I'd switch the tape recorder on and go round to the bog door and knock, and they'd say 'Wait a minute,' and you'd get these conversations going through the door, followed at the end by applause, and then the next person would come in. That's the sort of thing we were into. Real down-home.

"We're trying to get this band off the ground without any real hope. At this time the Beatles' first record comes out and we're really brought down. It's the beginning of Beatlemania. Suddenly everybody's lookin' round for groups, and we see more and more groups being signed. Alexis Korner gets a recording contract, splits from the Marquee Club, and who gets his spot, the Rolling Stones. For just about enough bread to keep alive.

"We really need a bass player now. I'm not sure what happened to Dick Taylor. I think we kicked him out, very ruthless in those days. Nobody could hear him because he had terrible equipment and he seemed to have no way to get anything better. Everybody else had hustled reasonable-size amplifiers. There was the scene of how much bread you were makin' and why split it with a cat who couldn't be heard anyway. Advertised for a bass player. The drummer we've got says, 'I know a bass player who's got his own amplifier, huge speaker, plus a spare Vox 130 amp'—which at the time was the biggest amp available, the best. He got one of those to spare, fantastic. So onto the scene comes—" William Perks, a bricklayer's son from Penge, in southeast London "—and we can't believe him. He's a real London Ernie, Brylcreemed hair and eleven-inch cuffs on his pants and huge blue suede shoes with rubber soles."

Bill met the Stones at a pub called the Weatherby Arms, in King's Road, Chelsea. "Bill came down there," Stu said, "and they were in one of their funny moods, and they didn't even bother to talk to him, and Bill didn't know what was going on. They were living in Edith Grove together and, um, I used to dread goin' round there because of some of the weird things that used to go on. I used to think they were fuckin' insane at times. When people live together all the bloody time they begin to develop virtually their own language and you're never sure whether you're gettin' through to them, or whether they mean what they say or whether they're laughin' at you all the fuckin' time. So Bill wasn't one bit impressed."

A few years older than the other Stones, Bill (born October 24, 1935) had received, along with his brothers and sisters (two of each), a sound musical education. By the time he was fourteen he could play clarinet, piano, and organ. "He was very good," his father said. "In fact, he was in line for the job of organist at our local church." The elder Mr. Perks, who played accordion "just for fun" at neighborhood pubs, told his children that "if they learned to play an instrument they'd never be short of a pound." But even though Bill's parents both worked, his mother in a factory, at sixteen he had to leave Beckenham Grammar School to find a job. Drafted into National Service, Bill started playing guitar while stationed in Germany with the Royal Air Force as a file clerk.

After his discharge, Bill found a job with an engineering firm in Lewisham. When he met the Stones he had been married for a year and a half and had a year-old son, Stephen. Bill was working for the engineering firm and playing part-time with a rock and roll band called the Cliftons. "We had a drummer and three guitarists," Bill said. "One played rhythm, one lead, and I'd tune the top two strings of mine down seven semitones and play bass Chuck Berry–style. We got away with it, but then we'd hear groups with real basses, and we knew there was something wrong. So we bought a bass guitar from a fellow, cut it down, took all the metal off, made it very light and easy to play. I still use it sometimes." The Cliftons played weddings, youth-club dances, "picked up a fair amount of money, considering we weren't all that good."

Bill used part of the money to buy the equipment that the Stones admired. "They didn't like me, they liked my amplifier," Bill said. "The two they had were broken and torn up inside—sounded great, really, but we didn't know that then. But I didn't like their music very much. I had been playing hard rock—Buddy Holly, Jerry Lee Lewis—and the slow blues things seemed very boring to me."

But Stu "got on all right with Bill, really, and as I was the guy that was taking him home each night, I managed to sort of talk him into staying."

"It also turns out," Keith said, "that he can really play. At first it's very untogether, but slowly he starts to play very natural, very swinging bass lines. But it's not a permanent thing, he does play with us and he's coming to rehearsals, but then he can't make the gigs sometimes, because he's married and's got a kid, and he has to work. So it's very touchy one way and the other.

"Stu gets us a regular gig down where he lives, at this pub, the Red Lion, in Sutton. We're playing around west London, Eel Pie Island. Nearly all the same people would follow us wherever we went, the first Stones fans, all doing the new dances. The clubs held a couple of hundred. Things were beginning to look up, we were making like fifty quid a week, playing about five nights a week, every week the same places, and it's getting good. Brian's trying to find out about recordings. We know that because of the Beatles thing that's happening, there's no time to lose if we want to get on records, which is what we really want to do. Every musician wants to make records, I don't know why. It's got nothing to do with the bread, they just want to see what they can lay down for posterity, I guess.

"We've got a steady scene going in London, and we get hooked up with our first manager. Nothing was signed, but he was Giorgio Gomelsky, who owned the Piccadilly jazz club, a terrible place, nobody much used to go there, but we played there a couple of times. At one of these gigs we decided to get rid of our drummer and steal Charlie from this other band he was working with, because we were now in a position to offer Charlie twenty quid a week."

Charlie Watts, the son of a lorry driver for British Rail, was born in London on June 2, 1941. "My grandparents moved from London before I was born, when my father first got married. And they lived not in Wembley but near there. We moved to Wembley when I was about seven," Charlie said. "It was like there was nobody there. There were greens and things, which twenty years before were farmland. I remember as a kid there was a farm in Wembley that's not there any more. It's an estate. That was the last farm in that area producing milk and having pigs and a farmhouse, with barns. It's all gone now, and that's in my lifetime. I mean how far can you go? The world's going like that.

"I went to infants school in Wembley. Junior school's where you start to play football. You go to a secondary modern school for an ordinary education, which is what I had. We used to have forty in a class. I specialized in art. If I hadn't, I'd have just played football all day long. That's all I would have been living for—and cricket.

"I started playing when I was fourteen or fifteen. We had a choir, which nobody liked singing in much, didn't have a band. Music was a guy lecturing, and nobody understood what he was saying. Fortunately my parents were perceptive enough to buy me a drum kit. I'd bought a banjo myself and taken the neck off and started playing it as a drum. I don't know how it came about, I started learning the banjo, and I just got pissed off with it, I didn't like it. There was a little period of four weeks and by the end of it I'd already taken the neck off. Played newspaper with wire brushes. My parents bought me one of those first drum kits which every drummer knows only too well. But you have to have them, or you'd never get any appreciation of the other ones. I used to sell records to buy bigger cymbals and whatever was in vogue at the time. I used to waste money like mad buying equipment. I practiced at home to jazz records all the time. The only rock and roll I ever listened to was after the Rolling Stones turned me on to it. I used to like Jimmy Reed and Bo Diddley and from there I went on to, who's that guy, 'Ooh Poo Pah Doo,' and slowly I got on to hearing how good the early Elvis records were.

"When I was older I used to play at weddings, but then I was working in the day. I used to be a designer. Well, I don't know what I used to be, I used to do lettering, that's what I used to do all day. For three years, sit down and practice that. For a little guy who made his living at it, and I was his apprentice. And then from there—I'd done three years apprenticeship and wanted more money, being Jewish, so I moved to a bigger firm, which sent me to Sweden, ah, Denmark. Actually it was a big con because I went over there and got paid and did no work because nobody knew what I was supposed to be doing, as usual. I should have gone to New York. That was my big ambition in those days. But instead of that I went to Denmark. I'm glad I did— I got straight in with a band there—but I had no drum kit, had to borrow one all the time.

"Prior to that I used to play at the Troubadour with this band, and that's where I met Alexis Korner. Then I went away and came back and he's starting a band. He said he wanted me to play, so I said okay. Three of us lasted through the first rehearsals. Well, the first six months. They all became friends of mine. 'Cause it wasn't for bread. You never made bread, none of us did. We went all the way to Birmingham once and got five shillings. Time went on and I left that band and I'd left my firm, I was out of work, playing sometimes with another band, Blues by Five, just a mixture of stray people, and I joined the Stones."

. . .

"We'd come to a club," said Bill Wyman, who changed from Perks, taking the name of an air force friend, when the Stones began announcing their names onstage, "when we could get one to take us, and set up our amps. The others were dressed in sweaters, leather jackets, blue jeans, and I'd be in the clothes I'd worn to work. The manager would tell us, 'Look sharp now, only ten minutes before you go on, better go and change.' We'd tell him that we were going on as we were, and he'd say, 'Very funny, now go and get dressed.'

"We carried three stolen metal stools with us, and with Mick out front and Charlie in back we'd just sit down, Brian, Keith, and me, and start playing, just as if we were rehearsing. Each of us would have a beer by his stool, and when we finished a number we'd all drink a bit and light up a fag. Customers couldn't believe it. They'd stop dancing, come stand around the stage and stare at us. Didn't know what to think. The managers would say, 'Right, pack up your gear and get out in five minutes or I'll set my boys on you.'

"We'd finish playing after two A.M., and I'd have to be up at six to go to my job. I averaged three hours' sleep, and didn't know where I was a good part of the time. But I had to go on, because I had Stephen. Finally, though, I had to choose—the people at work told me to cut my hair or pack up. I had had long hair before going with the Stones, but now it was longer than ever. It seemed such a silly thing. Everybody—the people at work, my friends, my parents, my wife—said I should keep my job and not go with the Stones. Later, when we were a success, they said, 'See, I knew you could make it.' "

"The first time I saw them," Glyn Johns said, "I'd never seen anything like it, ever." The chief engineer at I.B.C. recording studios in London in January 1963, Johns helped the Stones to get a recording session. "I can remember taking them to I.B.C. for the first session and being frightened of introducing them to George Clouston, the guy who owned the studio. I see photographs of them then and they look so tame and harmless, I can't associate it with the effect they had on people. It was just their appearance, their clothes, their hair, their whole attitude was immediately obvious to you as soon as you saw them playing. It was just a complete *pppprt* to society and everybody and anything."

"At the start of the Stones it was Brian who was the monster head," Alexis Korner said. "Brian was incredibly aggressive in performance. By then his hair was pretty long, and he had what was almost a permanent pout, crossed with a leer, and he used to look incredibly randy most of the time. He used to jump forward with the tambourine and smash it in your face and sneer at you at the same time. The aggression had a tremendous impact. Also, he was a very sensitive player, Brian, at his best, and could play slow blues exceptionally well.

But I remember him most for his 'I'm gonna put the boot in' attitude. Brian achieved what he wanted to achieve by his extreme aggression, and it was extreme, it was incitement, when Brian was onstage playing he was inciting every male in the room to hit him. Really and truly that was the feeling one got. At the start Brian was the image of aggression in the Stones much more than Mick."

"But it was always Mick who would take people on," Stu said. "When we used to get fucked up every week by *Jazz News*," which seemed purposely to misprint the Stones' ads, "it would be Mick who'd go up to their office and have it out."

"But onstage," Alexis said, "it was Brian who made blokes want to thump him. He would deliberately play at someone's chick, and when the bloke got stroppy, he'd slap a tambourine in his face."

"Brian could have been killed a few times," Stu said.

9

She said, "Daddy, this old World Boogie
Gone take me to my grave
Gone take me to my grave."
BUKKA WHITE: "World Boogie"

BEFORE TEN O'CLOCK in the morning I was sitting in the living room with my back to the sweep of Los Angeles, talking on a beige telephone to a travel agent, who said that Kerouac's funeral could be reached only by taxi or rental car from Boston. There wasn't time, but with the letter mailed and the Stones, Sandison said, planning to spend the next week in the studio finishing *Let It Bleed*, I could go home and try to prepare for the tour.

After a day of shopping—a leather jacket, an ounce of grass—I rode to the airport with Chip Monck and Ian Stewart, who were going to inspect the hall the Stones would play in Chicago. Stu's neat black hair with short back and sides, his khaki trousers, golf shirt, and Hush Puppies made him and Monck, in his California cowboy drag—red suede jeans—a curious pair. Monck had again fallen asleep sitting up. He was the only person I had ever seen who could make falling asleep pretentious.

I asked Stu, who was driving, whether the Stones would charter a plane for the tour. Nobody knew yet, but it might not be a bad idea, Stu said; Keith was banned from Alitalia "for stayin' in the restroom from Rome to London punchin' that crazy Anita."

At eleven P.M. I flew to Memphis with a quiet planeload of tired old people returning from a synagogue-sponsored vacation in Singapore. Christopher met me at the gate. "Are you a child or an adult?" people have asked her. Christopher is four feet eleven and a half inches tall, but like Hermia in *A Midsummer Night's Dream*, "though she be but little, she is fierce."

Today Christopher worked for Omega Airlines from three o'clock till midnight, talking to machines and people, and her eyes, that change like the sea, looked tired and red.

When I met Christopher, the great-granddaughter of a Mississippi River steamboat captain, family fortune gone, she and her mother were living like ruined Russian royalty in a federal housing project in Memphis. Her mother and father separated before she was born, and she never knew her father. They had lived in the project since Christopher was a little girl. Her mother, having neither the breeding nor the inclinations of a servant, did not cook or clean. They ate at a place called Mae's Grill, or else ate tuna sandwiches and Vienna sausages at home. When she was very young, Christopher went to a private day school in much the same way that Fanny Price went to Mansfield Park. One day —she was about five years old—her father called the school and told Christopher that he was coming to get her. He never came, but she was terrified.

Christopher grew up in perfect ignorance of men. She saw photographs in books of Roman statues wearing fig leaves and thought men were made that way. She never had a date in high school, but she read Thackeray, Henry James, Jane Austen. She knew more about life then than I do now.

I was nineteen when we met, and a more arrogant young fool never drew breath. Without the handicap of learning or experience, I saw no reason not to become equal to Poe or Melville. (Not Mark Twain—I didn't foam at the mouth.) I was also a great and cynical lover. Christopher forgave me.

Nearly ten years had passed. Christopher had worked her way through college and freed her mother from the housing project. She had been a private tutor, ward clerk in a hospital, secretary at a savings and loan company. I had taught karate, been a state welfare worker, a Pinkerton operative, lived off my parents, and tried to learn to write. Now I was something called a journalist. Christopher had wanted to work for an airline so she could travel. We had travelled, but Omega changed Christopher's schedule every few weeks, giving her jet lag when she'd been nowhere. We both worked constantly, but the only money we had saved was $2000 from the *Saturday Evening Post*, hoarded against the Stones tour.

Christopher handled money strangely. Coins poured from her purse. I would find them in the car (we lived in a little white house, whose door would be kicked in by Detective J. J. Wells of the Metro Narcotics Squad, and drove a maroon Mustang) and ask, "What's this?"

"People throw money at me."

Later I would come home from England to find Christopher gone and only a cold wind in her closet, and when I found her and asked where she had been, she would say, "The birds and the animals keep me warm."

But on this night I was drunk and happy, full of good news and romance. Frowning, Christopher touched with her doll-like fingers the swell of her belly, now fubsy, once perfect as a peach. She had a stomachache and didn't want to play ducks and fishes, and who could blame her?

On Friday, while Christopher was working, I had dinner with my mother and father. I felt good because my agent's first lieutenant had told me on the phone today that the contract with the publisher would soon be ready. My mother offered me turnip greens, my father passed the cornbread. If I could keep Klein and Schneider out of the deal, and if the Stones would let me work, then after the tour Christopher and I would go to England and be happy ever after. I wasn't sure what to expect, but I didn't think the Stones cared about the money. My father slid the platter of fried chicken toward me, and I saw in his eyes, the eyes of a man who started out in the world plowing a Georgia mule for fifty cents a day, a sad, wise look, a look that said, Nobody doesn't care about the money.

Saturday morning I went to the bone doctor to see if I had broken my little finger on the swing-chain last Sunday in L.A. The fat girl at the reception desk asked what's wrong, I told her in complicated terms, and she wrote, simple but eloquent, "injured in fall."

The waiting room was nearly filled with patients, mostly young. One beefy high school football player, in a cast from ass to ankle, was talking about how he wanted to get back out there. The doctor X-rayed my hand, glanced at my chart, said "You're a writer?" and tried to enlist my help in saving the world from "the Chinese Reds." He began by asking whether I was an optimist or a pessimist, but he couldn't wait to tell me that he was a pessimist and couldn't see any better solution than bombing ourselves back to the Stone Age and starting over.

I told him something Margaret Mead had said about the current younger generation being the first global tribe and that these new kids didn't believe in military solutions, half a million of them spent three days in the mud at Woodstock without so much as a fist fight. The doctor, a polite man for all his bombing plans, did not mention the half-million American boys in Indochina fighting the longest war in U.S. history.

"I hope you're right," he said. "Myself, I don't see any hope." He looked at the X-rays, said nothing was broken, my finger should be all right in a few weeks or months, and prescribed some pills I never took.

On Sunday, when Christopher was at home, our friends Jim and Mary Lindsay Dickinson came to see us. Dickinson was one of the last musicians to record on the Sun label of Sam Phillips, who made the first recordings of Elvis Presley, Jerry Lee Lewis, Howlin' Wolf, Ike Turner, and Charlie Rich, among many others. We had known each other since college, and every now and then we would get together, listen to music, take drugs, and talk. This time we took sky-blue mescaline tablets—not Christopher, who again said she was not well, touching her stomach once more. I was worried about her, but she and Mary Lindsay left for Overton Park, Memphis' central park, Mary Lindsay's eyes dancing circles as they went out the door. Jim and I listened to a special history of rock and roll radio broadcast and I told him what I had done in California. He was so pleased that when Mary Lindsay came back he would tell her to quit her job, thinking I suppose that we would all soon be rich and famous. Christopher and I were proceeding with care, acting like white people, always a mistake.

"I just want to live through this tour and see what happens," I said.

"You got to go to the top of the mountain and see the elephant," Dickinson said.

On the radio Ike Turner was talking about Phil Spector: "Sometime he use fo'-five drums, twelve guitars, twenty-five or thirty voices, the guy is, uh, really a genius, you know." I thought of Spector's statement, in the interview I'd read at Sunset Sound, that English musicians have soul like black folk because soul comes from suffering, and when you see a little English kid in a World War II newsreel, it's probably Paul McCartney—which sounded silly, but there was something in the image, blackout, a child, screaming firebombs.

I remembered when I was very small, waking in the winter morning from a dream of Mickey Mouse to hear on the radio Grady Cole's doleful tones and a country song, "Hiroshima, Nagasaki"—the syllables whose meaning I didn't know, the cold morning, dressing for school, filled me with dread. That fear was part of our lives; we had come into the world when, for the first time in history, man had achieved such power that any child, no matter where, no matter who, could lie in his bed and be afraid for his life.

We knew in our cribs that something was wrong. Now some of us by acting together were beginning to defy the forces that made war and to get away with it. With the grandiose sweep of mescaline vision, it seemed that the Rolling Stones might be part of a struggle for the life or death of the planet.

1 O

One of the most popular of these combinations . . . was a company of boys, from twelve to fifteen years old, who called themselves the Spasm Band. They were the real creators of jazz, and the Spasm Band was the original jazz band. . . . The Spasm Band first appeared in New Orleans about 1895, and for several years the boys picked up many an honest penny playing in front of the theaters and saloons and in the brothels, and with a few formal engagements at West End, Grand Opera House, and other resorts, when they were advertised as "The Razzy Dazzy Spasm Band." Their big moment, however, came when they serenaded Sarah Bernhardt, who expressed amazement and gave them each a coin.

HERBERT ASBURY: *The French Quarter*

"THEN WE GOT that Richmond gig that built up to an enormous scene," Keith said. "In London that was *the* place to be every Saturday night, at the Richmond Station Hotel, on the river, a fairly well-to-do neighborhood, but kids from all over London would come down there."

"The Station Hotel was the most important thing," Stu said, " 'cause it was at the Station Hotel that you really started seeing excitement. It was at Richmond that they finally started to get up off their backsides and move, and within two months they were swingin' off the rafters.

"The Station Hotel only lasted about ten weeks, because they wanted to pull the place down, and it's still standing there yet. So they moved us to Richmond Athletic Club, which had a very low ceiling, with girders, so of course they're leaping about among the girders, they're going barmy. I'd love to see all that again. Because it was so good. There was never the slightest nastiness about it. Everybody really sort of dug each other, and—we never wanted to stop playing. Half past ten would come, and they'd say Stop, and we'd say Aw fuck, and play another three or four numbers. Some of those numbers used to really, really move. By this time, having lived together and done nothing else but listen to their records and tapes and play together, Brian and Keith had this guitar thing like you wouldn't believe. There was never any suggestion of a lead and a rhythm guitar player. They were two guitar players that were like somebody's right and left hand.

"Still rehearsing three times a week. Nobody had any money. They were spending everything they got on either equipment or records. Those days were hard enough, but there was a thrill about being involved with it all. Even though at this time the Beatles were filling the Albert Hall with screaming kids, they were still over there with Gerry and the Pacemakers and Billy J. Kramer and that lot, there was no guts to it. But you were aware at the time that you were really starting something."

"I went to the Station Hotel—how old was I? Fifteen—yeah, fifteen," said Shirley Arnold, a pretty auburn-haired English girl. "It was fairly cold. It must have been February. I was about to leave school. There were six of us went down to Richmond. We walked around all day there and then went to the Station Hotel. Two of us ended up in the club, but I didn't actually see the boys, I just heard the music. There were quite a few people there. I was a fan of Tommy Steele and Elvis before that, I think they were the only two. The Beatles did come along just before that, and I was a fan of the Beatles. I don't think I knew what rhythm & blues and rock and roll were at the time. 'Route 66' was the first thing I heard the Stones do. We loved it. Then we came back and I said, 'Oh, I must see them again.' Apparently Mick and Keith went down to Ken Colyer's jazz club one afternoon and said, 'Look, can we play when Ken has his break, can we go in and play for nothing?' So they said, 'Yeah, you can do it.' No one was really interested, it wasn't that packed, and I could see them, and I just fell in love with them. The music was so exciting. Then, bang! It happened so quickly, everyone knew who they were."

Charlie almost hesitantly told me, "At Richmond we became sort of a cult, in a way. Not because of us, it just happens. We were there the night that everybody—it sort of works both ways. We followed them and they followed us. There were so many people, and because there was no room to dance they used to invent ridiculous dances. There was no room for Mick to dance onstage and he used to just wiggle his arse, which sort of made . . . I don't know, but it sort of created—it was a lovely . . . I mean the Crawdaddy was like—it was nice to have a dance. It was nice to be there, and the Crawdaddy was always like that. That was really the best time for response of them all. I mean, it got a bit wearing, if you did the same set, and you knew at a certain time every-thing would explode. And sure enough it always did, and it always ended up in an absolute . . . gyrating . . . riot. When the last Encore, or More, would die down—when you were nearly dead with sweat, you can't do more than four hours, and they had to shut the place up. That's what it was like."

"Singlehandedly, we discover," Keith said, "we've stabbed Dixieland jazz to death, it's really just collapsed, all because of us. Brian was so pleased to see the last jazz band disband and us taking over the clubs, it was his happiest, proudest moment."

The Crawdaddy Club was operated by Giorgio Gomelsky, the Italian of Russian ancestry who liked to think of himself as the Stones' manager. "We had no such illusions," Keith said.

"There were all sorts of people wanting to manage us," Stu said, "but they could never get through to us, because there was no phone at Edith Grove. There was no phone ever anywhere near it. The only phone number was in the *Jazz News,* I.C.I." The Stones' ads carried the tele-phone number of Imperial Chemical Industries, where Stu worked in the shipping department. "So one day this very pushy little guy called Andrew Oldham phoned up and said that he was very interested, and he was in partnership with Eric Easton, rhubarb rhubarb. So I said, The only way you're gonna get hold of them—I don't want to get too involved in this 'cause I've got enough to think about at the moment, shipping whole shitloads of explosives—I said, Look, why don't you just get on your bike, or whatever you've got, and go round to Edith Grove? And so he went round there and saw Mick, and that was the start of a very close relationship between him and Mick. We used to smuggle Andrew into the Station Hotel without Giorgio knowing, 'cause there were huge queues to get in, they'd start queuing about half-past six at night."

"Andrew is very young," Keith said, "he's even younger than we are, he's got nobody on his books, but he's an incredible bullshitter, fantastic hustler, and he's also worked on the early Beatles publicity. He got to-gether those very moody pictures that sold them in the first place, so although he hasn't actually got much he does have people interested in what he's doing. He comes along with this other cat he's in partnership with, Eric Easton, who's much older, used to be an organ player in that dying era of vaudeville after the war in the fifties, when the music hall ground to a halt as a means of popular entertainment. He had one or two people, he wasn't making a lot of bread, but people in real show biz sort of respected him. He had contacts, one chick singer who'd had a couple of Top Twenty records, he wasn't completely out of it, and he knew a lot about the rest of England, which we knew nothing about, he knew every hall."

Oldham and Easton had a Decca recording contract for the Stones, but the Stones had already signed a contract with George Clouston at I.B.C. in lieu of paying for the session they had recorded there. I.B.C. had done nothing with the tapes. "They had no outlet," Keith said. "They didn't know how to cut them or get them onto discs, and they couldn't get any record company interested in them. This recording contract, although it's nothing, is still a binding contract, and Brian pulls another one of his fantastic get-out schemes. Before this cat Clouston can hear that we're signing with Decca, Brian goes to see him with a hundred quid that Andrew and Eric have given him, and he says, 'Look, we're not interested, we're breaking up as a band, we're not going to play anymore, we've given up, but in case we get something together in the future, we don't want to be tied down by this contract, so can we buy ourselves out of it for a hundred pounds?' And after hearing this story, which he obviously believes, this old Scrooge takes the hundred quid. The next day he hears that we've got a contract with Decca, we're gonna be making our first single, London's answer to the Beatles, folks."

On April 28, 1963, Oldham brought Eric Easton to Richmond to see the Stones, who came the next day to Easton's Regent Street offices, where they made a handshake deal that Oldham and Easton should manage them. Within three or four days Brian had bought back their I.B.C. contract, and on May 10 the Stones went to Olympic Studios in London for their first professional recording session. It was also Oldham's first try at record producing. In about three hours, the Stones recorded two sides for their first single release: "Come On," a Chuck Berry song, and "I Wanna Be Loved," by Chicago songwriter Willie Dixon, both done in a style much lighter and less potent than they usually displayed onstage. Oldham left the mixing to the engineer, a young man aptly named Roger Savage. The tape of the session didn't sound bad, considering that Oldham came into the studio thinking that guitars should be plugged into wall sockets, but the old gents at Decca listened to it and then rang Oldham to suggest that he and the Stones try again at Decca's West Hampstead studios. "It was a big Decca session," Keith said. "All the big Decca heads were there, listening and going 'tsk tsk' and shaking their heads."

The results, while nowhere near the equal of any of the tapes the Stones had made previously, including the bathroom tapes, were released as the Stones' first single record on June 7. The record hovered around the middle of the Top Fifty records charts of the English music trade papers for more than three months. The Stones performed "Come On" in their first television appearance, on a show called *Thank Your Lucky Stars,* taped in Birmingham. They wore matching houndstooth check jackets Oldham had provided to make them look more like a group and there were only five of them.

"This is where Brian starts to realize that things have gone beyond his control," Keith said. "Before this, everybody knows that Brian considers it to be his band. Now Andrew Oldham sees Mick as a big sex symbol, and wants to kick Stu out, and we won't have it. And eventually, because Brian had known him longer than we, and the band was Brian's idea in the first place, Brian had to tell Stu how we'd signed with these people, how they were very image-conscious, and Stu didn't fit in. If I'd been Stu I'd have said fuck it, fuck you. But he stayed on to be our roadie, which I think is incredible, so bighearted. Because by now we were star-struck, every one of us, the Beatles have been to see us play ['They were just back from Germany,' Bill said, 'and they stood in front of the bandstand, all in long black leather coats, looking like cut-outs.'] and we've been to see them at the Albert Hall, and we've seen all the screaming chicks, the birds down in front, and everybody can't wait, you can't wait to hear the screams. . . ."

"That is what I *want,*" Brian told Giorgio.

"The next time I saw them they were the five of them," Shirley Arnold said. "I'd seen them at Colyer's once, and it was about three months, the record had been released by the time I saw them again. The next time we went we begged the girl on the door to sell us tickets the day before. She let us have the tickets. The queue next day was fantastic. Colyer's is a long room with a very small stage at one end, low ceiling, you could touch the ceiling. We were in early, so we were at the front of the stage, but we were packed so tight that I was pushed up against the stage. People were standing, and sitting on people's shoulders. Every inch was packed. Sweat was pouring from the walls and the amps kept going wrong, but the music was fantastic, the boys were fantastic. I didn't actually faint because of them, I fainted because it was so hot. And they just passed me over everyone's head into the tea room. One of the bouncers was pourin' water on me and I was thinkin', 'Oh, my makeup's gonna run.' My friend came in to see about me. She said, 'The music's stopped, they're comin' in.' So I went in a swoon like I wasn't strong enough to leave, because I wanted to see them. It was Brian who was the first one that ever spoke to me. He said, 'Are you the girl that fainted?' I was such a fan—there was never anything I wouldn't do for them, and at the time there weren't many girls like me who were freakin' out, so they were quite surprised. I asked Andrew about the fan club. He said, 'I don't know what's happenin' about the fan club. Do you want to do the fan club? Go up and see Annabelle Smith, I'll tell her you're coming, what's your name?' Annabelle was Andrew's secretary. She was older than any of the boys. I think she was about twenty-nine, which was old to us 'cause we were all so young. The fan club was started in her name, but I don't think she was really interested. So we went up to see Annabelle. She was only too pleased to give it to me. She gave me a stack of postal orders and said, 'It's yours, do it from home.' Things were happening so fast with Andrew and the boys that they had no time to think about the fan club anyway. So there was me goin' home with two hundred members and a stack of postal orders that came to about sixty quid. Well, sixty quid, you can imagine, I had it under my pillow every night 'cause it was a fortune. I tried to pay them into the bank, and they said, 'No, no, you've got to open an account through the office.' Weeks went on, I kept calling Andrew's office and saying, 'Look, I must do a newsletter and write to everyone—' but everyone was so busy, I never really got to speak to Andrew, so I had all the fan club things and still wasn't in contact with anyone. I was working for the boys and I'd only seen them once."

On July 13 the Rolling Stones played their first date outside London, at the Alcove Club in Middlesbrough on a bill with a group from Liverpool called the Hollies. "And in those days—what the Liverpool groups do must be right," Stu said, "and Andrew had the Stones convinced that he was going to make them London's answer to the fuckin' Beatles, and they were gonna be a really fantastic pop group, which pleased Brian no end, because it meant money, and I think the others were quite happy, 'cause they appreciate money, same as anybody else. Andrew knew nothing about music, he was only interested in the money.

"So anyway, here were the Hollies on, doing their three-part vocal harmony, and we had never heard anything like it. Brian immediately said, 'Right, everybody's got to sing.' Andrew and them changed the group right round, and the emphasis became on 'Poison Ivy' and 'Fortune Teller,' numbers like that. For a while the Stones lost their identity, I think, because they were playing all these novelty numbers and trying to sing them like Liverpool groups. That was Andrew's idea, which was a bit of a drag. Those ballrooms were awful. We used to go to these terribly thick places like Wisbech and Cambridge, and all the yokels, they'd heard of these Rolling Stones, but they hadn't the foggiest idea what to expect in the way of music. To start off with, some of them just gawked.

"There was a little bit of uncertainty in those days as to what should be played. They thought of more numbers like 'Poison Ivy' and that didn't seem to be doing much, and eventually they got everybody with the Chuck Berry stuff, and they reverted more to what they had been playing, till after a year or so some of these ballroom dates began to get really fucking wild. It was the *sheer excitement of the music*. Oh, Christ. No dressing rooms, no stages, no electricity, no security, fuck-all, used to be a hell of a fight every bloody night. They all said, 'We've had the Beatles here, we can handle anything.' You'd say, 'Well, you haven't had the Stones yet. You wait,' and they'd say, 'Oh, we can handle everything,' so everything used to get destroyed. The boys themselves never used to help matters much, because they resisted for a while the idea of all travelling together. Brian had something to do with this. Nobody wanted to be in the same car with Brian for any length of time. He began to feel as if he'd been eased out. He became difficult to live with.

"Brian, being Welsh, had always got a very obnoxious streak in him, and he used to be very tactless, and say things like, 'As I'm the leader of the group, I'm gonna have an extra five pounds a week.' We used to stay in cheap hotels 'cause we didn't have any money, but they never stayed in real shit, once they'd got a little bit of money. So we'd stay in a medium-class hotel, but Brian would say, 'In a few months' time, when we're earning more for a gig, I'm gonna stay in the Hilton because I'm the leader, and everybody else will be staying with you somewhere.' So eventually they got sick to fuckin' death of him. He would change with the wind as well. Brian was very pretty, but a very silly boy really. Eventually it became obvious that Mick was the leader of the group. In those days Brian was simply a very, very good guitar player, and he was very mercenary too, very keen on money. So when Andrew comes along and says It's time you started playing numbers like 'Poison Ivy' because you'll sell more records, it was Brian who immediately said Yeah, groovy, great. But having done this, after about the first six months of playing ballrooms in Stoke-on-Trent and Crewe, it was Brian who said, 'I think we ought to play at Eel Pie Island twice a week again, and play the blues.' Brian would change from one day to another, and they just got fed up with him.

"It was a pity. Brian was brought up in the worst possible way. He had a very good education, was very clever at school, but somewhere along the line he decided he was going to be a full-time professional rebel, and it didn't really suit him. So that when he wanted to be obnoxious, he had to really make an effort, and having made the effort, he would be really obnoxious. But his nature was really quite sweet. Brian was really quite a sweet person, but he took everything to excess. It's a shame, because he was really a good musician. I don't want to be too hard on Brian. He was a very difficult person."

What Keith remembered best about the night the Stones played with the Hollies was the drive back to London, three hundred miles in the back of Stu's Volkswagen van with Charlie, Mick, Brian, and all their equipment, Bill in the front with Stu because he lied and said he got carsick in the back, where they had to piss out the ventilator because Stu, "a sadist," Keith said, wouldn't stop except when he wanted. Thinking about that night and how they all had to sing because that's what the Hollies did, Keith said, "Brian collapsed straightaway to commercialism. He shattered."

The Stones were playing nearly every day, sometimes twice a day, and when they weren't playing or recording, they were rehearsing for their first concert tour of England, with the Everly Brothers and Bo Diddley. On July 19 they were booked to play a debutante's ball, but Brian was sick, the Stones all got drunk, and another band played. The next night the Stones, with Brian, played their first ballroom date, at a place called the Corn Exchange in Wisbech. "Come On" was at number 30 in its struggle upwards in the Top Fifty. The Stones were a gathering sensation and were averaging less than £5 per man for each job. On August 10 they played two shows near Birmingham, and the next day, after playing the Studio 51 Club in the afternoon, the Stones played at the third National Jazz Festival in Richmond. Stu had left his job at the chemical company because there was no time for anything but driving, setting up equipment, taking it down, and driving.

On August 17 the Stones played in Northwich, up near Liverpool, on a bill with Lee Curtis, who according to Keith "pulled an incredible scene to steal the show, where he'd do Conway Twitty's 'Only Make Believe,' and he'd faint onstage. Guys came and carried him off, and he'd fight them off and come back, singing 'Only Make Believe.' Then they'd carry him off again." The craziness was a part of the time, the beat craze that carried thousands of acts along for a while. Coming home on this same night, Bill mentioned in his diary, they met Billy J. Kramer and his band the Dakotas at a café on the M-1. "Doesn't sound very exciting now," Bill said. "Billy J. Kramer then was as big as the Beatles." And the Beatles were on their way to being, as John Lennon later said, more popular than Jesus. That week the Rolling Stones played six dates, not counting rehearsals and photo sessions, and each man got paid £25. The pace was killing, but they all managed to maintain it except Brian. On August 27 the Stones were booked to play at Windsor in a room over the Star and Garter pub. Brian, sick again, was not there, and for the first time the band that had been "Brian's idea in the first place" played without him.

11

Yes, it was some terrible environments that I went through in those days, inhabited by some very tough babies. Of course, wherever there is money, there is a lot of tough people, no getting around that, but a lot of swell people, too.

Speaking of swell people, I might mention Buddy Bolden, the most powerful trumpet player I've ever heard of or that was known and the absolute favorite of all the hang-arounders in the Garden District.

ALAN LOMAX: *Mister Jelly Roll*

I STAYED in Memphis until the next Friday, October 31. Each day I sat at home waiting for the publishing contract that failed to arrive. It was no fun, but I stayed, maybe because this odyssey could have begun only on Halloween.

I woke up late and rushed to the airport to make the L.A. flight. I kissed Christopher twice, she drove away, going to work, and I ran for the plane.

You can get used to anything, and in the years of magazine writing I had become accustomed to spending time in the pastel plastic innards of giant fire-belching jets, getting drunk. On this plane I threw down my black flight bag and set in to drink champagne, not the best champagne but not bad, and to read about the World Series in *The New Yorker,*

developing a strong attachment to the New York Mets, who this year
came from last place to become world champions, and to the stewardess,
who kept filling my glass. Yesterday I talked to Jo, who said that someone would meet me at the airport, but when I arrived I looked around,
found nobody, and called the Oriole house. Sandison told me that they'd
sent a driver named Mimi and that he, Sandison, was going back to
England, "ignominiously recalled." I'd heard Keith and Mick talk about
Sandison, and I was not surprised he was leaving. I sat down to wait
for Mimi. I had forgotten to ask how I'd recognize her, but I didn't
need to know because she never showed up. After the better part of an
hour I took a taxi.

At Oriole the back door was unlocked. The first person I saw was the
glamorous Shirley Watts, who was in the kitchen pressing a blouse.
"Delighted to see you ironing," I said, and proceeded to the living room,
where on one couch David Sandison and Glyn Johns the sound engineer
(dark-haired, bearded, wearing a lime-green fedora) were sitting and
on another was a girl reporter from *Time* magazine, wearing a neat red
tweed suit. Glyn was saying, "He can be very nice and put you at ease,
or he can put you very uptight. He has a remarkable, umm—"

I put my bags in the Oz room. On the way back down the hall I saw
Charlie shuffling along in his meditative cuticle-chewing 1950s hipster
slump. He went into the living room, stood listening to the lady from
Time and then said—closing the terrace door, it was getting dark and
the air was cool—that he would find it hard to do her job, that he
thought rock and roll had been inflated out of value. "A jazz bass
player died recently," Charlie said, talking about Paul Chambers, "and
compared to rock players he didn't make much money, and I can't
justify that."

The *Time* lady said that everything is inflated here, it's a matter of
the difference between countries, advertising in America is very exaggerated compared to that in Britain, everything in Britain tends to be
understated.

Yeah, Charlie said, but how do you know about all that if you're a
kid, gesturing at Los Angeles outside the window.

If you come from here you know about it, she said, and Charlie said,
Yeah, but—

Sandison, peeved at being sent home, warned me that no matter what
I wrote, Mick would say that he had never seen me. "One of the publicity
agents he talked to this week asked Mick about an interview with him
in the *Playboy* that's out now, and Mick said he'd never even spoken to
anyone from *Playboy*."

Charlie was going up to the Laurel Canyon house to rehearse, and I
went along with him, in a station wagon driven by Phil Kaufman. We
rode down Doheny to Sunset, up Laurel Canyon Drive to Shady Oak,

and stopped at a wide metal gate. A big black young man was coming toward the car. "That's Tony," Kaufman said. In his graded-tint shades and purple tie-dyed T-shirt, Tony looked like a Hollywood dream of a Black Panther, shapely and cool and slightly less colossal than King Kong.

Tony peered in at us, said "Secret agents twenty-seven, thirty-nine, and forty-five," and opened the gate. As we drove past he said, "Man, it's really a mess up there."

"What?" Phil said. "Why?"

"They forgot to open the chimbley and the fire smoked up the house."

"Oh, yeah?"

"Yeah, and some creeps got in."

"What happened, you throw them out?"

"No, when I got there they was all havin' a party."

Most of the people at the house were outside because inside the big fireplace was still filling the air with smoke. In the kitchen Phil Kaufman's quadroon girlfriend Janet was serving onto plates spaghetti with what appeared to be cocoons floating in it. Meals at the Oriole house were not very festive, but this one was about as cheering as a cremation, though not as warm.

"Are we getting rid of the smoke?" Jagger asked Phil, standing before the fireplace.

"Yeah," Phil said. "We're moving to Topanga Canyon."

"We are getting it together, right?" Mick said, not smiling.

"Yeah, right," Phil said. He and Sam Cutler stared up the chimney, trying to look competent.

Jagger went into the rehearsal room in the rear of the house and started playing an acoustic guitar. Charlie started playing drums, Bill picked up a bass, and Mick Taylor, a guitar. Jagger told Janet to tell Keith they'd started. She found him smoking languidly in a chain-suspended wicker chair out by the pool. "Keith," she said, "they've started."

"Oh, yeah," he said, not moving. "Tell them they're sounding great."

But in a few minutes Keith came in through the back door of the little rehearsal room and soon chaos became tuning, became a chord, a pattern, a riff, a twelve-bar blues that collapsed after a couple of minutes. Jagger put his guitar down and looked over a list of tunes. "How many are there?" Mick Taylor asked. "Eighteen," Jagger said. " 'Carol,' 'Jumpin' Jack Flash,' 'Bad Boy'—"

" 'Bad Boy'—that goes back a ways," Wyman said.

"Let's do it," Keith said, and they did it, a blues to inflame every girl-child within hearing: "I'm a bad boy, come to your town—"

Next they did "Street Fighting Man." From the big Altec speakers sound was pounding this coffin-shaped room, built to take abuse: lined at the top with fiberglass home insulation mats, the walls covered with carpet pads and one oriental rug.

When the song ended, Keith said, "We should have the black light come on next—"

"And police come on with truncheons, clubbing each other," Jagger said. "To be followed by showers of petals."

Jagger said the Stones would open their shows with "Jumpin' Jack Flash," the song they released the week of Brian's final arrest, but now they played it with difficulty and finally it fell apart. Keith told Mick Taylor, "On that one you'll want to use the Flying Arrow—"

"Lying farrow," Jagger said.

"Mia Farrow," said Keith.

Mick Taylor said, "Well, we can just take all the guitars onstage and see which we want—"

Jagger laughed. "Horrible thought."

Then Wyman had an idea—for an invention, an instrument that could be attached to a guitar and would light up when a string was in tune. Jagger and Keith insisted it was impossible. Charlie said it was possible and so did I. Keith was down on the whole idea. "Use your ears," he said.

"Yeah," said Jagger. "That's what you've got your god-given talent for."

"Actually I was thinkin' of it for you, man," Bill said to Keith. "I don't have any trouble stayin' in tune, you're the one."

As they started to play "Monkey Man," Phil Kaufman called me to the telephone. Pete Callaway was calling, a friend from Georgia. Later Pete and I had lived together in New Orleans, where he was a student and I was a dropout at Tulane. Now he was married and inching toward a Ph.D. in philosophy at Columbia while sometimes getting his head cracked by police at student demonstrations.

I took the call in the kitchen. We had a short version of the same phone conversation we had had every few months for years, a ritual of private jokes to let each other know that we were still ourselves, nothing had changed. Pete's little sister Nicole was with him. She told me hello and asked me to come see her when I was in town with the Stones. She was twenty-two, had just left graduate school without taking a degree, and was living in Greenwich Village. The last time I saw her she was a ravishing seventeen. Because of the way she sounded, a certain quality in her voice, on my fatal yellow pad I wrote her number.

The rehearsal room was a charging freight of sound. Jagger was the key—when he was sailing, screaming or moaning, he couldn't do anything in between, the Stones sailed; when he stopped, the music disintegrated.

"On 'Sympathy for the Devil' we'll need another drum, some congas,"

Mick said. "Maybe we can get some sort of black person to come along and do it."

Mick was trying to decide whether "Sympathy" should be "quite short or very long," his voice shaky, insecure. I had the feeling it might have to do with me, watching them in this small room. Mick's voice dragged until one by one they stopped playing. None of them looked at the others. Then Mick Taylor played a few notes, Keith played a chord, another chord, a bright pattern of notes, and everyone was playing, Mick singing at the end of the room, his back to me. They sounded like Louis Armstrong and the Hot Five, except that Mick Taylor was playing horrible Bo Diddley noises and Keith was playing a solo with a scream lost in it. Finally Mick sat down on the piano bench, Keith stopped, they all stopped: "Still falls down at the end," Mick said.

Waiting to go to what would be a dull party in Bel Air, we lounged around the house. Jagger and I were sitting with Wyman on the black leather couch, looking out the big window at the black hills of Halloween. Wyman said it was a holiday for kids, mostly, and Jagger disagreed: "They're real, those spirits, and the people to come after us will know about them."

"If the world survives," I said.

"We'll blow it up eventually," Mick said. "That's inevitable."

David Sandison woke me in the middle of the morning, carrying his bags out of the Oz room as he left, jaw firmly set, for England. I told him goodbye, showered, and dressed. On the coffee table in the living room was a magazine with a cover photo of Jagger and a story that ended, "The Rolling Stones are in town and everyone seems to be waiting for something to happen." The lead story was about the Beatles' financial problems with Allen Klein.

A young man from *Newsweek* was sitting on the back terrace with a notebook and a telegram of questions from his bosses in New York. Charlie and I joined him, Bill and Astrid showed up, and finally the three other Stones arrived, stumbling across the back lawn. Keith was wearing snakeskin boots, a red snakeskin belt, and a rose-colored shirt, torn off like most of his shirts above the kidneys to keep the tail out of the way of his guitar playing. The reporter dutifully followed the telegram—How do you feel about touring again—and received minimal answers. He asked what happened to Brian, and Keith said, "We couldn't figure it out. He was getting in touch with musicians, trying to get a band together—"

Newsweek didn't press any points, no interviewers did with the Stones, they hung back from the dark places in the Stones' past. The Stones had learned that nothing of any interest was likely to happen in the presence of interviewers and managed with near-perfect success to ignore them.

When the *Newsweek* talk ended and the reporter left, we all decided to have lunch together on the Strip. Charlie and I went inside for a minute and came back to see the other Stones driving away in a turquoise Continental. "Really, they are the rudest people," Charlie said.

Later, at Shady Oak, while the Stones rehearsed, Gram Parsons and I stood out back, leaning against his iridescent blue Harley-Davidson motorcycle, the hills dark behind him as he talked, seemingly against his will, about the Okefenokee country. Gram was born in Florida but grew up in Waycross, going hunting and fishing in the Swamp with his father. After his mother remarried he learned about other places, attended Harvard for a while. "You might say I was lucky," he said. "I got both sides of it."

I said nothing. Anyone who heard Gram sing "Do You Know How It Feels to Be Lonesome" had an idea how lucky he was.

Gram was going to play with the Burritos tonight, and I wanted to hear him. He wished I could, only he had to carry a lot of instruments and equipment, his roadie, equipment handler, in his car—but Sam Cutler wanted to come too, and Sam Cutler was not to be denied. So we commandeered the station wagon, the roadie loaded it, and I was nominated driver because the others couldn't believe I drove as badly as they did. Waiting a few minutes in the wagon for Sam and Gram, who were inside, Gram's roadie was bitching about what a drag Gram was to work for, unreliable, not punctual, his rich stepfather gives him a tremendous allowance—

The servant's grumbles subsided as Gram and Sam came out and we set our course south on the freeway for a club called the Golden Bear in Huntington Beach, but soon the roadie told me that if I was going to drive this slow I'd better get in another lane. Yeah, but it's driving funny, I said, and we had to drive for miles, the left rear end wobbling worse all the time, until we could stop at a gas station. Phil Kaufman's girlfriend Janet, now they tell me, had a flat tire, changed it herself, the wheel had never since been tightened, and had almost cut through the lug nuts. The station attendant said he didn't have any lug nuts, and we tightened up the worn ones and rolled slowly with our fingers crossed through Huntington Beach to the Golden Bear.

While Gram and the Burritos were getting ready to play, the proprietor, George Nikos, a courtly man, not young, invited Sam, Gram's roadie, and me into his office, gave us glasses of red wine, and Sam called Hertz about the wagon. He'd asked me to call them and I'd advised him that Americans would do anything for a person with an English accent. "Not one loik moin," Sam said, but I explained that in California they didn't know the difference. He finished the call and sat back like a lord in his library after dinner, the blaze on the hearth, and talked about his experiences with bands as if they were military campaigns. "But the Stones are the best," he said. "They're the best because they're the scaredest: they're the most worried band I've ever seen."

I spent the night drinking wine and watching Gram sing. His step-father was there, soft and prissy, with a large table of guests. Everybody got drunk—during the last set it seemed that Gram, his hair-frost glisten-ing, would fall out of the spotlight. But he glowed. He was radiant. He was covered with star-frost like Elvis Presley in his white suit on *The Jackie Gleason Stage Show* in 1956.

> I started out younger
> At most everything
> All the pleasures and dangers
> What else could life bring?

"You all are really gone be a success," I said after the first set.

"I think we already are," Gram said.

We went out back to smoke a joint, where it was not cool at all, Gram said, they love to bust you for dope down here. There's a garage down this alley, I'll go first and you follow me in a minute.

The garage was open and empty, with a dirt-and-cinder floor. I smoked while Gram peed in the alley, then he smoked while I peed, then we both smoked. Though we both tried to be cosmopolitan as hell, Gram, whose adrenalin was pumping from being onstage, was declaiming in the manner of Eugene Talmadge: I know one damn thing, I love the Rolling Stones and Keith Richards. We were both staggering pretty good, but I paid close attention.

What it comes down to, Gram said, is a man and a woman. I've got a little baby girl, beautiful, she's with her mother—I passed him the end of the joint and he said, What we got to have in this world is more love or more slack.

Late the next afternoon, the Stones rehearsed at the Warner Brothers movie lot, on soundstage four, copped by Al Steckler, who'd dangled before the Warner record company the Stones' soon-to-expire recording contract. Past the gates, down the central drive (wide concrete, lined with firs and palms), the soundstages all looked abandoned, their ex-teriors cracked and faded mauve. Inside soundstage four the Stones, minus Wyman (who wasn't coming: "Nobody told me what time"), were rehearsing on a partially dismantled set, a marathon dance ball-room on a pier, made for the film of Horace McCoy's *They Shoot Horses, Don't They?*, a reproduction of a place where people danced themselves to death.

The atmosphere was that of a deserted carnival, overarching beams braced by orange and red pilings topped with female figures of gilded stucco, draped in low-cut ancient Greek gowns, carrying gilded baskets of fruit and playing gilded trumpets. At one end of the ballroom set were bleachers, with this sign above them:

> ? HOW LONG WILL THEY LAST ?
> DAYS   COUPLES   HOURS   DAYS
>   Remaining Elapsed

In front of a row of amplifiers—twenty-five of them, courtesy of the Ampeg company, twenty-one in operation—Mick Taylor and Keith were tuning their guitars, and in the center of the ballroom, beneath a huge mirror-chip sphere, Mick Jagger was singing Chuck Berry's "Carol":

> I'm gonna learn to dance
> If it takes me all night and day

Charlie was playing hard and tight, all business. Mick Taylor knew the song but was having some sort of trouble, playing in fits and starts, shaking his head. After "Carol," they did the Jagger/Richards songs "Sympathy for the Devil," "Midnight Rambler," and "I'm Free," Jagger singing with his arms folded, then in the instrumental breaks walking to the far end of the ballroom floor to listen. They played each song three or four times, and finally, on his own "Stray Cat Blues," Jagger began to show a little enthusiasm, doing microphone monkeyshines, spinning the mikestand like a baton, throwing it up in the air and catching it. None of the others seemed to be having fun except Keith, who played louder and louder. They kept stopping to diddle with the amplifiers, and Stu, who had a new blue station wagon loaded with equipment parked right center stage, talked to Mick Taylor in hushed tones. When they started again Keith turned his amp all the way up and, standing in the movie set's leftover confetti, made godawful loud noises on a clear plastic guitar. In a world with guitars made from all different kinds of woods, stainless steel guitars, tortoiseshell guitars, guitars inlaid with gold and ivory, Keith chose to play one that looked as if it were made of hardened unflavored gelatin.

Next the Stones played Chuck Berry's "Little Queenie" and more Jagger/Richards songs: "Satisfaction," "Honky Tonk Women," and "Street Fighting Man," the song banned last year in Chicago during the riots at the Democratic national convention. Keith, a concave figure, eyes nearly closed, bent over his ugly guitar, was making a deafening mad racket. I remembered seeing, back at the Oriole house, an interview in an old issue of a music magazine with Jim Morrison asking the interviewer, "You were in Chicago—what was it like?" and the interviewer saying, "It was like a Rolling Stones concert."

When the Stones took a break, Charlie came over and asked me, "What do you like about this band?"

"That's a very hard question to answer," I said.

"Do we sound—like one of those bands at the Whisky? I mean, Mick's something more than that, and Keith is, but the rest of us . . . do we sound like one of those bands?"

"No," I said.

The Stones had rehearsed all the songs in the show except three old blues that Mick and Keith would do without electric guitars. They started one, sitting down, Keith playing a National steel-bodied guitar, but Keith said, "We can't do it." "It's a wank," Mick said.

"Right, Mick," Keith said, standing up. "It's a wank, everybody." He put on his fringed leather jacket and purple bug-eye sunglasses, and everybody left except Charlie and me and Stu, who would give us a ride home as soon as he finished packing up the guitars. "Really," Stu said, putting the guitars in their velvet-lined cases into the station wagon, "I never heard the like. A musician told me his amp was *too loud*. I simply told him Keith Richards is a very strong guitar player, and if you don't play as loud as he does, you'll be just as well off playing rhythm.

"I'm getting so fed up," Stu muttered to himself as we got into the station wagon and headed out. "You get them new amps, new guitars, new everything, and it still goes wrong, then what do you do?

"Mick asked what I'd wear onstage and I suggested what about dressing like this" (golf shirt, blue jeans, and Hush Puppies) "and he seemed to think that was completely laughable, not to be taken seriously at all." Stu was quiet for a moment, as if even he could not believe what was coming next: "It seems I'm to wear a white tuxedo." After another moment of pregnant silence he said, very matter-of-factly, "It's going to cost them a bloody fortune to have me play with them" (Stu who knew hardly any chords by name and was reluctant to ask Keith since Keith didn't know their names either and would just as soon have people think he did) ". . . and even more if I have to wear a tux. Cash every night one thousand dollars, two thousand with the tux."

At Oriole there was nothing in the house to eat, so Charlie and I were driven to the Aware Inn, a restaurant on Sunset, by Mimi, the girl who hadn't shown up to meet me when I arrived at the airport. Her performance then was typical, because she did pretty much as she liked even if she chose to show up, tall, skinny, barefooted, rat-faced, really like a rat, a face flat on both sides concluding in a sharp and most often displeased nose, seemingly displeased just to be there. On this tour we would have many idiosyncratic drivers, including me, but none quite so bored, so butch, or so belligerent as Mimi. If she showed up when she was not needed she made it no secret that she could be having a better time elsewhere, and if she was needed her attitude was about the same. While most drivers would, if your luck held out, get you to your destination and wait or come back to pick you up, Mimi would if she cared to, and she cared to, accompany you wherever you went, so that she sat down to eat at the Aware Inn with Charlie and me, both of us struck numb by the violent chicness of the place. We were, it was clear, barely worthy of being accepted as customers—in fact the Japanese waiter poured wine on me to put me in my place—while Mimi, perfectly not to say blissfully unimpressed, somehow managed to chew gum and rattle her car keys throughout dinner. Charlie and I gulped a few bites and escaped, but the management was superciliously slow to take our not-with-it money, and we both registered disappointment when, once outside, we saw our car, left by Mimi at the curb, being towed away by an L.A. county sheriff's department tow truck.

"Isn't that our car?" Charlie asked.

"Yeah," said Mimi, engaged as assiduously in smacking her gum and rattling her car keys as a Hindu mystic in the tintinnabulation of his little prayer bell.

"Well, tell them to stop," Charlie said.

"Hey, stop," said Mimi, as the car was pulled into the swiftly moving traffic to disappear in the night. A white Jaguar stopped at the curb before us, and we moved aside to let some aware people enter the Inn. It was late Sunday evening on the Strip, the sidewalk busy with kids who looked so strange that the police, walking by in pairs, gazed blankly into space trying not to see. "Maybe you'd better do something," Charlie told Mimi.

"Right," she said, went back into the Inn, and vanished. Charlie and I spent what seemed a long time standing first outside the Inn, then outside a place where they sold beads and drug paraphernalia, finally outside a closed boutique as we sought shelter of increasing darkness from the kids who approached, their eyes weirdly peaceful wastes of drug-ridden urban madness, saying, "Wow, you're Charlie Watts, far out."

Charlie listened to them with kind dismay. One girl said that San Francisco was much better than Los Angeles because around Haight Street you could get all the speed you wanted, and you could sit on the sidewalk and roll joints and nobody would bust you, and you could go to the Family Dog at night and drink this great punch that's usually filled with acid, it's great, you know, it's a great place. How old are you? Charlie asked her, and she said, Seventeen.

When we made it back to Oriole, the phone was ringing. Jo was already talking to Jagger on another line, so I answered it and found myself talking to the popular music critic of *Esquire* magazine. He told me that he and *The New Yorker*'s pop critic, a girl with whom he had been living for some time, were coming to interview Jagger. "Actually we're not together anymore," he said. "I don't know if you've heard about all this."

"Not really," I said. Jo was saying goodbye to Mick.

"We're going to have a joint interview with Jagger where we'll try to patch things up between us. Is Jo Bergman there?"

"Yes," I said. "Talk to Jo. Please."

Next day I sat out in the sunlight with Charlie, Shirley, and Serafina Watts. Serafina held out her arms with delight to Charlie and me. "*Two daddies,*" she said. Since coming to California Serafina had begun to learn to walk, and now she started across the lush lawn toward us, her plump little legs getting farther apart until, bottom-heavy, she sat with a plop.

Shirley was writing a letter to a friend in England. "I'm saying that I'm going to meet Mae West tomorrow."

"Are you?" Charlie asked.

"I'm being taken to the set of *Myra Breckinridge,* and even if I don't meet Mae West I shall say I did."

I went inside, smiling in this soulless house for a change, and saw Ronnie Schneider coming in with suitcases, wife Jane, and infant baby boy. I stopped smiling.

At rehearsal, with the first concert, the Stones' Return, four days away, just two more rehearsals after this one, a general depression prevailed. Jagger, the emotional barometer of the group, was having little physical problems, a toothache, sore throat, and dozed sadly in a chair, then lay prostrate on the amp covers, spread out in front of the bleachers. Finally he dragged himself up to say, "All right now, not too loud, we'll do the whole thing, I'll shout out the titles." Suddenly the band was playing "Jumpin' Jack Flash" deafeningly loud, Mick croaking, doing little handclaps for Keith's playing. The next song, "Carol," started at a decibel level well above the human pain threshold. "Bit loud," Keith said, turning his amps down slightly. He was playing crisp Chuck Berry licks on his plastic guitar, Mick with two fingers in the air, "gonna learn to dance——"

Then Charlie got up from his stool to talk to Stu and they switched a cymbal. "Come on," Mick said, "we're tryna get this fuckin' show together." With the new cymbal in place they did "Sympathy for the Devil" and then "Stray Cat Blues," Jagger lowering the age of the girl in the song from fifteen to thirteen. Charlie was hitting the drums as hard as he could with the wrong end of the sticks.

A copy of the *Los Angeles Times* was lying on a folding chair, showing the front-page summary of national news: "Assassination: A report by the National Violence Commission said the threat of assassination seems to be growing and urged protection for all public officials believed to be in danger. View of Abortion: A majority of American doctors questioned in a poll say that a woman should be able to have an abortion if she asks for one. Most also said that discreet homosexual acts between consenting adults should be permitted without legal restriction, but the doctors overwhelmingly rejected the idea of legalized marijuana."

"Midnight Rambler" was ending, Mick dancing in front of the bass drum, chanting to Charlie "Fasterfasterfaster—" Next Mick sat down to sing "Love in Vain," a blues Keith found on a bootleg Robert Johnson album, and then, still sitting, Mick sang "I'm Free," seeming tired and glum again. He stood up to start "Let It Bleed," but it sounded bad and he said in a parody north-of-England accent, "Noo noo noo, lads, all oota toon." Mick and Keith talked about whether they should do the song. "Either it's out of tune or it's just a mess," Mick said, but they tried it again and it worked, Mick did little kicks and bumps and grinds. While singing "Satisfaction" he leapt and spun, sick throat forgotten. The band cooked through the next two songs, "Honky Tonk Women" and "Street Fighting Man." Then Mick and Keith kicked Bill, soiling the seat of his white trousers. Bill retaliated by kicking Jagger as soon as he turned his back, but Mick's trousers were black anyway and he said, "Go right ahead, dear, you can put it up there anytime." Bill appeared uncertain how to respond and wandered a few steps away, tuning his bass.

Keith, using a Sinex inhaler, answered Mick's question, "What'll we do?" with "Under My Thumb."

" 'Under My Thumb,' " Jagger mused. "Some people think that's quite nice."

"Rather quiet," Keith said.

"Must be joking," said Mick Taylor.

"It doesn't matter what we decide to do," Jagger said, "once we get onstage all the plans go by the board anyway."

After supper at Oriole we sat, a little band of strangers, around the coffee table in the living room. Jane Schneider, a pretty girl with dark eyes and dark auburn hair, was telling me about an antique Rolls-Royce she and Ronnie had recently bought: "It's really gonna be a fun car. It's in a show in Boston this weekend, and if it takes first prize we get our names in the book, which I hope."

Her mother, Jane said, had the world's largest collection of china shoes, and her friend, who had marketed a special rack to hold recipe index cards, was now selling her latest idea, a key chain with your loved one's picture. "I had another friend," she said proudly, "who made a pile on jigsaw puzzles with your own picture."

When she returned to the book she was reading I noticed that it was the best-selling pornographic novel *Naked Came the Stranger,* written as a hoax by a group of writers, each of whom did a chapter without consulting the others. She saw me looking at the book and said with a shrug, "It doesn't matter what you read these days, it's all trash."

When I woke up in the morning, the first person I saw was a tall young man who had a big circle of black curly hair and was here to interview Jagger for ABC radio. With him was an engineer who told me that he usually worked on things like basketball games, but the ABC stations were programming "a kind of love-rock, and they want to interview Mick and insert clips from the interview in their programming. It's really very effective."

The interviewer was in a tizzy: "I've got a deadline, I can't wait around here. I've got to answer to ABC in New York. What's with Mick, where's he at, should I pack up and go home, or what?"

"We'll do the interviews tomorrow," said Ronnie Schneider, standing in the hall, talking to Jagger on the office phone. "Here's the movie deal: they pay for all the film and equipment and you own the film. If they do it and you see it and you don't like it, that's it.

"Also—about the photographer—he wants us to pay all his expenses, which will probably run a thousand a week, that's pretty expensive. Do you like him that much that you want him to do all the pictures? . . . Yeah. Okay. I understand. Well, we can probably recoup the expenses from the deals he makes with magazines and things.

"If you say that you'll give all the proceeds, the donations, to charity, Pete Bennett says that Nixon will endorse the free concert." Ronnie hooted with laughter. "Yeah, well, you can't donate it to the Marijuana Grower's Association."

Arranging the interviews was complicated by Mick's tonsilitis or "tonsilitis." Charlie said it was a nervous complaint that Mick got when he had to sing. "Like Maria Callas, that sort of thing. I get it too, before we go on, it affects my feet, at first I don't feel my feet will work right, but with him it's his throat."

Later I drove to the Stones' rehearsal with Jo, first stopping by a tie-dye establishment in the woods, where Jo was taking some of Wyman's and Taylor's clothes and picking up some of her own, and where, outside a cabin near the tie-dye shack, bouncing on a brown canvas trampoline, was Ken Kesey. A girl stood by the trampoline talking to a boy who was holding a football as Kesey bounced, his expression like that of a serious hard-working three-year-old, curly, blond, and plump.

Jo and I went down to the tie-dye place, where things were smoking in galvanized buckets. I didn't like it, stepped outside and here came the football, sailing past the house and the trees to end up in the creek. I stepped down and from the rocks in the creek bed threw it back. It sailed up through the trees, I couldn't see anyone, then Kesey jumped into the air and caught it. He tucked the ball under his arm, we met at the tie-dye porch, said hello. I thought of Kerouac and their mutual friend Neal Cassady, who died last year, but what was there to say?

When Jo got her clothes we went to the Stones' rehearsal. It was five o'clock. Keith came onto the ballroom set riding a bicycle with a sign on it saying PROPERTY DEPARTMENT, carrying a sign that said RESERVED PARKING FOR KIRK DOUGLAS. He put the sign in front of Jagger's mike and cycled away.

The band was tuning up, making their usual awful squawk, and Mick was away at the back of the soundstage talking to Jo, beating the first two fingers of his right hand into his left palm, looking directly into her eyes, hypnotizing her. She was nodding, nodding. She left him and walked toward me. I felt the approach of doom, as if the ground were falling away behind the steps of her small, tightly shod feet.

"Mick says you have to have a deal together by Friday," she said.

"What does that *mean?*" I shouted, over the dense music. Mick, walking past, heard me, as I intended him to, cupped his hand round my ear and shouted, "Got to get it together."

"Get *what* together?" I asked.

"Get a *deal* together," he shouted.

"I'm *getting* a deal together," I said in a tone that asked, What's it to you?

"By *Friday*," Mick said and was gone to the microphone. I sat down, sweating a little, though it was not warm. On his way across the ballroom floor Mick passed Astrid and patted her gently on the seat of her black suede slacks.

Suddenly the Stones were playing "Jack Flash," Mick's tonsils jumping, his hips bumping. Things were moving faster, the order of songs was set and they did each only once. There would be just one more rehearsal.

In the middle of "Satisfaction," Jagger jumped up, threw the bottle of Löwenbräu he was holding through the air to clatter without breaking on the cement floor. The music was soaring. They finished with "Honky Tonk Women" and "Street Fighting Man" and then Mick and Keith at the piano performed an impromptu "Tallahassee Lassie." I had been standing behind the drums, listening. Charlie, wiping his sweaty face on his shirttail, said, "This is ridiculous."

"What is?" I asked.

"All this," he said. "It's fuckin' ridiculous."

Charlie and I needed a ride, but Stu couldn't help because he had to go to a music store. Charlie said, "We'll get a ride with Bill." Then we noticed that everyone had left except Bill, who was getting into his Continental with Astrid. "Did you ask him?" Charlie asked me.

"No, did you?"

It was out of their way, they told us, but they'd take us. A warm group. As we rode Bill was talking about Jagger: "He keeps turning around and looking at me like this, like I'm playing bad notes or I'm out of tune, and I'm not—"

Bill missed his seven-year-old son Stephen, who was in boarding school: "A very nice one, a hundred boys, an old house with a very good telescope and eighty-two acres of playing grounds for sports. Most of the boys are older; Stephen's one of the youngest. The older ones show the others how to play cricket and things. It's quite nice, they have little dormitories with about six beds in them, little flowered bedspreads and matching curtains. It's quite lovely, actually I wish I were going there—"

At Oriole Charlie and I found ourselves alone on the couch, smoking.

"I played with Benny Goodman once," he said. "Do you want to hear about it?"

"Please."

"When I was with Alexis Korner we played a party in Park Lane. If you know London, that's the rich bit. It was at a friend of Prince Philip's —he was there—and Benny Goodman came in and played a bit with us. We were just terrible behind him, but he played four or eight bars that were incredible—"

Below us were the lights of Los Angeles. I thought about what Mick had said. I had heard nothing from my agent and didn't expect to have anything together by Friday.

A little later, Shirley joined us. We were discussing the frantic business machinations of the ones she called "the bought people," and Shirley said, "And it's just a tour, after all, just a group of people going around getting up on stages and playing music for kids to dance."

"If you don't put that in your book, I'll kill you," Charlie said.

12

Every folk song is religious in the sense that it is concerned about the origins, ends, and deepest manifestations
of life, as experienced by some more or less unified community. It tends to probe, usually without nailing down
definite answers, the puzzles of life at their roots. The
real issue, for example, in the Jesse James song-legend is
not that a "dirty, little coward" shot Jesse when he was
defenseless; it is to ask the question why it is allowable
that a thing like this can happen, especially to a man
with a loving wife and three brave children. The fact that
Jesse had killed defenseless people while robbing banks
and trains is not part of the song-legend's ethical system,
although such facts are reviewed. In essence, the only
point to be settled at this particular juncture is, What
kind of a world will permit the rank injustice of Jesse's
death by obvious cowards? At heart, it is a religious
question.

JOHN LOVELL, JR.: *Black Song*

BRIAN WAS STILL SICK the next night with an asthma attack
—"He used to just collapse," Keith said—and the Stones played their
regular Wednesday night at the Eel Pie Island club with Stu on piano. At
seven the following morning Brian left in the van with the others, going

to do a television show in Manchester. That night Bill wrote in his diary about being "mobbed" by fans at the television studio and afterwards at a nightclub. "Mobbed," Bill said, meant that you lost some hair or part of your clothing.

The Stones played a club in Manchester on Friday and a ballroom in Prestatyn on Saturday. On Sunday, when they came back to London to play first at the Studio 51 Club and then at the Crawdaddy, Brian, who controlled the band's money, advanced £3 to each of them, because they were all broke. By Wednesday night Brian was sick again, reacting to some medicine that had been prescribed for him, covered with blotches, "decomposing before our eyes," Keith said. Brian left the Eel Pie Island club in the interval, and the band again finished the show without him.

About this time, September, the Stones left Edith Grove, Mick and Keith going to live in a flat with Andrew, Brian moving into a house in Windsor with Linda Lawrence, a girl he'd met at the Ricky Tick Club, and her parents. They all lived together for years, Brian and Linda in one bedroom, Linda's parents in another. Brian had more than the comforts of home and never paid any rent.

Brian stayed sick for the next three days, while the band played ballrooms in Deal, Lowestoft, and Aberystwyth. On the way to Aberystwyth, Bill had a girl in the back of the van and didn't get carsick, so the others tumbled, and after that they took turns riding in the front with Stu. At Aberystwyth there was a skirmish backstage with a man from the local musicians union, because the Stones weren't members. They promised to join, did their show, and drove all night to Birmingham, where they were to make their second appearance on the popular music show, *Thank Your Lucky Stars*. When they arrived at the television studio, the night watchman, the only person there at that hour, told them they couldn't come in: "We don't open until nine o'clock." Finally he relented, the Stones slept a bit in the viewing room and then, joined by Brian, who had come up from London by train, performed "Come On," which they disliked and refused to play on their shows, giving Andrew high blood pressure. The Stones shared billing on the show with such acts as the Searchers, Brian Poole and the Tremeloes, and Craig Douglas, who had a weekly television program where he plugged his own records, some of which became hits. Douglas, who before going into show business had been a milkman, was very rude to the Stones, refusing to speak to "those scum." They left outside his dressing room door a milk bottle with a note in it saying "Two pints, please."

Then they drove back to London. Stu would usually take Bill home last, and sometimes afterwards he would wake up alone by the roadside in some totally irrelevant part of town. A couple of days later, Andrew

Oldham, walking down Jermyn Street on his way to the Studio 51 Club, where the Stones were rehearsing, was accosted by John Lennon and Paul McCartney, who were making their way in a cab from the Dorchester, where the Variety Club of Great Britain had given a lunch in the Beatles' honor. Andrew mentioned that the Stones were having difficulty recording a second release, and along to the Stones' rehearsal come Lennon and McCartney—"who are by that time very much into hustling songs," Keith said. "Everybody was doing Beatles' songs and they were going straight into the charts." McCartney played on the piano part of a song he and Lennon were writing. The Stones liked it, so Lennon joined McCartney at the piano and in a few minutes they had added the middle eight bars, finishing "I Wanna Be Your Man."

On this night the Stones played the ballroom of the Thames Hotel; Bill, broke again, was advanced £10 by Brian. The next night they played at Eel Pie Island, and on the next at a place they'd never been, the Cellar Club in Kingston, where the audience was friendly, but once the show was over and the people had left, the promoter told the Stones, "You've got five minutes to get out." They thought he was joking and paid no attention, but he went into his office and came back wearing one boxing glove, raging: "I said, 'Pack up!' " As they drove away the man came outside brandishing a shotgun.

It was an auspicious send-off for a busy weekend. On Friday, September 13, the Stones played to an overflow crowd at the California Ballroom in Dunstable. On Saturday their second appearance on *Thank Your Lucky Stars* was aired, and they played afternoon and evening shows at two ballrooms in Birmingham. On Sunday something called a Pop Prom took place at the Albert Hall, the Stones opening the show, the Beatles closing it. The show carried more prestige for the Stones than any in the fourteen months since they started their professional career by filling in for Alexis Korner at the Marquee Club. One of the music papers printed photographs of the Stones and another of the evening's acts, Susan Maugham, the most popular girl singer of the year in Britain: Susan in her permanent wave, her satin evening dress, Brian sucking a harp jammed against a microphone in his cupped hands, Mick howling, shaking maracas high at his temples, all the Stones in black leather vests, looking like sex killers from a Spanish Western of the future, grinning in an orgy of rhythm.

A part of their lives was ending; none of them knew exactly where they were going, but they could feel themselves taking off. One afternoon in late September, after paying the band £20 each for the past week, Brian went shopping with Bill and bought fifteen blue shirts for the Stones to wear on their first national tour, coming up in less than two weeks, with the Everly Brothers and Bo Diddley.

Within the week the Stones played the last of their regular club dates at Windsor, Eel Pie Island, the Studio 51, and the Crawdaddy. As the tour approached, the fast pace of their lives quickened. They played a ballroom in Morecambe, the coldest place they'd ever been, got back to London about one o'clock the next afternoon after driving all night, and that evening played what Stu recalled as "a riot" at the Walthamstow Town Hall. Next day they rehearsed and did two shows on the opening date of the Everly Brothers–Bo Diddley tour of the Rank Cinema Circuit.

"I remember it was the New Victoria 'cause that's where the Black and White Minstrels were showing," said Shirley Arnold. "My friend Paula and I had tickets about six rows from the front for the eight o'clock performance, but we came about eight o'clock in the morning just to hang around the stage door and catch a glimpse of the boys. About two o'clock in the afternoon they started to arrive. I never had the courage to go up and speak to them. You see girls run up and grab Mick—I could never have done that, I'd have felt too embarrassed. The boys were in and out all day. And then Stu arrived. I'd seen Stu before and I knew that he was the roadie and he would be the best one to talk to. So I said, 'I'm doin' the fan club,' and he gave us tickets to the first show and told us to come backstage after."

The tour, an attempt to cash in on the current, ill-defined, "beat-music" craze in England, opened with a vocal group called the Flint-stones, followed by Mickie Most, who sang three Chuck Berry songs, after which a girl singer named Julie Grant, and then the Rolling Stones. It was a great occasion for them; mothers, fathers, uncles, and aunts—Bill's and Charlie's, anyway—came to see their boys pump out the rhythm on the giant stage of the New Victoria.

"By the time the boys came on we were so excited," Shirley Arnold said. "Then they did 'Route 66.' It was too much. People were screaming. Paula and I ran to the front of the stage and went 'Aaah . . . ' " The Stones were amazed, Shirley said. "If you could have seen their expressions—because nobody had done it before. Men were pulling us back. Finally we got back to our seats."

Though the Stones were playing regularly, and their names were frequently in the newspapers, they were a long way from being a familiar act. The same was true of Bo Diddley, who closed the first half of the show. He had appeared on the Ed Sullivan television program, but not even in America was he a familiar performer. He worked with a maracas player named Jerome Green and his own sister, who wore sheath dresses and was called the Duchess. They usually travelled in a Cadillac, with fishing poles.

After the intermission, the Rattles, "Germany's answer to the Beat-les," opened, followed by the Everly Brothers, themselves not exactly household names in England, having had only minor hits there. But they were known to have influenced the Beatles, and they closed the show.

"Then we went backstage," Shirley Arnold said. "They all came in and I was nervous, but they were so nice. Mick said, 'You were the girls who came to the front of the stage.' Keith and Brian were talking about it. I told them I was doing the fan club and Mick told me, 'If you're gonna do it, you've got to do it properly,' blah blah blah. I'd already been a member of Tommy Steele's fan club, so I knew how things would go. So I started doing it from home.

"Everyone was saying they were ugly at the time—I was working in a warehouse and all the people were older than me, and I had this photograph, one of the very first ones, from *Mirabelle*. I was such a screaming fan. I'm not embarrassed by it because I'm not now, I never freak out now. There was me goin' around saying, 'Look at their faces, don't you think they're fantastic?' I always loved them."

When the tour was announced to the press "spokesman Brian Jones" had said that "It won't be a case of the pupils competing with the master. . . . We're dropping from our act all the Bo Diddley numbers we sing." Playing on the same bill with Bo Diddley might have paralyzed the Stones—"He's been one of our biggest influences," Brian said—but they were too busy, too many things were happening to them as the tour began. At the Southend Odeon Keith left a bag of fried chicken in the dressing room after the first show and returned from where he'd been—"with a well-known groupie," he said—to find the bag of chicken now only a bag of bones. "Who et me chicken?" Keith asked, as well he might. "Brian et it," said Bill, telling the truth but telling. "And just at that moment," Keith said, "the stage manager sticks his head in the door and yells 'You're on!' So we're picking up guitars and heading for the stage, and as we're walking downstairs Brian passes me and I say, 'You cunt, you et me chicken!' and bopped him in the eye. We went onstage, and as we're playing Brian's eye starts to swell and change colors. In the next few days it turned every color of the rainbow, red purple blue green yellow. . . ." Before the show the next day, at the Guildford Odeon, Brian, only slightly daunted, joined the other Stones, Bo Diddley, and the Everly Brothers' backing group for a bit of playing backstage. "I'll never forget Bo's face when Brian played some of those Elmore James things," Stu said. If the Stones were astonished to be playing with Bo Diddley, how must Bo Diddley (born Ellas McDaniel near Magnolia, Mississippi) have felt, seeing a blond English cherub with a bruised and swollen eye, playing guitar just like Elmore James, who had learned from Robert Johnson, who had learned at the crossroads from the Devil himself.

Every day brought new marvels. On Saturday Little Richard joined the tour: Richard Penniman, from Macon, Georgia, the Georgia Peach, who went from washing dishes at the Greyhound Bus Station in Macon to the throne of fame and fortune—at his peak, he had a throne carried with him and sat in it wherever he went—singing his superpowered songs such as "Tutti Frutti," "Long Tall Sally," and "Slippin' and Slidin'." In the early 1950s he was, like Chuck Berry and Bo Diddley, one of the founding fathers of rock and roll, dressed in his mirror suits that threw little rainbows of light all over the house, playing the piano with two hands and a white-slippered foot. Then, in 1957, when he was on a tour of Australia with Eddie Cochran and Gene Vincent, the Russians sent into orbit the first man-made earth satellite, Sputnik, and Little Richard said, "I had a dream, and I saw some turrible things in this dream." He threw away his fancy clothes and jewelry, and when he came back to the United States started preaching and singing gospel songs in churches. Now, in England, he was coming out of retirement, back into show business, and everyone was looking forward to seeing him because they had heard that during his performances he ripped off his clothes and threw them to the audience. Jo Bergman was there that night, and she remembered hearing Little Richard tell the manager of the Watford Gaumont that he wanted the place, the entire theatre, perfumed with lavender so it would be smelling nice when he came onstage. He was still dressed in his church clothes, performed in a little mohair suit, Little Richard who used to appear at the Beaux-Arts balls in Macon dressed in a leather G-string and a giant feather headdress, but he was still Little Richard and the audience screamed for his tie, his shirt, anything.

"This is our first contact with the cats whose music we've been playing," Keith said. "Watching Little Richard and Bo Diddley and the Everly Brothers every night was the way we were drawn into the whole pop thing. Before, there was this division between people who played in clubs and people who played the ballroom circuit. We never had to present ourselves onstage before, we'd just gone out there and played where people danced. But now we were playing for an audience that was sitting. That was when Mick really started coming into his own. We didn't feel we were selling out, because we were learning a lot by going into this side of the scene."

The day after Little Richard joined, the tour went to Cardiff. The Stones drove there in a new Volkswagen van, one with a seat and windows in the back, provided by Eric Easton to replace Stu's dilapidated, comfortless one, "which I thought was very good of him," Keith said, "considering he was making a heavy fortune off us." At an S-bend in Salisbury the van went out of control, thumped off a bridge but stayed upright. "We nearly died," said Stu, who was driving. "We should have all been dead."

The next night, a night off from the tour, the Stones went to Kingsway studios in London and recorded their second release. Easton produced, Stu said, "because he didn't trust Andrew," who was in the south of France, pouting. "Poison Ivy" and "Fortune Teller," planned as the next single, had been cancelled four days before the scheduled release date, and the Stones cut as replacements an instrumental called "Stoned" with Stu on piano and the Beatles' song "I Wanna Be Your Man," which is unforgettable only because Brian Jones plays on it an eight-bar break like nothing ever before played on a record by an Englishman. "I quite dig that steel solo," Keith said, years later. "I think Brian made that record, really . . . with that bottleneck."

The next day, before going to play a tour date in Cheltenham, the Stones went to Easton's office, where a new way of getting paid was started. They were to be paid every Thursday, with the money coming from the office and no longer from Brian. As October lengthened, the Stones' lives consisted of two shows a day at an Odeon or Gaumont cinema in another British town. They loved Bo Diddley and especially Jerome Green, his maracas player, and spent as much time with them as they could. On Halloween night George Harrison, one of the Beatles, came to see the Stones at the Lewisham Odeon. Bill's diary for these days is filled with such notations as "plagued with fans," "loads of fans again," and Keith remembered this time as "the start of a siege that went on for years."

With the release on the first of November of their second record, which naturally they couldn't find in the stores for days, there were reviews and articles about the Stones in the *New Musical Express, Melody Maker, Pop Weekly, Beat Monthly, Teenbeat,* and national and local newspapers. Giorgio Gomelsky, through whose fingers they had slipped, published an interview with them taped some months before, in which "Brian Jones, the leader," answers the question, "How did you come to play R&B?" by saying, "It's really a matter for a sociologist, a psychiatrist, or something. . . . If you ask some people why they go for R&B you get pretentious answers. They say that in R&B they find 'an honesty of expression, a sincerity of feeling,' and so on, for me it's merely the sound. . . . I mean, I like all sorts of sounds, like church-bells for instance, I always stop and listen to church-bells. It doesn't express damn-all to me, really . . . but I like the sound. . . ."

The tour ended on November 3 at Hammersmith. "There we were again at the dressing room, screaming up at the dressing room window," Shirley Arnold said. "They were about four rooms up and we're screamin' and they were lookin' out the window and I was sayin' to Keith, 'I do the fan club! I do the fan club!' so excited—'cause he was talkin' to me out the window. He said, 'Oh, yeah, I remember.' Finally they came out, we'd seen the show, we'd done our screaming, we chased their van up the road."

There was no time for the Stones to rest. The night after the last show of the tour, they played, still in their black leather vests, at the Top Rank Ballroom in Preston, where the stage revolved; the night after that, they played the Cavern, the Liverpool basement nightclub where the Beatles used to play. "It was like playing a Turkish bath, all stone, had a terrible sound," Keith said. "You can't imagine what a myth was built around it." Then, after playing a ballroom in Leeds the next night, the Rolling Stones had a day off, their first in ten days, another not to come for ten more days.

On their day off, the Stones drove from London to Newcastle, where the following two nights they played the Whisky-à-Go-Go and Whitley Bay clubs, both places run by the same people, who had for the Stones what Keith called "unbelievable devotion." Bill said, "They'd lay on birds, guard you with dogs, one guy yelled at us, 'Get a haircut,' and about eight bouncers took him out and creamed him."

The Stones were playing almost every night, to steadily increasing decibels of screams. On November 13 three thousand people showed up at the Sheffield City Hall and the Stones threw away their black vests. The next night they spent at Kingsway Studios, where with Eric Easton "producing" they recorded their first extended-play record, a stepping-stone to a long-playing album. All the songs were cover versions of American rhythm & blues or rock and roll hits. A newspaper had quoted Mick as saying, "Can you imagine a British-composed R&B number—it just wouldn't make it." But Andrew, with plans to publish Jagger/Richards songs, was according to Keith "very much into hustling Mick and me to write songs, which we'd never have thought of doing. Brian wrote one once. . . ."

The next day the Stones played two shows at the Nuneaton Co-op, the afternoon show filled with little kids throwing cream buns, something different happening all the time. The others were able to move around and do a bit of dodging, but Charlie, rooted to his drum stool, by the end of the show was "covered in cream cakes," Keith said. "So pissed off." To show how far beyond the bounds of reason the Liverpool-Beatles myth had gone, sharing the bill with the Stones at Nuneaton were four girls from Liverpool called the Liverbirds, who did all Beatles songs, regular female Beatles. "Real slags," Keith said.

In Birmingham they taped a television appearance on *Thank Your Lucky Stars* with, among others, Cliff Richard and his band the Shadows, and the American singer Gene Pitney, who was being publicized by Andrew Oldham. After a day off the Stones played the State Cinema in Kilburn, and next day on the front page of the local newspaper there was a photograph of the mob of girls held back from the stage by beefy brass-buttoned ushers with their arms clasped together, their backs to the keening crush. "When, finally, the spotlight was switched off them," the accompanying story said of the Stones, "there was a chase for the dressing room. Who would win, the group or the girls? Four of the group made it but the drummer was pulled to the ground and lost his shirt and half his vest. Girl fans fell on top of him. . . . Eventually the bouncers employed to keep patrons in order managed to free him and rush him to the dressing room, where his own girlfriend looked after him." His own girlfriend was Shirley Ann Shepherd, an art teacher, his wife-to-be. But Charlie was for the moment inconsolable, walking around holding a few shreds of cloth, muttering, "They tore me shirt."

Next they spent a day in the studio cutting song demonstration tapes for Andrew, who had returned from France. That night they played once again at the Richmond Athletic Club for auld lang syne. The following day they went to Swindon, where Andrew took physical-culture photos of himself in one of those three for a half-crown machines. On the next day, November 22, 1963, the Stones taped an appearance on the television show *Ready, Steady, Go!* in Manchester. Because of the time difference, they were finishing their performance about the time I walked in the graduate students' cafeteria at Tulane University in New Orleans. The Canadian girl who worked there came out of her office and asked, "Have you heard?"

" 'Papa gone buy me a mocking bird'?" I said, making the conversation conform to the lyrics of the song "Bo Diddley."

"President Kennedy's been shot."

"No, he hasn't," I said, because in those days such things didn't happen. Then from the office radio I heard Walter Cronkite's voice, and he wasn't kidding. The Stones were upstairs at the television studio having a drink when they heard the news on the radio. That night in Manchester they played on the same bill with the group of black American girl singers called the Shirelles. "I remember them crying onstage," Keith said.

The Stones went on playing nearly every night, sometimes twice a night. In December they played four dates second on the bill to Gerry and the Pacemakers. The third of the shows was at Fairfield Hall in Croydon. According to plan, the Stones closed the first half of the show. Then the audience stomped for fifteen minutes until the Stones did a two-song encore. All but about five hundred of the three thousand in attendance left without seeing Gerry and the Pacemakers, who must have been pleased to end their association with the Stones the next night.

Life on the road, Keith said, "drives you completely crazy," but it did have its compensations. Bill's diary entry for December 12 reads: "Liverpool, Locarno dance hall, Exchange hotel for night, first colored birds."

On December 14 the Stones visited Carshalton Hospital, where there were many children with fatal diseases. "It was nice to go and see them," Stu said. "I think Bill went back later on by himself. Most of them looked perfectly normal. Their faces lit up something awful." Keith and Brian got the giggles.

At Guildford the Stones played a rhythm & blues concert with the Graham Bond Quartet, the singer Georgie Fame, and a band called the Yardbirds, who before they were a band would come to the Richmond Crawdaddy Club each time the Stones played. Each of the future Yardbirds would watch the Stone who played his instrument, ask him questions, and by the time the Stones stopped playing at Richmond the Yardbirds knew their whole act. Giorgio Gomelsky was their manager.

On Christmas Eve night the Stones played the town hall in Leek. It was snowing, Mick and Andrew were two hours late, and the Stones did a single one-hour set instead of two shorter ones. At 4:00 A.M. Brian called Windsor and asked Linda Lawrence's father to come pick him up. Then he asked Stu to take him home. At seven o'clock Christmas morning, Linda's father was still in London looking for Brian.

The Stones played each night except one from Boxing Day through the end of the year. On New Year's Eve, they played a ballroom in Lincoln, and later, with the other Stones in the Trust House Hotel (from which the Stones were later banned—Brian again—and still later the place burned down), Charlie fast asleep after having talked for hours on the telephone to Shirley, Bill in bed also but not asleep and not thinking about his wife, and Mick and Keith up writing songs, Brian, along with Stu and somebody else (who is the third that walks beside you?) went in the dead of night to visit Lincoln Cathedral. Alone in the darkness outside the locked, deserted church, they heard the organ playing, a long sustained wail. "Just one note—very creepy," Stu said. "Just a trick of the wind, I imagine, but very frightening. At least it scared me and the other bloke with us, I remember. It didn't seem to bother Brian."

1 3

At any rate he calls us to come outdoors; Dionysus calls
us outdoors. Rise up, my love, my fair one, and come
away. For, lo, the winter is past, the rain is over and
gone; the flowers appear on the earth; the time of the
singing of birds is come, and the voice of the turtle is
heard in our land. Out of the temple made with hands;
out of the ark of the book; out of the cave of the law;
out of the belly of the letter. The first tabernacle in Jeru-
salem; the second tabernacle the universal Church; the
third tabernacle the open sky. "Only when a clear sky
looks down through broken ceilings will my heart turn
again toward the places of God."

NORMAN O. BROWN: *Love's Body*

THE WORLD, beyond the hedge outside the bathroom window,
was once more invisible, shrouded by dense, dirty gases. Scrubbed and
scraped as if I could wash away the poisons that surrounded us, I walked
the length of the house to the kitchen. The office and the living room
were aswarm with people I tried not to see, but in the kitchen I had to
look around to find food, and there at the Formica-topped counter was
Jane Schneider, holding a big red-yellow pomegranate, turning it over
and over, looking for the zipper. She asked if I knew how to open these

things, and of course I did, being from the South and all, so I went to work on the pomegranate with a paring knife and soon my cuffs were spattered with the rose-colored juice of the clear red kernels inside, each with its little white seed. "I don't think that'll come out," Jane said cheerfully. Pete Bennett, also in the kitchen and looking, as usual, like Murder, Incorporated, was talking about the uncanny attraction he exercised over famous people and photographers. "I was at a party at the White House," he said, "and somehow I didn't know, they didn't tell me, that everybody would be in dinner clothes, and I was wearing a regular"—anodized uranium—"business suit. It was terrible, like a bad dream, and then this photographer asked me to be in a picture with President Nixon and Neil Armstrong. Stuff like that keeps happening to me. Did you see the picture of me and Elvis Presley in *Cashbox*? I was in Vegas, see, and Presley is in Vegas, and he never sees anybody—"

"I know," I said.

"—and never has his picture taken with anybody. The club manager asked if his wife and daughter could have their picture taken with Elvis, and Colonel Parker said that Elvis would be happy to do it for five thousand dollars. So I ask to see Elvis backstage, and the club manager says, 'He won't let you in, he's got this Memphis Mafia, you'll just be embarrassed.' I say, 'I'm Italian Mafia, tell him I'm here.' Presley invites me into his dressing room for about three hours, and I get a picture taken with him that later comes out in *Cashbox*."

Standing in the kitchen doorway munching toast, looking over the menagerie in the living room, I wondered whether the mail had come and if so, who had it? I had nothing to do but take notes and wait for my contract. Today was Wednesday. On Friday, my deadline, the tour would begin.

The place was swarming because Jagger had chosen, so the Stones could concentrate on rehearsing, to postpone the pretour interviews until today and tomorrow. All of the Stones except Wyman were in the living room, talking to radio people (after the bushy-haired ABC love-rock interviewer left, Jagger said, "You can't tell by looking anymore, can you?"), periodical press and book writers. Keith, talking to a hungry-looking interviewer from an "underground" newspaper, said as I passed, going to sit on the couch, that the Stones' contracts stated that no uniformed police were to be allowed inside the arenas where the Stones would play: "Uniforms are a definite bad scene."

I sat beside Kathy and Mary, two blond locals who had been driving the Stones' cars for the last few days. "The Dynamic Duo," they called themselves. "We drive the Stones around and fill in during the lulls." They got up to go out to the kitchen as Sam Cutler sat down, nodding at Kathy: "I've screwed that girl ten times today," he said.

Finally the swarm buzzed off and so did we, a bit earlier than usual, to the last rehearsal. Gram Parsons showed up, wearing a furry brown beaver ten-gallon hat. We stood atop a wooden tower facing the marathon ballroom set. The music was so loud we couldn't talk, so we smoked Gram's marijuana and felt the floor patting our feet.

Talkin' 'bout the Midnight Rambler

A few days ago in Memphis a young man named George Howard Putt was arrested for the "sex-slayings" of five women. Still at large were Northern California's Zodiac killer and the killer or killers who this past summer had terrorized the Los Angeles area with bloody massacres like the one at the home of the actress Sharon Tate. Murder seemed to be in the air these days, like the scent of flowers in the spring.

The Stones, under the glittering mirror-chip ball and the gold-fringed red hanging lights, looked like a ghost band playing to a deserted ballroom. I remembered the line they tell you when you lose at the carnival: "At least you got to hear the band play."

After the rehearsal Charlie and I rode with Stu to Oriole, where a long-haired, blue-jeaned reporter from the *New York Times,* Michael Lydon, was listening to stagehand Bill Belmont set the scene: "Two towers . . . three trusses . . . Supertroupers . . . Chip Monck directs an *ambience.* No psychedelic crap. No 'blue spot on the slow songs, red spot on the fast songs.' "

Lydon nodded soberly. Then he heard Jane Schneider telling me, "The Stones' third tour, when I was eighteen, opened my eyes to—everything."

I hate to ask questions, but "Everything?"

"Men with men, girls with girls, I walked into this room and all these people were fornicating, right out in the open. I didn't know about anything like that, and I was knocked out. I'm blushing, Ronnie's saying, 'Do you want to leave?' " Lydon tiptoed away to get something to write with. I made a note myself, of something I heard Ronnie say on the telephone this afternoon: "He did the worst thing you can do to anybody. Sure you know what that is. He turned him in to the Internal Revenue."

Keith said that I didn't need Klein's or Schneider's approval to write a book. Mick said I had to have a deal by Friday. Every day Schneider said that he couldn't get in touch with my agent and asked me about the contract. Every day I liked this place less.

The morning was foul, surf breaking just the other side of the hedge. I staggered through another lobby crowd to the kitchen. A glass of orange juice gave me the strength to walk to the hearth and sit facing the fire, my back to the room. Michael Lydon, appearing at my elbow, wanted me to meet a man dressed in rumpled brown corduroy trousers, a blue shirt with buttondown collar, a wrinkled silk necktie, and glasses with tortoise-shell rims. He looked like a parody of a 1957 college student, and he was, I was told, the correspondent from *Esquire*. I returned to my orange juice and the fire, the licking blue flames. After a while I noticed *Esquire* still beside me.

"How're you doing?" I asked him, just to make a noise.

He shook his head like a movie actor showing despair. "It's over."

"Oh?" I said, wondering what could be over so early in the day.

"It's hopeless," he said, looking toward the couch where a girl who resembled Emily Dickinson with leukemia stared into smoggy space. *The New Yorker.* "Sorry to hear it," I told *Esquire*.

What must readers believe, when writers for periodicals regarded as standards of sophistication could believe Mick Jagger so purified the air around him that in his presence they would receive absolution for their past lives? It like to overcome me, being as it was a cloudy day, and I went to the Oz room for help. I came back to find Jagger, in a white velvet suit, reclining on a couch, discoursing. "Been on the musical stage since I was foive," he was saying in a broad cockney accent, "and I've missed it for the past few years. So I said to meself, 'Back to the boards where we belong—' "

Someone asked whether the Stones' music was nothing more than imitation black blues. I was lighting the reefer I got from the Oz room. "We're an imitation, certainly," Mick said, "but so is black blues—of *some*thing—but by being derivative, a new music results." He could get away with talking like this because on stage and records he seemed to be the Prince of Darkness. I passed the joint to him. Between hisses he said, "When we started, we'd go in clubs, they'd say, 'You don't play blues, you play rock and roll.' We said, 'Yes, fuck it, we play rock and roll.' We never thought we'd be big. Thought we'd do blues for fanatics. When we heard 'Love Me Do'—" Smiling now, he passed the reefer to *The New Yorker,* who took it as if it were a torch. " 'Love Me Do,' right, we thought we might have rock and roll hits, because it was obviously changing."

"May I ask a question?" I asked.

"If it's good," Michael Lydon said.

"He always asks good questions," Mick said. I was almost—but am never—too surprised to talk. "Do you ever think about the effect of what you're doing on kids—I mean, the effect of the awful things you do on children?"

"Can't think about that," Mick said, laughing.

"I don't blame you," I told him. The reefer had come back to me. The press conference had become a conversation. Someone asked about the days of drug-induced musical unity.

"The era of playing on each other's records was a joke," Mick said. "We may be all one, but we're not all alike."

This inspired *The New Yorker,* who was sitting well apart from *Esquire,* to ask about the Stones' politics.

"I was much more involved with politics before I got into music," Mick said. "At the London School of Whatsis I was always in arguments, pounding on tables—which is what you do at college."

"But when you wrote 'Street Fighting Man,' " said *The New Yorker,* "you must have been involved in the politics that was happening at the time."

"But you're always involved with what's going on around you," Mick said, beginning to mutter. "There is a certain political, I suppose, content to that song—"

"But it's just a song," I said.

"Right," Mick said, and knowing an exit line when he heard one, he escaped.

The magazine writers left, and I went at Jo Bergman's request to the Sunset Boulevard offices of Solters and Sabinson, the public relations people, to pick up copies of the tour itinerary. There I met David Horowitz, who could have been the "Under-Assistant West Coast Promo Man" of the Jagger/Richards song, except that he was not wearing a seersucker suit. But he did have horn-rim glasses and a suit that looked as if it had become shiny from lying on the couches of expensively upholstered psychiatrists. Jagger had hired Solters and Sabinson after talking to several firms, lying to them all to test their stupidity. For five hundred dollars a week, Horowitz told me, Solters and Sabinson were going to handle the Stones' media conferences, being careful to include the underground press. "We are aware that the Stones know the underground press are their friends. Our job in the case of an act like this is not to make news, the Stones are news, a tour like this is big news. We see our job as facilitating the dissemination of that news as widely as possible."

But when Horowitz's secretary gave me the itineraries and I thanked her, saying, "I have to send my wife one of these, so she'll know I'm not lost," Horowitz broke into little beads of sweat and refused to let me have the itineraries until he had approval from the Stones, so alarmed was he at the prospect of all this big news being in the hands of somebody's wife. He telephoned Jo, who told him to fork over the paper, and he did.

Back at Oriole, nothing much was happening. There were left-about signs of the times, managers' ads in the daily *Variety* saying "No groups please," and screenplays ("star vehicles") sent for Jagger to read, such as *The Adventures of Augie March* and another called *Children at the Gate*: as its first scene opened, Theresa, sixteen, climbing back into her cotton underpants, said to her naked nineteen-year-old brother, "God damn you, Angelo! How many times do I have to tell you not to hang your God-damned tie on the God-damned cross?" Scripts we never finished reading.

At nightfall Jagger showed up again to check some last-minute details with Jo, who told him that for the big L.A. opening show at the Forum they needed more free tickets than had been reserved for press and friends. "They'll be free to the press or free to your friends, that's the choice."

"Why is *that* the choice?" Mick asked, and paid for the friends' tickets himself.

Dinner with the Wattses, the Schneiders, Jo, and a few other people, was pleasant, even though tomorrow would be Friday, and the odds were not getting any shorter. Afterwards, with the doors locked against the cool air and the Midnight Rambler, Charlie and I were sitting on a couch in the living room, listening to a Columbia collection of 1920s records ("Varsity Drag," "Black and Blue"), when Schneider approached, wielding a deck of cards, asking us to take one, any one. Charlie said, in his deadly honest way, "When I started out playing, I played weddings and that sort of thing, where there was always someone interrupting with card tricks, just like that."

Looking through the wide windows of the President's Club at Continental Airlines in Los Angeles International Airport, under an ocean of smog, we seemed to be, but weren't, in the very early morning. The President's Club had low tables, quiet couches, solitary chairs, like a waiting room in a nondenominational mortuary.

Keith, wearing sunglasses with giant purple bug-eye lenses and a moldy green leather military greatcoat, was listening to Sam Cutler: "We've got all sorts of makeup and two very nice little hair dryers—"

"Good boy, Sam," Keith said.

In an alcove where a man in a dark suit watched, eyes wide, Mary was sitting on Kathy's lap, stroking her gently.

Keith, who had gone to see Bo Diddley last night and got to bed at six A.M., said, "Sam, bring me a vodka."

"But you said you didn't want nothing till you got on the plane," Sam said.

As if he were speaking to himself Keith said, "Must get used to my— unpredictability."

Several men wearing dark suits came in together and signed the guest list. I ambled over and did a little reading. National Aeronautics and Space Administration, Manned Spacecraft Center, Houston, Texas. I went back and sat on a couch with Keith and Mick, no time to worry about contracts today. Keith, having finished his vodka, was adding teaspoons of sugar to a cup of coffee, one two three four five. Jagger and I read the ads for inflatable party dolls in the back of *Cavalier*. Keith got up for a bit of a stroll, coattails trailing.

Bill and Astrid, sitting near us, were joined by one of the men in dark suits, who sat on a table beside Astrid. Deeply tanned and, now I notice, deeply drunk, he thrust a ball-point pen and a piece of paper toward Astrid and said, "Little lady, would you sign my thing?"

Astrid looked at Bill as if the least he could do was to challenge this madman to a duel. Bill smiled and said nothing. He was in Blackpool the night the audience tore the whole auditorium apart. Two others in dark suits came over and said, referring to the drunk, "You *need* this guy. He's a full-blood Indian harmonica player. You ought to hear him." I asked them if they really worked for NASA and they said sure. What are you doing, I asked, going to Mars?

"That's where we're headed," one of them said. "Just waiting for Nixon to turn us on."

I looked out at the fog, said, "I don't think he's going to turn me on," and the NASA men stopped smiling.

Across the room a middle-aged woman who had been reading *Palm Springs Today* looked up and asked Kathy and Mary, who were following Keith, "Are there girls in the group?" The girls smiled like the sisters of Dracula, and the woman asked, "Which one had the two babies with two different women in this month's *Cosmopolitan?*"

Whirling to face the woman, Keith said, sounding like Bea Lillie, "You talkin' 'bout me babies?"

"Are you the one in the magazine?" the woman asked.

"You read too many goddamned magazines," Keith said in the same high voice.

"I know *he's* not the one," the woman said. And she was right, Keith was not the one, the magazine article could only have been about Brian. But Keith growled, "Try me sometime, baby."

"Why are they so goddamned hostile?" the woman asked her husband, who was staring at the *Los Angeles Times,* pretending that he was alone on a tropic island. "I'm not hostile, am I, Chuck?"

Then, without warning, at 12:00 noon, only forty minutes late, our plane was ready. We boarded what the plump blond Passenger Service Director called over the intercom "The Proud Bird for Denver and Kansas City" and were airborne, headed for the out-of-town opening, our first contact with what was to come. Jagger, across the aisle from me, was pushing away, back to Schneider, a movie contract. "I can't read it," Mick said.

"It's in layman's language," Schneider said.

"I can read legal Latin easier," Mick said, putting on a pair of headphones. I put on a pair also and dialed the same channel, to hear Otis Redding. "Nice," I said, but Mick said, "Bad karma for a plane ride."

We were flying eight hundred miles over the Colorado River, Lake Mojave, across the Continental Divide, into the heartland of America. Over the Grand Canyon we heard Count Basie; Stan Getz accompanied us in the blue sky above clouds that brushed the dark snowcapped Rockies. All at once there was Denver, sunny and, so the P.S.D. said, sixty-six degrees Fahrenheit. The last time I was in Denver I was nineteen, stole poems from the library and a Bible from the YMCA, met girls in parks and bums in bars. As we touched down John Lee Hooker was singing: "Losin' you to my best friend."

In the Denver airport there was a Mercury Cyclone GT on a pedestal. All around were characters in cowboy boots and hats. Outside the weather was, sure enough, clear and cool. Parked at the curb were two limousines for the Stones, rented cars for the rest of the party. I selected the fastest one, a Dodge Charger, raring to fly into the dry brown flat fall.

After the urbanity, the flash, the cheap stylishness of L.A. it was awesome, the rurality that surrounded us: dry corn fields, barns, leafless trees, fields plowed under for winter. We were driving a hundred miles an hour a straight sixty miles to Fort Collins, where the Stones would play at Colorado State University. On the radio a nineteen-year-old man or boy was being sentenced for selling amphetamine. Along the road, passing pickup trucks and station wagons, we saw Black Angus cattle huddled around silos, a motel with two-hour prices, mobile homes, a spreading junkyard, a dog-racing track, haystacks, many signs: Green River Wyoming, Foaming Gorge Creek, National Forest . . . Looking? Ft. Collins has it . . . Bacon Hill Pig Farm, little Quonset huts by the road. . . .

At the turnoff (Ft. Collins I-25, Prospect I-14), a girl in blue jeans waving from the roof of a barn welcomed us to Fort Collins. As we entered the city we saw the magic American names, Rexall, Coke, Gulf, 7-Eleven, Safeway. In the distance we could see the Rocky Mountains, just as we were passing a grade school, bicycles parked outside, a chubby little girl riding past on a bicycle delivering newspapers, the whole town like a painting by Norman Rockwell.

Away from the downtown area, among modern, monolithic buildings, we pulled into a parking lot at the rear of the campus, a guard showing us outsiders, show folk, where to park. The sun was a red ball just starting to drop beneath the rim of the purple mountains.

Students in blue jeans and sweaters watched us, the carny bunch, enter a metal door with a sign saying NO ADMITTANCE FOOTBALL ONLY ACTIVE PERSONNEL. We walked down the concrete-block halls to the place the Stones would play, the basketball gym, filled with rows of grey metal folding chairs, next thing to playing a prison. Hanging behind the high stage was a big American flag. In the center of the gym a green electric scoreboard was suspended from the ceiling:

TIME OUT	TIME OUT
VISITORS	HOME
FOUL	FOUL

The Stones and Stu were on the stage among guitars, cases, amplifiers, wires, microphones. Some funky-looking hippies were watching, wearing yellow scarves to distinguish them as security guards, so one of them told me—a girl with straw-colored hair and light blue eyes, their pupils opened big and black by LSD. She asked if I would like some, telling me, as if there could be any doubt, that she was ripped to the gills. I said thanks but no, I need my paranoia intact.

Over by the back door were some jocks in yellow baseball caps and green Colorado State warmup jackets. Leaning against the front of the stage were a couple of the hippie guards. They were all watching Mick and Keith lounging onstage in their perverted public sprawl. Uniformed Colorado campus police were watching, too, licking their lips.

Charlie started playing and the others began tuning up, Mick playing harp, Keith turning up his amp. The lead wire of his guitar was tangled with Bill's, and they stopped playing to pull them apart. A balding man in a silk suit, holding a load of programs under one arm, was waving his free hand at Jagger. "Hey!" he shouted. "Harrisburg, PA." Mick waved, laughing.

"You know these guys?" I asked the man.

"I was with them on the 1964 tour, the first time they came to America. My name is Irving," he said, pronouncing it Oiving. "Pleased to know you. They remember Harrisburg, PA. There were about three hundred there in a hall bigger than this. I sold twelve programs."

The Stones were running lightly through the songs they would do. Schneider was walking the length of the hall, putting his left hand on each row as he stepped forward, counting the house.

Outside the lights were on and a crowd of young people were gathering. When the Stones stopped rehearsing we went down a hall, passing athletic trophies in big glass cases and a ticket office with bank-window glass, to a big room behind a door with a sign saying ACTIVE LETTERMEN ONLY. It was just a room where active lettermen had whatever they had like other people had cocktail parties, with couches and low tables littered with copies of *Sports Illustrated, American Rifleman,* the *Colorado State Alumnus* with Marine General Lew Walt on the cover. The Stones left at once, going to the Holiday Inn, not touching the big buffet, with all sorts of wines, liquors, meats, cheeses, and Alka-Seltzer, as required by their contract. They were going to get ready for the show, and that had little to do with having a nice tea. I poured a glass of wine and lit a reefer.

Once oiled, I went back to the gym. Oiv was selling programs.

"After I did the Stones' first tour," he said, "then they broke up with Oldham and Easton, and Klein didn't want to—what's the word?—the contract. Honor it, right. Because he gets a twenty-thousand-dollar guarantee from this other program guy. So I get a lawyer and he gets a court injunction: the other guy can't sell the programs, and if he does sell any programs he has to give the money to me. They can't sell nothing nowhere. So the guy calls me: 'What are you doing to me?'

" 'What did you do to me?' I asked him.

" 'Look,' he says, 'I've got printers, everything—'

" ' 'S not my fault,' I tell him.

"So he says, 'How about we go partners?'

"I tell him, 'All right, we'll be partners, but I won't pay you.' So it turned out we went partners after all. Then the next year Klein does his own shitty program—"

The hall was filling and I was beginning to wonder if I'd find a place to sit when Michael Lydon came over with two tickets down front, stage left. We found our places in the press of youth, some in little pullover sweaters, some hairy mountain freaks, all seeming gentle. The Bob Dylan song on the public address system ended, a fraternity-brother voice boomed Welcome and introduced the first act, Terry Reid, one week shy of his twenty-first birthday, who looked gentler than anybody. Though he never arrived, Terry and his trio had been for the past year or so the coming thing in English blues. But his act seemed not to move this crowd, who may not have known that English blues bands were supposed to play and scream as loud as possible. Knees pressing into my back, a girl in a sorority blazer sat beside a boy with short, neat hair and a tan sports jacket. I was seated on the aisle; to my right were three pretty girls in three sizes, each with dark hair and dark eyes.

As Terry screamed "I Got a Woman," the girls, Spanish-blooded, told me they were sisters: one fourteen, one twenty, and as Terry, with one blue spot on him and his flat-top guitar, introduced a song called "Bunch Up, Little Dogies," the third sister, too cute to be a minute over seventeen, a little guerrilla in the battle to see who will wear a crown, came to my side, and I began to see what the tour was about. When we are young, innocent, and ignorant, and we look and smell good, all that is required is a little rhythm—what could be more revolutionary, more troublemaking, than bringing rhythm to the scent of the classroom? We looked at each other, our heads, our hair touching in the crowd, and clasped hands, her skin soft as you might expect, nearly any seventeen-year-old is soft, but not every one is so serious and quiet.

Terry Reid was followed by the blues singer and guitarist B. B. King, who was backed by his usual rhythm section and hip, bored-looking horn players. Then the crowd, now under a haze of marijuana smoke, heard Sam Cutler's voice in the darkness saying, "All right, Fort Collins, we made it, we're here, and now I want you to give a big western welcome to the Rolling Stones!" Keith, in black suede pants with silver conchos down the legs and a red jersey shirt dazzling with rhinestones, played the opening notes of "Jumpin' Jack Flash," Mick, all in white, leapt into the air, and the crowd came to their feet.

The show was fine, it all worked, except—with my arm around my little guerrilla, feeling that way, two strangers suddenly together, I felt also, when Jagger sang "I'm Free," saying "You know we all free," that she, no hand-clapper, in this lonesome western basketball gym was not free, and she knew it. The song, written by Mick as a declaration of sexual independence, now seemed to be about many kinds of freedom. As the Stones started their last song, all the crowd standing, jumping on chairs, I held her against me so she could see the stage, and I looked into her happy, hopeless face—just a memory now, with the feel of her hair, her shy turning-away smile—and touched her shoulders, her hair, whispered to her, and she said, What? In the noise, the cheering, the music, it doesn't matter how much I love you, I can't stay, one small kiss and I'm gone, back on the road, Holiday Inns and airports, sad, tired, drear, ugly mechanics of transportation—to L.A. in the dawn, with the lights in the city below us, under the smoke and fog, going out like the last small fires one by one.

THE ELEPHANTS' GRAVEYARD

They lock the gate behind us. We are inside, but where are we? A plateau of dusty red clay. The road leads downward again, away from the Altamont Speedway clubhouse, as we follow a couple of Chip Monck's production crew. A station wagon meets us in the road and Sam Cutler gets out, phosphorescent from speed and cocaine. He hugs Keith, is dodged by Mick, swaps hellos with Ronnie and me, and glances at Tony. Warily. He has not forgotten what Tony said to him in Miami.

We all get in the wagon and drive to another basin where there are more cars and trailers, scaffolding going up, and a big orange bonfire. The people around the fire make room for us as they recognize us coming out of the wagon, walking toward them. The wind whips the fire high, great blasts toward our faces, the people quietly saying hello. Someone hands up a jug of California red wine and Mick drinks, then Keith, holding the jug in both hands, leaning back. I drink a long pull holding the jug moonshine-fashion with thumb through ring on neck, jug resting on forearm, and think of all the people coming to rest around glowing coals on these hills and of all the roasted hotdogs and marshmallows that will be consumed before daybreak, and if there are this many here now, how many will be here tomorrow afternoon? I can taste the roasted marshmallows. The Maysles brothers have followed us in another car and once more announce their presence with the bright quartz lights, circling the outside of the crowd so that the light is always shining directly into someone's face.

"Turn off the lights," Mick says. "No lights." They again ignore him, and Mick turns to Ronnie. "Tell them no lights," he says.

"Mick says no lights," Ronnie shouts into Albert's ear. Al, peering through the camera lens, says "Sync it" to David, who hits the microphone with his notebook, and for the moment their film stops. Al, the cameraman, the older brother, leaves the business deals, the con artistry, to David, thirty-seven, who was very upset when the New York Times identified him as the one who is forty-three, but now Al is staring at

David over his Ben Franklin half-glasses, saying eloquently without words, "What the hell? Here we are on some god-forsaken hillside with these strange people, this Jagger you've got a crush on, spending our own money to make a film about them, trusting them to look after our interests, these people who just skipped the hotel bill in Miami, and now your crooked pansy friend Jagger is telling us to stop? This is crazy!" Al says all this in a quick perplexed palms-up peep over his glasses, camera balanced perfectly on his custom-made shoulder, hair falling into wrinkling pissed-off boyish forehead, and David answers, lighting a cigaret and throwing the match over his right shoulder in a favorite movement of his that is almost but not quite too fast to be debonaire, "Far oot," a slogan with us now, the California-ism pronounced with the Maysles' Boston accent, because it fits so many situations. We use it so often that it has become a joke, we all say it, Jagger has taken to saying it about everything. By now we are so crazy that, as in the combat army, language has become code, because we are all thinking and feeling the same things, can read each others' minds, but the Maysles brothers, who have been together all their lives, have refined their conversational code so that David can say "Far oot" and mean "We can't worry about that now," and anyone who can tell you something like that is so incontrovertibly right that you can only shrug, as Al does, and go with the flow: A girl brings round a joint, the tiny end of a joint, too small to smoke, and this plain girl holds the joint between her fingertips, tells Mick to open his mouth and blows the smoke into Mick's open thick pursed lips, everyone watching the ritual tableau. Then she does the same for Keith, as Mick walks away, toward the stage rising on the slope.

Away from the fire, it is windy and dark. Chip Monck is on the stage, the scaffolding for the PA system is growing, Chip says that it will be finished by dawn, which, we see by Chip's watch, is not far off. We walk behind the stage to the trailer that is to be the Stones' dressing room and shelter in the stormy blast of the day to come, and there in the trailer, smaller but less shabby than the one in Miami, are some of the finer comforts of home, from grass and cocaine to a girl who offers us chocolate chip cookies and is heating coffee in an electric skillet. Sam looks at his watch: "Ten minutes to foive," he says, rolling his eyes like a madman. Grateful Dead factotum Rock Scully is here, grimy, saying, "Well, we've got a lot of work to do," sounding like someone who would go right on saying that forever.

"A cold shower and a few laps around the quad, lads," Keith says. Mick, standing in the doorway with smoke, in the movie lights, boiling *out around him, is talking to a radio interviewer: "I think the concert's just an excuse. It's just for everyone to come and have a good time. The concert is not like the proscenium of a theatre, it's just an excuse to get together and talk to each other and sleep with each other and ball each other and get really stoned and have a nice night out and a good day, it's not like just getting up there and seein' the Grateful Airplane and the Rolling Dead—"*

1 4

To know the reality of politics we have to believe the myth, to believe what we were told as children. Roman history is the story of the brothers Romulus and Remus, the sons of the she-wolf; leaders of gangs of juvenile delinquents (*collecta juvenum manu hostilem in modum praedas agere; crescente in dies grege juvenum seria ac jocos celebrare*); who achieved the rape of the Sabine women; and whose festival is the Lupercalia; at which youth naked except for girdles made from the skins of victims ran wild through the city, striking those whom they met, especially women, with strips of goatskin; a season fit for king killing, *Julius Caesar*, Act I.

NORMAN O. BROWN: *Love's Body*

I WOKE UP just in time to glimpse the first sunlight I'd seen in days, very edgy because it was Saturday and Mick had told me I had to have a deal by yesterday. When we came in last night, some of us found stagehands in our beds. I slept on the floor, and Stu slept fully dressed, curled in the fetal position, on the circular, vinyl-covered seat of the kitchen table, where I was sitting now, eating a ham sandwich and writing in my notebook about the little guerrilla. My fears were like Chinese puzzle boxes, one opening into another: Jagger might simply want to know for sure that if they carry an extra man, an actual book will appear, but he might want what Schneider wants, to censor my manuscript and take my money. As night fell I sat in the kitchen with the lights out and worried.

Al Steckler had come out from New York for the first big show, and I rode to the Forum with him, Michael Lydon, and a young woman who also worked at Klein's New York office. She said that she hated Klein, and that she was quitting. I did not have the luxury of that option.

The conversation about Klein lasted through our leaving Oriole and getting lost and ended as we came upon the Forum, a giant concrete building, rising like a monster toadstool from an asphalt desert. We parked and walked down a slanted ramp to the backstage area, passing at a gate a broadly smiling helmeted policeman. Just past him a girl in a black jacket and a boy in a brown suit were wrapped in a deep ravenous kiss.

The Forum had been used this afternoon for an ice hockey game, and the first show was being delayed while they covered up the ice. I stopped by the locker room where B. B. King was dressing to say hello. The year before, I had written a magazine profile about B.B., who had an office in Memphis, and had come to admire his honesty and humility as I had long admired his great talent. We talked for a bit, B.B. showed me a new guitar made for him by the Gibson company, shapely brown polished wood with gold fittings, and then he excused himself to go to "prayer meeting," opening the bathroom door to reveal the table, the musicians, the cards.

I stepped into the hall and saw the Stones coming in. Jagger had a tall black girl on his right arm, Allen Klein at his left. With them were a tall, thick-necked man with a vacant stare and Pete Bennett, the thickest-necked man I'd ever seen. They all went into the Stones' dressing room, and I let them go.

Out front Terry Reid was opening the show. The Forum was just another basketball gym, the view overhead the same as last night's, girders radiating like mushroom-spines in smoky space. But last night the mood had been gentle—now, ice underfoot, cops everywhere, you can't stand here, you can't do this, you can't do that. I retreated backstage, where Klein, Steckler, and Bennett were having a conclave with a Forum staff man who said, "I'm more worried about crowd control than anything else."

"I'm not," Klein snapped. Behind them four different varieties of uniformed police were standing around eight large trunks labeled Riot Helmets, Gas Bombs, and Masks. Nothing about the scene appealed to me, and I walked out front, where B.B. was having trouble starting his set because his voice microphone wasn't working. A young black man who worked for B.B. came out from backstage, and we said hello. I had befriended him in a small way, and he said, "Come on back here for a minute." We strolled like little colored gentlemen past the cops and war gear to B.B.'s dressing room, nobody there, and into the bathroom, also vacant, where he carefully unfolded a piece of tinfoil. "Hey, man," he said, "this *here* shit is *her*oin, you don't do this shit, do you?"

Four light brown sniffs on a shiny knifeblade, and we waltzed out of the bathroom, just as a plump black lady in a red dress was coming in. Better insulated from the cops, I listened to the rap B.B. had developed for the flower crowd: "Laze and gennlemen, if we just had more love, we wouldn't have no—wars." (Applause.) "Than kyou— And if we had more love, we wouldn't have no—jails." (Clap, clap, clap.) " 'An kyou"—and so on. The simple wisdom of a master musician in this frantic, expensive air cheered me up. I looked around and saw Schneider and Klein standing nearby. My eyes met Schneider's, mine laughing, his not.

Then B.B. stopped talking, was quiet for a moment, played eight searing bars of blues, and sang, "When I read your letter this morning, that was in your place in bed." The crowd, white city people, hooted and hollered, and for the moment even the cops seemed to stop harassing bystanders. Rising on his toes, B.B. lifted the guitar neck on the ascending notes. With his blue suit shining in the blue spotlight, so intent on what he was doing, B.B. was, for all his eight children by six different women, a saint of the blues.

After B.B.'s set, the Kings of Rhythm opened the Ike and Tina Turner Revue. The Ikettes (one of whom was the black girl who had been with Mick earlier) were going on as I started back to B.B.'s dressing room and noticed the backstage heavies talking to a fat man in one of the orange mini-togas worn by the Forum ushers, making them look like a fag track team. Klein was telling him that there must be no uniforms near the stage while the Stones were playing. The fat man nodded in disbelief and asked, "What happens when twenty thousand kids rush the stage?"

"We'll cross that bridge when we come to it," Klein said, and the man in the toga said, "Oh, I see. Great."

Everyone's attention was diverted as here came Tina down the hall, wearing a gold-and-silver-fringed dress, very short. With her was a big black young man in a white trench coat. Beside him she looked like a tiny, sexy doll, red-skinned, red-haired, filling the air with a scent so sweet, so musky, as to equal the evil black funk of her husband Ike.

B.B., in his locker room, was talking with his three sisters and his daughter Gloria about his father, a no more than average-sized man, telling B.B.'s very large brother what he could and couldn't do, shaking his finger upwards in the boy's face. But I remembered Tina's perfume and the way she looked and had to see her. She was telling the women in the audience, "Yo' man may not be taking care of you 'cause he has three or four other ladies he be takin' care of at the same time, puttin' yo' love in the *street*. You just have to say, 'Give it *tuhh* me—' " Tina made a long, rising moan, holding the microphone between the palms of her hands in a rolling caress, bringing her pursed lips near it, exhaling hot and damp on the head of the microphone. She and the Ikettes started to dance in their near-Egyptian way, and with my body sensitized by the heroin, it got all my attention, their hieroglyphic sexual writhing, arms folded over breasts, bucking, making little grabbing movements with their thighs as their skirts rose higher, higher, almost high enough to reveal the heavenly mink-lined wet black cunt. The lights went out, a strobe started to flicker, Tina and the Ikettes writhed and thrusted, caught in their mad nigger poses, crotch flashing, smoke bomb—

Next, the Rolling Stones. The aisles were cleared, those of us among the Elect were gathered in a gaggle behind the stage, and in Shirley Watts' opinion there was far too much fuss over what might have been worthwhile—fun, even—if kept simpler. But it was too late for that; we were in a mammoth arena with many different kinds of cops, rental cops, regular Inglenook suburban L.A. police, Forum guards in orange skirts, and, leaning against the back wall, a lady cop wearing under her white uniform shirt a black bra wide as a motorcycle belt.

Out front the lights were down again and the crowd were on their feet, stamping, the high metal arches ringing. In the backstage doorway Jagger was standing, dressed in black trousers with silver buttons down the legs, black scoop-neck jersey with white Leo glyph on chest, wide metal-studded black belt, long red flowing scarf, on his head an Uncle Sam hat, his eyes wide and dark, looking like a bullfighter standing in the sun just inside the door of the arena, seeing nothing but the path he walks, toreros and banderilleros beside and behind him, to his fate.

> I was born in a crossfire hurricane
> And I howled at my ma in the driving rain
> But it's all right now . . .

It is possible that to know the essence of this moment you would have to be part of the most Damoclean time yet seen on earth ("This could be the last time," says an early Stones record), to have come to this music in the innocence of youth because of its humanity (Alexis Korner called the blues "the most *human* music" he had ever heard), to have followed it steadfastly through all manner of troubles, and to have found yourself in a huge dark saucer-mushroom, doing it again, playing for survival, for your life. You had to be there. Twenty thousand people danced together. The big Ampeg amps blasted, lights (red, this was a fast number) sliced the darkness, Mick whirled in a white sunburst at the center of a purple carpet.

At the end of the first song, "Jumpin' Jack Flash," the crowd settled back. There were more cops than ever hovering around, Pete Bennett making them all superfluous as he strolled back and forth in front of the stage smoking a cigar, no one daring to approach for fear of instant mental picture of diving underwater wearing cement over-shoes. Jagger asked, "Has it really been three years?"

"Nooo," the crowd yelled, as the band started "Carol," Mick dancing, leaping high in the air like Miss Twinkletoes of 1969, not stomping booted feet and barking into microphone with abrupt James Brown monkey gestures, prancing, the Black Prince, swirling flowing scarf, blue-beaded Indian moccasins quiet on the soft carpet. Keith was wearing the same thing he wore last night, ear-tooth hanging in spot-light, the King of the Wraggle-Taggle Gypsies. As the Stones began "Sympathy for the Devil," I noticed Klein standing beside the stage, lighting a briar pipe.

When the song ended, Stu, who had been hidden by the piano, came across the stage carrying two high stools, wearing a pale yellow swallowtail dress suit. He set the stools around one microphone, Jagger sat on one, Keith on the other, and the two of them did the Reverend Robert Wilkins' "Prodigal Son" and Fred McDowell's "You Got to Move," Keith bent over his National steel-bodied guitar, stiff chords rising from it, rhinestones on his haggard shoulders sparkling in the blue lights. Charlie joined them for Robert Johnson's "Love in Vain," Shirley watching him stomping his pedals, love and pride in her green eyes.

The crowd, quiet during the slow songs, screamed for "Midnight Rambler." They were standing for the next song, "Under My Thumb," and the next, "I'm Free," which still didn't ring true. During the next two songs, the crowd surged steadily forward. I was pressed up against the right aisle wall with Shirley, Schneider, and the cops, Schneider helping the cops push the kids back.

"I wish I could see you," Mick said. "You're probably even more beautiful than I am. Chip, could you turn on the lights?" Mick peered out, hand over eyes, Indian fashion. The lights came up, the crowd, bright with color, surged forward, and I saw that I was about to be trapped between the numerous cops and the crush of bodies. I could be in only one of three places: in front of the stage with the cops, backstage with the cops, or onstage. I shoved my notebook into the front of my britches and swung up onto the stage like swinging out the bathroom window, Stu's piano ringing in my ears, Jagger leaping straight up, genitals visible, almost palpable. He landed at the rear of pretty little Mick, hands behind head, hips grinding, screwing little Mick's guitar solo. As the song ended the lights went down for a few seconds and back up again, the crowd a bobbing, swaying mass of heads against the stage. Looking from right to left I saw Jagger and the Stones inciting the audience to orgasm, and Klein, beside the stage, grabbing people in the crowd by their shoulders, throwing them down the aisle that led backstage, screaming "Out! Out!"

"Street Fighting Man" was the last song. "I'll kill the king and rail at all his servants," Mick sang, he and Keith facing Charlie, giving him the boogaloo beat, Charlie pounding it out, the whole place vibrating, Mick running around the stage throwing from a basket rose petals, as in the aisle below me, Klein faced the crowd with a long pole, the kind that fits a heavy push-broom, a fat little man, holding the pole in the middle, slamming it into people who were trying to dance.

Down the backstage hall (where I was allowed to be because I had two metal badges, one like a European stop sign, the other a reproduction of a Massachusetts road sign saying Rolling Stones—except that I had given them away to a Swiss photographer who seemed to need them worse than I did) I walked without credentials, thinking of Alfonso Bedoya, the bandit chief in *The Treasure of the Sierra Madre*, saying to Bogart, "Bodges? We ain't got no bodges. We don' need no bodges. I don' have to show you any stinkin' bodges."

Al Steckler was standing, more or less alone, outside the Stones' dressing room. I asked him why he didn't go in, and he said, "Ask him," nodding toward Tony, looming like a mastodon in a wide stance before the door. "No, thanks," I said.

The second show was an hour and a half late getting started. Backstage the atmosphere was terrible; it seemed every other person was wearing a purple fringed suede vest. I was talking to Steckler and Jo Bergman when a tall blond girl came up and said that she had lost Gram Parsons, he was supposed to meet her here. I went to the Stones' dressing room to get Phil Kaufman to find Gram. The girl led us to the door on the upper level where she had left Gram, and he was still there, the guard wouldn't let him in.

Phil failed to intimidate—"Who's your boss?"—the adamant guard, finally told Gram, "Go downstairs and I'll let you in," and then I saw, where he had been standing behind Gram, the Memphis blues singer Bukka White, whom I had last seen a couple of months ago at Furry Lewis' house. I had seen a handbill advertising Bukka and the Burritos at the Ash Grove the night the boy talked about having fun with niggers, but I'd forgotten it, and now here was Bukka, and I felt like Huckleberry Finn. We embraced, I welcomed Bukka to the Forum, and the stiff-necked guard said not a word. None of the guards did. Big jolly-looking old fat man with gold teeth in his smile, B.B.'s older cousin, convict freed from Parchman Farm because he sang the blues, Bukka White. At the Stones' dressing room, Tony threw open the door. I introduced Keith and Mick to Bukka. Gram and Bukka were drunk. Bukka reminded me to let him know when B.B., who had been starting his set as we came in, went offstage. "What you doing out here?" he asked me.

"I'm with these guys," I said, nodding at Mick and Keith. "They play some blues. They ain't bad. For white boys." I showed him Keith's National guitar, and Bukka, who played a National, an uncommon guitar, was surprised, but not too surprised not to play it. Bukka took the guitar, fumbled a few notes, and said, "I lef' my finger picks in the car," because the white boy has to play first, that's the way it goes. Bukka handed the guitar to Keith, who started playing "Dust My Broom." Mick joined him, singing a couple of choruses; then they did "Key to the Highway." Bukka listened, his head cocked to one side, and said, "That's good. These boys is *good*. Has you ever made any records?"

"Yes," Keith said, looking startled.

"I knew good and well you had. This a star, here," Bukka announced to the room, holding his open hand over Keith's head. "This a Hollywood Star. If I'm lyin', I'm dyin'."

B.B., coming in to ask about something, saw Bukka, and we had Memphis Old Home Reunion. "My wife want to see you so bad she takin' medicine," Bukka told B.B., who lived with Bukka when he first hitchhiked to Memphis from Mississippi.

Mick Taylor, then Charlie and Shirley, came over to me and asked to be introduced to B.B. "They're lovely, aren't they?" Charlie said, meaning men like Bukka White.

"This a world traveller, here," Bukka said to B.B., talking about me. "This a globetrotter."

B.B. went away with a bottle of tequila, Bukka went away with Gram's girl, Mick was down to his underpants, changing for the show, and I left the dressing room. Halfway down the hall Pete Bennett borrowed my pen to write the name and address of a girl he had trapped there. "I want her face for an album. She's got an album face."

I leaned backstage against an equipment wagon and wrote, hundreds of people milling about, all of them wearing badges and stick-on credentials that hardly any of them were entitled to wear. People talked to me but I went on writing, no one could reach me in my Poe-like drugged creative sweats. The place was so crowded with phonies that the people who belonged there were herded into a bunch, and over my shoulder I heard that the badges would no longer signify, we would have a sign, and the sign, I am not making this up, was the Boy Scout three-finger salute. I kept writing, hoping that I'd be left alone, which writers spend their lives hoping, but it never happens. The fat guard in the orange toga spied me writing, asked, "Is he all right?" and was answered by the entire group: "No!" I flashed the Boy Scout salute over my head and kept writing.

Ike and Tina Turner came offstage, the audience roaring. Shirley Watts, having been pushed by a cop, was standing against the back wall, furious. Schneider was talking about busted heads and cracked ribs given to fans by cops—and Klein, I wonder?—during the first show.

As five A.M. approached, the lights went down. "Here we go," Mick said. As the Stones started to play the crowd swelled forward. All our tiredness seemed to lift, as if we were dreaming and not subject to ordinary physical limits. I saw no uniformed police, nor Klein, but many guards, and Schneider pushing people away. The music ripped through the smoky air, and Mick said, "Wake up a little bit, you been waiting so long, we might as well stay on a long time."

Now Schneider, holding a briefcase, was on the stairs leading up to the stage. People were climbing onto the stage and being carried off by Tony. Some people in the crowd had crossed eyes from lack of sleep, others were staring, bright-eyed. Pandemonium reigned. At the back of my mind was a paranoid vision of being trapped, saying, "I know the sign!" to uncomprehending guards who would smash me as I gave the Boy Scout salute.

The lights came up for the raving end, a giant sign in the audience, JESUS LOVE AND PEACE. Darkness again, and then the spotlights washed over the stage, over the crowd, and the crowd broke forward as if the light had released them like the moon releasing locked-up secrets of the mind, letting out the demons. They came up against the stage, past the line of guards who were there to keep them back. Sam Cutler pushed Schneider aside to save a boy who was being dragged backstage by guards.

Mick, silhouetted above squirming, screaming bodies, was dancing at the edge of the stage, pouring pink champagne into a glass, raising it high, a toast, a toast, hands waving like undersea flowers before him. A boy being manhandled by guards beside the stage closed his eyes and put his hands together in a gesture of prayer. The whole building was jumping; I thought it might collapse like a bridge from lock-step marching. "We'll kill the king," Mick sang again, but when the show ended Sam told me he had been backstage rescuing kids from cops who were beating them on the feet with clubs.

1 5

The blues is a lot like church. When a preacher's up there preachin' the Bible, he's honest-to-God trying to get you to understand these things. Well, singing the blues is the same thing.

LIGHTNIN' HOPKINS

THE FIRST WEEK of January 1964 the Stones opened a tour of England, billed second to a trio of black American girl singers called the Ronettes, who quickly saw that to follow the Rolling Stones onstage was to commit professional suicide. After that the Stones always played last and got top billing.

Things were going well for the Stones, except Brian, for whom things were going to hell. Linda Lawrence, to Brian's alarm, was pregnant with his third child. At this rate he could father fifty bastards: Look at him, the teen idol, strolling the sidewalks of Windsor arm in arm with his pregnant girlfriend, his bloody pet goat, Billy G., following like a puppy dog.

Brian was still missing performances, excusing his absences because, for example, he and his chauffeur were "lost in a fog." The day after that one, the Stones played Shrewsbury, a grim place, and Brian was complaining that he needed something for a sore throat. Stu, who was driving Brian and the other Stones, turned toward a chemist's in a one-way street. Brian jumped out of the car and ran into the chemist's, as Stu and the others noticed that they were headed the wrong way, the traffic was coming toward them, and they had been recognized, fans were swarming. "Leave him," Keith said. Brian had lost considerable hair and clothing by the time he managed to reach the Granada Theatre.

On this same day, two fourteen-year-old schoolgirls—having written to the manager of the theatre in Aylesbury the Stones had played the night before, asking permission to see the dressing room the Stones had used, or if that were not possible, could we please just touch the door handle—were photographed for a local newspaper, one of them looking reverently at the door, the other kneeling, eyes closed in ecstasy, nuzzling the handle. The Stones' rhythm pounded sex tremors through the floor and the upholstered seats into the white cotton knickers, into the dews and damps, freeing the ripeness that presses outward against the skin, a wildness from within, knowledge in the flesh, old and devout and perverse, and with eyes shut tight she kneels as her hot cheeks press and caress the cold doorknob.

Other fans were now breaking out the Stones' dressing room windows, stripping the van of its lights, mirrors, even the rubber window mounts; popularity had become hysteria. Stu said, "It wasn't pleasant to see what the music did to people." It was the looks on their faces that had changed, that you did not like to see, the straining, screaming faces of young English girls, sweating and squealing like pigs, not loose and happy like raving together at the Crawdaddy but reaching out for something separate from themselves, not the music but the musicians, to touch them, tear them asunder to find out what manner of magical beings have let loose this madness.

But while the Stones were playing concerts almost every night and appearing on at least one national television program each week, the three records they had released were not chartbusters. The week the tour with the Ronettes ended, the Stones' first extended-play record was number 2 in the popular EP charts, "I Wanna Be Your Man" was the number 9 single. It would go no higher, but it was still a hit, a Top Ten record. Now they had to do it again.

On the day after the tour ended, the Stones were scheduled to record, but Andrew Oldham cancelled the session, and they all went to a reception for Phil Spector, the Ronettes' record producer, the boy genius from the United States. Young, talented, and rich, he was everything that Oldham wanted to be. The Stones had tried several times to record "Not Fade Away," the Bo Diddley-inspired song by Buddy Holly, and when they tried again a few days later, Oldham invited Spector to the session. But the session didn't go well, and Oldham telephoned Gene Pitney, who was in London on his way to the United States from an appearance in Italy. Pitney had written "He's a Rebel," the first hit record on Spector's Philles label, and he knew a lot about the record business. "Andrew called me and said, 'Listen, we gotta record a follow-up, and they all hate each other, and I don't know what to do,'" Pitney said.

"'I'll be over in a minute,' I said, 'I'll work it out.' So I took a big bottle of Martell cognac, and I got there and told them that it was my birthday, and it was a custom in my family that everybody had to drink a water glass of cognac to celebrate the birthday. It was the happiest session you ever saw in your life. Spector wound up playing an empty cognac bottle with a half-dollar."

It was such a happy session that the Stones recorded a song for the B side of their next single and two more songs for album cuts. But Pitney saw "a standoff thing. Mick and Keith were always close together, and Brian was like—in left field. God bless him, but I think he always had a problem with—I think just society in general. He was very paranoid even with the other guys in the group, not just from people outside the group. When you have that, there's giant problems to begin with." The Stones had no time for problems. Almost every day they were entering further realms of wealth and fame. A couple of days after the record session, they made more money than they had ever made in one day by recording a television commercial for Rice Krispies, a breakfast cereal that talked to itself in a three-word vocabulary, snap, crackle, pop.

Meanwhile the Beatles left England for their first performances in the United States, on the Ed Sullivan television program and two concerts at Carnegie Hall. Fifty thousand people requested the Sullivan show's 728 seats, and the Carnegie Hall shows sold out in a matter of hours.

Two of the Beatles' records had been released in the United States a year earlier to scant response. But steady publicity in the British press had been picked up by the London offices of the U.S. news media; *Time, Newsweek,* and the *New York Times,* as well as NBC and CBS television, did stories about the Beatles. Capitol Records, who distributed the Beatles' records in the United States, spent fifty thousand dollars for what they called a "crash publicity program." They plastered five million THE BEATLES ARE COMING stickers on telephone poles, washroom walls, and other appropriate places throughout the country. They tried to get a copy of the Beatles' current single, "I Want to Hold Your Hand," to every disc jockey in the country. They made up a four-page newspaper about the Beatles and sent out a million copies. They photographed their top executives wearing Beatle wigs, offered Beatle haircuts free to all their female employees, and persuaded the actress Janet Leigh to get one. They even tried, unsuccessfully, to bribe a University of Washington cheerleader into holding up a card reading "The Beatles Are Coming" before the television cameras at the Rose Bowl football game. "There was," said one Capitol vice president, "a lot of hype."

The Beatles' appearance on the Sullivan show was reported to have been seen by seventy-three million people, and to have reformed the United States' teenagers for as long as it lasted, since across the country during that hour not one major crime was committed by a teenager.

The Rolling Stones, on tour with some peculiar English acts, did not seem to be doing much to deter crime. Rather the opposite; fans attacked the Stones, separately and together, and their van, breaking the windshield. "Some of those crowds were too much," Stu said. "They began to get used to the idea that the Stones dropped their bleedin' guitars the last number and ran for it. And then the crowd from the first house would hang about till the second house had finished, and they'd be waiting for you as well. It got to be quite a problem. This is something they never really got credit for, that even at this stage they were causing bigger riots than the Beatles ever caused in this country. You see, nobody liked them. The establishment hated them, so they never got any good publicity."

The Stones did their part to alienate people. On this tour, after playing the Stockton Odeon, they stayed at one of the more pleasant English hotels, called Scotch Corner. "That was a hotel from the past," Stu said. "Lovely hotel, always wanted to stay there, but they didn't appreciate Brian at all. Brian would walk around the halls in his underpants, making noise, and just be a fuckin' uncivilized idiot. At most of these British hotels, people go to bed at ten at night. But these people made the effort. They said, Yeah, fine, okay, we'll lay on a nice cold meal, and there'll be waiters here when you come back. So we come back from Stockton at twelve midnight, and there are two waiters there, a great big table, fresh fruit salad and melon and cold meat. But Brian's got to start throwing bread rolls around the room, and demanding all sorts of bloody things they didn't have, and then he'd be obnoxious when they didn't have it. And instead of somebody sit—well, sometimes they *would* sit on him and they wouldn't go along, but at other times, once he'd start, the others'd start as well, and oh, I used to get so bleedin' embarrassed."

On February 21 the Stones' EP record was number one in the EP charts. "Not Fade Away" was released and went into the Top Ten. They were still touring, causing riots of sexual frenzy each night. At the Sophia Garden in Cardiff, a man came into their dressing room, offered to sell them hashish, and they had him thrown out. Sexual frenzy was all right, but hashish was illegal. A few nights later at the Wolverhampton Gaumont, Jagger found among the fan letters left in the Stones' dressing room a note addressed to him, containing a stick of chewing gum and the request, "Please chew some and send it back!" Beyond the perverse and illegal into the unsanitary.

Same day and place, a reporter from *Melody Maker* interviewed the Stones, and the resulting story had probably the most-quoted headline of their early career, the headline that asked the musical question WOULD YOU LET YOUR DAUGHTER GO WITH A ROLLING STONE? Consciously or not, the headline echoed the racism directed against people of African descent in the United States. It also fit the image of the Stones held by many people—leering Rolling Stone locked in savage embrace with fair young girl. True or not (and it was both), the image was too strong to be forgotten, especially by newspaper writers. A couple of weeks later, another headline asked: MARRY YOUR DAUGHTER TO A STONE? The article mentioned that Brian was moving to a flat in Belgravia. He had left Linda Lawrence. "I think Brian got scared," Shirley Arnold said. "It was the thought of another baby. They packed each other up, and then I think Brian got scared again 'cause she was having the baby and he decided to stay with her."

During this time, besides playing to berserk crowds twice and sometimes four times daily, the Stones recorded their first long-playing album, were given scripts for their first film, signed to tour the United States, and Mick and Keith became more skilled as songwriters, "though we didn't like anything we wrote," Keith said, "and we couldn't seem to get anybody else in the band to play it." But Gene Pitney had a hit in England with one of their songs, "That Girl Belongs to Yesterday," and Oldham produced a hit on another Jagger/Richards song, "As Tears Go By," recorded by Marianne Faithfull, a girl they had recently met at a party. She could barely sing, but she was very pale and blond and had a pseudo-virginal sadomasochist charm that was not wasted on Jagger's philosophical eye.

The Rolling Stones, their artily untitled (Oldham's idea) first album, was released and went directly to the top of the popular music album charts, a position held by the Beatles for almost all the previous year. "Not Fade Away," their first release in the United States, entered the *Cashbox* magazine Hot 100. It was number 98, but it was there.

And every day, in every sense, the crowds kept coming. In some towns the Stones would find the places they were going surrounded and couldn't get inside to play. At other places, where there were low stages, the Stones would start, the little girls would run right over the bouncers in front of the stage, and the Stones would drop their guitars and run. Oldham discovered one night between shows that the seats were dripping with liquids deposited by female fans. Dozens of girls fainted at every show; in the places where tickets were counterfeited, or promoters sold more tickets than they had seats, things were even worse.

"The first time Chuck Berry came to England," Stu said, "we were supposed to be doing two spots at the Savoy Room in Catford, and the first one was supposed to be about nine o'clock, and the next one at half-past ten. Berry was at Finsbury Park, and we'd never seen Berry live. Catford is south London, Finsbury Park is north London. So we're all looking at each other and saying, 'Well, what's it gonna be?' Of course we went off to see Chuck Berry. And these things were running a little bit late, and it must have been well after nine o'clock before Berry was finished. And he was very weird, he wouldn't talk to us, wouldn't say a bloody dickybird." The Stones then drove down to Catford.

"You couldn't see the bloody ballroom for ambulances," Stu said. "They were carrying girls out one after another. The promoter had let far more people into the hall than it would hold. And they were passing out right, left, and center. The boys had to come in through somebody's garden, up a ladder, through a window. I think it'd originally been a cinema, and there was this vast great wide stairway on one side of the building, and when we left, it was covered in bodies. Just gone. Flaked out. They carried hundreds out that night. It was awful. All fuckin' Chuck Berry's fault."

The next night the Stones played in Bristol, and Brian, driving down alone from London, missed the first show. "That caused one hell of a row," Stu said. Brian's retribution was so swift as to seem compulsive. Three days later the Stones played Saint George's Hall in Bradford, across the street from the Victoria Hotel, where they stayed. Between shows, Stu said, "They didn't want to sit around their dressing room until the second half. No cops about. They said, Shall we chance running across the road to the hotel? They all made it except Brian, who chickened out before he got to the hotel entrance because there was people running after him. He eventually turned round and ran the other way. So all these people are chasing Brian through the streets in Bradford, tearing clothes off him. The police finally brought him back without a jacket, without a shirt, and he'd lost a shoe and handfuls of hair. All the others got across easy, but not him."

Two days before, the Stones had taken smallpox vaccinations for their trip to the United States, about three weeks away. Before leaving, they did more television appearances and frantic concerts in Scotland and England. One newspaper review said, "Never before has there been a sound to rival this—except, perhaps, in the jungles of darkest Africa!" Their mounting success brought reporters to write about the individual Stones. Wyman, who for months had been writing "stuck in fog" in his diary as code for spending the night with a girl, complained in one story that the Stones' busy schedule kept him from his family: "We had a dog once but we couldn't keep it because I was never at home and he used to bite me when I turned up. That's rather sad really, isn't it?"

In another story, Brian answered critics of the Stones' effect on their audiences. "The Rolling Stones do not incite violence," he said. "I deny it categorically."

On June 1, the Stones left for the United States, where they were not unknown but not exactly known. Their LP had been released, and London Records, English Decca's U.S. chapter, had distributed news clippings, photographs of the Stones, and T-shirts with THE ROLLING STONES on the front. London had also hired Murray "the K" Kaufman— a Manhattan disc jockey also called, because he liked and helped them, the Fifth Beatle—to like and help the Stones. Kaufman met the Stones at Kennedy Airport, conducted a press conference for them there, and took them to his program on WINS, where they spent most of the evening. He also gave them a record he thought they might like, called "It's All Over Now." The Stones planned some recording, as well as touring and television, while in the United States. They would stay two and a half weeks, much longer than the Beatles' first visit, with greatly inferior planning and promotion, and with, as Keith said, "disastrous results, almost."

The Stones spent their first night in the U.S. trapped in the Astor Hotel by screaming girls outside, whom they believed had been hired. The next day they were taken out and shown to interviewers and photographers. They saw David Bailey, the fashionable London photographer, and met Jerry Schatzberg, the fashionable New York City photographer, and Baby Jane Holzer, a Warholite who was blond and fashionable all over. "The first people to catch onto us in New York, thought we were just bee-yoo-tee-full," Keith said.

Next day the Stones flew to Los Angeles. There were crowds of girls, probably a few hundred in all, waiting for them at the airport, as there had been in New York. The Stones appeared that night at the taping of a television show called *The Hollywood Palace*, whose guest host, Dean Martin, a musician of a different school, ridiculed their performance, appearance, ancestry, you name it. Partly because of this, and partly because they were billed among a trampolinist, a great many King Sisters, an elephant act, cowgirls, and so on, the Stones discussed walking off the show. But the dress rehearsal had been taped and could be shown, so they decided they might as well go on.

The Stones had a distinct feeling that they were not taking off in the United States like a rocket, but after a day of swimming at Malibu and a night of relaxing, they played a concert in San Bernardino that was a riot, just like England, except that the cops wore white motorcycle helmets and carried guns. San Bernardino raised the Stones' spirits so that they could fall the next night, at the Texas Teen Fair in San Antonio with George Jones, Bobby Vee, circus acts, and rodeo riders. Nobody came. It was so hot in San Antonio, not far from the Mexican border, that Wyman had Keith cut his hair. The tour was taking on a deep aura of gloom, and they were thinking of cutting it short. By the time they reached Chicago, Andrew Oldham was in hysterics or at least histrionics. At the hotel, after a scene with a revolver, Mick and Keith told Andrew to shape up and go to bed. He kept begging them for "just one bullet."

By the next day Andrew was in sufficient control to accompany the Stones to the morning television interviews and to Chess Recording Studio, where the Stones, with the help of Ron Malo, Chess' expert engineer, recorded four songs, including their next single, "It's All Over Now," a fine, spontaneous fourteenth take. The group ended the day with more radio and television interviews. The problem was that the Stones were making no national impact. Andrew used one of the oldest techniques a hustler can use when his act is too cold to get arrested: he got arrested.

The next morning Andrew called the news media and invited them to a press conference the Stones planned to have on a traffic island in Michigan Avenue, and did have, until the police came. It was on the national television news that night, which was the idea in the first place.

After taking their leave of the police, the Stones went back to Chess and recorded twelve more songs. Muddy Waters was there and helped them carry in their equipment. The graciousness of Muddy, from whose song "Rollin' Stone" Brian had taken their name, was touching. The Stones were recording Chuck Berry's "Around and Around" when Berry walked in. A week before they left England, Mick and Charlie happened to confront Berry, after he had snubbed them backstage at Finsbury Park. They were in a hotel elevator: the elevator stopped at a floor, the door opened, there stood Berry, who stepped aboard, saw Mick and Charlie, turned his back, when the door opened again he walked out, wouldn't speak. But this time he was trapped. "Swing on, gentlemen, you are sounding most well if I may say so," he said, sounding like Duke Ellington at his most unguent.

The next day the Stones, back on tour, played to four hundred kids at a fair in Minneapolis, the following day to six hundred in an Omaha auditorium. These were the days of Scotch and Coke, and there was always a bottle of Scotch in the dressing room, but the auditorium in Omaha was public property, where alcoholic beverages were prohibited by law, in the person of a cop who looked into the dressing room, saw the whisky bottle, made them pour it out, and made a couple of the Stones pour out their drinks. He told Keith to do likewise. "The thing is," Keith said, "I wasn't actually drinking whisky, the other two were drinking whisky and Coke, and I was drinking a Coca-Cola. He told them to pour it down the bog, and I refused to pour mine down because I said, Why the fuck is an American cop telling me to pour the national drink down the bog? Cop pulled a gun on me. Very strange scene to me, a cop ordering me at gunpoint to pour a Coke down the john."

Then, Scotch gone, cop gone, the Stones watched grimly on a television set in the dressing room the network broadcast of their visit to *The Hollywood Palace*, cut to near forty-five seconds among the elephants.

"That was the thin end of the wedge for Eric Easton," Stu said.

"Easton, we suddenly realized," Keith said, "wasn't big enough to handle anything outside of England." The next day, Keith bought a .38 revolver, in case he might want to drink a Coke backstage again sometime.

Just as things were going badly, they became worse. The hotel in Chicago threw them out, something about girls in some of the rooms, and called the police, who discovered that the Stones planned to go to Canada for a television appearance and that Keith had lost his passport. The police assured them that if they left the country they would not get back in. So instead of Canada, they went to see B. B. King at the Twenty Grand in south Chicago, and on following nights played to tiny groups of people in mammoth halls in towns like Pittsburgh, Cleveland, Hershey, where hardly anyone knew who or what the Rolling Stones were. The Stones didn't know what Hershey Bars were, and they called Phil Spector in Los Angeles to ask why the town was painted brown and there were trays of chocolates everywhere.

The next night they played to three hundred in Harrisburg, Pennsylvania, where Irv the program man sold his twelve programs. Driving from Harrisburg in a bus, the Stones saw a house get struck by lightning. Then, so swift it could give you the bends, they were back in Manhattan to play Carnegie Hall, "just screaming with kids," Keith said. "We'd almost forgotten what it was like, 'cause we were used to that every night, every time we played, and suddenly we were brought down, bang, everybody saying, What a fuckup, we've blown it. America was still very much into Frankie Avalon. There wasn't any thought of long-haired kids, we were just entertainment-business freaks, with long hair, just like a circus show. And we get to New York and suddenly we realize that maybe we—that it's only just starting."

In New York Brian told a newspaper man about a vision he'd had, coming out of a nightclub in the London dawn. "It was," the writer wrote, "as if the heavens had called him to look up and see the face of a goddess angel telling him to work for human good."

1 6

MANIFESTO

Greetings and welcome Rolling Stones, our comrades in the desperate battle against the maniacs who hold power. The revolutionary youth of the world hears your music and is inspired to even more deadly acts. We fight in guerrilla bands against the invading imperialists in Asia and South America, we riot at rock 'n' roll concerts everywhere. We burned and pillaged in Los Angeles and the cops know our snipers will return.

They call us dropouts and delinquents and draftdodgers and punks and hopheads and heap tons of shit on our heads. In Viet Nam they drop bombs on us and in America they try to make us war on our own comrades but the bastards hear us playing you on our little transistor radios and know that they will not escape the blood and fire of the anarchist revolution.

We will play your music in rock 'n' roll marching bands as we tear down the jails and free the prisoners, as we tear down the State schools and free the students, as we tear down the military bases and arm the poor, as we tattoo BURN BABY BURN! on the bellies of the wardens and generals and create a new society from the ashes of our fires.

Comrades, you will return to this country when it is free

from the tyranny of the State and you will play your
splendid music in factories run by the workers, in the
domes of emptied city halls, on the rubble of police stations, under the hanging corpses of priests, under a million
red flags waving over a million anarchist communities. In
the words of Breton, THE ROLLING STONES ARE THAT WHICH
SHALL BE! LYNDON JOHNSON—THE YOUTH OF CALIFORNIA
DEDICATES ITSELF TO YOUR DESTRUCTION! ROLLING STONES
—THE YOUTH OF CALIFORNIA HEARS YOUR MESSAGE! LONG
LIVE THE REVOLUTION!!!

> —Broadsheet distributed at the
> Rolling Stones' concerts in Oakland

LEAVES AGAINST THE WINDOW woke me, and I looked
out to see birds flying away in the wind. The heroin aftermath made
everything as slow as an anxiety dream. It was Sunday. I showered,
dressed, and called my father to ask if the contract had been sent to
Memphis, but it hadn't been. I didn't know what I would do with the
contract once I got it, except try to protect it. I had told the agency to
send it in a plain wrapper. I didn't know what else to do.

I flew to Oakland with Jo Bergman, David Horowitz, Michael
Lydon, and the photographer Ethan Russell. As we left the plane,
photographers on the runway took our pictures, until they saw that
we were not the Rolling Stones. In the airport, passing another car
on a pedestal, we saw a little old black woman wearing a straw Sunday
hat and a shin-length brown dress, walking with a cane, carrying a
hymn book. I thought of her at the time as a good sign, but didn't
stop to think that she was headed away from us.

In a couple of rented cars we drove to the Edgewater Inn, down
the freeway from the airport, past the Oakland Coliseum, where the
Stones would play in a few hours. The Inn was small, one story behind
a two-story front, like a car wash behind a church facade. Jo picked
up a handful of keys at the desk while Horowitz conferred with press
people who accosted him as we came in. He came back, saw Jo, and
asked, "How'd you get the keys?"

"I just have that kind of face," she said.

A board walkway extended from the back door of the lobby to the
swimming pool and on to a rear addition to the motel. Beside the pool
there were a steam shovel and a sign saying DANGER POOL FULL OF
CHLORINE. On the double glass door at the back of the motel smaller

signs said DANGER backwards twice. So much for the little old colored lady.

The rooms (five plus a suite—we wouldn't be staying the night) were done in *le style* Holiday Inn, plain brick walls painted beige. Jo ordered beer and bottles of whiskey from room service, and after a drink, we tried driving to the Coliseum, but a constant stream of cars leaving the football stadium next door prevented our turning left, so Jo, Michael, and I got out of the car and crossed the street into the stadium's parking lot. We were looking for a place to cross the deep ditch that divided us from the Coliseum's parking lot. Two men and two women were getting into a car as we passed, and Michael asked how we could reach the Coliseum. "You can get across up there," one of the men said, pointing farther up the asphalt. I walked to the spot and saw a wide stretch of dirty water running in the ditch. I walked back and said Thanks for the help, sport. You can make it, he said, swim across. Fuck you, I said. Oh, come on, Jo said, and we walked along the edge of the freeway till we could reach the Coliseum.

Hours before the show, kids were crowding outside. Stu was on-stage checking the equipment. Bill Graham, the show's promoter, born Wolfgang Grajonca in Berlin, walked to France to escape the Nazis, came to the United States, became involved with theater in California, now had two rock concert halls, one on each coast, and was at the moment walking around the Oakland Coliseum, killing time. He had wanted to promote the whole Stones tour, and in New York discussing the matter with Schneider had cited a long list of the attractions he had presented, to which Schneider had said, "Yes, Bill, but what did you ever do big?" We visited for a while, then left Graham to go back to the Inn. The setting sun was gold over the distant grey-green hills.

In the motel's restaurant, done in red and black, Naugahyde and flocked velvet, we found David Horowitz with a fat young man who said his name was Jon Jaymes. He was at the Forum last night. I didn't know whom he worked for, but he had a kind of authority. He was sitting at the red linen, speaking into a white telephone, preparing the Oakland airport for the arrival of the Rolling Stones. "I've notified the police," he said. "People must stay in their seats and let the Stones off"—his voice rising—"or there'll be *chaos* at the *airport*—

"Now what I want to do is notify the plane as soon as it's on the ground to let one of our people on to expedite getting the Stones off with our security people."

Jaymes' younger partner, Gary Stark (they both spent last night on the living room couches at Oriole, why I don't know), joined us as Jon hung up the phone. "How many kids are there at the airport?" Stark asked, excited.

"Seven hundred kids flew in from Harlem," Jaymes said, smiling. "Whaddya want from me?"

As we started to leave for the airport, I said to Jaymes, "Wow, you're a *real* con man, that's fantastic."

"One word like that and I cancel the whole deal," he said, "cancel all the cars, all the transportation. . . ." He was working for Chrysler, he'd been saying, and as we walked out I told him I'd intended the phrase con man as a compliment. He didn't quite know how to take that, but he was pleased to hear that I wasn't his enemy.

I rode to the airport with Jaymes, who drove insanely as he explained that he was Chairman of the President's Committee for Lowering the Voting Age to Eighteen, before that chairman of two other presidential committees, "a former FBI narcotics agent, and I have an obligation—to a company called Chrysler—to see that this tour is kept clean." Ah, not more no-dope stupidity, I thought, but Jaymes said, "This means that, through political influence if necessary, if everybody gets busted, I can get everybody off."

Jaymes said that Chrysler wanted nothing from the Stones in the way of endorsements or promotional photographs, they just wanted the Stones to use Chrysler equipment so that, at the end of the tour, Chrysler could say that they had transported the Stones and tons of equipment around the United States. If all went well and there were no scandals, there'd be a happy tie-in with the youth market. We were careering through red lights, Jaymes blowing the horn, stepping on the gas and the brake at the same time, as he said of Jagger (who'd changed plans abruptly, deciding to take a later flight to Oakland than the one he'd scheduled), "With all due respect, and I think he's due it, I think he has the idea that he's Mick Jagger, Rolling Stone, and he can do anything he wants, and he's surrounded with people who tell him he can when he can't. And someplace on the tour, that's gonna blow up on him."

We lurched to a stop at the curb and ran through the airport, a cop with us holding his gun under his coat steady in its shoulder holster, to gate number one, where the Stones should have been but were not. Horowitz was at the gate, saying, "There should be press here, where are they?" A birdlike little old lady was looking at him as if he were something strange and wonderful. Gary Stark ran up and said, "Gate three," holding up four fingers.

From a window I saw the plane landing. Almost at once the Stones were coming toward us, walking down the aisle, not too fast, flutter flutter all around, people stopping to watch—the pace picking up till we were past the front lobby and outside, where there were four more cars, rented by Jaymes in the couple of minutes we'd been in the airport. The passenger side door of one car was open, and I slid into the driver's seat. Keith was right behind me, followed by Mick Taylor, Jagger, Wyman, and Watts. Away we zoomed. I had not been expecting the hottest act in show business suddenly to pile in the car with me, so although you could nearly see the motel from the airport, I went off the wrong way, followed by a couple of cars.

It was like being gypsies. I remembered the gypsy boy buried by the roadside on the way down to Wyman's house from London. He had been hanged for a crime the gypsies say he did not commit, and each year on the date of the hanging, the morning finds fresh flowers on the grave, the grave now more than two hundred years old, but the gypsies' memory is older than night. We were like gypsy boys, I thought, in spite of the false con and the real con it was exhilarating to be with the Stones, millions of dollars worth of talent and notoriety, wheeling through the darkness, looking for the REGNAD REGNAD motel. I turned down a dark side road, pulled right, hit the brakes, and threw the front end left, placing us directly athwart the highway. Cars were coming from both directions. Jagger was groaning, "What you up to?" But we made it, turned around, went back to the main road, and in a minute we were at the motel.

Sam Cutler came out to greet us. "Raise the portcullis, let the knights enter the castle."

We went in, some of us had drinks, and then in the Stones' suite there was a press conference: more long-haired kids with cameras and tape recorders. One asked, "Why haven't the Stones made any state-ments concerning the U.S. youth movements, marches, and pitched battles with the police?"

"We take it for granted that people know that we're with you," Keith said.

"We admire your involvement," Jagger said, "but we're primarily, um, musicians, and last night for instance the crowd needed to rel— weren't ready to re*lax*. They wanted to be cool and intelligent, and it took them a long time to get to the frame of mind where it's just fun. We just want them to get up and dance."

The press, sitting on the floor, looked as if they'd never be able to get up and dance. Someone asked if the Stones had any trouble getting into the United States, and Jagger said, "No, because none of us has any convictions." The conference ended with, once again, little said.

As we left for the Coliseum I asked Horowitz if he was getting any good publicity. "Both the wires covered the Forum show," he said. Then he got himself under control and said, "Of course, with the Stones, you don't have to create news."

We drove to the Coliseum and in the back entrance. Inside the Stones' dressing room, above the table covered with cheeses, meats, beers, wines, champagne, was a large poster of Bill Graham smiling broadly, holding his middle finger aloft to the camera. The Stones came in and deployed themselves around the room, looking at the food as if it were a display of artificial flowers.

Ike Turner stuck his black, greasy head in the door, and Jagger said, "How are ya?"

"I'm lookin' good, workin' hard, starvin' to death," Ike said, and closed the door.

The Oakland Coliseum was smaller than the Forum, with amber roof lights. Ike and Tina had already played, and the crowd was stomping for the Stones. Sam on the microphone was saying, "We're sorry we're late, there were no cars to meet us at the airport, we'll be here in two minutes literally."

I wandered the aisles looking at the kids, hairy and wild but at the same time healthy and fresh, smelling of aromatic herbs and incense, stomping in time-honored fashion, like on Saturday afternoon when the projector would break before the cavalry could arrive. Then—it had been no more than five minutes—the cavalry arrived, to whistles and yells of pleasure, just like Saturday afternoon.

Keith hit the opening chords of "Jumpin' Jack Flash," Mick Taylor chiming in, Charlie bashing, Wyman's small, light bass (a Fender Mustang) creating a mountainous sound with great reverberating overtones. How he did it was a mystery. That Wyman was a Rolling Stone was a mystery, but there he was, a little old man, and just listen. He never danced, never even moved. "Once in a while I sweat a little bit under me arms," he said. Jagger sashayed around the stage, waving hello with his thin, elegant arms. Another factor was present tonight, and I walked to the back of the stage to see it: a giant closed-circuit television screen above the stage, a big black and white Jagger above the real one.

The joint was jumping, but in the middle of the second song, Keith's amplifiers died, and the band ground to a halt. "It seems electricity has failed us," Jagger said, "so we're gonna do some acoustic numbers." Keith was trying to coax an amplifier to work, Stu was dragging two stools onstage. Mick sat down, Keith picked up his National, and they did "Prodigal Son."

> Po' boy took his father's bread,
>   started down the road
> Took all he had and
>   started down the road
> Goin' where God only knows

When the acoustic songs ended, the stools were removed. The equipment men had been working on the amplifiers, but they weren't finished.

"When we all get ready," Jagger said. Then Keith hit the first chord for "Carol," and the amplifiers blew again. In anger and frustration, Keith broke his guitar, a Les Paul Custom. The band kept playing, Keith picked up another guitar, the music staggered on. "Sorry about the amp problems," Jagger said. "You'll just have to hear it in your heads." At the end of Chuck Berry's "Little Queenie," with the house lights up, the Stones started "Satisfaction." The kids rushed forward, carrying the guards with them, surrounding the cameramen in front of the stage. Bill Graham, onstage, rushed forward to protect the cameras as the cameramen climbed onstage, handing their cameras out of a sea of rocking flesh. Sam Cutler, watching Graham, thought he was too rough with the kids, tried to stop him, and Graham tried to throw Sam offstage. The Stones made it through "Honky Tonk Women" and "Street Fighting Man" and beat it to the dressing room, Keith kicking the table as he came in. "That *cunt*," he said.

In the press room next door, Jon Jaymes was on the phone trying to line up some airplanes so we could get back to Los Angeles, because we were going to be very late if the Stones did a second show at all, which was doubtful. I was drinking bourbon and offered Jaymes a drink. In the middle of a speech about how Graham's cameras cost $2500 apiece and he had every right to protect them, he stopped to say, "Never get me drunk." Just a jolly fat man. The Stones would, as it turned out, do another show, but it would take a while.

In the early days the Stones could and did handle a riot every night, night after night, kept on going, taking no dope of any kind. "You couldn't," Keith said. "You couldn't keep going if you did, not even booze, no pills, nothing." But in 1969 things had changed. It would be impossible to endure a world that makes you work and suffer, impossible to endure history, if it weren't for the fleeting moments of ecstasy. As you get older, it's harder to cook up the energy, even if your life is composed of distant beaches, soft female skin, plane rides, cold concrete arenas, cops, fatigue, cocaine, heroin, morphine, marijuana, busted amplifiers, riots. You have to get it from somewhere, which is why Jagger said, "All right, San Francisco, get up and shake your asses."

But now Jagger was sitting glum, the famous lips pouting, on the floor in the dressing room. I went out to the bathroom, where I encountered Bill Belmont's family, wife, cousins, because Belmont is from San Francisco and his family come to see him light a show when he's in town, I suppose, but why the bathroom?

When I came back to the Stones' dressing room, Jagger was gone. Bill, Charlie, and Keith were talking with Rock Scully. Scully was, I'd heard, a sort of manager for the Grateful Dead, the San Francisco band who had hung out with Ken Kesey at the Acid Tests and who had rushed their equipment to the Stones to replace the blown Ampegs.

Scully was wearing Levi's and a plaid cowboy shirt, and with his beard and his bright eyes, he appeared a pleasant open-faced charming western guy. He was talking about the proper way to give a free concert, how it might be done, with whose help. The Dead had done this sort of thing many times, and Scully might actually have known how to give a free concert in, say, Golden Gate Park. The Be-In, a mass gathering, had taken place in the park with no unpleasantness. The Hell's Angels, who had attended the Be-In, had acted as security at some Grateful Dead concerts, and it was natural (not to say organic) to have the Angels help you do your thing, or so it seemed to Rock Scully. He was saying, sitting on a couch in that oblong room where our destinies were being formed, though we were too tired to give much of a shit, "The Angels are really some righteous dudes. They carry themselves with honor and dignity." He was so wide-eyed and open about it, it seemed really convincing. Nobody was even particularly paying attention, but I noticed the way he used the words *honor* and *dignity*, these high-flown words here but *you* know what I mean.

Uppermost in people's minds in the dressing room was Bill Graham and what an ass he was. Keith was furious, and when Keith was furious, everybody else had better be at least indignant. Scully was running Graham down for being a capitalist pig, and Keith was saying that Ralph Gleason was obviously "Graham's bootlicker. Why don't he go on writin' about Art Blakey and Monk and people like that, he's just an opportunist who's climbed on the rock bandwagon." The poster of Graham above the banquet table was spattered with thrown cheese dip.

Jagger came in, still in his black stage garb, opened a bottle of champagne, and sat down on the floor. "I've been watchin' Tina," he said, "and she is so good, she's fucking fantastic, the way she is onstage. I mean, she's so *cocky*. I used to be cocky, but I ain't anymore."

Ike and Tina burst in, and Mick got up to greet them. "Tina, you were fantastic." They talked briefly, Ike and Tina left, then Tina looked back in to say to Mick, "Watch it with the Ikettes. Last time, we got ready to go, and no Ikettes."

"Whaddya want me to do?"

"Do what you want, but be cool."

"I haven't done anything yet," Mick said, sounding like a little boy.

B. B. King had missed the first show and was late for the second, scrambling the show's order. Ike and Tina went on first, followed by Terry Reid, then B.B. The shows, supposed to start at 6:30 and 10:30, started at 6:50 and 1:15. It was nearly 2:30 A.M. when the Stones took over the stage. In 1966, the last time the Stones had played San Francisco, the audience had been twelve-year-olds, kicking seats over and wetting their pants. Tonight, just across the Bay, there were anarchists passing out a manifesto. And the Stones just wanted people to dance.

But after the fast early numbers and the acoustic blues interlude, when the band was playing "Little Queenie," as Mick was saying, "Come on, San Francisco, let's get up and *dance*, let's shake our *asses*," Bill Graham was crouching before the stage, pointing to kids who were dancing, shouting, "Down! Down!" Finally he took his cameras and left, as the crowd surged to the stage. There was no feeling of violence, only the desire to get close and boogie. "Street Fighting Man" ended at 3:45 A.M. The Oakland Coliseum was ringing with the same sound I had heard the last two nights. It was not the band, not the crowd; it was a third sound. I didn't know what it was, but I liked it.

The days were starting to have a uniform strangeness; they all took place in the dark, we lived from dark to dawn. Each night we went someplace new and strange and yet similar to the place before, to hear the same men play the same songs to kids who all looked the same, and yet each night it was different, each night told us more. In three days, the Stones had played to nearly eighty thousand people. None of the shows had been without problems, and yet the screams got screamed, the sweat sweated, the shows done. That might be the whole point, the only victory might be in simple survival. Or so it might seem if Mick didn't keep leaning out over the stage each night, singing, as if it were a Sunday School song, "I'm free—to do what I like, justa any old time—and I ain't gonna give you no bullshit— ain't gonna give you no lies—we're free—you know we all free." It never sounded true. If it were true, true just once, if ever you had the feeling that you could let go, jump up, sing "Honky Tonk Women," dance, do what you like, without the fear of a cop's club or Klein's mop-handle against your skull—that would be a victory. As long as Mick kept saying "we all free," that was what he had to achieve. If he wouldn't say that, if he'd settle for less, then maybe victory would be easier; maybe there was a simpler and easier victory. Maybe.

Tonight we were going to San Diego, a big service town where they burned the dope seized at the Mexican border. It was Monday, and my contract hadn't arrived. I knew it took some time to prepare a contract, but I didn't know how much time I had left.

As I was going to bed this morning, Jon Jaymes was in the living room on the telephone to New York, having a tantrum. I couldn't make out all the details, but it was clear that Jaymes, the president of something called Young American Enterprises, was being called home by his mother, back to New York, and he was getting all red-faced and blustery about it, like a child who doesn't want to leave the party while there's still all that ice cream and cake. As we left for the Burbank airport, Jaymes was still with us, and besides Gary Stark he now was accompanied by an older man and a woman with black permed hair and lacquer on her lips and nails as bright as fresh blood. She looked the same age as Jon, twenty-odd going on fifty, and he introduced her to me as Grace, so it was not until Jo told me that I knew she was Jon's mother, come out here, no doubt, to look over the ice cream and cake.

The Stones met at the Golden West charter flight service. Jagger was with a girl who looked just like Jean Harlow. Kathy and Mary were along, too, Kathy angry because Sam hit her earlier today. As we walked out in the chilly air to board the little gold and white jet, she was saying to me, "They're just going to have to get another girl to drive. This is all fun and everything, but believe me, the novelty wore off the first week."

We arranged ourselves, about a dozen of us, among the plane's twenty seats. I was sitting behind Mick and Harlow, who had taken her hairbrush from her purse and was brushing Mick's hair, to his obvious displeasure. His hair was all greasy and parted; he washed it when it needed it and not before, sometimes a day or two after.

Soon we were 4500 feet above L.A., as the pilot told us in his low western drawl. We could see fifty miles around, all fifty miles alive with darting lights of traffic. We were over Anaheim, the pilot said, and "In two minutes you'll be able to see Disneyland." That brought cheers from some of the passengers. Encouraged by the enthusiasm, the pilot gave us a bit more local color: "We're flying just outside the four-mile restricted area around the West Coast White House. You'll be able to see it, the blue lights all in a clump to the left of the plane." Our silence on receiving this news made him add, probably remembering that these were Englishmen, "That's Nixon's West Coast residence." After which more silence.

It took only about half an hour to reach San Diego. The door of the plane opened and there on the tarmac were four black limousines. "Looks like a funeral," Kathy said. We all piled in and rode to the San Diego International Sports Arena, where a big sign read ROLLING STONE TONIGHT, like a menu advertising the *plat du jour*. The Arena was smaller than the last two halls, capacity about ten thousand, and it was not filled, though there would be only one show. B. B. King was playing when we arrived. The arena seemed cold, the audience distant. The place smelled like an old pea coat.

When the Stones came on I stayed behind the stage. People yelled and applauded but stayed in their seats. I looked around and saw standing beside me a woman wearing a white blouse and a blue serge skirt. Her overseas cap read Tipton Patrol and she was carrying an oiled billy club over two feet long. I went out front, found a seat, and sat down.

It was a dreary night in San Diego, but it wouldn't last long, Jagger had already sung "Under My Thumb" and was starting "I'm Free." In this atmosphere it seemed less true than ever, a man saying he wouldn't give you any bullshit telling people they were free. But they were kids mostly and loved it and may even have believed it. Mick sang "Live with Me," and at the line, "Don't you think there's a place for you—in between the sheets?" there was a rush forward, the children all dancing. "Little Queenie" was next, then "Satisfaction." A girl who had fainted down front was being lifted onto the stage— but she was awake, a Mexican girl, looking around wildly, rolling her head, and then I realized that she was blind. She was lifted onto the stage and led away.

As "Street Fighting Man" started, Mick said, perhaps sensing the militarism of the town, "Sometime we may have to get up against the wall." Mick was making a V-sign with each hand as Keith ripped the opening chords: "Everywhere I hear the sound of marchin' chargin' feet, boys." I had left my seat and was by the stage, a helmeted cop beside me putting his fingers over his ears, grimacing. In the roar, the keening, as the song ended, Mick danced along the rim of the stage just out of reach of the clutching hands, skipping along like Little Bo Peep, throwing rose petals from a wicker basket. When the petals were all gone he threw the basket, it arced high over the crowd, we hotfooted it out of the arena, jumped into the limos, raced back to the plane.

Not a particularly good show, it was brief and it was over. We were headed home. A sort of camaraderie was beginning to grow among those of us who had sat around the L.A. houses too long with too much hype raining down on us. On the earlier Stones tours, a small group battled the world. Now that we were starting to be a small band against the world of cops and promoters, striving to make the gymnasiums of America flower with savage young passion, we were starting to enjoy each other's company. When we got into our seats Keith held aloft a fifth of Old Charter and said, "Cocktails, anyone?" Jagger took a long swallow and leaned over Shirley's seat back to say, "Shirley Ann Shepherd, faithful Stones fan, follows her heroes from Halland to San Diego."

Seven hundred years ago, Halland was the Archbishop of Canterbury's hunting lodge. Now it was where Charlie and Shirley lived their pastoral life, with Merlin and Belle, the horses; Louise and Blackface, the cats; and Jess, Tru, Jake, and Sadie, the Welsh collies. Halland to San Diego was a long way to go in one lifetime.

As we taxied out, Ronnie Schneider, all lapels and crinkly sideburns, leaned over the back of the seats where Mick and Keith were sitting and asked, "Do you want to do another show in Detroit?"

"Yes," Keith said without hesitation.

"How fast did they sell out?" Mick asked.

"About a week."

"No, not if it took them a week," Mick said.

"But it sold out with no promotion," Schneider said. "The guy's guaranteeing a full house."

"It's the first date of the second half," Keith said. "We need the two shows to get into it."

"The guy's guaranteeing a full house—"

Mick still looked doubtful. "If there's one empty seat we won't go on," Keith said.

With the Fasten Seat Belts and No Smoking signs lit we started to ascend. "Ladies and gentlemen," the pilot's fine voice said, "we are now leaving the San Diego airport—" and most of the people in the plane hooted for silence. We could tolerate that stuff on the way down, but now we couldn't abide life at the intercom level. Jaymes, sitting in the front, leaned inside the open cabin door to ask, "Could we dispense with that, please?" It was so quiet then that even Jagger took pity: "Poor guy, he already had that speech thought out. Tell him we love him. We love you!" We were reaching the top of our climb to flying altitude, and Keith called, "Is it cool to smoke?" The No Smoking light went out and at once half a dozen joints were circulating in the tiny cabin, where the air space was so limited that everybody must soon have been stoned, including the pilots. Mick was talking about the blind girl who was lifted onstage. "All those kids are so *stoned*," he said. It was true, the Stones were for the first time playing to kids who were under the influence of dope, almost all of them stoned every night.

Mick handed me a reefer that I soon passed to Charlie, reaching him in the window seat around Shirley, who did not indulge but who had to breathe like everybody else, so that she turned her glazed lovely eyes to me and asked, "Will you dedicate your book to me?"

Jo had told me that Keith and Mick were thinking about going south for a few days between the halves of the tour. She suggested that I might "get it together," so I talked to Mick about it. He said that if they had only a couple of days off, because of coming back to L.A. to record, then they'd just want some rest, man, you know what I mean? I suggested Mountain View or Eureka Springs, Arkansas.

"What kind of music do they like?"

"Old mountain fiddles, handmade cherry wood dulcimers, in Mountain View they have community sings every Friday night."

"Would it be cool? Would there be any trouble?"

"No, I've never had any trouble, it's cool."

"I mean physical violence," Mick said, leaning closer. "That's the kind of trouble we get into."

I started to ask why—then gazed past Mick to see, sitting beside him, head lolling on chest, bottle cradled over crotch, joint dangling from mouth, the grandson of Gus Dupree. "Oh. Yeah. Keith."

"Y'see wot oi mean?" Mick said, laughing. "I mean, 'e always travels with a gun, y'know?"

Keith, who had appeared to be asleep, stood up and was grappling over the seat back with Charlie, who was sitting in front of him, trying to protect his chest. "The nipple-pincher returns!" Keith cried.

"After three years," Charlie said, dodging.

Shirley was saying, "You may put in your book that Mrs. Watts was once again brutally manhandled by a security guard." She had been sitting with Astrid, and as they were going backstage when the aisles started to fill up, a guard knocked her to the ground, then went to get a helmeted cop to throw her out. The cop recognized her and the guard apologized, saying, "I didn't know who you were."

"That's no way to treat any girl," Shirley told him. I was properly indignant over the abuse to Shirley's person, but I couldn't help thinking that any red-blooded cop might make such a mistake. Shirley loved rock and roll music and got excited and when she did she might have been any pretty teenager, and that was enough to make a cop want to hit her, to strike out at her pretty pleasure which had nothing to do with him or anything like him.

Then the Fasten Seat Belts sign was on and we were back in L.A. I rode home with Charlie and Shirley and Bill and Astrid. Bill was talking about the sound-balance problem which afflicted poor Mick Taylor, who wouldn't turn up his amplifiers. "In order to get a little more reaction out of 'ooever's diggin' it, Keith turns up so loud at the end that you can't hear the notes. When Brian was there, he'd turn up louder than Keith and balance it, but now Mick Taylor says it's too loud, and Keith says, 'Yeah,' lookin' at me. So what you do is pretend to turn down and Keith does turn down and it's cool."

Shirley, staring at Bill as if she were thinking of something else, said, "I read something that said all that's left for the Stones now is to die before they're thirty, and I thought it was terrible, I was very upset, and then I remembered Bill's already thirty, so that's all right."

At 6:00 A.M. I called home and woke Christopher. "So far, so good," I told her.

"Can I buy a new dress?" she asked.

Then I went to bed. When I woke up, trouble was waiting.

1 7

De old bee make de honeycomb
De young bee make de honey
De Good Lord make all de pretty gals
An' Sears Roebuck make de money

FURRY LEWIS

''I GOT SETTLED in my office, and they were away, which was probably America, and I was thinking, Ah, how many days before they come back and I get to see them," Shirley Arnold said. "By this time the fan mail was ridiculous, stacks—you know a post office sack, we had about eight of those in the office unanswered. We used to ring up the GPO, and they would come round in a van and take the letters back. I think we had about sixteen thousand fan club members within about three months, so when we sent the newsletter out we had to have members in to help address envelopes. Fans were coming up to the office, and I was all excited, 'cause I was there and I was working for the Stones, and then they came back, and they came into the office and said, 'Hello, how's it going?' They sat and talked to me, and I thought, This is me, sixteen, working for who I want, really loved them, and there are all the fans that come to me with their problems and that write me letters, so I just sort of changed. When I first went I was more interested in working for the Stones than in anything else, and then I realized that I was working for the fans. I got fond of the fans and was really interested in them, which was a good thing. The fans used to say, Who's your favorite? And I'd say I haven't got a favorite, and I think that's why they liked me, 'cause if a Mick fan walked in and I said Mick's my favorite, she would have hated me, 'cause I was inside, working for them. My money was quite good, and there were fans who had no money and I used to give them money, and take them to lunch, and buy them coffee. I really loved them, I wasn't doing it for someone to say thank you, but it was just nice, because I was a fan, and I think that was the greatest thing, because I was a screamer, that's why I understood the fans."

Returning from the United States, the Stones drove from Heathrow Airport to Oxford for a booking at the university, made a year ago, "and don't think they didn't try to get out of it," Stu said. They slept all the following day and met the day after with a solicitor to discuss forming a limited company and having the bass player's name legally changed from Perks to Wyman. Two days later they played an all-night Welcome Home show with at least fifty other performers, not much fun, and "It's All Over Now," their version of the song Murray Kaufman had given them, was released. Then they took two weeks off, and before the holiday was over *Melody Maker* had the record listed as the best-selling single record in England, the Stones' first number-one single.

On the second night after the Stones started back to work, they played the Queen's Hall in Leeds, a place that once had been a tram garage, but now was a concert hall with a revolving stage. "It was in the center of the hall, and they had to run for it," Stu said. "And again it was Brian who got left behind, because they had it all worked out, a gang of bouncers round them, and they just ran. Four of them got themselves together in and amongst these bouncers. Brian's fuckin' about onstage, 'arf asleep, doin' something or other, and all the bouncers take the four off the stage, and all the kids go after them, and there's Brian still on the stage with his guitar and just me, pickin' up instruments and fuckin' about. Brian realized, Ah, they've gone, and panics: '*Do* something,' and of course within seconds the kids realized he was still there, and ka-pow. Brian destroyed again."

Brian was by now a father once again—Linda had given him another son named Julian—and at times he seemed to like it. "There was one time when Brian and Linda were gonna get married," Shirley Arnold said. "They actually told people that they were going to get married. This was after the baby—they were still living in Windsor. Whenever they came in town, I looked after the dog, a white poodle called Pip. One day they came to the office, and they said they were gonna get married, and Brian was all excited. Maybe he did want to marry, maybe he wanted to settle down and know where he belonged. But he never quite made it. I was a friend of Linda's, and they were rushing around, Brian saying, You're gonna be chief bridesmaid. Linda and I went out that afternoon; she was looking at wedding dresses and I was looking at bridesmaids' dresses—and I don't remember what happened after that. They just split up. She decided to stay at home with her mum and they left each other again."

All this happened with a near-nightly chorus of screams and attacks of varying intensity. One night in London, while the Stones recorded, Stu and I talked about the time the Stones played Blackpool: "July 24, 1964, which was very nearly the date on my gravestone," Stu said.

"They got out, and you had to stay there, right?"

"Yeah, but they only just got out, believe me. I'll tell you roughly, what happens is this, that this city up in Scotland called Glasgow, which is the roughest city in the world—"

"In the *world*?"

"Yeah. I'll guarantee that. They'll thump-up anybody, these people, they'll take on the U.S. Marines, anybody, put 'em away without any difficulty at all, because they just live for fighting. They're not cowardly about it, they don't have to do it in gangs, one guy'll take on three any time he feels like it. In Glasgow, all the factories and all the construction companies shut down the same fortnight of the year. This is what's called the Glasgow Fair. In that fortnight, they move out of Glasgow. Glasgow shuts down, literally, and the rest of the country trembles.

"One of their pet places is Blackpool. A lot of them have run out of money by the end of the fortnight, but those with money spend all of it on the last night on drink. They get drunk themselves— Scotch, beer, Scotch, beer, like that—and anybody 'oo 'asn't got any money, they buy drinks for. Once they're outside of Glasgow, they all stick together—and if one guy 'as a go at a bloke from Glasgow, then they all jump 'im. So, unsuspecting, we agree to do this dance at the Empress Ballroom, which holds about six thousand people."

"You didn't know of these folkways at the time?"

"We knew what they were like, but we didn't connect the end of the Glasgow Fair and Blackpool. We get into the town, and it's absolutely full of these ravers from Glasgow, and I thought, Oh, this should be fun. It's the last night, and so they all, or as many as possible, or as many as were still sober by eight o'clock at night, and many who were drunk, crowd into this Empress Ballroom. There was some sort of funny agreement whereby police in uniform were not allowed inside the ballroom, some sort of thing between the people that operated the ballroom and the police. The police stayed out of sight backstage, and they were bloody trembling.

"The only thing that saved us was the stage was about six feet high, and these people from Glasgow are pretty small. They're rarely much more than five foot six or seven. In Germany they call them poison dwarves, because they're so little, and they do so much fuckin' damage. All these Glasgow regiments, like the Black Watch, in Korea and in the last war, they gave them all the deadliest jobs going, because nothing's too much for them, they never run away, they just go straight, they love it."

"I wonder why they're like that."

"I think it's just the awful deprived way—it's just Glasgow. Glasgow is one big mistake. They built these fantastic tenements that they all live in. But unlike most slums—I mean, a slum house in say Baltimore is usually leaning over and ready to fall down, but the tenements weren't. They were built of granite during the industrial revolution, and they'll still be standing yet. They'd have a hell of a job knocking them down. No hot water. In fact, no running water at all in the actual living accommodations, only on the hallways. One toilet to maybe three flats. Hopelessly underpaid. Very susceptible to slumps, because Glasgow's built round ship-building and heavy industry, and in a slump, that just goes. That's the way these people are brought up. You go into Glasgow and you see a bus queue of men coming out of a factory, they've all got scars, all been cut, all had their noses pushed in. Horrible place.

"This night there was a bit of an anti-Stones thing going on, not really quite sure what, and they were all very drunk, and the feeling was getting nastier and nastier, and you could tell it. They were really looking for bother, and eventually some of the ones—"

"What was the distribution of the crowd? Were there some little girls?"

"No. These guys had their girls with them, but they weren't the sweet little big-eyed, long-haired fans from London. The girls carry the knives. The Stones'd play a number, and there'd be big cheers and claps and things, and a little bit of screaming, but there's also a lot of derisive cheering as well. No cops, no bouncers. There was the Stones on this stage and a couple of old retainers in uniform at each corner of the stage. Another thing about these people in Glasgow, they won't normally just walk up to a guy and hit him. They need a spark—you got to detonate them. I think this kept them off the stage, 'cause they could have come up anytime they felt like it. Some of the guys in the crowd, some of the ones that had been booing—Keith can't stand being booed, anything like that, he was sayin' 'Aw fuck you' to them and they could hear him. So they started spitting, and eventually Keith is literally covered by these cobblies at the front spitting at him.

"I could see all this going on. I was standing on one side of the stage nearest to Keith, and Keith and these guys started exchanging words. I thought, 'Right, they've got one more number and they'll be off if they're lucky.' There was one guy right in front, he was a bit taller than the rest, and he spat at Keith, and Keith just kicked him in the head. And that's it. Good night. The whole hall just ee-rupted. One of their people had been kicked, and that was the spark. These guys' reactions are pretty quick, he probably got out of the way all right. I'm surprised they didn't get hold of Keith's leg and pull him off the stage. He wouldn't be here now, if they had. Keith still thought he was God and that he could kick one of these guys and get away with it, but I was next to him—the other guys already turned, realizing they're gonna have to get off the stage—I just pushed him, said 'For fuck's sake get out of here while you're still alive,' and I went off as well.

"The cops got rid of them all right, and luckily between the back-stage area and the rest of the hall there were some fairly heavy doors. We could hear cymbals going through the air, thumps as all the amps got smashed up, and then there was the most glorious fucking crash of all time—there'd been a grand piano on the stage. The cops stood it long enough and sent for reinforcements. And they wouldn't go near them. They wouldn't look at these guys. After there was about fifty of them, they went in with truncheons. By this time a lot of the steam had gone out of it. Charlie wasn't using his drums, he'd borrowed a drum kit off this guy, and the guy was sitting there crying, his lovely Ludwig kit— we never saw it again, got one cymbal back. They didn't steal them, they just smashed them. Of the amplifiers, there was bits of wood, and I think we got one loudspeaker chassis. Without any cone in it, and that was all. Everything else was totally mangled. They took about a dozen people to hospital. Not having been able to get hold of the Stones, they started fighting amongst themselves.

"We'd booked a hotel in Preston, which is about twenty miles up the road. We drove to the police station, the boys had their own cars at the police station. Cops walked round and round the hotel all night."

Interviewed after Blackpool, the Stones called it the most sickening night of their lives, but what difference does it make whether one is torn apart by one's enemies or one's friends? One week after Black-pool, the Stones went to Ireland. "The first time we went to Ireland," Stu said, "we did this thing in Belfast and the whole city turned out, they couldn't get near the Ulster Hall to get in. And when they got in they couldn't defend the stage. The stage stretched the full width of the hall. There's kids everywhere. Lots of kids hurt that night. Bloody horrifying. Show lasted twelve minutes. Cops didn't want it to go on in the first place. There was space for seating up behind the stage, and they were getting on the stage at either side and going up behind the Stones, more and more were doing this till the Stones just got surrounded. Quite a night. Never been nearer. We should have got mangled that night."

On August 7, 1964, the Stones went to TV House, Kingsway, London, where they appeared on *Ready, Steady, Go!* Twenty policemen and more on motorcycles tried to control the mob waiting outside, but girls broke through the police lines after the show as the Stones ran for their limousine. One policeman climbed off his motorcycle and onto the Stones' Austin Princess to stop fans getting in. As the chauffeur drove away with the Stones, one of the car doors came open, knocked down a policeman, struck a lamppost, and the fans tore it off its hinges.

The Stones flew to Holland for a concert in The Hague. There were police onstage, but after three songs the fans attacked and it was closing time, gentlemen. Back in England at the Tower Ballroom in New Brighton, a ballroom on top of a tower, "the stage was so high that they had to use a block and tackle to get the gear up there," Stu said. "The kids were pressing the front, getting underneath the stage so they couldn't see anything, and the trouble started." Two hundred fainted, and about fifty were thrown out for fighting. A girl pulled a switchblade on two guards who were trying to subdue her two escorts, and four guards were required to disarm her and carry her out of the hall.

In the next place the Stones played, the Palace Ballroom in Douglas, on the Isle of Man, the only police dog on the island was onstage to protect them from seven thousand teenagers, but the dog got excited by the music and the screaming and was led away, snarling at the crowd and the Stones. "I thought he was going to take a bite out of me," Mick said.

At the ABC Theatre in Hull, two dozen rugby players formed a line in front of the orchestra pit, but when Mick walked along the edge of the pit shaking his maracas, a girl grabbed him, arms around his legs, and he fell into the pit. He crawled back onstage unhurt.

Part of the Stones' charm was that they lived in an atmosphere of danger, and one came near them at one's peril. Near the end of this tour, at the Gaumont Theatre in Ipswich, Stu watched as "the barrier in front of the stage collapsed and a girl got a broken back. I saw her go down and I heard her back break. But a lot of them you never heard about. They were in the local papers the next day and that was all."

Charlie Watts and Shirley Ann Shepherd barely had time to get married (secretly, by a Bradford registrar) before the Stones were off for Belgian and French television appearances and their first appearance at the Olympia Theatre in Paris. "Even as late as this," Stu said, "Brian was thinking of himself as a leader, 'cause he wanted a bigger amp than Keith's, the day before we went to Belgium I remember driving down especially to get him the same size amp the Beatles used, just to keep his little Welsh mind happy."

With a successful Paris concert behind them—a spokesman for the Olympia said that the theater had suffered £1400 worth of damages—the Stones came home and had a day to pack before leaving for their second assault on the United States. About this time the Stones had four records on the British charts, including a new EP, "Five by Five," recorded at Chess. Wherever there were popular-record charts, the Stones' records were on them.

Trying to make up for the mistakes of their first U.S. tour, the Stones began this one by appearing, after rehearsing for two days, on *The Ed Sullivan Show*. "We'd got it into our heads that Ed Sullivan was the thing to do," Stu said. "The only thing worth doing." *The Ed Sullivan Show*, in the beginning called *The Toast of the Town*, every Sunday night for twenty years was the phoenix of vaudeville, bringing to U.S. television the most various collection of acts that could be imagined, the finest ballet dancers and opera singers doing two and a half hot minutes, comedians, jugglers, animal acts—all stars who had reached the top, because in its time and place, the Sullivan show was the top.

When the well-rehearsed Stones were on the Sullivan show, the reception from fans inside and outside the theater was so enthusiastic that Sullivan said he'd never book the Stones again. The Stones were pleased, knowing that probably meant they would be invited back. The next day they flew to Los Angeles. They played Sacramento, then took a day off, noticing that in the five months they had been away, the men had grown their hair longer.

After rehearsing for two days at the Santa Monica Civic Auditorium, the Stones appeared on the Teen Awards Music International (T.A.M.I.) show, recorded before an audience by a new process called Electronovision. The Stones closed the show, following, among others, the Beach Boys, who wouldn't speak to them; Marvin Gaye; the Supremes; the Miracles; Chuck Berry, who was pleasant, talked with them and even gave Wyman a pair of cufflinks; and, ultimately, James Brown, who said he would make the Stones wish they'd never left England. The Stones had never seen James Brown. "The kids were eating out of his hand," Stu said. "Mick and them were trembling, having to follow this. But they did it, they got canned and bowled on and did it." It was one of their most spirited performances; even Wyman moved a bit.

In the next few days, the Stones did shows in a couple of Southern

California towns, recorded six songs at RCA Studios in L.A. with Jack Nitzsche, who worked with Spector and conducted the stage orchestra for the T.A.M.I. show, and then they left for Cleveland. They were preceded by an address on Cleveland radio from the local mayor, advising the citizens that the Rolling Stones gave immoral performances and that no teenagers should be allowed to see them. In spite of this the show was poorly attended, perhaps because on this night Lyndon Johnson was elected president of the United States by the greatest percentage of the popular vote in the country's history. Next, New York City, the Astor, then to Providence and a cinema where no live act had ever played. The management had covered the orchestra pit with thin plywood, and when the Stones started playing, girls ran down the aisles, jumped onto the plywood and disappeared into the pit.

The Stones went back to Manhattan that night by train, getting out at Grand Central Station, where the black porters yelled, "Are you the Beatles?" and the Stones yelled, "Are you the Harlem Globetrotters?"

They were in New York City for the next two days, but did no more concerts. They had a new single, "Time Is On My Side," from a new album, *12 × 5*, on the U.S. charts, and they paid a friendly visit to London Records. That night Brian and Bill went to a jazz club in Greenwich Village where they met Julian Adderley, called "Cannonball" because of his rotundity, a man of enormous appetites, considered by some musicians the greatest alto saxophonist since Charlie Parker, and the man after whom Brian had named all his sons.

At midnight of the next day the Stones flew to Chicago, where they would spend most of the next week, and Brian would spend all of it. On their first day the Stones went back to Chess Studios and cut five tracks. Among the tracks they finished, Stu said, "there was a thing called 'Stewed,' on which Brian didn't play. He was pissed. But I don't think that was ever released, it was just an instrumental. And I think the great mysterious 'Key to the Highway'—we know we did it, but we can't find it. I can hear it in my head. But nobody's got a copy of it, and it was never released, and Decca say they ain't got it. I remember playing on it."

For the next four days, mostly doing interviews, the Stones were in Chicago, except for a drive to a press reception in Milwaukee to promote the shows there. Brian didn't make it to that pair of concerts, nor to the one the next night in Fort Wayne, Indiana, on a bill with the Shangri-Las and a band with green hair, nor to the one after that, in Dayton, Ohio; Brian was in Chicago at the Pasavant Hospital with a temperature of 105 degrees, delirious, the doctors said, from bronchitis and extreme exhaustion.

"He was certainly ill, all right," Stu said, "but he didn't do anything to help himself, he aggravated it by taking too much of something, and generally behaved very stupidly. I tell you what, he nearly got hoofed out there and then. He hadn't really contributed anything on those record dates. He was either stoned or pissed or just sick, and they got fed up with him."

The Stones, carrying on without Brian, drove four hundred miles from Dayton to Louisville, Kentucky, in a bus, played two shows at the Memorial Auditorium, sent their equipment back to Chicago, slept in Louisville, and followed the equipment the next morning. The Stones had scheduled two shows at the Aire Crown Theatre in McCormick Place. "The Aire Crown Theatre's got one of these stages that rise out of the pit," Stu said, "so Brian decided he was all right, and he was gonna leave hospital, and we thought it'd be groovy if we didn't make any announcement, we just came up out of the pit with Brian playing, and the kids all went stark raving out of their minds."

The Stones flew the next day to New York City, where they had their picture taken for the cover of *Cashbox* and were taken to lunch, to nightclubs, saw a rough cut of the T.A.M.I. show. Then back to England and the release of a new single, "Little Red Rooster," a song done earlier by master bluesman Howlin' Wolf. News, no longer new, of the Wattses' marriage appeared, with Charlie denying it. It was a small lie; the Stones hardly had any time to be at home. There were plenty of girls if you wanted them, but very little home life.

"Brian finished with Linda," Shirley Arnold said, "but he didn't actually finish, full stop. They used to go back and finally when they did finish there were lots of girls."

Brian seldom heard from Pat, the girl who had left him after Jagger had been with her, and their son. "Brian had a few letters," Shirley said, "which meant I had a few, 'cause any letters that were sent to them came to me and I dealt with them. I think he was paying her some money every week. She sent a letter one year with a photograph of the baby—well, he was growing up then—he was the image of Brian. It wasn't a very nice letter. It was Christmastime and she said, 'This is a photograph of your son. Would you send him a typewriter—a kid's typewriter?' I told Brian about it and he said, 'Okay, you can send it, but say that you opened the letter and that you sent it.' So we did that."

On January 6, 1965, the Stones flew to Ireland, did interviews, a television show and two concerts in Dublin, "another of these occasions when Brian got separated from everybody else when they were trying to get out of the theatre and got lost in the crowd," Stu said.

"He used to really dig being mobbed," Keith said. "He'd be dead scared of it, but he used to really dig it, too. He used to demand to be surrounded by heavies, and he'd take his jacket off, and 'Now. Now. Now. Now!'"

From Dublin the Stones took cars to Cork, one hundred and fifty miles, passing people with donkeys, like going back centuries. The number of centuries was revealed when they stopped at an "old clothing shop, sort of army surplus, in a little village on the road to Cork. We went in," Keith said, "and this old Irishman grabbed hold of Brian's balls and dragged Brian outside and pointed to the church tower, there's these huge holes in it, and he said, 'Cromwell's balls did that, now let me see what I'm gonna do to your balls.' So Brian got his cock out and pissed all over his old overcoats and everything. We all went haring out of the shop and leapt in the car, and—he was very old, this cat—and suddenly he leapt up across the street and onto the bonnet of the car and started kickin' the windscreen with his huge boots." Andrew nicked the man's hat and they careered off toward two shows in Cork.

Next day back in England, and the day after, the Stones played the Hammersmith Commodore on a bill with Marianne Faithfull. Two television shows done, and the Stones left for a tour of Australia and the Far East, stopping over in Los Angeles to record "The Last Time," taken by Mick and Keith from an old gospel song.

They left L.A. early in the morning for the eighteen-hour trip to Sydney Airport, where hundreds of fans, most of them little suntanned girls in tight shorts, were crashing over police barricades to see the Stones. In Sydney Mick met relatives he hardly knew existed, people with names like Shopp and Pitts. His aunt, whose last name was Scutts, and whom he had met when she visited England last year, had a letter from Mick's mother saying, "I solemnly advise you to take earplugs, because after the last concert I saw, my doctor had to treat me for perforated eardrums."

The Stones had an entire floor at the Chevron Hilton, with an excellent view of Sydney Harbour and the fans outside. "That's where you stay in a Hilton hotel and the staff send the birds up to you instead of trying to keep them out," Stu said.

"Amazing number of birds there," Keith said. "In Melbourne, too, in that weird motel, all glass. Bill on the phone to the hall porter, 'Send me up that one in the pink.' Nine in one day he had, no kidding, he just sat all day long in his bedroom looking out the window, and he's right in with the hall porter, 'No, not that one, the one with the blond hair, not that 'orror.' Used to tell him off for sending up uglies. It was in Melbourne we kept calling up that blind DJ and asking for songs like 'I'm Beginning to See the Light.' "

The Stones' first Australian shows went well, and they left for New Zealand. They arrived at Christchurch in a downpour, had a press conference and went to the best hotel in town, which was terrible. "Our hotel has too few bathrooms," Mick said to the audience next day at the Theatre Royal, "so you can't blame us if we smell." They hired three bodyguards for New Zealand, but lost one in Christchurch when a police dog bit him, lost a second when his arm got jammed in a door, and the third couldn't guard all of them by himself, and so he left.

At 7:30 A.M. the Stones flew to "Invercargill, the arsehole of the world," Keith said. "The southernmost town in the world."

"You could put your bed in the middle of the street at five o'clock in the afternoon and nothing would disturb you," Stu said. The audience at the Civic Theatre was as dead as the town, and the Stones cut their performance short.

They were in New Zealand ten days, in near hundred-degree weather, being refused admittance to hotels, watched in stony silence by the crowd at Dunedin, pelted with eggs by the exuberant fans in Auckland, and with Brian and Bill carrying on a competition among the suntanned legs.

"They were the only two who used to actively go out looking," Stu said. "Bill would usually be the first one to find summink, and then Brian would move in."

"Bill had an absolute compulsion," Keith said. "He had to have a bird, otherwise he couldn't sleep, he'd get homesick, he'd start shaking, really, he'd collapse completely if he didn't have something in bed with him, no matter what it was."

The Stones returned to Australia for more shows in Melbourne, Adelaide, and Perth. At a party after one of the Adelaide shows Bill picked up a girl and again Brian nicked her away. She had been in Bill's room at the Akabar Motel, but she went away with Brian, leaving her coat and jumper. When she came back for them the next morning Bill told her to look off the balcony. Her clothes were in the ground-floor rock pool.

Next day, in Perth for the last shows of their first tour of Australia, Bill, whose suite adjoined Brian's, came in through the connecting doors to Brian's bedroom, where Brian was already in bed, about to be joined by a girl who was sitting on the side of the bed in her bra and panties. Bill greeted them cheerily, sat beside the girl in the dark room, whispered in her ear, and away they went together. Those girls couldn't give themselves up fast enough, but to have one taken out of your bed was funny, and people made sure Brian knew how funny it was.

Returning to L.A. by way of Singapore and Hong Kong, where the Stones played concerts, Charlie met Shirley, who was waiting for him; Mick re-recorded his singing of "The Last Time"; Wyman flew back to England, and soon they all went their various ways. The day before "The Last Time" was released in England, the Stones reunited there to do a live television broadcast of the song. Millions of viewers saw

Mick dragged by fans from the rostrum, twisting his ankle, getting stabbed by stiletto heels.

The Stones took almost a week off before starting a new tour, their fifth of England, with both "The Last Time" and *The Rolling Stones No. 2* high in the charts. The tour ended in one of their finest moments, Wyman's Weakness versus a certain garage in Stratford. "Nothing would have come of it," Stu said, "if it hadn't been for some local super-zealous idiotic youth club leader who happened to be getting his little Morris 3 fart-box filled up with a gallon and a half of paraffin."

After another scant week off, the Stones started a short Scandinavian tour, flying to Copenhagen, where they had the entire nineteenth floor of the Grand Hotel. "And I'm afraid," Stu said, "the Grand Hotel, which is still the best hotel in Copenhagen, ever since that week will not have anybody who even looks as if he's got long hair inside the door. Nineteen floors up, they were throwing empty bottles out the window. To the fans down below."

During rehearsal at Odense, Mick received an electric shock while holding two microphones and fell into Brian, who fell into Bill, who was knocked unconscious. They all recovered, and the show went on. After more concerts and television appearances and more girls and eviction from a Gothenburg hotel, the Stones returned to England. They spent a few days without working, did a television show and closed the *New Musical Express* Pollwinners' Show at Wembley Stadium. On the sixteenth of April they flew to Paris to play the Olympia Theatre. The Stones had played there before, and Paris was not especially exciting. Diane Wyman and Stephen came along with Bill. Brian was with a French model named Zouzou. After one of the shows, a girl came backstage. She said in a German-sounding North Italian accent that her name was Anita. She was a model and had acted in Italian films. A few years before, when she was seventeen, she had gone to the United States and had lived in a house in Greenwich Village where the poets Frank O'Hara and Allen Ginsberg also lived; at the time, she had been scared to death. Now she was no longer seventeen, no longer scared to death. Brian knew nothing about her and had no thought that he would die loving her.

18

Nearly everyone who wrote about Bolden followed . . .
in saying that he was a barber, and in addition that he
edited a scandal sheet called *The Cricket.* These unsub-
stantiated facts became part of the legend. . . . Buddy's
widow, Nora, said that ". . . he did not run a scandal
sheet and was not a barber, although he drank a lot and
hung out at barbershops."

DONALD M. MARQUIS: *In Search of Buddy Bolden*

STEPPING INTO THE OFFICE to find out when we would be
leaving for tonight's show, I collided with Schneider, who asked, in a
tone more abrasive than usual, whether I'd talked to my agent. "If you
don't get something together by tomorrow, you're not going any farther
with the tour."

"I 'spect Mick will have something to say about that," I said, eyeing
his neck, reminding myself that to throttle him would likely cause
trouble.

"When did you talk to Mick?"

"Every day."

"Well, it's getting expensive carrying everyone around."

"I'll be happy to pay my bill."

"No, but there are all these people talking about deals, and the
deals don't get together."

"I am not one of those people."

"Then why isn't it getting together?"

I said that these things take time and went into the living room to seethe. Months later, when he was drunk in the underwater atmosphere of a mod London basement restaurant called Barracuda (lit by tanks of green water containing lazy, cool-eyed killer fish), Ronnie would explain that his business technique derived from classic high school sex moves: outside the bra, inside the bra and so on. I saw him cruising, waiting to rend off hunks of my book.

In a corner of the room a television set was giving the news, sending into the room horrors of oriental wars, zodiac killers. Charlie, on one of the couches, was watching, smiling his pleasant amazed smile.

Ronnie came into the room from the office, where he had been screeching into the telephone, and sat in the chair next to mine. "Why can't I get your agent on the phone?" he asked. "He doesn't return my calls."

The last time Ronnie told me this, I said, "He never returns my calls either." But now, pushing back, I asked, "What do you do for the Stones, Ronnie? Or is it Klein? Who do you work for?"

"I don't do anything for Klein," Ronnie said. "I work for the Stones."

"What do you do for them?" I asked, sounding like Mr. District Attorney.

"I'm a groupie," Ronnie said, getting up and talking over his shoulder as he left the room. "I crave their bodies."

When he had gone, Charlie asked, "Don't you like Ronnie?"

"Do you like him?"

"He's not so bad, really."

He was bad enough for me.

At the Burbank airport we had to wait because the plane (borrowed for us by the redoubtable Jon Jaymes) wasn't ready. Everybody except me joined the Stones in the restaurant. I didn't want to be with Jagger where he could be influenced by Schneider.

In the waiting area, a man in a business suit, carrying an attaché case, said to another man outfitted the same, as he pointed out a tall blond young man standing ahead of them in a line to the ticket counter, "He's Jagger, the singer with the Stones."

"Oh, yeah?" said the second business suit. "The Gallstones?"

As I was writing this dialogue in my notebook, Jo Bergman appeared at my side. "I thought you hadn't made it," she said.

"No, here I am."

"Have you—what's going on with you and Ronnie?"

"Nothing," I said. "Ronnie doesn't understand and doesn't care what I'm trying to do, and I am not going to discuss it with him."

"He might surprise you," Jo said.

"In a dark alley," I said.

"We'll talk about it tomorrow."

The plane was ready: it was a giant plane for our group (even though the group tonight included friends, cooks, groupies, and Mick's Ikette), a Boeing 707 from Air California, with 115 seats and three stewardesses in orange ruanas, all ours till six A.M. After the show in Phoenix we were going to Las Vegas for some late-night action.

Jagger and Keith huddled with Sam Cutler in the rear of the plane, then Mick joined the Ikette a few seats back of me and offered her a small drift of snow on the back of a magazine. "Try it, you'll like it," he said and sniffed through a rolled-up twenty.

Schneider came forward, talked to Mick for a few minutes, then came to me and rested one hand on the arm of my seat. "Mick says you got to get it together," he began. I dropped my notebook and grasped his lapels, looking deep into his eyes, thinking how much I would enjoy throwing him off the plane. "Ronnie," I said, "leave me alone."

I let go of him and went to speak to Mick.

"Don't worry about it, man, don't listen to him. In a funny way he wants to get it together for you. I mean, he wants it to happen."

"So do we," I said, hoping I was right, "but we want to do it right. I don't want you to think I'm bullshitting you—"

"I know you're not bullshitting me."

As we came down the steps of the plane in Phoenix, the cool night air brought with it the strong odor of fresh cow manure. The Sports Arena had a rodeo feeling, with earth, not ice, under the floorboards, and I was starting to relax. I stepped over a rope stretched across the doorway to the dressing rooms, but Ronnie stopped me. "What did Mick say?" he asked.

"Listen, Ronnie, this is a small matter to you, but to me—"

"No, it's not small, but your agent is no good, he's not getting it together."

I started to answer, but he went on: "I know somebody at your publishers, so I'll know what kind of deal you've got."

There was no way to tell when he was bluffing, but to me he was a total bluff. He was trying to stop me from doing my work, and I had to remind myself once again not to scrag the bastard. He must have seen something in my eyes then, because he said, "You shouldn't take anything I say personally." It was true, I shouldn't, any more than a cheerleader in high school should have taken it personally when he grabbed her tit. I walked away. Ronnie had nothing and I had everything to lose.

We arrived late and missed the opening acts, Terry Reid and Ike and Tina Turner. Now the lights were down and Sam introduced "From England—the Rolling Stones." Mick strutted a tour of the stage, waving his Uncle Sam hat, then clapped it on his head and began singing "Jumpin' Jack Flash."

The show—just one tonight—went quickly. I had spoken to Jo about the badness of "I'm Free," and on the drive to the airport, Glyn Johns, on the tour to plan a live album, was complaining about it: "Mick's recently come across the word *messianic*, and he's quite fascinated with it. It's in this new song, 'Monkey Man,' you know. He can be as messianic as he wants, but as far as I'm concerned, when he says we're all free, he's talkin' out his arse."

On the plane to Phoenix Jo told Mick and Glyn told Keith that the shows seemed to drag and suggested cutting "I'm Free." Keith's reaction was negative—"Bollocks," he said—but they left out the song, and it seemed to help. The show's pace was steady, even though the crowd seemed quiet, almost docile. When they stood up and the guards, blue-uniformed and beefy, started sitting them down by making head-knocking gestures with flashlights, Mick said, "Why can't they stand up? It's all right, you can stand up if you want to." So for the last few songs the crowd was jumping and swaying together, girls were riding their boyfriends' shoulders, people were shouting and dancing, it was a rock and roll revival. Mick congratulated the crowd down front. "You *did* it," he said.

Through a slit in the back curtain a cowpoke wearing a straw hat poked his sunburned head, looking at the crowd with wonder, as if he were sitting on a church steeple watching a cattle stampede. It ended with the petals falling as we ran out the back. Jon Jaymes, swinging his arms, directed us into the Phoenix collection of rented cars, and we raced teenagers and motorcycle cops to the airport.

In minutes we were aloft and headed for Las Vegas. I sat back for the flight. Mick was standing in the aisle beside me with an open suitcase, trying to take his pants off. "It's really hard to move a slow audience like that," he said. "You feel as if you're moving a great weight." He put on a black-and-white checked suit and a gray tweed cap, an outfit that made him look like a parody of a music hall performer. "We can't get the old things together. People at the Forum want the most hip things, the things off the new album, but it's hard to move more remote audiences. They want to hear the hits—but we've had trouble getting them together." He closed the suitcase.

At the Las Vegas International Airport, we saw next to the gate as we entered a row of slot machines being fed by an airman and two drunks in business suits who bellowed and whistled at us as we passed. Four taxis took us to the Strip, among the hotels, nightclubs, casinos, with their dazzling neon signs that impoverished the stars, luring the average Depression-bred American with the promise that he could make things better overnight. The taxis stopped and Jon Jaymes beckoned us into the Circus Circus. Outside, fountains were spouting and crashing; inside, fun mirrors were waiting to distort your image. As we collected, stewardesses too, in the lobby, lined with photographs of celebrities staring into flashbulbs, James greased our way in, asking a Circus Circus host if they'd like the Stones as guests. "Certainly," the man said. "We'll put their picture on the wall."

A spiral staircase led down into a giant circular room, decorated in red, with circus acts going on all around. Halfway down the spiral we saw on a stage below us a sword balancer wearing black tights and a white blouse. Keith saw him, his glittering rhinestones, his greasy hair, and smiled; a light, tiny but intense, flashed from Keith's eyes. The swordsman's eyes flashed back. "Hey! I know jew!" he said. "I seed jew in the movies, yes?"

"Yeah," Keith said.

Leaning backward, closing his eyes, gesturing palms up with both hands, the sword balancer said, "Man, you out of sight."

"So are you, baby," Keith said, turning away.

"Stay—stay and see my show."

But Keith, heading down the stairs, did not look back. At the bottom were slots, various kinds of tables, the croupiers, dealers, all in red and white candy-striped shirts, staring at us. We attacked the tables and machines. Above us the sword balancing act began, two swords held by their points in the man's teeth, nobody watching. At a table above the slots, four women who looked like grandmothers were asleep. Mick and Keith played blackjack. Up a few stairs, black curtains hid an alcove under a sign saying Adults Only Sleeping Beauty Ball Toss. I couldn't stand the suspense and stepped past the curtains to find a young man behind a counter where baseballs were stacked inside billiard racks. About fifteen feet behind him was a green metal disc a few inches wide. Farther back, displayed on a couch under a rose-colored light, behind a gauze curtain, was a girl wearing tiny rose-colored panties and a chiffon shawl.

"What happens?"

"Try and see," she said, so I bought three balls for a dollar and hit the disc with the second. Music started and up she rose, a big strong girl who in quieter times might have gone to bed at sundown and got up in the cold morning to jerk warm milk from cows, but who was in Las Vegas twisting her pelvis for a stranger who hit a target with a baseball.

"How long have you been doing this?"

"Too long," she said, twisting.

On the public address system a sultry female voice said, "Gather 'round the Dingaling Room, where lots of fun is starting to happen with Kay King and the Yum Yum Reunion." The voice broke the spell. The Stones party regrouped and left the Circus Circus, followed by a man wearing a tuxedo, carrying a camera, asking, "Stones? Photograph? Which ones—"

Outside, no taxis, someone suggested we go to the International, a great hulking pyramid far away, so we walked, strung out like the wedding party in *Madame Bovary*, past the inhuman glitter. Once there, we were stared at by men in mohair suits and women in fur coats. More gambling, some winning, not much, but nobody lost much. Back to L.A. before five o'clock, asleep before dawn.

We had been to Fort Collins, Los Angeles, Oakland, San Diego, Phoenix, and after taking today off we would leave for Dallas, Auburn University in Alabama, the University of Illinois at Champaign, and the Cow Palace in Chicago, then back to L.A. We would be four days on the road. I called Christopher, who was coming to the show at Auburn with the Dickinsons, and she told me that she wouldn't be there because she was sick. I told her that I'd skip the show at Champaign and ride to Memphis from Auburn with the Dickinsons. Christopher was still working, and my book contract still hadn't arrived.

Mick came over in the afternoon to talk with Jo and Ronnie about the free concert. Rock Scully was coming down from San Francisco soon to help make plans for it. Mick mentioned that he and Keith were going to see Little Richard at a club tonight, and I told him I might see them there, but Jo went to dinner with me, and after we came back I sat up talking to Stu, so I was not at the club when Little Richard, toweling himself dry in his dressing room after his show, made to Mick and Keith what seemed a happy prophecy: "The angels will be watching over you."

1 9

August 2, 1965

Dear Keith,

We watched you on TV the other night and the first thing that grabbed our eyes was your lovely Hampton Wick. After that we did little besides studying it. We're not kidding; you've got a very fine tool, as a friend of ours puts it. From the way your pants project themselves at the zipper, we figure you've got a beauty of a rig. Sometimes we hoped you'd whip it out or something, but they don't have TV cameras that could focus anything that large, do they? Hey, tell Mick he doesn't have to worry about the size of his either; we noticed that already (well, who could help but?). Our favorite names for you are Keith the Giant Meat and Hampton Mick.

Keith, we're serious; we judge boys primarily by their Hamptons because they're so exciting to look at and contribute so much to a healthy relationship. We can hardly wait till you come into town in November, maybe then we can find out more about what's inside your pants.

We hope you don't think we ought to receive head treatment or be put away before we attack men or something. We hope you sympathize with us and agree that sex should be openly appreciated just like all other works of beauty and ingenuity. We like to say what we really think while other people just sit there all cringed up and inhibited inside, afraid they'd offend someone if they told them something complimentary about their Hampton or, as in your case, their shoulder boulders.

Would you like to write us back and confirm our beliefs about your Hampton Wick? Would you say, aside all humility, that it is as spectacular as your pants have led us to believe? Do you always wear your rig on the right side because you're right-handed or doesn't it make any difference? What is the first thing YOU look for in GIRLS?

If you're interested, drop by awhile, why don't you, when you're in Chicago or give us a ring. We're both 18 and like to wear tight-fitting sweaters. We think a girl should wear things tight on top to please a boy, and that a boy should do the same on the bottom to please us.

So please don't forget to answer us. And keep pleasing us by wearing those pants good and tight.

Reach us at:

> Cynthia Plastercaster
> Chicago, Ill.

AFTER PARIS the Stones had three days in London to get some sleep and pack their bags again before flying to Montreal, leaving a trail of screamers on the tarmac at Heathrow, for their third tour of North America. In Montreal they played to six thousand fans, some of whom attacked the stage, adding a familiar but always seductive element of danger. At the "Y" Auditorium in Ottawa, the next city on the tour, thirty police onstage, unable to keep back the audience of four thousand, pulled out the amplifier cords and told the Stones never to come back.

The crowd control force in Toronto were not so paranoid, and the Stones played to fourteen thousand at the Maple Leaf Gardens. The next day they drove three hours to the Treasure Island Gardens in London, Ontario, where the police, alarmed by the spectacle of three thousand people having a good time, stopped the show during the fifth song, inspiring the audience, many of whom had driven all the way from Detroit, to riot.

The following day the Stones went to New York City to stay a week and a half. They went to parties, saw Wilson Pickett at the Apollo Theatre and played in Worcester, Massachusetts, with the house lights on and the police constantly prowling. They played in the afternoon at the Academy of Music and that night at the Convention Hall in Philadelphia topped a bill including Bobby Vee, Little Anthony and the Imperials, and Freddy "Boom-Boom" Cannon, who had said, after his recording of "Tallahassee Lassie" sold over a million copies, that he had never been to Tallahassee but now thought he might like to go. The Stones taped their second appearance on *The Ed Sullivan Show*, took the next day off, had dinner at the Playboy Club, saw Dizzy Gillespie at the Village Gate, visited a radio talk show. On May 4, they flew to Atlanta, almost missing their plane, whose brakes failed as they landed in great clouds of smoke and fire. The plane was towed in, they took another to Savannah and drove under pines and oaks with long grey tresses of Spanish moss to the Georgia Southern College Auditorium in Statesboro, where the sound system, not surprisingly, was wretched. They spent the night in a Savannah motel (Charlie went to Fort Pulaski in the morning to look at Civil War relics), flew to Tampa, and drove to Clearwater, Florida.

Charlie was lost without Shirley and had to be told to change his clothes and wash his hair. Bill and Brian had their girls (their only other mutual interest was in science fiction), and Keith and Mick, when they were not performing or sleeping, were writing songs. In England the Stones had two LPs, two EPs, and six singles in release. Each single after the first had contained a song—the last had two songs—by the Stones. *The Rolling Stones, Now!* and "The Last Time," the Stones' latest U.S. album and single releases, were at numbers 5 and 9 in their respective charts, but still Keith and Mick had not managed to write a hit song that was truly characteristic of them, though their song "Play with Fire," released as the B side—the side not expected to be a hit—of "The Last Time," was while very English as threatening as a Muddy Waters record, sexually threatening in a most un-English way. In Clearwater the Stones played on a stage built above second base of the baseball stadium and finished four songs before the fans swarmed over three rings of police onto the stage.

Back to the motel, nothing to do in Clearwater but sit by the pool. Charlie wished he were home with Shirley. Bill and Brian were with two girls they had carried into the South like prospectors taking extra canteens into the desert. Mick and Keith were working on a song that had developed from their failure, the last time they were at the Chess Studios, to record Martha and the Vandellas' "Dancing in the Streets." Keith didn't like the new song because the guitar figure was simple-minded, but the song expressed real feelings in strong, direct terms. While Mick and Keith wrote "Satisfaction," Brian quarreled with his girl, an airline stewardess, hitting her, and one of the road managers slugged him, cracking one of his ribs.

Taped together, Brian went with the Stones the next morning to Birmingham, played another stadium, and flew to Jacksonville, arriving at the Thunderbird Motel there at 5:30 A.M. That night they played the Jacksonville Coliseum, the next day flew to Chicago and went to the Sheraton Hotel for a press conference, but for an hour and a half were prevented by the fans from entering the hotel. The Stones kept phoning the hotel from a bar a few blocks away, trying again to get into the hotel, then going back to the bar.

They played the Aire Crown Theatre that night, and the next day spent eleven hours at Chess recording four tracks: "Have Mercy," "That's How Strong My Love Is," "Try Me," and a Nanker Phelge song based on the chord changes of "Fannie Mae" by Buster Brown, called "The Under-Assistant West Coast Promo Man." The song, inspired by a London Records publicity man, about "the necessary talent behind every rock and roll band," years later would be brought to mind by David Horowitz.

The Stones tried but failed to record "Satisfaction," flew the next day to Los Angeles, went the day after to the RCA Studios, started working at 10:00 A.M. and by 2:15 A.M., more than sixteen hours later, had recorded six new songs, one of them "Satisfaction." They went back to their hotel, slept a few hours, then Andrew and RCA engineer Dave Hassinger returned to the studio and began mixing the tracks. At 1:00 P.M. the Stones showed up to re-record certain parts, Bill, Charlie, and Brian leaving at 9:00 P.M., Mick and Keith staying at the studio adding vocals till nine o'clock the next morning. They had a new album and a single that would be the most popular they had ever done.

They spent the rest of May 1965 in the United States. They played in San Francisco, San Bernardino, San Diego; they did a *Shindig* television show and brought Howlin' Wolf as their guest. I saw the show and thought, Whoever these people are, if they have the Wolf with them they got my attention. They played Fresno, San Jose, and Sacramento, having in all these places the usual struggles with crowds, but in Long Beach they had one of the struggles of their lives. "Scaredest I've ever been," Keith said. There were eight thousand in the Long Beach Arena, and the show was tolerably mad. Two girls dropped twenty feet from the balcony to the stage. The Stones did five songs—they were approaching the height of their take-the-money-and-run period—and ran out the back way into a limousine, Mick and Brian in the front seat, the others in the back. Before they could leave, the car was covered with bodies, the roof collapsing, the Stones holding it up as the driver tried to inch the big car forward through the crowd. Finally cops with clubs climbed on the car, beating the kids back, hurting many of them. Once past the crowd, the Stones raced to a waiting helicopter. The crowd like locusts covered the car again and the Stones watched the car being torn apart as they ascended.

Billboard first listed "Satisfaction" on its Hot 100 singles chart at number 60 on June 4. In the next two weeks the Stones, back in Britain, did two television shows and a four-day Scottish tour June 15 through 18, in Glasgow, Edinburgh, Dundee, and Aberdeen. By the time they played Aberdeen "Satisfaction" was on *Billboard*'s singles chart at number 4.

26 Alnwickhill Road
Edinburgh 9

Dear fantastic "Stones,"

I thought I must congratulate you on your fab performance at the Usher Hall, Edinburgh, on Wednesday 16 it was terrific in fact I cannot find words to describe it.

Tell BRIAN that he was stupendous when he played the tambourine, it sent me in a whirl.

All my love,
Jane

A Hard Day's Night and *Help!*, two movies starring the Beatles, and *Don't Look Back*, not so much a movie as some film about Bob Dylan, had been released. Expecting Andrew to help them dump Easton and movie stardom to strike them like lightning, the Stones were playing only short tours. On June 23 they made their first trip to Norway. The fans who came to the Oslo airport to welcome the Stones were met by fire trucks knocking them down with high-pressure water hoses. The Stones played to three thousand at the Messehallen, while police with clubs knocked down those who didn't stay in their seats. One girl made it onstage, embraced Charlie, and fainted.

The Stones played Pori, Copenhagen, Malmo, and flew back to London. Their movie was postponed again, and except for a three-day English tour in the middle of the month, the Stones did next to nothing in July. On the first of August they starred in a show they had booked themselves at the London Palladium. *New Musical Express* reported police and ushers using "Gestapo-like methods" on girls trying to get near the stage, but outside Mick kicked a girl who attacked his date.

Their latest British EP, titled "got LIVE if you want it," recorded at performances in Manchester, Liverpool, and London, was selling well, so it was not until August 20, after "Satisfaction" had been number one on *Billboard*'s singles chart for three weeks, that it was released in Britain. The Stones did some television appearances and radio interviews to promote the record, which had caused *Newsweek* to describe the Stones as "tasteless" and "leering."

The Stones had, unbelievably, scheduled another show in Blackpool, but at the request of the local police and public safety committee the show was cancelled, and the Stones played Scarborough instead.

A few days later the London papers printed the news that Decca would in the next three years spend at least £1,700,000 to finance five films starring the Rolling Stones. It was also announced that an American, former accountant Allen Klein, thirty-one, had taken over the Stones' business management, replacing Eric Easton, who received "a golden handshake."

"He'd served his purpose—we'd done as much as we could in England," Keith said. "We could get a grand a night, and that's as much as you could earn, in those days. You think, What the fuck do we need him for . . . because that was the way it was. Onward."

The Stones' comanager Andrew Oldham, the papers said, would work with Klein as "creative manager." The papers didn't say that Klein was Andrew's discovery; he had lived in an orphanage and in poverty with his grandparents, been in the army, become a certified public accountant on the G.I. Bill. He did record-company audits for some entertainers, keeping half of any underpayments he found, and he found plenty. He did an audit at RCA Victor for Sam Cooke and became Cooke's manager, but Cooke was shot and killed in a motel scrape with a whore in Los Angeles. Cooke, whose first fame was with the gospel group the Soul Stirrers, was a popular symbol to black Americans, and it was as natural for the Stones to sign with Cooke's ex-manager as it was for them to record at Chess, or at the RCA Studios in Los Angeles, where Cooke had recorded. One of the songs on the Stones' latest album release in the United States, *Out of Our Heads*, was Cooke's "Good Times." The English papers did say that the Stones' reason for hiring Klein was "to further the group's financial success."

Andrew told reporters that the first of the Decca-financed Stones movies would be made within the next six months, but that it was "too early to say" what the movies would be like. Mick snarled at one reporter, "We're not gonna make Beatles movies. We're not comedians."

The Stones went back to work, doing three television appearances in four days, playing Dublin and Belfast on the weekend. The Dublin concert was stopped when part of the second show audience at the Adelphi Theatre leaped over the orchestra pit onto the stage. Mick was dragged to the floor; three boys were throwing punches at Brian while two others were trying to kiss him. Wyman was crushed against a piano at one side of the stage. Keith managed to get offstage, and Charlie sat playing the drums, his face expressionless. In Belfast the audience tore up the seats and threw them at the stage. As the Stones tried to leave, fans covered their car, but they got away with another collapsed roof.

The next morning they flew to Los Angeles for a few days to record at RCA their new single release, "Get Off of My Cloud." The Jagger/ Richards song, not about love or even love/hate, but about the frustrations of the modern world, was in the same vein as "Satisfaction," though not as memorable. But "Satisfaction" was the most popular song in the world, and it would have taken an airplane crash to stop the Stones now.

They returned to England, played a concert on the Isle of Man, were the hosts for a special edition of the television show *Ready, Steady, Go!* On September 11 the Stones began a tour of five German cities. Teenagers broke through a police cordon at the Düsseldorf airport when the Stones' plane touched down. About two hundred fought their way, breaking windows, wrenching phones off the walls, smashing doors, to an airport waiting room where the Stones were to give a press conference. Police cancelled the conference, and the Stones drove to Münster. Newspapers there described the show as "hell broken loose" and "a witches' cauldron."

Next day the Stones played the Gruga Halle in Essen and the day after that the Ernst Merck Halle in Hamburg. While six thousand fans rioted inside the Gruga Halle, two thousand rioted outside. The ones inside had the advantage of not being ridden down by mounted police. In Hamburg also there were police on horses with clubs and hoses keeping out the kids who were trying to get into the Stones' show. Cars were overturned, and kids were trampled by horses.

On September 14, with *Melody Maker* listing "Satisfaction" at number one for the second week, the Stones played Munich. Anita Pallenberg, the girl the Stones had met backstage at the Olympia Theatre in Paris, was there. She had some amyl nitrite poppers, and Brian was the only one of the Stones who would share them with her. He went home with her, but Mick and Keith had said something to him that made him cry all night.

The next day the Stones went to West Berlin and played to twenty-three thousand in the Waldbühne, where Hitler used to appear under the open sky. The following day, off to Vienna and then home to London. They took six days off, the British version of *Out of Our Heads* was released, and then they opened a four-week English tour at the Astoria Theatre in Finsbury Park. In a corner of the dressing room Brian sat alone, playing on his Gibson guitar Wilson Pickett's "In the Midnight Hour." Keith and Charlie were talking with friends, Bill was beside the stage watching the Spencer Davis Group, and Mick was talking to reporters. The Stones performed a new sequence of songs, with Brian playing organ on "That's How Strong My Love Is," playing with people who had humiliated him and reduced him to tears, and as he heard the screams of ecstasy from the audience in the darkened hall, Brian threw his head back in the spotlight, laughing.

At Liverpool thirteen girls were injured as they tried to climb over the canvas-covered orchestra pit to the stage. Theatre officers lowered the curtain, and the Stones accused them of panicking. In Manchester Keith was knocked unconscious by something somebody threw. He was carried offstage, woke up, and came back to finish the show. Mick was cut by something, probably a coin, and had to wear a plaster under his left eye for most of the tour. Brian was struck on the nose by a half-crown.

The tour ended on October 17, "Get Off of My Cloud" was released in Great Britain on October 22, and on October 27 the Stones left Heathrow Airport for New York City. The next day they held a press conference in the penthouse of the Hilton. To protect the Stones from the fans around the hotel, their limousine was driven onto the hotel's freight elevator, and they were carried to the top. Most of the Stones' fans in the United States at this time were quite young girls who thought that anything English was exotic and adorable, but a writer at the Hilton press conference said the Stones looked "like five unfolding switchblades," adding, "I left with the terrible feeling that if Kropotkin were alive in the 1960s he would almost certainly have had a press agent."

On October 29 the Stones flew to Montreal, handing over the passports in a bundle so the customs officers wouldn't notice that Keith's was missing. There were eight thousand in the audience at the Forum, thirty reported injured. The Stones flew back to Syracuse, New York, played the next afternoon to six thousand students at Ithaca College and played that night to eight thousand at an auditorium in Syracuse. On Halloween they played to thirteen thousand at the Maple Leaf Gardens in Toronto, fighting fifty-knot head winds to get there, sneaking Keith over and back. In Rochester the next night thirty police and thirty ushers could not control the crowd of thirty-five hundred at the Community War Memorial Auditorium. The Stones did six songs, during which the curtain came down four times. Finally Keith, furious at the treatment of the crowd by the police, shouted, "This is a hick town. They were twice as wild in Montreal. They won't get hurt. You're too rough with them." The police chief stopped the show, but "Get Off of My Cloud" was the most popular record in both the United States and the United Kingdom.

The Stones played Providence, New Haven, the Boston Garden, the Academy of Music in New York in the afternoon, and Convention Hall in Philadelphia the same night, the Mosque Theatre in Newark, Reynolds Coliseum in Raleigh, taped an appearance on the television show *Hullabaloo*, played Greensboro, Knoxville, Charlotte, and on November 17 came to the Memphis Mid-South Coliseum.

A teenager in the 1950s—I was twelve years old in 1954, the year Elvis Presley made his first recording—I had been given a new sense of life by rock and roll, a sense that diminished as the quality of the music diminished. Now musicians my own age, like the Stones, again were taking up the music. Christopher and I went to see them.

The audience consisted almost entirely of pubescent girls, some with Mom and Dad, all white, shrieking at the tops of their piping little voices. The Stones' show was not a concert but a ritual; their songs, compared in content or manner of performance with the material of other popular musicians, were acts of violence, brief and incandescent. Mick threw a tambourine into the audience, and hundreds dived for it. Years later I would get the Stones' autographs for the girl who caught the tambourine, its sharp-edged cymbals slicing her hands so badly that she had to be taken to a hospital emergency room and stitched together.

Four of the Stones left the next day for Miami, and Wyman stayed in Memphis. Cindy Birdsong of Patty LaBelle and the Blue Belles, one of the other acts on the tour, stayed there too. Wyman went to the Club Paradise and saw Big Ella and the Vel-Tones, but he didn't get to be such good friends with Cindy Birdsong as he would have liked. Anita Pallenberg flew to Miami to visit Brian. Anita and the Stones, staying at the Fontainebleau, rented motorboats from the hotel and floated in the ocean off Miami Beach until late afternoon. When they came in, there was no sign of Brian. Then they saw him, under a line of seagulls, a tiny dot in the sunset, headed out to sea. The hotel sent a boat after him, because he hadn't enough fuel to make it back. "I was chasing the birds," he said.

The tour resumed, to Shreveport, Dallas, Fort Worth, Tulsa, Pittsburgh, Milwaukee, Cincinnati, Dayton, Chicago, Denver, and Phoenix, where the Stones stayed in Scottsdale and went riding on the desert. This was the first Stones tour with Allen Klein and Ronnie Schneider. The Stones would meet in Ronnie's room before an outing. Better call Brian, he'll be left, Ronnie would say. Don't call him, Keith would say. Even Charlie don't like him. If Charlie don't like him there must be something wrong with him.

Anita would be meeting Brian at the end of the tour in Los Angeles, where the Stones planned to record an album. On the cover of the English *Disc Weekly* for the week the tour ended there was a photograph of Brian and Anita and the headline, BRIAN JONES WEDDING? Brian, telephoned during the tour, said that he had been going with Anita for about three months. "Anita," he said, "is the first girl I've ever been serious about."

2 0

Charles Bolden, a musician, of 2302 First Street, hammered his mother-in-law, Mrs. Ida Beach, in their house yesterday afternoon. It seems that Bolden has been confined to his bed since Saturday, and was violent. Yesterday he believed that his mother-in-law was drugging him, and getting out of bed, he hit the woman on the head with a pitcher and cut her scalp. The wound was not serious. Bolden was placed under a close watch, as the physicians stated that he was liable to harm someone in his condition.

New Orleans Daily Picayune, 1906

LATE LAST NIGHT Stu and I went out to a café, and I ate an omelet while he told me that he'd like to make a record of "Silent Night" with Keith on bass, Jeff Beck on guitar, himself on organ, Mick on harp—but you can't get them together. I slept, awoke, and all too soon, Shirley and Serafina Watts were leaving in the morning sunlight for England. The Stones and most of the rest of us were going later this afternoon to Texas. All long-faced, Charlie, Shirley, and I said goodbye.

Last night Stu said that they used to come to the United States, stay in hotels and with one Englishman and one American tour twenty or thirty cities. "*That's* a tour," he said. "When you start renting houses and putting people like Jo Bergman in them, you're *going* to have trouble, because that's their business." So we arrived after dark at the Hyatt House in Dallas to find our rooms already rented. Securing rooms was Bill Belmont's job, and as we rode to a Quality Court Jagger told Schneider that Belmont should be hauled on the carpet. It occurred to me that we were travelling across the country without one grownup person.

I went up with my suitcase and came back down to find Belmont and Michael Lydon leaving in a limousine for the Moody Field House at Southern Methodist University. Schneider had, clearly, spoken to Belmont, who said, "I don't have to take this dogshit! They're snobs, they don't care. I haven't talked to Jagger in three days, and I don't intend to. They think they're fucking gods. They started it all, but the crew might go back to the Fillmore and enjoy life. If I say, 'Let's ride,' they'll all walk out."

Belmont was operatic, but at the auditorium there was much to be done, and the crew stayed. I went upstairs to the Stones' dressing room, its walls decorated with photographs of SMU football and basketball players. Terry Reid was there, preparing to open the concert; he was twenty-one years old today. I watched his act from the balcony. The place was crowded, people sitting in the aisles and on the floor. I saw no police, just university campus cops. The crowd was throwing Frisbees, colorful little plastic saucers skimming over their heads from the floor to the balcony and back again. They cheered good Frisbee tosses at least as much as Terry's songs.

When his set ended I went back to the dressing room to wait for the next act, Chuck Berry. This would be the first show he had played on the tour, replacing Ike and Tina as well as B. B. King. But one of the promoters, a man in a brown suit, came into the dressing room and said that Berry wouldn't go on until he was paid $3000 in cash. I told the man he'd have to wait for Schneider.

The crowd, occupied with the Frisbees, didn't seem to mind waiting. Soon Schneider and the Stones showed up, and Berry went on. He was wearing white shoes that looked like albino alligators. He had the same bad white band that was with him at the Whisky-à-Go-Go, but he duck-walked, played with his guitar upside down and in various phallic positions and got a big ovation at the end of his set. In a minute he was in the Stones' dressing room, asking Jagger, "Where this gig tomorrow?"

"Um, Auburn," Mick said.

"Auburn University," Berry said. "I want to be sure, 'cause I ain't gone do no lookin' 'round, I'm goin' *straight* to that gig."

When Sam Cutler announced, "Ladies and gentlemen, the Rolling Stones," the crowd stood and cheered. Jagger tipped his Uncle Sam hat. "Very nice smells down here," he said, referring to the aroma of the marijuana being smoked in the front seats that went almost all the way up to the stage. The show was brisk. Even the line in "Sympathy for the Devil,"

I shouted out, Who killed the Kennedys?

passed without a ripple, nobody paying mind to Mick's heavy lyrics.

One girl, kneeling before the stage, kept yelling, "Take it off!" Jagger lashed her into silence with "Midnight Rambler," swinging his belt overhead, crashing it down onto the stage. There were shrieks in the darkness as Mick crawled on all fours, looking stark mad in a red spot.

As "Little Queenie" started, Mick said, "If you can move"—the place was packed—"why don't you shake your asses?" By the end of the show the place was rocking, ringing with that sound, like great organ chords. It was a good crowd, a good show, no hassles, no "I'm Free." We ran out, piled into limousines. Schneider, who happened to be in the car I caught, was carrying two rolls of movie film.

"Where'd you get that?" Michael Lydon asked.

"Some kid with a camera," Schneider said. "We'll develop it and see if there's anything good and use it in a documentary if we make one."

"You're going to develop that?" Lydon asked.

"No," Schneider said. "I'm going to expose it and wear it around my neck."

"You mean you just *took* it?"

"Tell him you're a thief, Ronnie," I said in exasperation, "so he'll understand."

At the Quality Court, where room service was closed, no one wanted to go out again, but I was hungry and went across the street to a steak and egg café and ate a hamburger. On the way back to my room I stopped by to see Jon Jaymes and ask what time we'd be leaving tomorrow. Jon was naked to his fat, hairy waist. With him were two girls, one dark-haired and quiet, one big and blond and loud. She was wearing plastic bracelets of red, blue, gold, yellow, and green, earrings that were each three great gold hoops. Jon was on the phone to Schneider, who sent the girls to him and who had another bevy of girls with him now. The blond had told Schneider that she had a pound of butter in her purse, and she wanted to spread it over Jagger's body and lick it off. Schneider had tried sending her to Sam.

"I saw him," she said, "he fucked me, he's a pig." She was angry, talking about the girls who were with Schneider: "I really hate those chicks. I really do, especially that one. She told a lie about me and if I go down there I'd probably knock the fuck out of her." Wrestling the phone away from Jaymes, she said, "Ronnie, do you know those girls are underage? What about Keith or Charlie or Bill? You can have Mick

Taylor," she said to her companion. "It doesn't matter, I'm not choosy, I just want one of their bodies, and I want it now. I can't wait around forever, I have to go pick up my little boy."

I gave up, went to bed and slept—to be awakened at 9:30 by a call from Jo, who told me to go back to sleep, we'd be leaving at 2:45 P.M. on a commercial flight to Montgomery, Alabama. Almost at once Ethan Russell called with the message from Jon Jaymes that the press should be in the lobby and ready to leave in fifteen minutes. Cursing, I got out of bed. I showered quickly and was shaving when the phone rang again. It was Jaymes, who said, "You and the rest of the press and your gear, downstairs, now." I gripped the phone, sputtering, then threw it back into its cradle. I finished shaving, dressed, and went down with my bags to find, as usual, plenty of time to lean and wait before we left—Jo, Stu, Michael Lydon, Ethan Russell, and I. The Stones were still sleeping and would take a later plane.

I rode to Atlanta with Jo sitting beside me as I got drunk on bourbon. Chip Monck, she said, saw Brian onstage last night, playing tambourine for about three minutes at the end of "Under My Thumb." I kept on drinking.

In Atlanta we rented a car, nobody tipping the black porter who loaded a half-ton of luggage into the trunk, and drove away, heading down to Auburn. I drove the car, a blue Dodge Charger, past pine woods and rolling Georgia fields. "Looks very much like Scotland," Stu said. "Very pleasant." But as we went deeper into the country, passing signs—DON'T LOSE YOUR SOUL BY THE MARK OF THE BEAST, JESUS WILL SAVE U—Mo-Jo gas stations, and tarpaper shanties, two banks of slate-colored clouds engulfed the sun, so that we entered Alabama under a morose blue-green sunset, and Stu said, "What a stupid place for a rock and roll concert."

"Apollo Twelve is three and one-half hours out at six forty-five P.M. Auburn time," the radio said. Men were going to walk on the moon for the second time in history, and none of us could be bothered. I was driving ninety miles an hour through the Alabama backwoods, but the sky had turned black by the time we reached Auburn, and it had begun to snow. As we drove onto the campus, the wind was whistling, snow whirling in the headlights. We parked behind the auditorium and ran to the back door, which we were happy to find unlocked.

Inside we were greeted by the head of the Auburn Special Events Committee, a graduate assistant who taught math and whose name was Jett Campbell. His helper was Mike Balkan; both of them were sober young white men with tidy haircuts. Terry Reid was here, but the Stones' whereabouts was unknown and there was a rumor, Jett told us, that Chuck Berry was not coming.

Two shows were scheduled, and Terry went on to start the first one.

The auditorium was not filled, and no one in it was black. Terry was booed during his first song, and some members of the audience yelled requests for irrelevant country songs. A few people stood and applauded when Terry went off, but it was a cold crowd on a cold night, and still no Stones and no Chuck Berry.

Then the back door opened and Chuck Berry came in with a white girl and my friends Jim and Mary Lindsay Dickinson, Jim carrying Berry's guitar. Berry's band was already present, and while he was on and I was talking to the Dickinsons, the door opened again and the Stones came in, all chilled from spending three hours aloft in an un-heated DC3 that leaked air, "freezing our asses off over the Mississippi Delta," Keith said.

Jagger, taking the weather as a personal affront, was reconsidering the idea of visiting the South between the halves of the tour: "If the South's going to be like this, I don't want to visit it, I thought it was warm in the South."

Friends of mine from Georgia had come to the show, and I was running low on marijuana, so I asked Keith if he had any to spare. He told me to let him know if I found some because the band had none left. Jagger, hearing me mention that my friends had come to the show, said, "It's not gonna be very good. The crowd's not good, and I'm not going to sing much, I'm fucking hoarse. And you have to have a night off sometime."

They did seem to rush through the show, it was the weakest one yet, no question of singing "I'm Free" under these circumstances. The hall was half full, and though the Stones played hard the place didn't shake.

Between shows I swapped the luggage from the car I'd been driving to another one, because I would be staying in Columbus tonight, and the others would be flying to Illinois. The Dickinsons and I sat in the car and smoked part of my dwindling dope. They had come in with Chuck Berry because they happened to stay at the same motel as Berry in Columbus, and Mary Lindsay had knocked on Berry's door and asked him if he knew where I was. Berry had been in the shower when she knocked, and his girl, Elizabeth, had let Mary Lindsay in. Berry came out of the bathroom and talked to Mary Lindsay while lying on the bed face down, nose buried in Elizabeth's crotch. But he did agree to take the Dickinsons to the show if they would guide him there. They had to stop for directions only once. "One of you Caucasians better do the asking," Berry said at an Alabama gas station.

The first show had been late, and the second show was already so late that Terry Reid was cancelled. The Auburn Special Events people were upset because the coeds had to be in their dorms by midnight. The girls here were not groupies or even fans, just coeds with Friday night dates, and the reason there were not more of them was that a lot of the boys were saving their money to take them to the big football game tomorrow night.

Berry started the second show with his first hit, "Maybellene," interpolating "Mountain Dew" at boring length. Then someone—a boy from Memphis whom I knew slightly and had given a ticket to the second show—called for "Wee Wee Hours," the B side of "Maybellene" and the first Chuck Berry blues. Berry, looking surprised, asked, "You want to hear some *blues*?" A small band of enthusiasts shouted "Yes!"

"You asked for it," Berry said and played "Wee Wee Hours" and then "Dust My Broom." The bad band was forgotten, and for about ten minutes the room was transformed. Then Berry went back to his old rock and roll songs, singing obscene lyrics to some of them and doing such other songs as "My Ding-A-Ling," a childish dirty ditty. He went on and on, as the Stones waited, Stu becoming outraged, threatening to turn off Berry's electricity. Finally Jett Campbell went onstage and thanked Berry, who left at last.

Jett, who had been on the phone with some higher authority, made the announcement that the Auburn coeds had been granted what he called "When-over permission," meaning that they could stay out until the concert was over. "While the Rolling Stones are getting ready to come out, let's hear a great Auburn cheer," Jett said, leading the crowd in a crescendo: "Warrr-EAGLE!"

I went backstage, where Stu was passing around tiny bottles of airplane Scotch. Alcohol was prohibited at the University, but Jett and Mike made an exception in our case, because we were exceptional. Jo was on the telephone, trying to reach the Stones' London office. Wyman, perfectly relaxed waiting to go onstage, told me that transportation and hotel problems always happen, no matter how well prepared you are.

The Stones' second set was better than the first; they were looser and warmer and the audience, War Eagles or not, were warmer too. Someone down front threw something at Jagger, who said, "You missed me with that joint."

"We love you," someone else shouted, and Jagger, tossing his long red scarf over his shoulder, said, "Thank you, sir—a man down here says he loves me."

When the lights came up for the last three songs, I went down into the crowd and danced before the stage. Wyman saw me and smiled, making one of his rare onstage changes of expression.

"It might happen," Mick said, "even in the streets of Auburn—"

> Everywhere I hear the sound of marchin',
>   Chargin' feet, boys

The Stones had come here through freezing cold for $35,000, out of which they would pay the other acts and all their own expenses. They could have made much more money someplace else, but they had chosen to play at Auburn University before a herd of fraternity pins. Though there were not even any campus police to be seen, most of the crowd were not dancing, and the Stones' brave effort seemed too weak to make a real difference.

At the end of the show, out the back way again, the Stones going to fly from the frozen South to Champaign, Illinois, where they would play another university tomorrow night. I drove with the Dickinsons to the motel in Columbus, hired a room and went to bed, leaving a call for nine o'clock in the morning. It was a long drive across Alabama and Mississippi to Memphis, and I wanted to get started as early as possible. But the call didn't come; I woke up after eleven, called the Dickinsons, and by the time we left it was afternoon. As we walked out through the lobby, a television set, tuned to Saturday cartoons, said, "Wait! It's not the giant pussy!"

I was eager to get home and see Christopher, but Dickinson drove slowly because today was his birthday and he was superstitious. My impatience was not lessened when, just past the Tallapoosa County Memorial Gardens, a cemetery in which several Jersey cows were grazing, we ran out of gas. Dickinson pulled onto the grassy shoulder and started to write HELP on a piece of paper. That message seemed a bit vague for the motorists of Alabama, so he made another sign saying GAS. I took it and tried to thumb down cars, but they sped up as they passed. Then an Alabama State Patrol car came along and stopped about thirty feet behind us. I walked back to the big grey Pontiac with the state outlined on the front doors and told the man in his grey twill shirt and sunglasses, "We just did the dumbest thing you can do."

"You run out of gas," he said.

Mary Lindsay joined us, and the trooper asked, "Is that a girl or a boy driving the car?" Jim's hair was quite long.

"That's my husband," Mary Lindsay said in her most mature tones. The trooper explained that he didn't want to leave two women alone on the highway, but that Mary Lindsay and Jim could stay and he would take me to where I could buy enough gas to make it to Birmingham.

As we rode along I was thinking that things were not as bad as they might have been; we could have waited a long time for someone to stop and help us. I noticed the trooper's name, Pilkington, on the black plastic nameplate pinned over his shirt pocket, and it occurred to me that I was carrying drugs that even in modest quantity could get me put away forever in Alabama. Pilkington looked serious, and I looked out the window, serious too, when the giant pussy came to my aid. I remembered the cartoons and knew there had to be football on a cold Saturday afternoon in November.

"Who's winnin' the game?" I asked.

Pilkington relaxed, grinned, said, "Ole Miss whippin' hell out of 'em."

As we drove, hundreds of thousands of people marched in Washington, D.C., demanding an end to the Vietnam War. Not until the summer of 1982, when a greater number demonstrated in New York's Central Park against nuclear weapons, would such a gathering occur. But the wars would go on, and so would the weapons.

Off the highway, down a winding asphalt road, at a crossroads with a post office and one gas station, we waited for Junior to get back with the truck, because the gas can was on it, but he showed up, and Pilkington drove me back to the car and wished us good luck. I was sorry I couldn't help him by telling him what a nice arrest I'd be, but I was in a hurry.

Dickinson drove slowly on, explaining things to me, for which I kept him around. "The Stones are trying to tour without a big agency booking them because they've been fucked by agencies," he said. "They didn't trust house PAs or equipment rental agencies, and they felt they should give audiences a record-quality sound, so they got their own PA and a mixing board. They're controlling their own tour. They haven't booked the typical cow palaces—some, enough to make money—but they're in the revolution, they'll play places the Beatles wouldn't. They wind up hiring their friends who are actually incompetent. My God, they were late. Only acts of God excuse musicians." I made a note to ask about that.

In Mississippi, as it was getting dark, I asked at a gas station if I might make a collect call to Memphis, and the man there said, "This a business phone." I turned around without saying anything more, and he said, "They a pay phone about a quarter-mile down the road."

"I can find a phone," I said. Down the road, at a pay phone leaning against a cow skeleton, I called Christopher. The situation was typical; for years we had been together, happy in the New York snows and the Caribbean shadows, but as time had passed we had run more and more on separate schedules. Christopher would come in from work and go to bed while I wrote, like the drunk man in the Don Marquis poem, "falling upwards through the night."

"What'd you tell her?" Dickinson asked.

"That I'd be home about nine."

"We'll be there sooner, you shouldna told her that."

But it was nine o'clock when I got home. I didn't know it yet, and it would have seemed insane, knowing as I did what I had been doing, but it was possible to suspect a man on the road with the Rolling Stones of having a real good time. And not without justice. We were very close. She knew I was guilty before I knew it myself.

2 1

At the beginning of the 20th century there were only six reliable and effective pharmaceutical preparations, namely digitalis (still helpful in many kinds of heart disease), morphine, quinine (for malaria), diphtheria antitoxin, aspirin and ether. Two other successful means of chemical intervention were also available: immunization against smallpox and rabies. This pharmacopeia remained basically unchanged until about the time of World War II. Since then, drugs and other substances that can, if employed wisely, usefully affect the chemistry of life have been produced in startling numbers.

SHERMAN M. MELLINKOFF:
"Chemical Intervention," *Scientific American*

ON DECEMBER 5, 1965, after forty-two days, the Stones ended their fourth tour of the United States at the Los Angeles Sports Arena. In a month and a half they had made two million dollars. They stayed in L.A. for the next week, recording at the RCA studios a single record and *Aftermath*, the first album composed entirely of Jagger/ Richards songs. Then the band went their own ways, all of them returning to England for Christmas except Brian, who was in the Virgin Islands with Anita and a tropical virus. But he made it back to play *Ready, Steady, Go!* on New Year's Eve.

I had left Tulane and was in Memphis, working for the Tennessee Department of Public Welfare, an outfit that confirmed every fear I'd ever had about the social system. I would come out of a house that stank with the ammonia smell of poverty, start my car, turn on the radio —there was interesting music on the car radio for the first time since 1957—hear the Beatles or the Supremes and have to turn the radio off. The happiness of popular music was unbearable at such times, but I could always listen to the Stones. I sensed the strong blues truth that underlay their music.

The new single, "19th Nervous Breakdown," contained what may have been the first reference in a popular song to what were called psychedelic, mind-changing, drugs. Mick and Keith, moving with the times, were no longer having people thrown out of dressing rooms for dealing dope. Marijuana, heroin, and cocaine were associated—in popular legend, at least—with black ghettos, jazz musicians, and beatniks. In the middle 1960s, with the white man's burden heavy again from Vietnam to Birmingham, Alabama, and Birmingham, England, adolescent whites began to display sympathy for what many of them saw as the colored victims of white men, and old wars were fought again in living rooms between disturbed parents and uncommunicative offspring wearing long hair and Indian headbands. The situation was complicated by the increased use among the young of certain substances, such as the peyote cactus (active ingredient, mescaline) and "magic mushrooms" (psilocybin), that had been in limited use among tribal "medicine men" and religious mystics for centuries. The easy availability of substances like these and many synthetic analogues (among them LSD, DMT, STP) far more potent than anything of the sort occurring in nature, alarmed parents and other authority figures. Taking such substances could cause, for minutes or days, sense impressions to overpower the mind. The generation that had fought World War II and had created the postwar baby boom found the use of such drugs dangerous and made it as illegal as possible. They knew in their calcium-deprived bones that you can't be too careful.

From the Stones' point of view, things were not so simple:

> On our first trip I tried so hard
>   to rearrange your mind
> But after 'while I realized
>   you were disarranging mine

On February 4 "19th Nervous Breakdown" was released in England. It hit the *New Musical Express* singles chart at number 2 on February 11. That day the Stones flew to New York to tape an appearance on *The Ed Sullivan Show,* refused to be photographed at the airport, and nearly got into a fight with the photographers. They split up for their

New York stay, hoping to avoid fans, or at least to spread them out. Mick and Keith stayed at the Essex House on Central Park South, while Brian, Bill, and Charlie stayed at the Regency on Park Avenue. No decent New York hotel would accommodate them all together. On February 16 the Stones flew into Sydney, where about three hundred kids were waiting in the rain to welcome them at the start of their second tour of Australia. The tour had been sold out in all the state capitals for days and extra matinees added to meet the demand. Mick sent a report to *Disc* magazine dated February 21, datelined Brisbane, saying that it had rained every day, the shows had been better than on the last tour because they had appeared then with Roy Orbison and drawn mixed crowds, the food was bad, the birds were all pretty and suntanned, but that Brian had asked him to say that he, Brian, was still in love.

The Australian tour lasted through February; on March 3 the Stones reached Los Angeles, where they stayed four days, long enough to record the Jagger/Richards song, "Paint It, Black." It was to be their next single. The comma was Andrew's idea. On March 13 all the Stones except Brian arrived in London. They had two weeks off before starting a European tour. When Brian returned to London, he said that he'd been delayed four days after the other Stones because the clubs in New York stay open twenty-four hours a day. He arrived at his Earl's Court Mews apartment wearing rose-tinted spectacles and carrying a dulcimer.

One bright, cold morning in March of 1966, I sat on a brown Naugahyde couch in the Welfare Workers' lounge, on the seventh floor of the M&M building in Memphis, at the corner of Beale and Main streets, reading the *New York Review of Books.* The week before, after working eight months for the Tennessee State Welfare Department, I had given my two weeks' notice. This morning I came into the office, left at once, went for a walk and decided that I couldn't take another week. Now, waiting for lunchtime, when the supervisors would go out and I would sweep downstairs, clean out my desk and disappear, I came upon an advertisement. At first I assumed it was for the Famous Writers' School, but then I saw that it was for *Playboy.* All firm-jawed and one foot in front of the other, it said something like, We're Looking for Men Who Eat and Sleep Writing.

Years later I would find in my old Welfare Worker's notebook the remains of the letter I wrote to *Playboy* that morning. I suggested writing for them about cars, airplanes, and sound equipment (because I had read *Playboy* and had an idea of what they would want their serious writers to take seriously), but the only specific subject I proposed to *Playboy,* back in ought 66, was the Rolling Stones. No wonder they didn't hire me.

On Beale Street, half a block from the Welfare Department, was

Reuben Cherry's Home of the Blues Record Shop. Reuben kept a rubber snake to scare people in the store, and Elvis Presley would come in, get the snake, take it out on Beale and scare the people in cars as they drove down the street. "The boy's a menace," Reuben used to say of Elvis, back when they were both alive, as Reuben had been the day he sold me a Folkways album recorded in 1958 by a Memphis street sweeper named Furry Lewis.

When I left the Welfare Department I took with me this note from Furry's Welfare file (which showed that he had been turned down twice): "Mr. Lewis has a pawn ticket in the amt. of sixteen dollars ($16) from Nathan's Pawn Shop 194 Beale Street which he states is for a guitar. He states he was an entertainer of some kind, as well as his work for the City of Memphis."

In the first few months after leaving my job I wrote a novel about poor people and some stories, one of which was about Furry. During the heyday of Beale Street, when the great Negro blues artists played and sang in the crowded, evil blocks between Fourth and Main, Furry, a protégé of W. C. Handy, was one of the most highly respected blues musicians. He was also one of the most popular, not only around the saloons and gambling dives of Memphis but in the medicine shows and on the riverboats all along the Mississippi. In Chicago, at the old Vocalion studios on Wabash Avenue, he made the first of many recordings he was to make, both for Vocalion and for RCA Victor's Bluebird label.

But at the close of the 1920s, Furry told me, "Beale Street really went down. You know, old folks say, it's a long lane don't have no end and a bad wind don't never change. But one day, back when Hoover was President, I was driving my cart down Beale Street and I seen a rat, sitting on top of a garbage can, eating a onion, crying." Since 1923 Furry had worked at times for the City of Memphis, Sanitation Department, and he kept on sweeping the streets.

Furry and I adopted each other. "Me and him just like brothers," he told people, pointing at me. Several years after I wrote it, "Furry's Blues" was printed in *Playboy* and won an award. Furry went on to make many albums, to appear in a Burt Reynolds movie, to be visited by celebrities from Joni Mitchell to Allen Ginsberg, to be honored by the Rolling Stones (who refused to go onstage in Memphis in 1978 until Furry had played), and to heaven in 1981, but he is still with me, saying, "Give out but don't give up."

I found Furry with the help of my friend Charlie Brown, who ran a Memphis coffeehouse called the Bitter Lemon, where old blues players sometimes appeared. Charlie took me to Furry's apartment, on Fourth Street half a block off Beale—I had been near there to visit welfare clients—went with me to watch Furry sweep the streets and hired Furry to play at the Lemon so I could watch him work.

The year before, Charlie Brown had come up with the first grass I'd seen since 1961, when I'd scored in North Beach and brought it—half a lid—back to Memphis. Charlie also had the first LSD I ever took, and I took it with him. I was somewhat prepared for the experience by reading Aldous Huxley, R. H. Blyth, and the haiku poets, and I had even eaten a large number of Heavenly Blue morning glory seeds, which didn't exactly free me from the temporal sphere—but on LSD I saw Charlie Brown change, become all races, all ages, I felt myself die, turn to damp clay, felt breath, air, come back into my body, was filled with a tender care—a new sense of the value, the preciousness, of life. When we could navigate, we drove CB's 1949 Ford that was rat-colored like Hazel Motes' down to an all-night eatery for a mild repast, marvelling at the city lights reflected in the raindrops on the windshield. At the café there was a cop, all dark blue, black leather, and menacing devices. He was sitting at a table with a cup of coffee, talking to someone on a walkie-talkie. There had been a burglary at a warehouse in a black neighborhood. The burglar was a black teenage girl. The cop said he'd be right there, his tone loaded with sex and sadism. The only way he could be intimate with a black girl was to punish her. After he left, the place still reeked with his lust, if you had taken acid.

At the end of March and into April, the Stones toured Europe, including Amsterdam, Brussels, Paris—where Brigitte Bardot came to their hotel to meet them, a rather embarrassing scene since only Mick spoke French, and her beauty made him speechless. On the next day the Stones played Marseilles, and Mick's forehead was gashed by a chair thrown from the audience. "They do it when they get excited," Mick told reporters.

In April *Aftermath* was released in the United Kingdom, and "Paint It, Black" was released in the United States. Years later Charlie would recall how Brian "sat for hours learning to play sitar, put it on 'Paint It, Black' and never played it again." The new single was amazing, a nihilistic outburst that would be a number one popular record. The Stones performed the song on *The Ed Sullivan Show,* and Mick, interviewed by the Associated Press, said that teenagers in the United States had changed, were asking more questions of their elders, becoming more independent in their thinking. "When we first came here in 1964, the kids wanted to be what everyone wanted them to be. . . . They were all satisfied by convention. They gave each other rings. They never thought about whether politically anything was right or wrong."

At this time, London was the most fashionable city on the planet. The Beatles, James Bond novels and movies, photographs by David Bailey, clothes by Mary Quant, haircuts by Vidal Sassoon, all contributed to a period of great international popularity of things British. Headlines about the Stones were changing. Mick and Keith had been photographed by Cecil Beaton, who said they reminded him of Nijinsky, of Renaissance angels. For years Keith kept a newspaper clipping of one of the Beaton photographs of himself with the caption, "Wonderful Head and Torso."

Time magazine had a cover story dated April 15, 1966, titled "London, the Swinging City." It shared space in the magazine with news of the increasing intensity of U.S. bombing attacks on North Vietnam. The Rolling Stones' music was the most "In" now, *Time* said, making it official.

Plans for the Stones' film, supposed to have started in April, had changed again. The film was now to be taken from a novel called *Only Lovers Left Alive,* by Dave Wallis, about England taken over by teenagers after a nuclear attack. Mick told *Melody Maker,* "I can't see, for instance, Ringo with a gun in his hand and being nasty in a movie and going to kill somebody. It just wouldn't happen. But I don't think you'd think it was very peculiar if you saw Brian do it."

In the same interview, Mick had further thoughts on the United States: "Vietnam has changed America. It has divided it and made people think. There's a lot of opposition—much more than you think, because all the opposition is laughed at in American magazines. It's made to look ridiculous. But there is real opposition. Before, Americans used to accept everything, my country right or wrong. But now a lot of young people are saying my country should be right, not wrong."

Mick was living in a furnished flat in Baker Street, and Keith, the papers stated, had bought Redlands. Wyman had bought a house at Keston, near Bromley, Kent, three months before. Because of the Stones' schedule, Keith would not actually live in Redlands until the fall. In June *Aftermath* was released in the United States, and they went back for their fifth tour. Fourteen New York hotels, fearing the fans, refused to have the Stones as guests. Allen Klein made a show of threatening to sue all fourteen for $5 million, claiming the Stones were discriminated against because of national origin. They solved the immediate problem of shelter by renting a yacht at the 79th Street Boat Basin.

The tour opened at Manning Bowl in Lynn, Massachusetts, with a riot in the rain. Eighty-five police held back fifteen thousand fans until the opening notes of the last song, "Satisfaction." Fans broke through the police cordon, and cops threw tear gas that the wind blew away from the crowd and back toward the stage. The Stones beat it for their two limousines, but the fans caught up with the cars, which were nearly torn apart. As the cars took off, one girl, clinging to the rear bumper, lost two fingers. "Brian, Brian," she screamed, not knowing that her life—or at least her hand—had been changed forever.

The Stones' shows lasted little more than half an hour and consisted mostly of their hits: they did ten songs, "Not Fade Away," "The Last Time," "Paint It, Black," "Stupid Girl," "Lady Jane," "Spider and the Fly," "Mother's Little Helper," "Get Off of My Cloud,' "19th Nervous Breakdown," and "Satisfaction." They played in Cleveland; Pittsburgh; Washington, D.C.; Baltimore; Hartford; Buffalo; Toronto; Montreal; Atlantic City; the Forest Hills tennis stadium in Queens, New York; Asbury Park; Virginia Beach; and Syracuse, where at the War Memorial Stadium Brian tried to steal an American flag that had been spread out backstage across a chair to dry, and a stagehand snatched it back, creating a small scene and a few headlines. It wasn't the time to kid around with the American flag.

The atmosphere on this tour was more friendly, not just because Mick and Keith and Brian were now, like many of their generation, smoking grass. (An album of the Stones' hits had been in release in the United States since March; it was called *Big Hits (High Tide and Green Grass)*. Charlie, a jass player, smoked marijuana now and then, and Wyman had tried it, but it made him ill.) The Beatles came to the United States for their last tour this summer, 1966, and after talking and listening to them at a press conference, I had the feeling that we were all of us in the same struggle, all of us who wanted to (the slogan had appeared) make love, not war.

The Stones' tour continued, with little regard for geography, to Detroit, Indianapolis, Chicago, Houston, St. Louis, Winnipeg, and Omaha. At the next stop, Vancouver, the police, alarmed by the forward surge of screaming youngsters in the Pacific National Exhibition Forum, even though there was a riot fence between the audience and the stage, shut off the sound system. The Stones, police told reporters, then "began making obscene gestures that incited the crowd even more." In Seattle the next day, Mick denied inciting the crowd: "What's an obscene gesture? I don't know any American obscene gestures. They're different all over the world."

After Seattle the Stones went to Portland, Oregon, where they refused to talk to reporters at Portland International Airport. United Press International reported, "Mike Gruber, from the Stones' New York-based publicity agency, said interviews 'would ruin their image.' " As the Stones started back up the steps of their chartered plane, a television cameraman asked the Stones' business agent, Ron Schneider, to stop blocking his camera. Schneider and Gruber ordered the cameraman off the field. From inside the plane the Stones yelled, "Give 'im a knuckle sandwich, Mike."

The end of the tour was approaching, and the madness increased. In Sacramento the Stones threw desserts all over a motel room and each other. Schneider gave a hundred dollars to a maid and asked her to clean it up. Then, dripping with whipped cream, they all went out and jumped into the pool. The manager came out, furious. Send us a bill, they told him. They played Salt Lake City, Bakersfield, and the Hollywood Bowl. Charles Champlin, the *Los Angeles Times* critic, reviewed their performance as if it were some kind of art, calling them "talented and inventive musicians," and referring to Brian as "lead guitarist." On July 26, Mick's twenty-third birthday, they played San Francisco, then flew to Hawaii, where they ended the tour and spent eight days waiting for an air strike to end. Then they went back to L.A. and recorded "Have You Seen Your Mother, Baby, Standing in the Shadow," at RCA Studios with Dave Hassinger engineering as usual. They also recorded most of the tracks for *Between the Buttons,* the album that would come out in the USA and England in January 1967.

After the recording sessions were over, the Stones went on holiday. Mick and his girlfriend Chrissie Shrimpton were reported in a car crash in Great Titchfield Street near Marylebone, both shaken up but no real damage done. On September 2, the story appeared that Brian Jones, "lead guitarist of the Rolling Stones pop group," had broken his left hand while on holiday in Tangier. When the Stones appeared on *The Ed Sullivan Show* to perform "Have You Seen Your Mother," Brian's hand was bandaged. On the sleeve for the new single the Stones were pictured dressed in women's clothing, looking like five matrons of the day, Keith a gossipy birdwife, Charlie a leggy policewoman, Bill a crippled WAC in a wooden wheelchair, Mick a Harlem housewife with white plastic cat's-eye glasses, Brian a blond WAC looking like Judy Holliday. They were posed in front of a window with a gold star sticker indicating a World War II death in the family. It was a remarkable picture to appear on a sleeve designed to be sold to schoolgirls by the millions. The English music papers added another classic headline to the Stones collection: HAVE THE STONES GONE TOO FAR? The answer was, not quite yet.

It was announced in the papers on September 14 that the Stones had added £231,000 to the profit of Decca in the last fiscal year. They had not received Orders of the British Empire, as the Beatles had, but people who were making that kind of money for a small country with a bad balance-of-payments situation would have to go a ways before they could be said to have gone too far. Still, they were heading there as fast as they could.

Brian and Anita were living together in a large flat in Courtfield Road, near the Gloucester Road tube station. With their circle of friends, they were a center of activity in "Swinging London." Soon Keith started living with Brian and Anita, all of them friends, taking lots of drugs, going down to Redlands for the weekends, not looking back.

At the end of September the Stones toured England with the Yardbirds and Ike and Tina Turner. They still went onstage in whatever they happened to be wearing, but on the day they opened the tour at the Albert Hall Mick happened to be wearing an orange shirt, white bell-bottom trousers, black sequined Chinese-style jacket, and Brian wore silver-grey velvet trousers, a purple velvet jacket, a red silk shirt, and a white cravat.

In October, while the English tour was going on, Decca announced that the Stones movie would start shooting in November. It was to be the first film solely financed by a record company. The Stones would earn from it, the newspapers said, a million dollars. On October 11, "Have You Seen Your Mother" started down the charts. It had hit at number 6, climbed to 4, and now at number 5 it was going down and out. It was the first Stones single after six straight number ones not to reach the top. There were some empty seats on the tour, but when it was over, Keith and Brian told *Melody Maker* that it was "an enormous success." They seemed to think that this was partly due to their having purged the ranks of their followers. "In the 'It's All Over Now' era," Keith said, "we were in danger of becoming respectable!"

The Stones' movie naturally did not start shooting in November. On November 14 the London papers carried pictures of Brian in a Nazi uniform with Anita kneeling in front of him. "These are . . . realistic pictures," Brian said by way of explanation. "The meaning of it all is there is no sense to it."

The phrase *to blow minds,* meaning to astound, was current. Brian and Anita were into blowing people's minds. In an interview with *Melody Maker* after the last English tour, Brian had said, "My damaged hand is mending well. It has worried me a lot, but I am now able to leave the bandages off although I am still a bit limited in my little finger."

At the time of the accident, the newspaper stories had said that Brian had hurt his hand in a fall down a hillside, but years later Anita told me that Brian had broken his hand on her face, during a fight. "He always hurt himself," she said. "He was very fragile, and if he ever tried to hurt me he always wound up hurting himself."

2 2

The only way to avoid murder is by ritual murder.
NORMAN O. BROWN: *Love's Body*

AFTER EIGHT HOURS I woke up with just enough time to re-pack and leave for Chicago, where I would rejoin the Stones. I drove with Christopher to the airport. She sighed, looking out the Mustang windows.

From O'Hare Airport I phoned Jo at a hotel that called itself the Ambassador East. Jo told me to meet them at the International Amphitheatre, where the Democratic Party selected a presidential candidate last year, an occasion that provided much sport for the police. A cab driver, an old man in a grey cap, told me about the place: "Down by the stockyards. Built it for a cow barn. Three blocks long." McCormick Place burned last year, and while it was being rebuilt, the Amphitheatre was being used, the driver said, "for conventions and shows."

I arrived primed for a battle to get in, but there was no one in sight, and the back door was open. Inside, only the stage crew was on hand. Bill Belmont showed me around. Belmont always looked the same, dressed in Levi's and a blue shirt with a button-down collar, black-haired, dark-eyed, and he was always ready to show you around. Belmont would talk to anybody. (Much later I learned that Jon Jaymes had passed from Belmont to Chip Monck's manager and met the Stones with cars at the Los Angeles airport after the Fort Collins shows.) He didn't leave the tour until the stage was clear of corpses. This part of the Amphitheatre, where the Stones would play, was the Arena. On the rear wall, a painted sign said HOME OF THE INTERNATIONAL LIVESTOCK EXPOSITION. In this dusty old rust-colored barn the obligatory U.S. flag was huge, hanging in the dead center of the room. If it fell rows of customers would smother.

I found the ambience a mite oppressive and went backstage to the dressing rooms, really just the business offices of the Amphitheatre, with filing cabinets, shabby desks, and tables. On the walls hung a couple of paint-by-number still lifes, *Cake with Rose* and *Vegetable Plate*. One desk was brightened by a bouquet of dusty blue plastic flowers. Thumb-tacked to another wall was a list of this year's Amphitheatre attractions: a Jehovah's Witnesses convention, wrestling bouts, livestock shows, roller derbies, the Boy Scouts of America Fun Fair. On a table in a back room were a few packages of pre-sliced American cheese, Saltine crackers covered with plastic wrap, and some apples. The Jehovah's Witnesses probably hadn't even got that much, a point (with just exactly whom we are dealing, here) emphasized when Stu came in and I asked him, because Dickinson had told me that performers' contracts include fines for lateness, whether the Stones had been fined so far on the tour.

"No promoter would fine the Stones because they're too big," he said. "They could tell all the English groups not to work for this or that promoter and he'd have no acts."

The Stones hadn't arrived, and once again Chuck Berry, who was due onstage, refused to start his set until he was paid $3000 in cash. Stu went to Berry's dressing room, returned with a receipt signed by Berry and gave it to me for safekeeping. Ten minutes later, with the crowd stamping in eagerness, Berry went on. In the dressing room, I heard the crowd cheering as Berry started to play, and I decided to go out and watch him. But as I opened the door, there were the Stones, Jo, Schneider, Sam, Tony, David Horowitz, Michael Lydon, and Jon Jaymes. Mick and Keith asked how was Memphis, and how could I tell them?

Schneider asked me for Berry's receipt. Business as usual. Yesterday the Stones played two shows in Champaign-Urbana at the University of Illinois Assembly Hall. At least this place was not another basketball gym. Behind the stage curtains a small neon sign read, SIRLOIN ROOM NEXT DOOR.

The old brown hall, filled with folding chairs, had a low ceiling, compared with some of the space domes the Stones had played, and the atmosphere was more old-fashioned and theatrical. The Stones' first set seemed more like the old days, with Mick twirling the microphone and stomping. There didn't seem to be any cops pushing people around; Stu pushed the ineffectual blue-capped ushers offstage. It was as if, after what had happened here last year, nobody in authority cared about a little old rock and roll concert. The crowd stood, danced, sang, shouted. The show seemed over in no time, and we ran out the back door to the limousines, the same limousines which had brought the San Francisco-based rock group, the Jefferson Airplane, who were crouched at the back entrance of the theatre with movie cameras, filming the Stones' departure.

At the hotel Jo phoned the dining room with our order, to be eaten there after a press conference and after a call to the Stones' English office, instructing them to find two places in London for the Stones to play concerts before Christmas and to send telegrams to each of the Beatles, asking them to play the shows, offering them the closing spot. The Beatles, who were coming apart, would not reply.

In Keith's suite there were fuzzy-headed people with cameras and tape recorders, as we'd come to expect at press conferences. One of them asked, "Do you notice any difference in the crowds you have on this tour compared to your previous ones?"

"Yeah," Keith said. "The audiences used to be composed ninety percent of chicks twelve and thirteen. My first thought on this tour was, 'Where are they now?' The audiences are much more intimate now. They listen more, we can play much better."

"We got a guy we heard was good for sound and lights," Mick said. "If you're gonna play ice hockey stadiums and huge abattoirs, you really should do something to make it better."

There were questions about the still-unreleased album, and Mick said they expected some trouble getting airplay: "Some people find some of the lyrics rude. Some of the lyrics are rude, actually."

Mick sat on a couch, crosslegged and barefooted, giving polite answers to dimwitted questions until someone asked how long it had taken him to learn sitar, an instrument he does not play.

We were soon seated in the Pump Room, waiting for dinner. It was a large room with great crystal chandeliers, midnight blue walls, candelabras bearing three points of light on each white-clothed table. We sat at a long table near a small dance floor and a quintet—tenor saxophone, trumpet, rhythm section—playing songs like "Yesterdays" and "Willow Weep for Me." Jon Jaymes—sitting with his mother, Mike Scotty (the older man who'd been along in San Diego), and a handsome young blond girl at a table to our right—was talking as usual into a telephone. The band was good, and the place was not bad, but the sedate clientele regarded us as if we were a circus troupe with our own Mafia rep. You couldn't blame them.

Ordering early did no good; we sat and waited for our food, Michael Lydon grabbing the chance to ask Mick some questions he had been saving up about "Midnight Rambler."

"I write," Mick told him, "just to confuse people like you." And because the service was slow, he added, "I don't really like 'Midnight Rambler.' I don't dig singing about killing people. Taj told me '32-20' by Robert Johnson's not where it's at." But making love and death into songs was exactly the Stones' business.

When the food finally arrived it was good, pâté, rijsttafel, caviar, cannelloni, wines, cognac, and we ate quickly, because the hour drew nigh. Then we went back to the barn, drove in the back, and as I was going into the dressing room, Stu stopped me. He asked if I knew someone named Abbie Hoffman. Not really, but close enough. Most people knew Abbie because, after the Democratic convention was over and the troops were gone and the tear gas had drifted away, Abbie and seven others, "the Chicago Eight," were charged by the U.S. government with conspiring to cross state lines for the purpose of starting a riot. Abbie had come to the Convention as a nonleader of a nonpolitical party, the Yippies, who held a funeral for their nonmovement and nominated a pig named Pigasus for President. For this he was on trial.

Stu said that Mick wanted to see Abbie, so I went and found him, bushy-haired, jovial, intense, sitting out front with his pretty, dark-haired wife, Anita. We went backstage, where Abbie told Mick, "We're in the same business. Your thing is sex, mine's violence."

"Yeah, I love a good fight," Mick said.

"Say, do you know where you are, what happened here, the Demo—"

"Sure, I know," Mick said, brushing his hair.

"Who's the man with the bread?" Abbie asked me, and I pointed to Schneider, sitting at the table with the Saltines doing addition.

"Why don't you give us some bread?" Abbie asked.

"No," Ronnie said.

Abbie repeated the question to Mick, who laughed and said, "For what?"

"The trial," Abbie said. "The Chicago Eight."

"I've got to pay for my own trials," Mick said.

"I'll pay you back," Abbie said, "when the trial's over."

"Please," Sam was saying in his officious cockney manner, "will everybody except the Stones leave the dressing room, they have only about five minutes."

Abbie shrugged, and we went out. "He didn't say yes, but he didn't say no. I've been trying to talk to him all day. I even called the Ambassador East and told them I was Elvis Presley. 'Jus' wanna see how ole Mick is a-gittin' along.'"

I watched the first half of the Stones' set from onstage, standing behind Keith's amplifiers, then after "Prodigal Son" I went into the crowd and joined Abbie and Anita, sitting with them and, as things got hectic, standing with them on chairs. Abbie kissed Anita during "Little Queenie" and sang harmony off-key on "Honky Tonk Women." The conspirator was just another rock-and-roll-crazed kid. "I may come to California for the free concert," he said.

After the show the Stones travelling party went back to the hotel to pick up luggage. Charlie and I would have liked to stay in Chicago and go to some jazz clubs, but we were going back to Los Angeles. The Stones were going to record an appearance on *The Ed Sullivan Show* there the day after tomorrow.

Keith and I were in his suite, talking as he packed. He dropped a pack of cigarettes, bent to pick them up, and dropped them again. "It's that time of night when you drop things and can't pick them up," he said.

Wyman, coming in, said, "I've got such a ringin' in me ears."

"I always have one after each show for about half an hour," Keith said. "A high-pitched ringin' sound."

The driver of one of the limousines that took us to the airport was the man who drove the judge of the Chicago Eight trial to court every morning. "What does the judge say about Abbie?" I asked.

"He hates him. Says he's going to jail."

On the plane, I reminded Mick that at the Woodstock festival Abbie had tried to address the crowd and had been hit on the head with a guitar by Pete Townshend of the Who. "I don't blame Townshend, I'd probably have done the same thing," Mick said.

We talked about the shows on the first half of the tour and the problem of controlling the people who try to control the crowds. "The press conferences are odd," I said. "It's as if nobody understands what you're trying to do."

"We don't know ourselves what we're trying to do," Mick said and went to play cards.

Charlie joined me and asked, "Is he good, that Abbie guy? Is he a good guy?"

"Well," I said, "it depends—"

"I mean, he doesn't carry himself like somebody you'd respect. He's like a clown."

"Maybe in politics these days the clowns are the most respectable people."

"Sad, isn't it?" Charlie said.

Stephen Stills' house had been returned to him, so the Stones were moving to the Oriole house. The rest of us were going to stay at the Continental Hyatt House on Sunset Boulevard, but I rode up to the Oriole house with the others because I wanted to see if my contract was there. I was drunk from drinking on the plane but managed to be the first person in the house, looking in the kitchen, living room, office, everywhere the mail might be. Though I'd told the agency to send the contract in a plain wrapper, there it lay on the desk in the office, the name of the agency on the envelope like a red flag. I was just shoving the envelope into the front of my trousers when Jo and Ronnie came into the office. I left quickly, went out the back door and stuck the contract in a low hedge of boxwood in the yellow light from the kitchen windows.

Back inside, I drank some raw milk, the first I'd had since we'd left for Dallas, hung about till it was time to go to the hotel, got in the car, waited for it to start, then said I'm forgetting something—ran around the corner of the house to the hedge, jammed the contract into my trousers, went back to the car. At the Hyatt House I put the contract in a drawer, fell into bed, and slept.

About three o'clock I got up, dressed, had breakfast in the coffee shop, then went to a drugstore and bought some stamps and a manila envelope for my contract. When I got back to my room the phone was ringing; it was Jo, organizing dinner for the Hyatt House contingent. I went along, with Jo, Ethan Russell, and some other people, but Jo had to stop by the Oriole house. Gram was there, and he, Keith, Charlie, and I started listening to records and the dining party left without me.

We listened to the Stones' first EP, then their second single, "I Wanna Be Your Man," with Brian's remarkable solo. Charlie was sitting on the couch with his back to the window, the lights of Los Angeles below. Keith flopped beside him. "What happened to Brian?" Charlie asked.

"He did himself in," Keith said. "He had to outdo everybody, do more. If everybody was taking a thousand mikes of acid, he'd take two thousand of STP. He did himself in."

Charlie nodded sadly. "It's a shame," he said. "Brian could do that"—nodding toward the record player—"without even trying."

Gram roared away on his motorcycle, going to get a record he wanted to play. Keith joined Jagger in one of the back bedrooms, where they sat hunched over guitars, Keith mumbling as he played, Mick listening. "It's the strongest thing they have together," Anita told me later. "Keith doesn't know what he's saying, but Mick can interpret it."

Charlie, Mick Taylor, and I listened to some jazz records and some by Furry Lewis, Fred McDowell, and Johnny Woods. Then Gram showed up with a Lonnie Mack record, and we listened to it while Charlie played a drum kit set up by the piano.

Earlier this evening Rock Scully and Emmett Grogan had been up to talk to Keith and Mick about doing a free show. Grogan was a founder of a San Francisco group called the Diggers, who supplied the community with food, clothes and political conscience. Now Gram, who had left a large chunk of hashish on the coffee table, couldn't find it, so we looked everywhere, under the sofa cushions, under the piano, in the icebox, all over the kitchen, in the office, on the floor. Keith came out then and searched in all the same places, finally deciding that Scully and Grogan had stolen it.

"Shit," Gram said. "I spent my last night's pay on that hash."

But Keith poured some cocaine onto a Buck Owens record sleeve and we forgot about the hash. Gram had a sore throat—the same sore throat Mick had created before the first show, everybody has had it at least once by now—and told us the Parsons Health Plan: "It's the drugs, they keep you healthy—that's what I tell all my health-food friends."

Gram left, and Keith and I talked about the still-unreleased new album. "The mastering fucked it up," Keith said. "We refused it. They equalized and limited it. Makes all the difference to a record."

Keith went back to play more with Mick, and Charlie asked me, "Is it worth going out to eat?" He was despondent now that Shirley and Serafina were gone. "It's not bad," he said, "I don't mind being on the road, I just don't like being in the house now that they're not here anymore."

We finally did go out, to the Times Square Delicatessen on Sunset and Doheny—drank Löwenbräu, ate blintzes and matzoh ball soup. Charlie cheered up a bit, told funny stories about English jazz players, but the beer came off the table at two o'clock, and we said goodnight.

Next morning at the Hyatt House I woke up at ten, called my agent, and asked what to do about the contract. "Just sign it and send it back," he said. I was eager to do that, but first we met—the lot from the Hyatt House and the Stones—at the Oriole house, from where we would go to CBS Television City, down by the Farmer's Market, and the Stones would tape two songs for the next Ed Sullivan show. "We wanted to do something more fah out," Mick had said at the Chicago press conference, "but there isn't anything more fah out. It doesn't matter what you do, because one minute you're a washing machine, the next, something else. It's like an antique show."

Up in the bird neighborhood, where the zoning codes were strict, it was a beautiful sunny day, flowers nodding in the gentle breezes. When we got to the house I made myself some toast and drank some milk. The city below us was hardly visible in the white smog. Furry Lewis was singing on the record player. Mick burst into the kitchen, remarked to the room at large, "I'm moving out tomorrow, this is a madhouse!" and went back the way he came. I followed him. Jo, on the couch talking on the phone to Steckler in New York, asked, "So when will the record be out?"

Keith, Charlie, Mick Taylor, and I sat around the living room listening to the blues while the sun shone. I tried to think of notes to make, but nothing was happening. Mary (of Kathy and Mary, the Dynamic Duo) had gone to fetch Wyman. Finally we decided to leave and let him meet us at the taping. We started out to the cars—being joined by

Michael Lydon and his bosomy red-haired girlfriend—as Mary drove up with Bill and Astrid. Standing beside the purple Continental, I said hello to Bill, sitting in the back seat close enough to touch, if he weren't behind a pane of glass, and he rolled his eyes toward heaven and appeared to pass out. Astrid, lowering her window, said, "Bill is seeck." We went back inside, Bill stretched out on the couch, and Jo called a doctor. The development seemed to have cheered Mick up, he was smiling.

"He's been taking antibiotics," Astrid said, sounding amazed at the peculiar little man she lived with. "He gets so afraid and starts imagining things—"

Jo told Mary where to take Bill and away they went. We went, Kathy driving the Stones, me driving Michael and his girlfriend, whose name was Lilith Leonards, out to TV City, a great grey building in the middle of a huge parking lot. Kathy drove to the gate, and I pulled up beside her. A guard told us there was no room to park inside; park outside and walk in. "I'm not walkin' any fuckin' place. Drive in," Mick said. Kathy did, and I followed, but there really was no place to park. I started to back out, nearly running over Mick, who was walking behind the car and slapped the trunk with his hand. We frowned at each other.

Inside TV City, we went past a desk, down a hall, and into the studio, passing men in rubber-soled shoes carrying small pine trees. Inside sound stage 31 there were a small audience, four Norelco color cameras, and lurking technicians. A little man wearing black lace-up shoes, white socks, gray slacks, a blue cardigan sweater, and horn-rim glasses said, "Mick, I'm Bob, your stage manager." He showed the Stones the way to makeup, and Michael, Lil, and I sat in the audience with Kathy, who told us more about herself. She had been living with Mary since she'd left Mary's brother, her husband, the father of her little girl. She and Mary had really got into rock and roll bands, and they'd known a lot of them. She gave us a long list including the Beatles, Led Zeppelin, and Terry Reid, but for two years they had wanted Mick Jagger. They'd be with a guy and then split and say, He was cool, but he's no Mick Jagger. When they finally got picked up by the Stones and were at the house, Mick went upstairs to bed, then came back down throwing Floris Sandalwood perfume on Kathy and Mary and asked Kathy, "Want to come upstairs?"

"My girlfriend has to come too," she said. (The Dynamic Duo had sworn to stick together.)

"Okay," Mick said.

"We were really disappointed," Kathy said. "He was so bad. When he's being himself, he can get it on. Fair. But we were just laughing at him. He tried to come on like Mick Jagger, all sexy—when he's himself, he's fair. When we came downstairs from Mick's room, we said, 'Well, he was cool, but he's no Mick Jagger.' We had to get Mick to get it out of our systems."

The Stones had returned from makeup and camera angles were being tested. Keith's gaunt face filled the monitor screen. "But it's Mr. Richards I really want," Kathy said. "He talks to Anita for like five hours every couple of days—their baby looks just like him, he has all these pictures of him. Anita puts the baby up to the phone and Keith talks to it and listens to him gurgle for hours."

While Kathy was talking, the background for the Stones had been set up: a lot of aluminum-foil-covered rectangles which looked—purposely out of focus on the monitor, with prismatic light-reflections—dreamy and rainbow-studded. Glyn Johns came in and came over to say hello. He had had a big hassle at the front desk trying to get in. "I told them, 'I have the Stones' backup tapes, if you don't let me in, they can't go on—' "

He went to set up the tapes, and Kathy continued: "Mick is so different from what I thought he'd be like— Sometimes he wakes up and says, 'Oh, Kathy, I feel so fragile this morning. Sometimes you feel butch and sometimes you feel fragile, and this morning I feel terribly fragile.' And I'd think, 'Wow, where is the Mick Jagger I used to dream about?' Mick drags himself up, shaves, puts on perfume, it takes him an hour to get up and then he usually doesn't say anything for an hour. Keith gets up, scratches his head, says, 'Hiya, Kathy,' bounces around—

"Mick says he used to playact and tell everybody to fuck off—'Now I'm being myself, and everybody tells me to fuck off.' He's great, so natural and sweet when we're alone, he'll tell me something he's going to tell Jo and ask me how it sounds, does it make sense, and I say, Sure, and I don't know what he's talking about. I mean, he's asking me, I can't believe it. But then one other person can come in and he's completely different; you can't communicate with him at all."

On the monitor, under the lights, behind Mick and Keith, both of them in black shirts, the tinfoil was glamorous. "But Terry Reid is the greatest," Kathy said. "He's ten times better than Mick."

The Stones had gathered around the drum kit, waiting to rehearse, nothing happening. Then the stage manager said, "Here we go, gentlemen," and the band track for "Honky Tonk Women" started. Mick skipped to the microphone, turned and started to sing. The others pretended to be playing, Keith taking all the solos. The record ended, Mick stopped singing and said, "Thank you, Mr. Sullivan, yes, we'll do another one, Mr. Sullivan," shaking hands with Sullivan, who wasn't there. But then, as if on cue, he was there; as they started taking the set apart and putting up another for the second run-through, Ed Sullivan appeared, a man resembling a fire hydrant, lighting a Winston, shaking the stage manager's hand. In Ed Sullivan's day there was hardly a comedian on television who didn't imitate his strange inflections, his unpredictable grinding of consonants, his stiff, spastic movements. Going from person to person, shaking hands, he seemed to be propelled by a silent mechanism that soon sat him down in a—chairr, to watch the changing of the—*tssett!* The tinfoil was being replaced by large flame-shaped pieces of plywood, painted white. Mick, laughing, leapt in the air, trotted over to us, and said, "D'you see that *set?*"

Sullivan, rising from his chair, asked, "Is Mick here?"

Mick stepped to Sullivan's side—one step—they shook hands and walked away together, Sullivan talking.

Michael and Lil were going to the Farmer's Market for a bite to eat, and they asked me if I'd like to come along. I wondered about getting back in, but I was hungry, and we walked across the parking lot to the Market. There were many stalls where they sold all kinds of vegetables and flowers and prepared food of different nationalities. We ate delicious Mexican and kosher food and went back to TV-Land. At the desk a woman asked us if we were on a list, and we said we were with the Stones and had just been out for lunch, so she quite reasonably let us pass. We went down the hall the same way we'd come out—but the place was so big and there were so many great orange doors that we forgot which way to go. Two guards, one old and tall, the other younger and squat, were coming down the hall. "Where you going?" the short one asked.

"We were with the Rolling Stones and we've sort of lost them," I said. "Just went out to lunch and lost our way back."

Neither of the guards said anything, and I turned to the tall one to see if I could make contact with him. "Could you show us the way to soundstage 31?" I asked, and suddenly like in a dream he grabbed my arm, saying in a light, dry, intense old-man's voice, "I'll show you the way you're going—you're going right back out the way you came."

I was frightened by this old lunatic who was tugging at my sleeve, trying to drag me away, and I started to pull away from him, all this happening in the underwater silence that seems at times to accompany violence. As I twisted my arm free, he started attacking me with his fists; weird, light blows like falling leaves, weightless as his voice, started raining down on my head. I was so embarrassed, humiliated, at being in this predicament, attacked by a mad helpless old man in a guard suit, that I threw my hands over my head and huddled against a wall. A puff of smoke would have toppled the guard, who stood flailing at me, his silly old hands flopping around my head and shoulders as Lil screamed in piercing tones, "Stop it! Stop it!"

Finally he stopped. "If you don't believe us, come to the front desk," Michael said to the other guard, who appeared a bit embarrassed himself.

I was trembling with the desire to throttle the old geek, but he was a weak old maniac and no great boot to destroy, and I knew if I did him in I probably wouldn't get to write the next scene. So I said, "You're an old man, you ought to know better than to behave like that." And he, lost in his mad fantasy of defense, like the last raving Confederate soldier, said, "I seen you swing at me. Come on! Come ahead! See what you get! Come at me!"

The other guard cleared his throat and said, "Well, if you are who you say you are, soundstage 31 is through the second door yonder."

"Well, we are," Michael said sincerely.

"Come on, let's get out of here," I said.

We went through the door and slipped into our seats beside Kathy. Nearly all the seats in the audience, maybe three hundred, were filled now, mostly with kids. Wyman had come in from the doctor's. He was smiling, he looked fine, wearing a red shirt, red suede pants, and a little brown suede vest of the sort he was partial to. Astrid sat down next to us. "He's still pale and trembly," she said. "The doctor gave him a vitamin shot, but he's very shaky. He'll talk to Stephen in the morning. That'll help him. He was the same way when Stephen was in South Africa with his mother. Bill had fever, he was all trembly—people can't understand him."

Coming in to sit in the row behind us was Little Richard (Penniman), the Georgia Peach. Richard was in green velvet, ropes of pearls on his bosom, hair puff-coiffed, got him a *do,* honey, Sheaffer Thinline mustache, cocoa makeup—he called himself "The Beauty." He was with two handsome black friends, a man and a lady. I said hello to Richard and told him that I was from Macon, where I did in fact graduate from high school. "Honey, you are jokin'! Did you know Otis Reddings?"

"Yes," I said, "Just before he died, we—"

"I give him his start! I give Otis Reddings his start! I was his idol! I give—you know Jimi Hendrix? I give Jimi Hendrix his start! He started out playing guitar with me in my band! I give the Beatles their first tour! I give the Stones their first tour! In England! Mick digs me, he came to see me—Mick! Come here!"

Mick loped over, shook hands, " 'Ello, Richard—"

"Why don't you tell the man to have me on his show, honey? Tell him he's had Liberace, now he can have the bronze Liberace—"

"Ohhh, Richard," Mick said.

"Rolling Stones insert, take one," a voice called over a loudspeaker, and Mick said, "I gotta go."

The lights changed and Ed Sullivan was barking at the camera: "You y'ngs'ers know, and of course your parents also, the Rolling Stones are the sensations of the of the of the—of the *world,* actually. Their last date with us was January sixteenth, 1967, with Pet Clark, Allan Sherman, and the Muppets. So let's have a big hand for the Rolling Stones! 'S 'ear it!"

And the Stones mimed while Mick sang "Gimme Shelter" to a backing track. As the song ended, Sullivan walked into camera range and shook hands with Mick: "Wonderful to have you here, and what are you gonna sing now?" Mick gazed into the sky as if he'd spotted a bluebird and said, "We're gonna go put on our flimsies and sing 'Love in Vain' and 'Honky Tonk Women.' "

The voice on the loudspeaker said, "Shelter—take two—stand by." Mick stood by, fidgeting thumbs across fingertips.

In the audience there were a boy in a red and green leprechaun suit and a fake long white beard and a tall, tanned, big-bosomed, blond girl, naked except for a few scraps of buckskin. She was dancing and clapping as Mick started to sing again. Kathy saw me watching her and said, "Mick saw her before you came back in and said, 'Oo's that cow?' "

On the monitor Keith grimaced, striking his guitar, ear-tooth shaking. "That Keith Richards is really a funky-lookin' cat, ain't he," Richard said.

When the second take ended, the Stones went to change. Richard asked me if I worked for the Stones, and I told him I was writing a book, travelling with them. He asked if my wife was with me, and I said, "No, she's at home."

"And you out here carryin' on, misbehavin'—"

"No, I'm bein' have," I said.

"You should get the Stones to promote your book for you! They should carry it around with them wherever they go! Listen to me! They can help you with that! Ed Sullivants came all the way out here from New York just to tape the Stones! Mick didn't want to go to New York, he and Keith wanted to stay out here and write music and rest, so Ed Sullivants had to come all the way out here!"

The Stones were back, wearing different clothes. Sullivan greeted them. "Mick, it's great to have you here with us, and what are you going to sing?"

"Ah, we're gonna sing 'Love in Vain,' " Mick said.

"All right," the loudspeaker voice said. "Let's take it."

A camera rolled in and Sullivan said the same thing. Mick started to repeat himself too, but it was silly answering the same question the same way, and Mick laughed.

"Cut," the loudspeaker said.

"Ed Sullivants offered Mick fifty thousand dollars to be on this show!" Richard said. "Mick don't care about the money, he just want to entertain the people!"

"Well, let's try it—" Sullivan was saying, "I won't ask you what you're gonna sing now, we'll just shake hands."

"Okay," Mick said, "we'll just shake hands."

"Mick don't care," Richard said. "He'll tell Ed Sullivants, Take that fifty thousand and buy you some shoes!"

The cameras rolled again, and Sullivan asked, "What are you gonna sing now?" Audience, Stones, cameramen all laughed.

"He a old man," Richard said, "and what he think of rock and roll it really like this"—gesturing thumbs down—"but he *need* the Rolling Stones for his *ra*-tings."

Sullivan and Jagger at last succeeded in shaking hands, and the Stones started "Love in Vain," Mick in an orange and black satin shirt with long trailing bat-sleeves and a wide black choker with dangling tiny gold coin medallions, glinting in the lights on the monitor. "That's beautiful," Richard said, "that choker." He lifted his ropes of beads and said, "I wear my pearls every day, honey. I say, if you got 'em, wear 'em."

"Love in Vain" ended, and Richard had to leave. He blessed us all and told me he hoped I sold "one billion." He was far too pretty to have gone on washing dishes at the bus station in Macon.

Before "Honky Tonk Women" started, Sam came up to Kathy and told her that the Stones wanted some chicks. "Just pick out some nice ones and ask if they'd like to meet the Stones, you know—"

"Okay," Kathy said. The song started, and there was a very pretty young girl, dressed in brown shirt and pants, very excited, standing up applauding. "That's the sort of girl Mick likes," Kathy said. "He really digs those young innocent-looking ones—but I don't think I can handle Sam's pimping duties for him."

"Honky Tonk Women" ended and the taping session was over. Kathy told Sam she thought he'd better handle it. In a moment he was leading away, back to the dressing rooms, the big blond in buckskin.

Michael, Lil, and I went out, the pretty little girl in the brown outfit ahead of us, smiling, lucky to be left with her dreams, into the purple dusk. Michael was going to his home in Elk, California, for the layoff between now and Detroit on November 24, six days away. We drove to Lil's apartment, on a side street off Sunset, to pick up Michael's green canvas duffel bag. He carried it across the sidewalk to the car, Lil watching him—not sorry, I thought, to see him go. I told her I'd call her later so she could help me mail my contract (since she's a local girl and knows the post offices) and took Michael to the airport in the same green Dodge Charger I'd driven before we left town.

On the freeway Michael was talking about women and how much he loved them and how sad it was for him and his wife to break up, but she was a writer and very jealous of his talent and so it didn't work out. He said he loved his little girl, he loved all women. "This girl Lil, she's a great girl," he said, "don't you think so?"

"Yeah, she's fine," I said. "I try not to get involved with people

myself, because it's all too fucking sad, you'll get your heart broken
enough times without going around looking for trouble."

"I've really been having a great time with women on this tour,"
Michael said. "I'm in love with them all, I guess I love all women."

Lots of luck, I thought. I let him out at the airport. It was night now
and I switched the lights on and headed back into the city. Just off the
freeway a billboard displayed a big book, a big can of paint, and the
message, "Harold Robbins paints with words in *The Inheritors*—The
best word in paints: Sinclair."

The car was almost out of gas, so I stopped at a service station. The
attendant was Indian, with blue-black raven hair, a redneck haircut, no
feathers, greasy green coveralls. I wondered what tribe he was from but
couldn't bring myself to ask, Who were your people, once-proud Red
Man?

I paid for the gas, drove to the Hyatt House and called Lil. She told
me to come over. I took the contract down to the desk and the night
manager let me Xerox it on the hotel's machine. Soon I was at Lil's
door. She opened it and said, "Oh! I thought you were the guy next
door, he's got some records the postman left with him because I wasn't
home." I came in feeling as if I were the wrong person. The apartment
was decorated to the hilt, like a set for Marlene Dietrich in a very lush
Von Sternberg movie. The front room was furnished with ostrich
plumes, fans, cushions, black gauze curtains. Lil was highly perfumed
and wearing a blouse that almost contained her bosom. She played
Frank Sinatra records and we talked about singers—Sylvia Syms,
Anita O'Day—and smoked excellent hashish. I didn't know exactly
what Lil did, except that she had designed covers for record albums.
She showed me collages she had made with photographs of the Stones'
faces and of parrots, dancing girls, various images that she seemed to
want me to "understand" in all their symbolic complexity.

The incense kept burning, and we kept smoking, and Lil played
peculiar music and finally announced that she was famished. I was too,
what with the length of the day, Ed Sullivan, apoplectic guards, and all
that, so I said, "Let me sign my contract and mail it and we'll go eat."
I was so stoned that moving was torturous, and the back of my neck
felt as if it were dissolving in hot water. I took the folded contract out
in its sky-blue wrapper and once again read every word, trying to believe
that after all the years since I was fifteen and, at Waycross High School,
decided that I was going to be a writer, and if I failed, I would die
trying—after all the time when I couldn't make a living at it and
Christopher and I had clung to straws of straight jobs and journalism—
here was the contract, its thighs open before me, and all I had to do
was sign it (or so, even if I didn't really believe it, I devoutly hoped)
and I would be paid real money, the kind you can live on. I couldn't

sign my name at first and wrote it several times on a sheet of notebook paper, then signed the contract and put it in an envelope addressed to my agent. I was also sending a copy home. "Where's the post office?" I asked.

"There's a box on the corner," Lil said, which wasn't what I'd had in mind for such a grand document, but I had some stamps and decided to risk it. Lil asked what sort of eating place I wanted to go to and I told her someplace where they left you alone. I know just the place, she said, and she did. On the plane to Oakland, in the *L.A. Times' West* magazine, I had read a story about it: Musso and Frank's Grill, a restaurant on Hollywood Boulevard favored by writers including Scott Fitzgerald, Robert Benchley, and William Faulkner, where in the 1920s Charlie Chaplin, too busy to leave the movie set, would send his Rolls every day to pick up his lunch. Hollywood Boulevard, in those days, "was . . . strangely appealing . . . with an avocado grove toward Sunset, a stream running down Franklin, a eucalyptus tree in the parking lot and a manager at a marble-fronted Owl Drug Store on Highland, who wore a morning coat with a carnation in the buttonhole. . . ."

In 1969, the place was probably very much as it was when Dorothy Parker, Nathanael West, and S. J. Perelman ate there. You got a table with clean white linen and it was understood that you had come in because you were hungry and thirsty. No music, only warm friendly ghosts. The waiter brought us drinks (tiny needles of ice in my gimlet) and delicate whitefish and roast spring lamb and sand dabs and cognac and coffee. As we ate Lil told me a story which, if I weren't hearing it in such a pleasant and comfortable place, would cause me to tremble. It concerned the time that Lil Leonards was in Los Angeles, her hometown, reading the best-selling war novel by Moses Ringer, a book called *Flying Backwards*. It seemed to her a good and funny book, and it seemed the man who wrote it must be a fine fellow indeed, and just the sort one would like to meet. "So I wrote him a letter," Lil said, "telling him that I was sitting at a bus stop on Sunset Strip, wearing a wet bathing suit, reading his book, and—"

"Were you?" I asked, naive child.

"Of course not," she said. "I told him a lot of things and he answered my letter and we got to know each other and he flew me to New York." She told me the details of how she had put him in a position where he'd had no choice. I was terrified by the story, but we finished the meal. Lil told the waiter how good it was and he asked her, "Have you ever been here before? I know *you* have," he said, meaning me.

"I've never been here before," I said.

"I thought you were a regular," he said. That cheered me up. We went back to Lil's, where the night turned mauve. We smoked hash until I was once again swimming in a sea of warm molasses. Lil asked me what I thought of the Stones. I said that they were a new band in a way since Brian died.

"Yes," she said, "now they know that they will die—"

Lil brought out some unpublished poetry by Jim Morrison and began to read it aloud. Since I just came over to mail a letter, I thanked her and left. It was after midnight, but when I reached the Hyatt House I drove past, deciding to check on the Oriole house to see what was happening.

As I came into the living room, Jo, Mick, and Ronnie came out of the office. Kathy, Mary, Sam, Tony, Keith, Gram, Mick Taylor, and Charlie were around. Gram was passing around a 35-millimeter film can of cocaine. Soon he and Keith were sitting at the piano singing. Mick joined them, and I relaxed in front of the fireplace, talking to Kathy about my peculiar evening with Lil. A couple of girls came in, one of whom, blond and rather pretty, was Linda Lawrence, Brian's old girl-friend. With her was a small boy wearing snakeskin boots, a velvet suit, and long blond hair—Brian's son, Julian, looking exactly like him, like a miniature Brian, same hair, same face, same eyes. Linda sat down before the fire, a joint was passed her, she took a couple of hits, and Julian went by, bouncing a large many-colored balloon in the air.

"Want something?" Linda asked him.

"No." He shook his head and went on across the room, following the balloon, keeping it in the air with his tiny hands that were, like his father's and grandfather's, almost as wide as they were long. Gram and Keith were on the piano bench, Mick on the couch, leaning over the back, the three of them singing unintelligible hillbilly songs. The room had a rhythm, but Julian didn't seem part of it. He wasn't bouncing around the room like a child, he was quietly and lightly, in an almost unearthly way, walking or dancing around the room, like a silent ballet dancer, following the balloon, which leapt and danced over his head, leapt at the touch of his fingers.

DANCE TO THE DEATH

We are in the trailer with the condiments and cookies, Mick in the doorway head down in the bright movie lights, his burgundy newsboy cap hiding his face, listening to the radio interviewer. "Mick, do you and the Stones intend to go on touring?"

"Yeah, we aim to stay on the streets. We dug doing this tour, actually, more than the others. We got into playing a bit more, we could hear ourselves occasionally."

"What do you think of this gathering?"

"It reminds me of when we were in Marrakech the—Keith and I were in Marrakech the last time, outside the city walls, there were a great many musicians and dancers, very medieval."

Sam Cutler, sitting at the trailer's kitchen table with Keith, Chip Monck, and Rock Scully, his eyes red in a grey-white bristly face, says, "You should go on about five P.M. Sunset's at twenty to six."

"Are you ready to split, Keith?" Mick asks.

"I'm stayin'," Keith says.

"Okay. See you soon."

We step down from the trailer. Ronnie is standing by in his grey business suit. Keith is staying. He likes it here. I can't get over feeling that it is a pity, even if we could save the world it is a drag to have to go into the desert to do it, which I suppose Moses must have felt also. And it is cold, the cold has finally reached us even in California, after days in Muscle Shoals, Alabama, where the people were sincere and polite and we had as a result a peaceful and pleasantly exciting time. Now we are back among the limos, the lead suits, the ring of the cash-box, the smell of the shill. And so we are out of gas, Bill Belmont scurrying around looking for a cop; the driver, hands folded, gazing heavenward like the Holy Mother in a pietà—as if he were (it is a look we have seen before) delighted to be singlehandedly bringing the whole of an enormous enterprise to a halt through his own ineptitude. An enormous enterprise—to save the world is a joke phrase but how *could you express what we are about, much less explain—I was about to say why salmon take such pains to spawn or grunion run headlong out of the sea on their little wobbly tails, but those are fish and we are—what are we? Who could say, and who could say how old was this instinct that led us to dance and get high and go mad? What brings us here is an impulse toward freedom as old perhaps as life, but still strong enough by the time man could threaten all life on earth to touch Brian Jones, he was more than a little touched by it and set out with a fanaticism that swept along Keith and Mick and Perks and Watts the noted brush-drummer, and Stu, and in fact all of us now standing around in the early morning hours of the day before Pearl Harbor Day's twenty-eighth observance.*

As the limo is loaded with fuel Belmont has found somewhere, Mick is asking the Maysles brothers if they'll be staying. "There should be filming starting at dawn," he says.

"Oh, sure," David says. "We'll stay." Al looks at him. They have been with us all the last sleepless night in Muscle Shoals, across the country with us, behind us in another car as we drove out from San Francisco, and now Mick on his way back to the hotel asks them if they'll be staying for a second sleepless night.

"We'll have a helicopter bring out some film stock," David says.

"See you later, Measles," Ronnie says, as he Mick and I board the limo, all sitting abreast on the wide rear seat.

"They will stay, won't they?" Mick asks.

"Yeah, they'll stay," Ronnie says. "I'll make sure they get some film."

Mick seems pleased and excited, and why not? This is what the Stones —all of us?—have been after all along (though I regret, as I stodgily kept saying, the necessity for abandoning all the good works of history along with the bad—the Ellington band, Bach, the flush toilet, and other great works of man's ingenuity seem to be undervalued by the rock audience), no matter what it took, abandonment of what refinements and conveniences, it was necessary to seek an alternative. So here we are, thousands of strangers coming together in a strange place like some mad sect prophesying Apocalypse—Shakers, Holy Rollers; roll over, Beethoven, dig these rhythm & blues. But why this place? Though it does fulfill Spengler's requirement that the Fall should come, the De-cline should reach its climactic moment, on the westernmost point of the West, and in fact they had first talked of Golden Gate Park, the Golden Gate to the Orient, as the site for this, this. . . .

"How'd we get this place?" I ask Ronnie. We are away from the

*stage now, driving very slowly, gently, through the steady onward press
of young people with their baskets and sleeping bags and jugs and dogs.
It is so late and we have been up for so long that, even with the cocaine,
Ronnie's voice comes and goes in and out of my hearing. Something
about no rock in the park, so this fellow offered this place mostly for
the publicity after they tried to get Sears Point Raceway, which was
owned by Filmways, which was partly owned by Haskell Wexler's
mother. Wexler had been in L.A. and had shown Mick half of* Medium
Cool, *his Chicago '68 Democratic convention riot movie, and he had
been asked to do the Stones film, but he had other commitments. Anyway, the Sears Point people had offered to let the Stones have the site
for just the weekend rental but then Filmways (who also owned Concert
Associates, who'd promoted the Stones' L.A. Forum shows) became
interested and demanded hundreds of thousands in deposits and
millions of dollars of insurance plus distribution rights to the film shot
at the festival. So here we are at Altamont. It doesn't make a hell of
a lot of sense to me, but it has been a while since much of anything has,
especially anything related to upper-echelon show-biz wheels and deals.
I can't see what Haskell Wexler's mother has to do with it. "So how
much is it costing the Stones?"*

"Nothing," Ronnie says. "The film rights will pay for it."

"That's nice," I say. "It really is a free show."

*"It's free," Mick says, slumped under his cap, "but it still has to be
paid for. Maybe we can sell bits of the film to TV—maybe Tom Jones
would buy a couple of numbers." We have come to a stop behind some
other cars lined up before the gate, and people are crowding around
the limousine. "I wanted to do all the shows free," Mick says, "but that
was before I talked to the accountants. I'd like nothing better than to
do a free show on the East Coast." There are kids at the window now,
knocking, and Mick finds the button to slide it down. The driver is
honking the horn, though the other cars are parked and empty and
are not about to move by themselves.*

*"Are you real?" a girl is asking Mick. She has long dark hair and
is bundled up in a heavy green stadium coat. "Is it really you?"*

"Yeah, I'm real, are you real?" Mick says.

*She reaches in, taking his hand—"Let us in," she says, "it's so cold
out here," but Mick is tired and wants to sleep, so he says, "Are you
havin' a good time?"*

"Yeah, who are they?" the girl says, looking at me and Ronnie.

*"Just some friends," Mick says, but the girl seems—though maybe
I'm crazy with dope and no sleep—sort of paranoid. "Are you havin'*

*a good time?" Mick asks again as the gate guard comes over, wearing
a beige rent-a-cop uniform, and says to the people around the limo,
Would you please move so this car in front here can move so this car
can move so the one behind it can move so we can get this other car
out? All right?* Grumbling gently, hip but tractable like in a 1956 movie,
Don't Knock the Rock *or whatever, the kids fall back and we pull away
and Ron with the gold heart says, "The kids are so lovely," and Mick
says, "Yeah, they're gettin' down with it, that's what you have to do."
And they really are—there really is something about them, they are
definitely getting down with it, and Mick's saying this while slumped
in the back seat of a Cadillac limousine on the way to the cool white
sheets of a Nob Hill hotel seems incongruous. I am by no means sure
why I'm going back to the hotel myself instead of staying out here with
this giant beast of humanity, and I say in reply, "Yeah, that's what
Keith's doing."*

*"I'd like to stay but I've got to rest," Mick says, and I say, "Yeah,
Keith's fantastic," and Mick says, "I've got to sing—if I had to play
the guitar tomorrow I think I'd stay, but I've got to sing."*

*The cars in front have been moved and we roll out the gate, the
guard locking up behind us against the hundreds of people who are
outside, hundreds or thousands of the hundreds of thousands who'll
be coming.*

*"If it's free, why are they keeping people out?" Mick asks, ever
the avenger of injustice.*

"They can come in at seven," Ronnie says.

*"Seven?" Mick says, obviously not thinking much of this answer,
but Ronnie says, "If you let them all in you'd never get the stage set
up," and Mick says, "Yeah," settling back, then asks, "What about the
people already in there, though?"*

"They have to go out in the morning."

"What?" Mick asks.

"Joke," Ronnie says.

*We are slowly proceeding the hell outa here, and now in the near-
dawn hour the pilgrims are increasing, a steady stream of them on both
sides of the car in their rough clothes and long hair, bleached out in
the headlights' glare. I'm wondering whether I should leave, whether
I should miss a minute of this mass phenomenon that I do not even
like the looks of. Wherever we have been before, none of us has ever
been alone in the desert with hundreds of thousands of other young
freaks, the Rolling Dead, all kinds of dope and* no *rules!* DO WHAT THOU
WILL: *that shall be the whole of the law. At Woodstock, a commercial*

event which turned into something else, a détente existed between people and police, because the police were outnumbered, but here you couldn't find the police even if you wanted, we are free, free at last.

But right now it is cold and uncomfortable and if I am not going to be among the walking dead when sunset comes, I have to sleep. I know we won't be at the hotel long, and I want to get my tape recorder and a little rest because I am tired, and I want some rest between me and what the dawn will bring. But still, uncomfortable and cold and mad and lost as it might appear, a lot of people are showing up, and anything might happen, just anything.

"I'd like to get some mescaline for tomorrow," Mick says, also watching the people stream past. "Like to take some after the show."

"Like to take some before the show," I say.

"No, I have to sing, I can't sing if I'm stoned, I'll be freakin' out all over the stage—"

"I've got some, we can take it whenever you want," I say.

"Do you? Great, I haven't had any psychedelics in a couple of years. I'd like to take some and just wander around in the crowd and talk to the people."

"All right, I'll take some with you," I say, "but I don't know, man, you believe all this generation-revolution hype a lot more than I do."

"No I don't; I don't, I'm just thinking about the film, that's all. It's going to be very interesting for the film. If we travel next year as well, and go to the East and maybe Africa—I'd like to have all sorts of different music, African music, oriental music, native things, if we do a world tour I'd like to show a lot of strange musical and exotic, uh, erotic things—like these chicks I saw in Bangkok—you went to this place, it was like a whorehouse only it wasn't, you come in and there are all these chicks on this red carpet behind this sort of glass curtain, and they're all wearing white socks and blue jeans and T-shirts with numbers, very weird, they all look like—what d'you call them, cheerleaders—and you pick the one you want, like, 'Numbah fifty-two, please,' and they take you away and do w'atever, tread on you, massage you, suck your cock—you can't make it with them there but you can make a date to take them someplace else and fuck them. It was so strange, like Alphaville, *sort of weird science-fiction atmosphere. There was a concert there too, native music, they were really gettin' it on—I mean it was much better than most rock and roll, more exciting. I think that would entertain people—I really do, I mean I'm entertained by that sort of thing, and you could cut in all sorts of things, us playing and then maybe some African drums—just do it like* The Ed Sullivan

Show, *I mean I don't think there's anything wrong with that form,
inherently, just putting one thing after another, as long as the things are
interesting—"*

"It would have to be done right, though," Ronnie says, "or it would
just be *Around the World with the Rolling Stones.*"

"Well, that—what's wrong with that?" Mick asks.

"Seems as if you'd need something more," I say.

"It'll develop as you do it," Ronnie says, "you don't have to worry
about it in detail now. First you should get some bread for it. Ahmet
can probably get you half a million from Warner's with a treatment."

"What could be in a treatment?" Mick asks. "An itinerary, maybe.
We don't know where we're gonna go yet. We've got so many things to
decide next year, which is the best record company—"

"Man," I say, "I tell you, Atlantic—"

"Only Atlantic is hip enough to—" Ronnie and I are in agreement
for the first time since we have known each other.

"We'll just have to talk to them all," Mick says.

I open my eyes. We are on the highway now, still in the pitch-black
night. We have been riding along talking with our eyes closed. Mick is
quiet. It is impossible to tell whether he is sulking or just trying to
sleep. Then he says, "I think a film of the Rolling Stones around the
world would be interesting. I'd go to see that film."

"Well, it just depends what's in it, that's what gets the people," I
say. "What the story is, what's at stake. Like that movie I hallucinated
about you all with Bill the Sinister Vicar and Charlie the Mute but
Honest Gravedigger and Brian the Wicked Renegade who lives with
some gypsies on the edge of your estate, the mad gleeful Spirit of Chaos
hangin' around the place, and Keith your evil Alter Ego and your wife
and baby under threat of death because of the ancient curse, you know,
there has to be something at stake—"

"Oh, my old lady and all that fell apart on me," Mick says. "If you
have children you have a family life and if you don't it all falls apart."

We ride on in silence. After a long time, or what seems a long time,
Mick says (on the plane to San Francisco he had been talking to Charlie
about marriage and loving one woman and how do you keep it together,
so maybe talking about it now reminded him of Charlie), "I wish
Charlie could have seen it. He was very upset, he thought it was all
going wrong."

I can't see what you could tell from what we saw that would be
reassuring—it is too vast and ponderously pregnant to be named yet—
but Mick says, "He felt he was sucked into it—because he really doesn't

have much money and they don't know that he really could use the money—I could have done the whole tour free because I'm big shit, y'know, and I've got money, but he hasn't and he has a family and could use it—wish he could have seen how nice it is out there—we'll leave a note under his door."

23

And when one can have no more brilliant dinners and make love to no more women, when one has no longer appreciative companions to listen to one's stories and can no longer travel and try one's luck—one can at least summon one's intellectual resources, work at problems, write one's memoirs; one can still test one's nerve and strength by setting down an account of life as one has found it, with all its anticlimax and scandal, one's own impossible character and all. The writing of the *Memoirs* represented a real victory of the mind and the spirit. Scoundrels like Casanova do not usually put themselves on record, and when they do they are usually at pains to profess the morality of respectable people. . . . But when all Casanova's obeisances to the established authorities have been made, life itself in his story turns out to be an outlaw like him.

  EDMUND WILSON:
  "Uncomfortable Casanova," *The Wound and the Bow*

ONE AFTERNOON at my grandfather's house near the Okefenokee Swamp, where I heard the sounds in the night, I was sitting on the front porch, listening to a Ray Charles record that I had played on my grandfather's Sears, Roebuck record player. I was just out of high school and about to move with my parents from Macon to Memphis. It was summer and I was visiting my grandparents. Their house was set in the shade under two sycamores at a crossroads in the little turpentine camp where the roads from Waycross and Homerville headed, past the shotgun houses of the quarters, toward Pearson and Mexico, Georgia. A black girl from the quarters heard the record and came and sat on the steps of the screened porch. We talked a bit about Ray Charles and Memphis before my grandfather came and chased her away. Neither of us had been to Memphis, but we knew it was the home of the blues.

"Memphis," Sleepy John Estes said, "has always been the leader of dirty work in the world." In the years I had lived in Memphis I had found the blues, though it wasn't easy. The first time I went to Beale Street I was thrown out of a Ray Charles concert for sitting at a table with some black classmates from newly integrated Memphis State University. But I had managed to sweep the streets with Furry Lewis, throw up at Elvis Presley's ranch (overdosed on Darvon by Dewey Phillips, the first man to play an Elvis record on the radio), drink Scotch for breakfast with B. B. King, watch Otis Redding teach Steve Cropper "The Dock of the Bay," and now I was raiding the country with the Rolling Stones.

I flew home from Los Angeles thinking of my grandfather and how he had loved my grandmother, who died last year. I thought, with the contract signed and payment in the offing, that we were very fortunate, Christopher and I, and as I drank as usual too much while thousands of feet in the air, I developed quite a mood, hopeful and elegiac.

Getting home didn't exactly shatter my mood, but it made me grim. Christopher was still waiting, still sick. It seemed that unless I was working in Memphis, the city affected me like a shot of morphine. I intended to get a passport, go to the dentist, do all sorts of things, but I spent the week sitting on the couch, staring into space, waiting.

On Monday, November 24, the Stones would play Detroit, but I wanted to go to New York, see my agent and find out when and how much I would be paid. By the following day the Stones would be at the Plaza, and I figured to meet them there.

My flight was nonstop, and I slept until the safety belt chimes rang and I woke to see muddy water only a few feet, it seemed, below the window as we came in for a landing at Kennedy Airport. I called the agency and talked to the first lieutenant, who said he was going out to lunch and I should call him when I got into town. I rode the crowded, dismal bus past drifts and piles of dirty snow to the East Side Terminal. It was raining.

New York always affects me in the same way—as I came into it I puffed up like a toad for protection against the coldness and lonesomeness of it, the giant apartments you saw coming in from Kennedy, one

great redbrick wasteland of the human spirit over on the right with
ancient whitepainted sign NOW RENTING APARTMENTS 2½ - 3 - 4 ROOMS
SUITABLE FOR RETIREMENT and just past there on the same side of the
bus a cemetery, white headstones stretching into the distance. Coming
into New York I got something like a mescaline rush, because whether
you came in through the miasma of industrial corruption in Newark or
the misery of little boxes on the Kennedy side, you were reminded of
the fragility and shortness of your life, and your blood began to pump
faster in order that you should be more alive. At least it was that way
with me. The first time I came to New York was in 1963, the year
before the Stones came to the United States. I went to see my friend
Danny Freeman, who was in Greenwich Village at Saint Vincent's
Hospital dying of cancer at twenty-three.

After the approach, Manhattan Island seemed at first almost pastoral
—old wooden houses, a bicycle on the stoop, a small supermarket with
the specials in the window—and you did not feel the girders pressing in,
the skyscrapers meeting over your head, until about 42nd Street. By the
time you reached one of the Terminals, any philosophic remove was
gone, and you could only confront all of it from your own small height.
I got off the bus and called my agent, whose assistant suggested I come
over in a couple of hours, leaving me with a moral dilemma. I knew a
place on 58th Street, not too far from the agency, where I could knock
two hours dead. I called my friend Cynthia.

In 1961, when I met her, Cynthia (she had had three or four other
names since then) was fifteen years old. I was nineteen, an intense
young karate student and teacher. Cynthia was theater-struck; maybe
she thought the karate school (dojo) was an oriental dance class. But
she came in with her slightly older friend Jane. The owner of the
dojo wound up marrying Jane, who wound up committing suicide,
dead by her own hand at the age of twenty-one. When Cynthia was
twenty-one—on her birthday—she called me from a hospital, where
she had been taken after attempting and failing suicide, though she had
made it look good, taking a colossal overdose of sleeping pills. I was
working so hard when I first knew her—going to college every day,
teaching karate every night and eight hours on Saturdays—that sometimes Cynthia would come up (second-floor dojo with a couch in back)
and I would be too tired to do anything but look. Then we both left
Memphis and I lost track of her for several years, but she always
called me. Six months or a year or two would pass and the phone would
ring at 2:00 A.M. and it was Cynthia, or whatever she was calling
herself. I was always, *almost* always, happy to hear from her—she'd be
having an abortion in Denver or escaping a narcotics bust in California
or being a beach groupie in Hawaii—I was living like a mole all this
time trying to become a writer, and it pleased me to hear from her, as

I would tell the telephone company when they'd call me to ask why she never paid the phone bills. She's too busy living, I'd say, Isn't it wonderful the good times these young folks can have.

The name she was using now, so pretentious and phony a stripper couldn't have stayed in business with it, nevertheless, combining the French words for alone, love, cat, and night, told you a lot about Cynthia and made her easy to find in the Manhattan directory. I rang and she answered. I recognized her voice, but just to be sure I asked if she was in, using her current name. She said, This is she. I said, I find that hard to believe. Come on over, she said, we never do anything but talk on the phone.

Oppressive and scary though it was, it was fun to be in New York. For the Rolling Stones and for me this tour, this time, was a test, to see if we could survive on our own terms. When I was nearly twenty-six years old, living in Memphis, unpublished, and fearful of loss, of failure, of a wasted life, I would awaken every morning and look into the mirror that sat facing the bed at the end of the room, see myself a day older and feel my fear and frustration lifting my body. I had the actual physical sensation of being lifted by the force of will and desire toward my life and work. As I rode in a cab up Fifth Avenue, I felt the same mixture of fear and exhilaration.

Cynthia lived on the seventh floor of a big apartment building. I stood in the hall with my suitcase, ringing the bell, but no one came to the door. I knocked, rang again, and finally, as I was about to give up, the door opened slightly. "Who is it?"

"Dewey Phillips," I said. The door opened a bit more; I looked in and there was Cynthia, wearing a towel. She had never looked so good. She had lost her baby fat, and Cynthia always had lovely white skin—a bit damp now, as she had been taking a bath. Her hair was still black, blacker than God makes it. I suppose Cynthia's hair was dark brown, but as long as I'd known her she had dyed it black. Paint it black, Cynthia.

"Bring your suitcase in," she said. "Put it down. Now that I've got you, you're staying for a while."

I dropped the suitcase and followed her through the big living room to the bedroom. Cynthia sat before a dressing table and started taking pins out of her hair, which fell onto her shoulders. Cynthia was from Boston; I'm not sure how she came to Memphis, but her permissive mother and father were divorced, and Cynthia's behavior appeared to be textbook simple, an attack on her absent parent. She had been very promiscuous, putting it mildly, had slept with me and most of my friends and a great many other people. What made Cynthia even more of a textbook case was that she herself never had an orgasm. For her sex was a compulsion that brought no satisfaction. To an idiot like me there was something appealing about a sexy girl who was frigid. As Cynthia raised her arms, reaching to the hairpins, her bosom rose, the towel dropped, and she was naked to the waist in the mirror, where our eyes met.

Some time later, when Cynthia asked "Did you finish?" I could hardly believe it. What was the meaning of all that screaming?

"Unh hunh," I said.

"If I could have you all the time, I think I could get over being frigid."

"You have me," I said.

"But for how long?"

"Well," I said, "I do have to see my agent—"

But not before a bath in a deep old enameled iron tub with Cynthia telling how she always knew one day I'd come to her because there I am in her fifth house of marriage, it's all in the stars, she wants to have my baby, that's the way God planned it. As she talked I was taken into her weird world; she'd been in New York for a couple of years, doing auditions. In all the time I'd known her, the only actual stage work that Cynthia had done was at Front Street Theatre in Memphis where in a special children's production of *The Wizard of Oz* she played a munchkin. Now she was ready for me to write her life story, she said as we bathed.

On the wall was a piece of poster paper with the word REVOLUTION, the R crossed out, and Cynthia wanted me to help her get it copyrighted or patented or whatever you're supposed to do. She didn't want much, just marriage and children and her life story and patents and copyrights and would I mind going out and buying a quart of milk and a hundred-watt light bulb? There's a little grocery right around the corner. . . . I did it, brought back milk and bulbs and said, I've got to go, see you when I get back from the agency.

"When will you be back?" Cynthia asked. "Are you going to take me out tonight?"

"Take you out? Out where?"

"To dinner, and then we could go someplace and dance. Are you going to introduce me to the Stones?"

Oh, Mick would love that, I thought, this is just what he needs. "Well, I'm not sure how long I'll be," I said. "I'll call you."

I went down to the street and hailed a cab, whose driver didn't want to go down Fifth Avenue in the four o'clock rush hour traffic, but of course he did, complaining all the way. At the agency I gave my name to the girl at the switchboard, who seemed to recognize it, but I thought she had probably been trained always to give writers that impression. She smiled at me as if she knew some secret I didn't know, and did she ever.

My agent's first lieutenant, a thin pale young man, told me that my book would have to sell thirty thousand hardback and three hundred thousand paperback copies to pay off the advance. If it kept on selling, if dreamy little *shiksas* kept coming out of the woodwork and wriggling down to the drugstore to buy the dark saga of the Rolling Stones, I might make more money. He took out his pencil and paper and worked it out, encouraging me in my delusion. Lessee now, thirty thousand here, three hundred thousand there—shit, boy, you gonna be rich.

I asked when I should meet the publishers and he said, looking at my jeans and leather jacket, Maybe we should get you some money before we let them see what you look like. Who was he protecting? Me, bless his heart. If the publishers had seen how fatheaded and ignorant I was, they wouldn't have given me two cents, would have swept me right out of the office. But there I was, young and dumb, walking out of the agency, looking at the clients' book-jackets displayed on the walls— books by geniuses, Nobel prize winners—and feeling good about it. just like I was supposed to. Step right up, folks, they're alive, they're on the inside.

From a phone booth on Fifth Avenue I called Pete Callaway, who told me to come up. I took a cab up the West Side to 157th Street, then under a motorbridge and up to where Riverside Drive goes off in seven different directions. Pete lived on one of that intersection's many corners in an old redbrick apartment building. He had been there for years, growing balder and wider, waiting in vain for a Ph.D. in Philosophy from Columbia University.

Pete and I had been among the very few beatniks in central Georgia. In 1961, when I was living in Memphis, we went to San Francisco together, met Lawrence Ferlinghetti and Alan Watts and scored our first grass and had a fine time. In the last five years—except for the Columbia riots—Pete had hardly moved. With his German wife, Edith, we smoked grass and drank Scotch and then went down to Pete's little sister Nicole's apartment in the Village, on Waverly Place.

The last time I had seen Nicole, she and her mother had come to New Orleans to take home Pete and his books. She was coltish and angular, seventeen and suntanned. We had admired each other. That was five years ago. But I remembered Nicole most vividly as an awkward child with funny spaceman glasses and a little starched yellow cotton dress, sitting on the floor at one of her mother's cocktail parties, eating great spoonfuls from a muskmelon filled with pineapple sherbet, one of her mother's friends saying, "Go right ahead, Nicole dear."

Now waves of chestnut hair spilled onto her shoulders that would, if they could have been seen in a 1930s backless cocktail gown in the smoky air of Café Society Downtown (a place distinguished among other ways by being the only nightclub Eleanor Roosevelt ever visited),

have caused the world to forget the shoulders of Myrna Loy. Nicole was
at the Sorbonne when its riots answered Columbia's, but her head was
too pretty to crack. She did graduate work at New York University
but left without taking a degree and was now working for *Newsweek*.
In her rose satin cowboy shirt and Naugahyde jeans she was not boyish
—she was tall and shapely, with small breasts, long elegantly tapering
fingers, startling iris-blue eyes, and an endearing tendency to get high
and mouth-breathe. We went out to dinner, then went back to Nicole's
apartment and smoked more grass, drank wine, and listened to records
—the Stones, the Burritos, Otis, Aretha—until the cold grey dawn.
When we left, I told Nicole I'd see her again before I left town.

Pete and Edith dropped me at Cynthia's. I had her key, but the chain
was on the door. She let me in, all wrapped with black gauze. She asked
where I'd been and I said I'd been to see a television producer and
had fallen asleep on his couch. I undressed and got into bed, exhausted.
"I think I'll take this negligee off, I don't really need it," Cynthia
said, slipping it off and sliding up against me. "Argh," I said, and fell
asleep.

I woke at eleven o'clock, when Cynthia got up, and someone rang the
doorbell many times while I lay with my head under a pillow, insisting
that I would go on sleeping. But it was no use. The Stones were now at
the Plaza, so I called and asked for Jon Jaymes. "Come on over," he
said, and told me my room number. Now that the Stones were here I was
feeling guilty about being away from the action, so I got dressed and
ready. Cynthia had put on her model face and garb, and I was impressed, she looked just like one of those girls in the magazines, except
perhaps for something unusual about the eyes. I asked her to come along
and have lunch.

When we got downstairs I started looking for a cab. But Cynthia
said, We don't need a cab, it's only about a block and a half to the Plaza.
But I'm carrying a suitcase, I said. You can carry it that far, Cynthia
said. I did, but it seemed silly, arriving at the Plaza on foot, carrying
your own suitcase, like Woody Guthrie arriving at a hobo jungle under
a railroad bridge.

We came in the back door. I told the two men at the desk my name,
they went away and came back all smiles, Sorry to keep you waiting. A
bellman took my suitcase and up we went to the thirteenth floor and a
small double room overlooking Central Park. You could see the dark
naked branches of the trees against the fallen snow and the circular ice
rink with tiny figures in bright-colored coats and mufflers skating
silently far below us.

The bellman left, and Ethan Russell looked in and said that nothing
was happening, the Stones were still asleep. I no longer felt guilty about

being away from the action, since there wasn't any, so Cynthia and I began to dally. I discovered that she was wearing wonderful purple underpants, decorated with drawings and names of the signs of the zodiac. A few moments passed, and Cynthia gasped. "I'm sure I'd get over being frigid if I were around you for a while," she said, slipping off my lap to kneel beside the bed. "You deserve to be thanked." But she had only begun to thank me when there came a loud knock and the door opened: "Maid service." Luckily I had chained it. We gave up for the moment and went downstairs to eat.

At the Edwardian Room they wouldn't let me in without a tie. "Try the Palm Court," the headwaiter said.

"No no, you must have tie and regular sport jacket," said the Palm Court's headwaiter.

"But at the Edwardian Room they said to come here."

"No no, you cannot—"

"But I'm a guest—"

"No no, you cannot—"

"But we're *hungry*," Cynthia said.

"Ah," said the headwaiter, "we cannot let such a beautiful lady go hungry—I lend you a tie."

I put on the Palm Court's skinny black necktie and the headwaiter seated us. "Thank you," Cynthia said.

"Madam," he said, "I am from Verona, a city of romance."

We ate salads and went back upstairs. I sat down on the bed, Cynthia sitting beside me. I was just starting to be rewarded when the door opened. I went into the bathroom to tuck in my shirttails. I heard a voice: "Hi, I'm Michael, who are you?"

"Don't start," I said, coming out of the bathroom.

"Detroit was far out," Michael said. "There were two thousand kids at the airport and the shows were great, very aggressively political crowds—"

We sat around talking as the day grew darker and the lights came on, the skaters in the park moving to unheard music on an island of white in the blackness, and it was time for Philadelphia. Cynthia wanted to go to the show, but I told her there wouldn't be room in the limos. She didn't believe me, but she let me walk her home. Inside her apartment, I sat on the couch in the living room, and Cynthia said, "I never got a chance to give you your reward."

Afterward, she went away to wash and came back smiling, brushing her damp clean hair. It was a pleasant moment. Cynthia was not going to get what she wanted, and I was not going to get what I wanted, but neither of us knew it yet. I struggled away from her, promising to come back after the show—I wouldn't—and walked in the cold, slicing wind back to the Plaza.

Michael and some of his friends were in the room he and I were supposed to share but wouldn't because Michael was staying with another girl. After belittling Michael for his womanizing, here I'd been doing the same thing. Michael danced around the room, telling me about Cecil Beaton taking photographs of Mick while I was out. I started to make a few notes, but as I began to write, the call came that we should go downstairs and board the limousines.

They were from a company called Head Limos, which catered mostly to rock stars and was supposed to supply dope and the latest eight-track stereo tapes for your en route entertainment. The car that Michael, Ethan, Tony, and I rode in had no dope, three tapes (Blind Faith, Chicago, Gladys Knight and the Pips), and a vague driver who missed the turn to the Lincoln Tunnel and had to U-turn to get back on the trail. I dozed on the way to Philadelphia, noting only the giant chain-fenced complex with huge signs—USAF Spacetrack Aero Defense Command and RCA Defense Electronic Products—and thinking that to compete with this sort of thing you really need big amplifiers.

The Philadelphia Spectrum was one more giant basketball arena, seating seventeen thousand. There were swarms of girls around the back entrance, where big metal doors opened for the limos. Inside, the backstage was dark, with big men in dark suits standing around, giving the place a precinct-boss smell. Michael and I walked down a narrow hall to B. B. King's dressing room. B.B. and his band were there, the musicians sitting and standing around, drinking beers from a picnic cooler, B.B. operating a new Sony tape recorder he had bought in Memphis. As we talked he recorded several voices around the room, then played them back. The musicians, hearing their voices, laughed like aborigines.

I watched B.B.'s set from the press box, where a few hippie types were smoking dope. Then I went downstairs and took up a position by the right side of the stage. When the Stones came on and started to play the entire crowd started to jump, and I jumped along with them. During the first couple of songs I found myself dancing with a pretty blond girl, but the crowd surged forward and she went backstage. I climbed up and stood behind Keith's amplifiers. The atmosphere was becoming frantic as the kids tried to give themselves to the Rolling Stones. Down front a girl fainted and was lifted onstage, where she opened her eyes and waved to her friends. Just across the amps from me, a rent-a-cop, about to throw a boy back into the crowd, was stopped by Tony, who helped the boy climb down.

The show was hard and fast without "I'm Free," but it seemed, in spite of all the action, like an old-fashioned rock and roll show of the fifties, people having a good time within the imposed limits. Ripping up seats expresses frustration, but it doesn't change much besides the seats.

As the lights came up and "Honky Tonk Women" started, I felt close to despair—it seemed that the tour had lost its focus; I didn't know what the Stones were trying to do, and I didn't know what I was trying to do. Whatever it was, it had something to do with love and something to do with death—and rape, murder, suicide. But it seemed that what was happening on the tour was not the transcendent expression of our feelings, but our attempt to have a good time, express the energies of our youth, in spite of the disadvantage of terrain. Onstage there were beefy men in light cotton jackets and Hush Puppies, Jon Jaymes' special security force, though I didn't know that yet. As the kids were crashing the stage full force and the evening was reaching its most hectic point, Jon grabbed me, yelled, Keep this till I ask you for it, and from his left armpit handed me a blue steel .38 caliber revolver. I slipped it into my jacket pocket, and as the last notes of "Street Fighting Man" rang in the rafters and the rose petals Mick had thrown floated down on the sweating ravers, we ran out the back, climbed in the cars, and roared out into the night.

Five limousines spread out on the turnpike at a hundred miles an hour. The show had revived us; there was no way you could fail to be excited by the great rush of energy. We talked loudly about music, sang Jimmy Reed's "Baby, What You Want Me to Do" and Fred Mc-Dowell's "You Got to Move" in the middle of which we heard the moaning siren of the State Patrol—on the New Jersey Turnpike in the wee wee hours.

All five limos whipped to a stop on the road-apron. I started to get out, and the driver said, Better stay in the car. I opened the door and looked out to see the cop reining his motorcycle and a man in a golf jacket, one who had been onstage, getting out of a limo. He hit the ground running toward the cop, taking something from his back pocket, holding it up—I saw the glint of a badge—and the patrolman waved him away, cranked his bike, sped off, and we were back on the road at a hundred miles an hour, passing the cop, gone like a cool breeze.

When we arrived at the Plaza the limos let us out at the back, where the doors were locked. The Plaza's not what it used to be, I said. It's not so bad, Mick said. Scott Fitzgerald used to like it, I said, but that was a long time ago. They didn't lock the back door at night when he liked it, Mick said.

We walked around the block in the icy cold. Inside, I went to Jon Jaymes' room and gave him his gun back. Tony stopped by to tell Jon that he wanted two things: a knife and a blackjack. You'll get them, Jon said.

We assembled—the five Stones, Tony, Sam, Ronnie, Astrid—in the lobby, preparatory to going out for something to eat. "Are you going?" Charlie asked me as we went out. "I hope you behave yourself."

"Come on in," Mick said, opening the limousine door. "Too bad you missed last night's concert, it was good. Here's a tape."

Mick turned up the volume control of a portable tape recorder he was holding on his lap. "Who made it?" I asked.

"A kid. It was confiscated."

"By Schneider?"

"Yes," Mick said. "He's awful."

"I saw you on *The Ed Sullivan Show*," I said. "That was very amusing." The show had aired only two nights ago, but it seemed a very long time. A track had been added to make it sound as if the Stones had been accompanied by an unceasing barrage of screams.

"Topo Gigio was very good," Mick said. Topo Gigio was a puppet-mouse who did a comedy routine with an Italian ventriloquist.

"Eddie Albert, too," I said. Eddie Albert had recited a prayer for the nineteen-seventies, very depressing.

We went to Reuben's, a delicatessen that stayed open late for show business types and crapshooters. Nick and Nora Charles had eaten there once in *The Thin Man*. The sandwiches on the menu were named after famous folk, one of which, the #32, was the Ed Sullivan. I pointed it out to Keith. Yeah, he said, the Ed Sullivan, I'd love to eat him—and coming from preposterous-looking Keith the statement had more of a cannibal than a sexual connotation. The walls were decorated with autographed pictures of celebrities and glum-looking stuffed fish on wooden plaques. A weary little old waiter schlepped around the long table taking orders, trying to explain the kosher menu to Tony. When the food finally came, it was terrible, canned orange juice, stale toast, cold soup.

As we ate, Ronnie wondered aloud how we were going to get from Miami to the West Palm Beach Pop Festival, where the Stones would play Sunday night, the last date of the tour. There were no planes from New York to West Palm Beach, all the planes stopped in Miami. Ronnie had looked into renting a plane for the last half of the tour, but the price was prohibitive.

"Jerry Wexler has a yacht down there," I said. "We could go from Miami to West Palm on his yacht."

"How big is it?" Keith asked.

"Big enough to take us."

"But we've still got all that equipment, guitars and stuff," Keith said, "and we'll need something that can take us out afterwards—"

"Where we going afterwards?"

"It's a secret," Keith said, "but we're going to the Deep South."

"Oh, yeah? And what in your opinion is the Deep South?"

"Muscle Shoals, Alabama. Goin' down there to record for a few days. Ahmet set it up." Ahmet Ertegun was the president (and Jerry Wexler the vice president) of the Atlantic Recording Corporaton, the biggest independent record company in the business, a great rhythm & blues success story. "We'll be down there four days," Keith said, "but don't say anything about it, to Michael or anyone in the press, 'cause it really is a secret."

Mick and Ronnie were talking about record companies, how to make the best deal—Ronnie was always discussing deals because that was how he made his living. "Why do you have to deal with them other mother-fuckers at all?" Tony asked. "Why mess with record companies and distributors? Why don't the heads put out their own shit?"

"Because it's too complicated," Keith said. "There's too much involved. You'd have to do all the pressing and distribution yourself, have to own a fleet of trucks. That's the problem. Phil Spector tried it, he cheated and bribed and did everything he could to get started, and that's cool, but he couldn't do it, it didn't work." He paused for a moment, then said, "Still it must be possible. How do bootleg records get around, how does grass get around, that's the way it's got to work—"

When we got back to the Plaza it was nearly five o'clock in the morning, and the *New York Times* for Wednesday, November 26, was in a stack by the elevators. I put a dime on the stack and took a paper, but the elevator man, coming to take us up, said, "That's fifteen cents," and I saw a little handwritten sign, PAPERS 15¢—a 50 percent price increase for the privilege of getting the bad news in the lobby of the Plaza. I said good night to the group and went up to my room. The park was wreathed in grey morning mist. There were gilt-wrapped chocolate mints and a fresh carnation on the nightstand, sheets turned back, a whole set of attentions you don't get at the Holiday Inn. I lay back on the bed and looked at the paper.

According to a story on the front page, in March 1968 in a village called My Lai in the South Vietnamese province of Song My, a twenty-six-year-old First Lieutenant named William Calley killed or caused to be killed one hundred and nine civilians. There were several related headlines: "Laird [Secretary of Defense] Says Top Army Officials Knew about Alleged Massacre . . . Thirteen Villages near Song My Razed in a Week . . . Ford [House Republican Leader] Charges the Previous Administration 'Covered Up' Vietnam Report . . . Laird 'Shocked and Sick' Over the Story." On page two, "A Beatle Returns Award as a Protest. London, Nov. 25. John Lennon, one of the Beatles, has returned his award of Member of the British Empire as a protest against Britain's role in the Nigerian Civil War and British political support of the United States in Vietnam."

At each Rolling Stones concert there were indications that we were fighting for something tender and lovely and free, but what a hell of a world we had to fight, when the land of the free and the home of the brave was sending its sons out to slaughter women and children, and the sons, men my age and younger, were doing it. As I sank toward sleep I made my last note of the day: God bless all children & old people everywhere. But as I closed my eyes, my last thought was that Jon Jaymes had handed me that revolver like a promise.

2 4

Buddy Bolden . . . had played himself out in a few years. Accustomed to earning only a few cents a day as a barber, he had begun to make real money, which he spent like a drunken sailor. Lack of sleep, liquor, women, hot music, gradually sapped his strength.

Only at certain moments did he still sound like the great King Bolden; at other times his sidemen noticed that he played his cornet as if mad. Possessed themselves, they came to fear this insane music which attacked their minds. Finally, in 1914, it became known that Bolden had to be put into an asylum.

ROBERT GOFFIN: *Jazz*

IN SEPTEMBER OF 1968, I went to England to write about the Rolling Stones. I did not know that taking place on my second day in the country would be Brian Jones' second—and, as it turned out, his last—drug trial. During the trial, Brian glanced into the spectators' gallery, and I looked into his eyes. A few days later, Brian and I walked in Kensington Gardens and beside the Serpentine, where Peter Pan landed, and Brian gave me a photocopy of an essay that he intended to use as liner notes for an album of music he had recorded in Joujouka, a village in the Moroccan Rif valley, where the word reefer comes

from. The essay, by Brion Gysin, was titled "The Pipes of Pan." I
knew then what I had seen in Brian's eyes—or whom I had seen
looking out of them—but I knew nothing about what had happened
the year before in Morocco between Brian and Anita and Keith, how
Brian had come to this music. You could have written a book about
what I didn't know.

But at the end of 1966, Christopher was working for Omega Airlines,
living in an apartment with her mother. Omega's peculiar employee
schedules made it possible for her to lie to her mother at times and
spend the night with me. I was trying to do the impossible—to start
making a living by writing before my savings from eight months with
the State ran out. Some people liked my writing, but no one would
buy it. *The New Yorker*, on returning "Furry's Blues," said, "The en-
closed has a pleasant tone, we felt, but. . . . "

Christopher and I wanted to be together, but I wanted to wait until
I was making some money. I also thought that if marriage wasn't good
enough for James Joyce or Pablo Picasso, it wasn't good enough for
me. That is, I shared their disregard for the convention that makes love
the business of bureaucrats. Christopher and I compromised. We had
our blood tested ("premartial," the receipt said), bought a marriage
license, and on December 20, Charlie Brown married us. He signed the
license with the name of a parson I had invented. Before he signed the
paper, Charlie asked us if we loved each other. We said yes. "You're
married," he said.

Two days later, Charlie was arrested for selling a small amount of
marijuana—an ounce, I believe—to an old high school acquaintance
who informed on him. He had been in the county jail for a couple of
days before I heard about it. By the time I managed to get him out,
it was Christmas Eve night. There was snow on the ground. Charlie and
I walked from the jail to the bailbond company—Charlie kept falling
on icy places and getting up with a big smile, happy to be free to fall
down—and then I drove him to his apartment. The front door was unlocked. Just inside, a search warrant lay on the floor. The air stank with
gas. We went through the rooms, opening windows and closing valves.
The police had turned all the heating outlets on and left them unlighted
in the hope that Charlie would come in and light a cigaret. In their
search they had knocked holes in the walls, poured chemicals into all
the liquids in the place, broken almost everything that would break.
Charlie looked at the wreckage, then walked to an overcoat hanging on
the bedroom door, reached into a pocket and took out some grass. We
sat on the broken bed and smoked and thought about things.

In January, Christopher and I flew to New York City on an Omega
Airlines Honeymoon Pass. Each day I would wake up and leave calls

for editors. *Esquire* had "Furry's Blues," and I had heard they wanted a story about Elvis Presley. Each night Christopher and I would go out, and the next day we would sleep till noon, missing any phone calls. Finally, on our last day in New York, I conferred with an *Esquire* editor at a Chock Full o' Nuts and came home with the Presley assignment.

The Rolling Stones were in New York for another Ed Sullivan appearance to promote a new single record. (The Stones' new album, *Between the Buttons*, was also a January release.) The problem this time was that Sullivan refused to let Jagger sing the title words to one of the songs on the new single, "Let's Spend the Night Together." There were news reports that the Stones might refuse to appear on the show. I kept hearing bits of the squabble on taxi radios. Finally the Stones went on and did the song and Jagger didn't sing the title words, just sort of hummed and mumbled.

The Sullivan show was broadcast on Sunday, January 15. The day before, there had taken place, in San Francisco's Golden Gate Park, the Human Be-In, where the Hell's Angels had been, as Rock Scully would tell us in Oakland, such groovy security.

The Stones flew back to London to prepare for the next Sunday, when they would appear for the first time on *The London Palladium Show*, British television's equivalent of *The Ed Sullivan Show*. That is, the Palladium show presented variety and watered-down nightclub acts, polite and ingratiating, for the Sunday evening of the English masses. The Stones had always stayed away from the Palladium, and when the booking was announced, a newspaper commented that "pop groups can no longer rely on teenaged viewers alone to get TV bookings, but must appeal to a wider audience." To which Jagger said, "Times are changing, and with the changing times comes a different market— one market. We think the Palladium is ready for the Stones, and the Stones are ready for the Palladium." He was wrong.

In the last year, as the pop "counterculture" had become more aware of itself—pacifist comrades of illegal sacraments—Mick, Keith, and Brian had grown closer. Oldham used illegal sacraments, too, but he was very fearful of being arrested and would smoke hashish while leaning out of the rear window of his office so he could drop it if the cops came bursting in. He was married, had a two-year-old son, and was quite devoted to making money. He had called the Rolling Stones, in a full-page *Billboard* ad, "the dividing line between art and commerce," but he told a reporter, "I want to produce good, progressive pop music, but music which is still commercial. I'm not interested in this psychedelic trash, or taking trips."

After the Stones came to the Palladium, things were never the same between them and Oldham. Keith and Brian arrived for rehearsal two hours late, both of them crammed with LSD. Brian, wearing a combination of his and Anita's clothing, played piano on one song and insisted on placing a large *hookah* on top where no one could fail to see it. Not trusting the television sound engineers, the Stones brought a tape recording of their instruments, in violation of a musicians' union ban of taped music. But the main issue was the roundabout, the Palladium's revolving stage, where each week's acts gathered at the end of the show to wave and throw kisses at the audience. The roundabout was a great English show-business tradition. Jagger had told the newspapers that the Stones would play the Palladium show, but they wouldn't go on the roundabout. At the end of rehearsal, Jagger and the Stones refused to revolve. Oldham told the show's producer, who said that they had to do it, they had no choice. Oldham agreed with the producer and called the Stones' behavior "atrocious." Jagger yelled at Oldham, who walked out, saying he didn't need the heartache.

If the Stones on the Palladium show offended Andrew Oldham, who took dirty pictures of himself at public photo booths, the rest of England was outraged. Last fall, about the time Brian had been breaking his fist on Anita's head, Mick had split up with his girlfriend of three years, Chrissie Shrimpton, the younger sister of Jean Shrimpton, the world's most fashionable fashion model. The week after the Palladium show, the newspapers revealed Jagger's "Secret Romance" with Marianne Faithful, another Oldham client. "I've known Marianne for years now, it wasn't until three months ago that we realised we had strong feelings for each other," Jagger told reporters at the airport in Nice. "I got Marianne's call in the middle of the night to come—so here I am." Marianne, twenty years old, mother of a fourteen-month-old son, had left her husband four months before. She had phoned Mick complaining of loneliness when her song, "The One Who Hopes," failed to reach the finals of the San Remo Song Festival. ("He gets the worst women," Keith said, "and when it's a black one it's the whitest one he can find.") "I'm fed up with the fuss and dancing in nightclubs until dawn," blond, blue-eyed Marianne said. Jagger hired a small boat with three red sails and Saturday evening found them sailing toward Cap d'Antibes "into a red sunset."

But by the following Sunday, Jagger was back in London and on a radio talk show defending the Stones against the show's two other guests, one of whom had a poodle named "Bobby's Girl" after her hit record, and against the tabloid *News of the World*, which that day had published a story about pop stars and drugs accusing Mick, among others, of taking LSD. Mick said he had never taken LSD and that his lawyers would sue. Two days later, the *News of the World* was served with a writ for libel.

The next Lord's Day the Stones would never forget. It climaxed at about eight o'clock in the evening, when nineteen policemen and -women descended on Keith's country house, Redlands. Mick, Keith, Marianne, Robert Fraser, and some other people were down from London for the weekend. "Anita and Brian were gonna come but Brian started a fight," Keith said. "We just left them fighting." The police took some substances from the premises and left.

After hurried contacts with lawyers, Mick, Keith, Brian, and their companions left England—left Europe—for Africa. Mick, Marianne, Fraser, and a few others flew to Morocco. Brian, Anita, and Keith went to France and headed south in Keith's blue Bentley, driven by Tom Keylock, Brian's chauffeur. At Toulon Brian got sick and checked into a hospital. After a few days, with an actress friend they'd picked up in Paris, Keith and Anita continued south into Spain. At Barcelona, after having a fight with some drunks and being held in a police station till 6:00 A.M., they got out to find Brian on the phone demanding that Anita return to Toulon. The actress left, and Keith and Anita, heading for Africa, went to Valencia and spent the night together.

"We took the ferry to Tangier," Keith said, "arrived at the hotel, and found a stack of telegrams and messages from Brian, ordering Anita to go pick him up."

Brian and Anita traveled to Tangier together and then—with Keith, Mick, Marianne, some more friends and a lot of LSD—to Marrakech. Brian brought a tattooed Berber whore to the hotel, outraging Anita, then went off to hear some Moroccan music with Brion Gysin. Keith and Anita left, going home together. "Where does that leave me?" Tom Keylock asked, and Keith said, "You can come to work for me." Brian had lost his band, his girl, and his chauffeur, and his cat would soon be gone.

When Brian came back to the hotel and found himself abandoned, he attempted suicide. Gysin got him a doctor and nursed him back to whatever he had instead of health.

Meanwhile, a London newspaper carried a story about a new modeling agency whose clients included Brian and Anita, available at $250 an hour for "very special jobs," and ran a photo of Brian in velvet and Anita wearing a miniskirt and a feather boa. She had dyed her hair blond and they could have been twins, beautiful blond twins.

Brian flew back to London and entered another hospital. The Stones' press agent—who had also worked for Frank Sinatra and Louis Armstrong—announced the release of a new German film, titled in English *A Degree of Murder*, starring Anita, with soundtrack by Brian. The report mentioned that Brian was in hospital, as if to say, Brian's having a bit of a total collapse at the moment, but his career's going great guns.

On March 20 Keith and Mick received court summonses alleging offenses against the Dangerous Drugs Act. Five days later, the Stones left for three weeks in Europe, their last tour with Brian. He and Keith were not speaking.

"There have been some nice riots," Mick said, talking to *Disc* magazine from Dortmund. "Here real bodily violence breaks out."

The Stones played Warsaw, taking what Mick called "a piddle of our usual fee," carrying full-scale rock and roll for the first time to Communist Eastern Europe. "The only scene I ever seen near it was when we tried to get out of the Long Beach Auditorium in 1965 when a motorcycle cop got run over and crushed," Keith said. "All the cops had white helmets and the big long batons. Exactly the same equipment. Exactly the same uniforms. Deployed in the same way."

The tour was a series of fights, featuring the Stones, customs officials, fans, and police, and involving thrown chairs and guard dogs and fire hoses. Back in London when it was over, Jagger said, "I see a great deal of danger in the air. . . . Teenagers are not screaming over pop music any more, they're screaming for much deeper reasons. When I'm onstage, I sense that the teenagers are trying to communicate to me, like by telepathy, a message of some urgency. Not about me or about our music, but about the world and the way they live. And I see a lot of trouble coming in the dawn."

Trouble was certainly coming to the Stones. On May 10, while Jagger and Richards were at a preliminary hearing in Chichester Magistrates' Court, putting up £100 bail apiece, pleading not guilty, and electing to be tried by jury, Brian was leaving his Courtfield Road flat surrounded by six Scotland Yard drug detectives.

In the early evening of the first day of spring 1970, I was at a flat in Duke Street St. James's, talking with Brion Gysin, who was in London visiting friends. Gysin had been telling me about taking Brian Jones to Joujouka to hear "the group of the Master Musicians. I've known them for twenty years, going up there since 1950, recognized that they are the people of Pan, and that's another whole long story—"

We were interrupted by William Burroughs, who came in and sat down, wearing a hat and overcoat. He was the drunkest man I had seen since I had last seen Furry Lewis. Reduced in Burroughs' presence as Keith was reduced by Chuck Berry, I found myself telling him about my prized copy of *Big Table 1* with its first U.S. printing of parts of *Naked Lunch*.

"Oh, wow," Burroughs said, seeming to awaken. "That's a real collectors' item." His eyes narrowed. "They are—now—quite valuable collectors' items—and—y'know—if you want to—I could autograph it, and we would—ah—share—"

"Make a little exchange," Gysin said.

"—anything—we could get—on the collectors' market."

I rested easier then, because I knew I was talking to men who, like Furry Lewis, would burn a guitar for firewood. Burroughs began to grumble about not wanting to be an artist, just wanting to make money; I quoted Shaw to Goldwyn: The difference between us is that you care only about art and I care only about money.

"There you go," Burroughs said. "No one who is an artist gives a shit about being an artist. They want to make a little money and have a little peace. Be an artist, indeed." He was struggling to unload a layer of clothing.

"Take off your coat, William," Gysin said. "There's a good move."

"At least I think I'll take off my hat," Burroughs said. He got to his feet, hung the hat on a rack, and sat back down. "Now I'll take off my coat."

"Excellent," Gysin said. "I wonder if I can get back to Joujouka. I really would like to talk about Joujouka and what the music is and what Brian got on tape and how it ever happened that he got there. How does he appear in your book?"

"Brian? As—well—sort of—as a little goat god, I suppose."

"I have a wild tale which I'll tell you about just that. A very funny thing happened up there. The setting was extremely theatrical in that we were sitting under a porch of a house made of wattles and mud. Very comfortable place, cushions were laid around like a little theatre, like the box of an old-fashioned theatre, and a performance was going on in the courtyard. And at one moment—dinner obviously had to be somewhere in the offing, like about an hour away, everybody was just beginning to think about food—and we had these acetylene lamps, giving a great very theatrical glow to the whole scene, rather like lime-light used to be, a greenish-white sort of tone. And the most beautiful goat that anybody had ever seen—pure white!—was suddenly led right across the scene, between Brian and Suki and Hamre and me, sitting on these cushions, kind of lying back, and the musicians out in the courtyard about ten feet away right in front of us, so quickly that for a moment hardly anybody realized at all what was happening, until Brian leapt to his feet, and he said, 'That's me!' and was pulled down and sort of subsided, and the music went on, and it went on for a few minutes like that, and moments lengthened into an hour, or two hours, or whatever it takes to get a great Moroccan dinner together, which sometimes can be three hours or four hours or five hours—"

"Long as it takes to kill a goat," Burroughs said.

"—and we were absolutely ravenous, when Brian realized he was eating that same white goat."

"How did he take that?"

"He said, 'It's like Communion.' "

" 'This is my body,' " I said. "But Jesus didn't eat himself, he fed the others."

"If he'd been sensible, he'd have eaten Judas," Burroughs said. "I'm gonna eat Graham Greene next time I see him. Gulp!"

2 5

All the beauty that's ever been, it's moving inside that music. Omar's voice, that's there, and the girl's voice, and the voice the wind had in Africa, and the cries from Congo Square, and the fine shouting that came up from Free Day. The blues, and the spirituals, and the remembering, and the waiting, and the suffering, and the looking at the sky watching the dark come down—that's all inside the music.

SIDNEY BECHET: *Treat It Gentle*

ON THE ROAD I was in the habit of wearing a wristwatch to bed. When I woke up this particular afternoon, it said ten minutes past one. The watch was a Timex on a brown leather strap, and—as I would learn—not the most trusty Timex. I took a shower in the stately Plaza bathroom and came out in a towel to find, sitting on the beds, Ethan Russell and Michael Lydon. They were going to Jon Jaymes' suite. I dressed and went along. The place was like a gypsy camp: bodyguards all over, waiters carrying trays of food in and empty plates out, an ex-Lawrence Welk child prodigy pianist touting his four older sisters' rock band (the Hedonists), and Barbara, a pretty girl with brown hair and Bambi eyes. She was a model but she didn't have that evil model look. Jaymes was going to have her travel around in a bikini and help him demonstrate *Laugh-In* body paint. "This is a real break for me," she said.

Ethan, Michael, and I went next to Jo Bergman's suite, but it too was full of people, and Jo was distracted.

"We came to see if you were ready to go to the press conference," Ethan said. I hadn't even known there was going to be another one.

"No, you go ahead," Jo said. "I've got to get some Valium for Mick."

In the lobby we ran into Charlie Watts and Mick Taylor. Charlie was wearing a white wool pullover under a pearl-grey leather trenchcoat. "We were just goin' out for a walk," he said, "when somebody happens to stop us and tell us about the press conference. It's a drag havin' to sit around not knowin' what's happening. And all this security around, havin' all these heavies, it don't look good—"

As Charlie and Mick left to look for the other Stones, the elevator delivered Jo Bergman. "There are some limousines outside," she said, but there weren't. It had snowed in the night, and now, if you stood still, the wind blew rain in your face and froze you, so we decided not to wait for the limos and hiked the eight blocks to Rockefeller Center.

The press conference was held on the sixty-ninth floor in the Rainbow Room, behind big windows looking out on the city; a *haut-bourgeois* setting. At the door a girl in a long-sleeved dress sat by a small white-clothed table, checking names against a list. Al Steckler, inside, saw us and waved us in. A long table, also white-clothed, held drinks and steak tartare canapés. The waiters wore dinner jackets, and a string quartet—one long-haired boy also in black tie and three girls in evening dresses—were sawing away at Mozart.

In the big square inner room were rows of chairs facing a long table that held bouquets of flowers and pitchers of orange juice. Before long the place was filled with press people who ranged in appearance from dapper black men in suits to scruffy hippies in dirty jeans. By the time you started to wonder what they had in common, the Stones came in and sat at the table, Sam Cutler with them, Pete Bennett and Allen Klein standing behind them. A writhing mass of media people, fighting and scrambling, thrust microphones and flashed photobulbs, groped and twisted like lost souls in Hell as the Stones sat with the flowers and orange juice, staring across the white expanse of tablecloth.

I went and hid in a corner. Jon Jaymes was standing beside the table, hands raised toward the press, looking like a man conducting the antics of a bevy of magpies. As the crowd grew quieter, though they didn't stop snarling and pushing, questions drifted across the room.

"Do you see yourselves as youth leaders?"

"What do you think of the Vietnam War?"

"What do you think of America?"

"Do you think it's getting better?"

"You look more beautiful than ever," Jagger said. That brought a laugh.

"Mr. Jagger," a woman wearing glasses and a tailored suit read from a notebook, "some time ago you recorded a song, 'I Can't Get No Satisfaction.' Are the Stones more satisfied today?"

"Sexually, d'you mean, or philosophically?"

"Both."

"Sexually—more satisfied, financially—" (thinking of Klein behind him) "dissatisfied, philosophically—still trying."

"Are you sadder but wiser?"

"Just a little wiser." I didn't know it yet, but about thirty minutes ago Jagger had learned that Marianne Faithfull had left him, left his house in London, and was living with a film director in Italy. "Do you have any Valium?" Mick had asked Jo, who scrounged one five-milligram tablet from a *Daily News* reporter.

"I have a question for Mick Taylor," someone said. "How does it feel to replace a member of the group who was loved by so many? I'm talking about Brian Jones."

Whatever Mick Taylor said was lost in the groan that arose in the room. Even in this crowd, bad taste had its limits. As if on cue, someone asked, "Are the Stones going to give a free concert?"

"Yes," Jagger said. "The free concert will be in San Francisco December sixth, but there is no exact location yet."

At the first press conference back in Los Angeles, the hippies had asked for a free show, and now on the other side of America the Stones had promised them one. The tone of the questions as they continued asked not for a statement of position but for a declaration of support. Once again the hippies were in their callow fashion asking whether the Stones were on their side in the battle against repression. In Europe the hip community was so small as to be hardly a community—young sports in blue python jackets strolled the Kings Road with no more herd instinct than pythons—but in America something was driving the people together, and the Stones were going along with it.

"What was your reaction to John Lennon's returning his MBE?"

"At last," Jagger said. "He should have returned it as soon as he got it."

"Or if you get one," Keith said, "you should wear it."

"What would you do if *you* got one?"

"We never got them, and I rather doubt we will."

"Mr. Jagger, in California you were wearing an Omega button, which is a symbol of draft resistance—"

"I thought it stood for infinity. I don't know."

"Mr. Jagger, what is your opinion of the mass concerts such as Woodstock and the Isle of Wight?"

"Well, they all happened in the same year—I think next year they will be more—huge and better organized."

"Why are you giving a free concert in San Francisco?"

"Because there's a scene there, and the climate's nice. Besides, it's unfortunate when Ralph Gleason has to pay fifty dollars to get in."

The questions dwindled to a halt, and Sam said, "That's all, folks."

"Thank you, New York," Jagger said, and the Stones got up to leave. Charlie, still wearing his overcoat, wandered off in the wrong direction, but he was stopped and put back on course. The Stones zipped away, and the freaks, straights, beards, sideburns, cameras, and recorders rushed for the elevators.

I stopped to talk to Lillian Roxon, who had written a book called *The Rock Encyclopedia.* An Australian, Lillian was a good-looking blond girl with pale blue eyes, but she had gained forty pounds writing her book—which seemed like a lot to go through for a rock and roll book, how little I knew—and soon she was going to be dead, another dead one. I told her goodbye and went down in an elevator with Michael, Jo, and Pete Bennett. We walked back to the Plaza, Pete in front cutting off the wind. "Pete," I asked, checking out something I'd heard, "is it true you're going to be in an Orson Welles film?"

"Yah," he growled over his shoulder, smiling past his tightly clenched cigar. "He says I'm a great nachal actah."

At the Plaza, I went upstairs and called Jerry Wexler, just to say hello. Wexler asked me to come out to his house on Long Island for a visit, but the Stones were playing Baltimore tonight, and tomorrow, Thanksgiving Day, they would play Madison Square Garden. I told Wexler that I had to stick pretty tight with the tour, but he said, Naw naw come on out and have Thanksgiving dinner with us. I told him I'd call tomorrow.

Now it was almost dark. Michael and I went again to Jon Jaymes' suite. Jaymes told us that we were taking a bus to Baltimore because the Stones were going in a seven-seat Learjet. We went down to the street and there was the bus. In it were the driver and some of Jaymes' federal narcotics agents and off-duty New York City detectives, big short-haired men in golf jackets and Hush Puppies. They had nice faces with sad wise expressions, sorrowful like very old priests or midwives, as if they had seen all the bloody consequences of man's folly. Also aboard were two greying Jewish boys, the film-making Maysles brothers, David and Albert. We introduced ourselves, and looking around in the failing winter light at the plastic seatcovers and metal walls, I asked, shivering, "Is there any dope on this bus?" The heavies looked at me, their mild pleasant eyes unblinking.

"Is it cool to smoke?" Michael asked.

"Sure it is," I said, loud enough to carry to the back of the bus.

"Is it?" Michael asked, turning to the cops. "Yeah, all right," one of them said. "Less go get some," Michael said to me. He was clearly delighted at the prospect of getting high with police protection. We went and ransacked the hotel but didn't find anybody who could help. When we got back and sat down, though by no means all of the Stones tour party were present, the bus pulled out. The Maysles brothers and I tried to work up a chat, but the bus was so grim—no food, nothing to drink—that we made the driver pull over by a delicatessen. David Maysles and some of the heavies went in and came back with beer and sandwich materials. We tore into them with picnic fervor. Then as we were about to leave Manhattan—approaching the exit ramp—I asked the driver how far it was to Baltimore. Too far. Michael and I said fuck it and got off the bus. We wandered through the streets, eating sandwiches, drinking long swigs of beer.

Michael was talking about women, his favorite subject. He was sad that his wife had left him and taken their daughter, but—taking a drink—this girl he was staying with in New York was really nice. I told him that I had a wife who cheered me up and never bored me and that all I wanted was to live through this fucking tour so we could settle down and enjoy what was left of our youth, our lives, together. I was going, though I didn't know it yet, to do extensive research on pain.

We went down the stairs to the subway, the Horrors lurking in the shadows, and boarded an uptown train. Michael collapsed on a seat and I stood reading the map. "Let's not figure out where we're going or when we'll be there, let's just relax for a minute," Michael said, but I already knew where we were going.

On Riverside Drive, its great stone lions staring west across the Hudson, stands Gore House, a grey stone cottage of thirty-two rooms. Built in the nineteenth century by a mideastern potentate, the place had been after his death an Episcopal nunnery (hence the haunted dormitory bathrooms). Now it belonged to someone named Gore, whose caretaker, a student at Union Theological Seminary, had usurped the name. Gore had been until a couple of months before an employee of the agency where I was a client. He had sold my work and told me the truth and always seemed to imply that there was more to be told. Now that he was away from the agency, I thought he might be willing to tell it.

Thin and blond, with tortoise-shell glasses, Gore opened the big iron doors, draped with ropes of garlic, to let us enter. In the dry precise tones of a grand aunt he directed us past the mosaic tiles of the entrance hall and up the dark staircase to an inner sanctum. There we sat and consumed great quantities of red wine and hashish as Gore, kneeling before his record collection on a cheap cotton rug made in the likeness of Leonardo's *The Last Supper*, played excellent music— Burritos, Ronettes, Crickets—disappearing now and then downstairs to the kitchen in whose refrigerator the Methedrine was kept.

Some friends Michael had telephoned came over, another writer and his wife, both so ugly they looked like a dog act. They talked to Michael

while Gore and I made war plans. I had the Stones' letter of consent,
I had a publishing contract, but I wanted to know—still thought I
could know—what else could go wrong. I told Gore that the Stones'
letter gave me their "exclusive cooperation."

"Then you have the authorized biography."

"I don't want that," I said, knowing that "authorized" often meant
"censored by the subject."

"Well, you have whatever you want, then."

I could feel the muscles relax in my shoulders and the back of my
neck. Michael's writer friend and wife were talking about their recent
trip to Peru, showing us a souvenir keychain figure of a little Indian
with a giant upstanding phallus. Meanwhile the Stones were in Baltimore, the Maysles brothers and the heavies were on the highway.
Hearing about the Baltimore show later, I was sorry (till I remembered
the cold grim bus) I hadn't gone along. The audience, for the only
time on the tour, were more black than white. "Spades always cause
trouble," the state man who'd come for the admissions tax told Jo. The
show was in the Baltimore Civic Center, whose orchestra pit on this
evening contained cops, against whom Mick protected the audience by
saying, If everyone wants to get up and dance, no one should hurt
them or bother them. The audience loved the show, cheering "You
Got to Move," and Mick, for the first time since San Diego, sang "I'm
Free" after "Under My Thumb." The white mayor of Baltimore sat in
the front row with his fingers in his ears, his blond wife beside him
rocking to and fro with the music.

At Gore House we drank and smoked, and Gore told me some
things I didn't know about my agent. Born in the Bronx, he had at
thirteen years of age started writing science fiction for pulp magazines
and at nineteen, deciding to rise in the world, had started his own
literary agency. Disliking his plainly Jewish name, he had taken the
last name of an English novelist and the (Anglo-sounding) first name
of his own little brother. Now the little brother, having proved unable
to support himself, worked at the agency under the original first name
of his older brother. My agent was, then, a man who'd lifted his own
brother's name. "Tell him you want photocopies of all the original
checks," Gore said darkly.

I filed the knowledge, but in the end it wouldn't help. Years later,
when the book came to be published, I would sign a contract paying me
exactly what I owed the original agent and publisher. I would leave the
girl in New York in the sunlight with snow coming down all around us.
The other girl would read my notes, and that ended that. All I got
was the story and, as they say, I got to hear the band play.

Finally Michael's friends left and we said goodnight to Gore. Michael
and I caught a cab and went to Max's Kansas City, where he was going
to meet his girl. On the back of the front seat a sticker read YOUR

FINGERS ARE IMPORTANT SAFETY FIRST DON'T CLOSE THE DOOR ON
THEM! above a drawing of an open hand with a stub where there should
have been an index finger.

Max's, with what Michael called "the young elite of the communica-
tions industry," was dark and noisy. I ate a hamburger and watched
people yell and wave beer mugs. Outside the front window a drunk
older man, who'd been thrown out for shoving people at the bar, stood
making faces, a lit cigarette in his ear—until up wheeled a young man
in a wheelchair, and a drunk with a fag in his ear is not as heavy as
a man in a wheelchair and everybody including the drunk knew it and
finally he wandered away. So did I.

When I opened my eyes the November sky outside the tall windows was
colorless and timeless—twilight morning or midday, impossible to tell.
My watch, stuck to my wrist like a clam, said eleven-thirty. Afraid I
would be late for Thanksgiving dinner, I called the Wexlers.

"Jello," a woman said.

I said who I was and asked for Mr. Wexler.

"He ees esleeping. Yo no sé cuando se levante."

"Oh. All right. I'll call back."

"Sí. Goo-bye."

If they're having Thanksgiving dinner, I wondered, why is he asleep?
Where I was brought up, Thanksgiving dinner came in the early afternoon, the siesta came afterwards. They order this matter better in the
South, I thought, going back to sleep. I woke up again, ten past one
by my watch, and again called the Wexlers. Shirley, Jerry's wife then,
answered.

"Jerry's asleep still," she said. "Come see us. The one fifty-four
Long Island train gets into Great Neck at two twenty-seven."

"But it's after one now. I don't know if I can make it."

There was a short pause. "Honey, it's only about ten o'clock."

"Oh my God," I said. "Damn this watch. Sorry. That'll be fine."

I tried to sleep more but couldn't, and got up feeling as you can
feel only on a cold day with a white sky when you are a little drunk
and drugged and lost in time. I showered in the high-ceilinged bathroom amid clouds of purifying steam, shaved, dressed, and went down
four floors to Jon Jaymes' suite. There Jo Bergman and Ronnie
Schneider were planning Thanksgiving dinner at Ronnie's Manhattan
apartment for the crew and cast (if any of them should care to attend)
before the Stones' show tonight at Madison Square Garden. I told them
to make sure I could get into the show, because I would come back
from Long Island to Penn Station, directly under the Garden, just
before it started. Jon gave me a button, yet another badge, this one for
the Garden shows, with the stars and stripes bordered by the words
GOD BLESS AMERICA—THE FLAG I LOVE.

I went downstairs, passing Mick Taylor in the hall; he seemed as fog-bound as I was, a sweet-tempered English boy staying blasted on grass and coke.

"Happy Thanksgiving, Mick."

"Thank you. My first Thanksgiving."

"How do you like it?"

"Don't know yet."

The doorman summoned a cab, and away we went. Times Square was crowded with traffic because the Macy's Thanksgiving Day parade had just ended. The driver hated everyone who'd come into town for it. "Bunch of stupid motherfuckers shouldn't be allowed out of Jersey," he said, trying to run over an old black man tapping with a white cane across Broadway. At a red light we stopped beside a car with a mama and papa and two little girls in white organdy dresses, white bows in their hair, white gloves, holding white patent leather purses.

"Mommy, where's the parade?" one of the little girls asked, and the cab driver, leaning out his window, said, "Forget the parade. The parade's over."

The girl threw down her purse and both of them began to cry, little mouths opening wide, tears starting to flow down contorted cheeks as we pulled away from the light and zipped on to Penn Station.

I stood in line, bought a ticket, boarded a train. Before it left the station its lights went out. All the Thanksgiving travellers sat silent, Muzak filling the darkness. Slowly the train rolled out to where the sunlight was starting to burn away the mist. Across the aisle a white-haired man was telling his two grandsons, who looked about nine and twelve, that for years their father worked for Western Union and had a free pass on the railroad, never had to pay. The boys rolled their eyes, bad actors expressing boredom. The grandfather went on talking, trying to get them to look at the scenery, to live life, to see, to care, but the boys ignored him, thinking they would live forever. To my right were two girls in miniskirts, one wearing black tights and the other red. In front of me a belligerent black woman in gold-rimmed spectacles was demanding that a small Chinese girl put her large suitcase out of the way on the overhead rack. I lifted it for her and when we got to Great Neck carried it off the train, partly because I had never carried a Chinese girl's suitcase.

At Great Neck I couldn't find Wexler, but as the crowd thinned I saw him, looking like Edward G. Robinson in shades, suntan, trim white beard. "Hey, mee-an," he said in his classic Washington Heights accent, "couldn't you push ahead of these Noo Yorkers?"

Where I come from, if you push people they are liable to kill you, but I didn't mention it. In Wexler's white Mercedes coupé (secure *thunk* of expensive doors closing) we drove through snowy Great Neck streets.

I had met Wexler the day after Otis Redding died, in 1967, less than two years ago, but we had become friends almost at once. If Wexler had known what madness I would bring into his life, he might have kept his distance, but I doubt it. At heart, we loved the same things. Wexler had published fiction as a young man, had studied journalism at Kansas State, had worked for *Billboard* (where he may have invented the term *rhythm & blues*), and was an aficionado of good writing. Before I was a teenager I had memorized Atlantic records Wexler and the Ertegun brothers, Ahmet and Nesuhi, made with such artists as Ray Charles, Joe Turner, Ruth Brown, LaVern Baker, Chuck Willis, Ivory Joe Hunter, Clyde McPhatter and the Drifters, the Modern Jazz Quartet, Charles Mingus, Phineas Newborn. Among his generation of American record producers—a number of whom, like the Erteguns and John Hammond, were from families with money—Wexler was the only one who had washed windows (as Sam and Judd Phillips were the only undertakers). *Blues from the Gutter*, a Champion Jack Dupree album produced by Wexler, was Brian Jones' introduction to the blues.

Wexler asked how business was, and I told him, including the contract-in-the-bushes story and the things Gore said last night. Wexler was interested but preoccupied. He and his family were going to spend the year-end holidays in Miami, and his older daughter Anita, nineteen, wanted to take her black boyfriend along. Wexler asked my opinion as a professional Southerner.

"Miami ain't the South," I said, but he was still uneasy. It was ironic, because if anybody brought black boyfriends into white girls' hearts it was Wexler, with all the great black artists he had recorded.

The Wexlers' house was not so big you got lost in it, and the sitting room had soft chairs and Magrittes on the walls. Shirley, blond and tanned, brought out Bloody Marys and little ham and cheese sandwiches, and we made small talk—though Wexler's talk was never small; as he spoke careers grew and crumbled, empires stretched and shrank. The last time I'd seen Wexler, he'd said, "The Stones sent me a tape of this song, 'Sympathy for the Devil.' They wanted Aretha to record it. The only artists on Atlantic who could record those lyrics are Sonny Bono and Burl Ives." Now I mentioned that the Stones were looking for a label or someone to distribute their label, and he said, "I'd love to have them, but I don't want to deal with Klein."

"I don't think you'd have to. I don't have to. He had nothing to do with this tour. I think they're breaking away from him."

"Tell Shirley about your book. He doesn't have to have anybody's approval, it's fantastic." Relaxation gave Jerry's accent some resemblance to that of Warner Brothers' Elmer Fudd, as it made mine resemble the speech of Erskine Caldwell's Jeeter Lester. Wexler did not

go from washing windows to owning yachts and living in such places
as East Hampton and Central Park West by being a pushover, and
his accent gave him a pleasant touch of humanity. Mine just made me
sound like a redneck.

I was too close to the action to see what a wonder it was that anyone could maintain a position as undefined and free as mine in the
presence of something so protected and pecunious as the world's leading rock and roll band. I didn't even know what my position was. I
just wanted to stay alive and see what happened.

Wexler asked Shirley to call Ray Charles at the Plaza. Charles had
left Atlantic at the end of the fifties, and now Wexler had hopes of
signing him again. The first era of rock and roll, rhythm & blues, ended
after the 1960 U.S. House of Representatives' investigation of the
music business. Atlantic stagnated in the early sixties until it was refreshed by the influx of Stax/Volt records from Memphis. More
recently Wexler had made a series of recordings with Aretha Franklin
and musicians from Memphis and Muscle Shoals. Atlantic had also
recorded various artists in Memphis, but having been squeezed out
of the studios there and now denied even the privilege of bringing
Memphis musicians to New York (by Memphis producers who said
they were tired of being raided by carpetbaggers), they had begun to
use a studio in Miami, staffing it with Cold Grits, a rhythm section from
Mobile. "But they can't cut it," Wexler said. "They don't even listen to
records."

"If you need a rhythm section," I said, fatheaded as usual, ready to
solve somebody else's problems on the spot, "the best one I know's
down in Memphis."

Wexler asked who they were. When I told him—Charlie Freeman,
Jim Dickinson, and the Dixie Flyers—he asked, "Do you think they'd
work for me?"

"If I were a musician, that's exactly what I'd want to do."

Wexler made a quick sweeping motion with the Bloody Mary in his
left hand, as if he were smoothing a dealing space in the desert sand. "Do
you suppose if I gave them a production percentage and paid them twelve
thousand a year and gave them an artist's contract as well that they'd
move to Miami and—we'd pay for that, of course—and work for me?"

"Wouldn't hurt to ask."

I made the phone call to Dickinson, and some of us lived through
what it caused and one of the best of us, Charlie Freeman, didn't.
Dickinson said he'd talk to the band, and Wexler, taking the phone,
told Dickinson they'd talk about it in Memphis or Muscle Shoals. We
said goodbye, a thunderhead of music, drugs, money and anguish
starting to gather out in the future, as Thanksgiving continued in Great
Neck.

"Those guys down in Miami now, they know nothing about what's happening in music," Wexler said. "They'd never even heard the Band till I played it for them."

Thinking of the Band, the group of musicians brought together by Ronnie Hawkins, the Arkansas Flash, that had been rustled from him by Bob Dylan and had then left Dylan to go on their own, Wexler recalled the session he'd produced not long ago with Hawkins in Muscle Shoals. Hawkins had come into the dry Alabama county in his private plane with his private case of booze and dope and Miss Toronto. "I got my pot, my pills, and my pussy," he said. "Let's go to work." Wexler played some of the tracks as we talked.

The Wexlers had seen things the likes of which would never be seen again, and I lusted to hear about them. They had gone to Café Society Downtown when they were too young to be served liquor. They'd been there the night Tallulah Bankhead came in and watched Billie Holiday's first set (Billie in the spotlight, trademark white gardenia in her hair) and then the two great ladies went into Billie's dressing room and didn't come out for the second set.

We were waiting for Wexler's mother to arrive so we could have dinner. Anita showed up with her boyfriend Jimmy, stayed briefly and left. The Wexlers' son Paul was in from some kind of experimental college in California, Norman Mailer on its board of directors. Finally Wexler's mother arrived, a small grandmother-shaped lady with darkened hair. She had just come from seeing an osteopath who'd given her an adjustment. "But I can't say what kind of adjustment."

"Sure you can," Wexler said.

"A coccygeal adjustment. And no more backaches."

Wexler sat her down and gave her a glass of sherry. She had taken a cab from the train station because Wexler's limousine driver was sick. Shirley called the driver to see if he could take Mrs. Wexler and me to the train later. The man's wife said he was still sick. "If he's sick, he's sick," Shirley said in Long Island double-talk.

"I'll see nobody misses the train," Wexler said.

Lisa, the Wexlers' younger daughter, fifteen, had joined us. Dark-haired, with shapely high cheekbones, she cast demure but intense glances from dark, long-lashed eyes. "I'd be glad not to ride in the limo," she said.

"Lisa hates the limo," Wexler said. "She makes the driver let her out a block from school."

Lisa made an elegant, feline shudder.

When it was time for dinner I lingered in the sitting room to telephone Jon Jaymes. "Be sure, you bastard, I can get in—put my name on the backstage pass list. I don't want to be standing outside in the fucking snow."

"You got your button? Nothing to worry about."

We ate goose, broccoli, potatoes, and drank fine red wine while Ronnie Hawkins sang "Down in the Alley" and other good songs. Wexler talked about how much he enjoyed recording with Southern musicians. "I've always wished my kids could grow up in the South," he said.

"My God, whatever for?" his mother asked. In spite of her years, she was, Wexler had told me, quite active on the political left—always out leafletting shopping centers, that kind of thing. She would call Wexler to tell him where she was going so he could bail her out if she got arrested.

"Because the good people in the South understand bwotherhood better than anybody else in this country," Wexler said, but his mother looked skeptical, knowing how fallible he was, her son the record millionaire.

Soon after dinner Wexler's mother and I said goodbye to Shirley and the kids and Wexler drove us to the station. Wexler and I made plans to meet at the Stones' show the following night.

On the train I heard how Wexler had made his mother suffer. Once again—or still—slightly drunk, I had been telling Mrs. Wexler what a great man her son was in the history of American music, and she said, "Do you really think so?"

"It ain't what I think, it's what's so. Haven't you seen all them interviews?"

"I don't know," she said. "I was very worried about Gerald when he was younger. He wanted to be a writer and I wanted him to be one— sent him to journalism school in the Midwest. . . ." She told me that Wexler didn't knuckle down and work hard in school and she finally had to come out to Kansas and extricate him from the clutches of the shiksa he was shacked up with and bring him back to New York where she locked him in his room to write. "But he started fooling around with music, and I guess he's done well enough at it." A worrier, like all good mothers.

At Penn Station I saw Mrs. Wexler safely to a taxi and walked around to the back door of the Garden. The streetlights were shining on the piles of dirty snow in the gutters and on the sidewalks. Outside the door long-haired boys and girls in warm coats crowded around a folding chair where sat a white-haired, ruddy-cheeked Irish cop. I showed him my flag badge and it meant nothing to him; just as I'd expected, I was a fool standing out in the cold with a GOD BLESS AMERICA button.

I asked the cop to check for my name on the guest list, and he went inside and returned to tell me that nobody knew nothing about no list. He was polite and unperturbed and in my frustration I had to admire his cool.

On that crest of mixed feelings, the door opened and Jon Jaymes beckoned me inside. I went down the hall to the Stones' dressing room, where for a moment I was alone with the concrete block walls and hard benches. I heard voices and in came the Stones with Jimi Hendrix. They were followed by the Maysles brothers, tape and film rolling.

Jagger took off his shirt and walked around; Albert followed him, filming. Mick Taylor and I sat on a bench with Hendrix, who seemed subdued but pleasant. I told him about seeing Little Richard, and he said, smiling as if it cheered him up to think about it, that once when he was with Richard, he and the bass player bought ruffled shirts to wear onstage, and Richard made them change: "I am the beauty! Nobody spoze to wear ruffles but Richard!"

Mick Taylor handed his guitar to Hendrix and asked him to play. "Oh, I can't," he said. "I have to string it different." Hendrix was left-handed, but he went ahead and played the guitar upside down, a wizard he was.

As Hendrix played I went into the bathroom, where Jagger was putting mascara on his lashes. Hendrix had tried to take Marianne Faithfull away from Mick, who wasn't about to stand around and listen to him play, upside-down or sideways. I told him about my afternoon with Wexler. He seemed distracted, I figured because he was about to go onstage. I didn't know that in the distance a black girl was telling him she was going to have his baby, and a blond girl (who two weeks ago had been threatening to join the tour) was telling him goodbye. Back at the Plaza in a few hours, Jo would write in her notebook, "Tried talk Mick imposs—concert fantastic—Mick better but must keep his mind on necessary things." He listened politely, or appeared to, till I finished talking about Atlantic and the Magrittes; then, with the Stones changing into their stage drag, I went out to see the show.

In the hall I saw another of the next year's ghosts, Janis Joplin, heading for the Stones' dressing room. Because I'd heard that something I had written about her had made her angry, I avoided her. The next day, when I came into the Garden for the afternoon show, Bill Belmont told me that Janis, being stopped at the Stones' door—because, as nobody got a chance to tell her, they were mostly naked—stuck her head in and gave the middle-finger salute to what must have been a surprised bunch of Rolling Stones. I think she was drunk, not an unusual state for her. Later tonight, when Jagger, onstage, sang "Don't you want to live with me?" Janis would yell, "You don't have the balls!"

It was cold in the Garden, under the high arches and giant mushroom spines. Terry Reid and B. B. King had already played and Tina Turner was onstage singing the Otis Redding song, "I've Been Loving You Too Long," her sleek red beauty shimmering in a black dress, back arched, legs bowed, one arm thrust out, testifying as she had been for years to drunks in juke joints and cuttin' parlors. Ike was standing back from the spotlight, small and black and nasty, eyeballs glowing under his shiny processed Beatle cut, chopping chords as if in anger. This afternoon Wexler, who often saw the Turners when they were in New York, said, "He's really got the fear of God in her." As you watched them, you couldn't help wondering if Mother Nature were married to the Devil.

Tina sang "Respect" and "Come Together," eyes bleached out in the spotlight, her pupils swimming white slits. When the band geared up for "Land of 1000 Dances," Janis Joplin stepped onto the rear of the stage, stomping with delight, and Tina called her to the front. Janis looked for once in her life completely happy; it was plain that she would love to nose around in Tina's crotch all night long. "Roll over on your back—y'know I like it like that," they sang together, Ike's guitar whipping them, and Janis pulled off her little crocheted cap and threw it into the air.

After Tina and Janis finished there was a delay during which the audience had contact flashes from what they had seen and the recording equipment was prepared for the Stones. How can they follow this, I asked myself, as I did at almost every show. After watching Tina in Oakland, Mick had said that he wasn't cocky anymore; but he was still following her. I went backstage, and Mick was wandering among the Coke bottles and folding chairs, looking rather lost and forlorn. The others kept their distance. He was about to be consumed, and there was a reverent silence between them. With his blue-beaded moccasins and black pants with silver leg buttons (only back here you can see they're not silver, just shiny in the spotlight), little black jersey, his scarf dragging, hair hanging limp, chin slumped over gold-medallioned choker, Uncle Sam hat in hand, Mick seemed not bored but not comfortable, making little sounds under his breath as if to say, What a dumb thing this is, waiting.

As time passed and nothing happened, I went out front again into the smoky darkness. No one seemed to mind the wait. "Ain't nothin' any good without it has some grease on it," Tina (the former Annie Mae Bullock, of Brownsville, Tennessee) had said, and she and Janis had left the audience greased and pleased. There were guards, but they weren't wearing togas, and the few police didn't seem intent on ruining a good time. The atmosphere was, if not relaxed, at least secure—perhaps because we were on an island in a giant tin can, concrete and metal shell, and no apparent threat to anybody.

Stu, walking across the stage to check a microphone, dressed in his pale-yellow tuxedo with shiny satin lapels, caused a ripple of applause, which he answered with a V-sign—very satirical, Stu. Then the stage was deserted and out of the stillness a disembodied cockney voice mused, "Everyone seems to be ready, are you ready?"

Yesss, the crowd answered in a snow-slide's whisper-roar, *Yesss*.

"For the first time in three years," Sam Cutler said, getting louder, "the greatest rock and roll band in the world, the Rolling Stones!"

The big yellow-blue-white spot bleached out Jagger as he came on-stage, twirling overhead his Uncle Sam hat, not smiling, gaze fixed on fate. In a breathless rush of silence the Stones came out, Charlie settling onto the drums, the others, quick and businesslike, plugging their guitars into the amplifiers, twisting dials, setting levels, until Keith hit the opening chords of "Jumpin' Jack Flash," Mick started to howl about being born in a crossfire hurricane, and the kids all stood up and screamed. Glyn Johns stopped me in the corridor at the Plaza the next day to say that he had been backstage in a sound truck and the truck was jumping on its springs. "So I got out to see who was shaking it—I thought there might be some kids on top of it—but there was nobody there, the truck was just picking up the vibrations from the house, the whole bloody building was shaking."

As "Jack Flash" ended, Mick, buttoning his trousers, said by way of greeting, "Think I busted a button on me trousers, hope they don't fall down. You don't want me trousers to fall down, now do ya?"

Yesss, the crowd answered, as Keith started "Carol," standing beside Mick in the spotlight, surrounded by a glimmering halo of rhinestones on his Nudie shirt.

"We are making our own statement," Brian had said in one of the interviews the publicity office arranged to keep him from feeling left out. "Others are making more intellectual ones."

What message would you get if you were fifteen years old, standing in a cloud of marijuana smoke inside a crowded, cavernous hall, face reflecting the red and blue and yellow lights, watching Charlie hit the drums as hard as he was able, Bill slide his tiny hands over the skinny neck of his erect light-blue bass causing a sound like booming thunder, little Mick stare with wide eyes as if he were hearing an earthquake's faint premonitory quiverings, Keith bend over his guitar like a bird of prey, Jagger swoop and glide like some faggot vampire banshee, all of them elevated and illuminated and larger and louder than life? A few years later, a *New Yorker* writer would observe, "The Stones present a theatrical-musical performance that has no equal in our culture. Thousands and thousands of people go into a room and focus energy on one point and something happens. The group's musicianship is of a high order, but listening to Mick Jagger is not like listening to Jascha Heifetz. Mick Jagger is coming in on more circuits than Jascha Heifetz. He is dealing in total, undefined sensual experience of the most ecstatic sort."

By the time that was written, Mick had sung "Midnight Rambler" in pink top hat and tails; after Altamont, the Stones would for reasons of self-preservation turn toward comedy. But in 1969, few people at

Madison Square Garden on Thanksgiving Day thought that what the
Stones were doing was a performance.

The Stones had first come to the United States in 1964, fewer than
six years before. They had done five U.S. tours in three years, then
were stopped for almost three years. Since then they had become
world-famous idols, outlaws, legends, relics, and one was now a
corpse. They had been more than lucky to find a guitarist who was
docile and played, though not as Brian once had, excellent bottleneck.
One problem they'd had preparing to tour was choosing songs that
Keith and Mick Taylor could play. Hence "Carol" and "Little Queenie,"
Keith's Chuck Berry specialties, and hence the difficulty Jagger had
mentioned of getting the old things together. The old things had
featured, as Stu said, "two guitar players that were like somebody's
right and left hand."

The people inside Madison Square Garden on this Thanksgiving had,
most of them, lived through a time of cold war, hot war, race riots,
student riots, police riots, assassinations, rapes, murders, trials, waking
nightmares. But Keith, Mick, Charlie, Bill, and the new guitar player
were impersonating the Rolling Stones, and the audience were impersonating their audience, both of them at the moment a great success.
Dancing under the circumstances ("Oh, Carol! Don't ever steal your
heart away—I'm gonna learn to dance if it takes me all night and
day!") seemed to have a transcendent value. Many people thought
then that dancing and music could have a major role in changing the
structure of society. They may have been naive, but they were much
more interesting than the sensible people who came along later. The
Stones would tour the United States every three years for a long time
to come, and the value of dancing would never be less than transcendent,
but at Woodstock, only a few months before and a few miles away,
music had seemed to create an actual community. There was—at this
time, for many members of this generation—a sense of power, of
possibility, that after Altamont would not return.

When "Sympathy for the Devil" began and it became clear that
nobody was going to sit down, I went around back and climbed the
stairs to the stage. Hendrix was sitting behind one of Keith's amplifiers.
Keith was a twisted figure, torturing his guitar strings in the red spotlight, his blistering solo saving the song now as it did on the record.
The lyrics were ponderous, but they were written by a man who'd
done some thinking on the nature of evil.

> So if you meet me
>   have some courtesy
>   have some sympathy
>   and some taste

Use all your well-learned *politesse*
or I'll lay your soul to waste

While Keith played, Mick took long drinks from a fifth of Jack
Daniel's and a can of Stauffer's beer. Ten feet in front of the stage
Jon Jaymes and Gary Stark were trying to hold back the crowd, among
them a tall, electric-haired boy in a bow tie, chewing gum with big
open-mouthed smacks. A couple of yards to the rear Pete Bennett
prowled, cigar in jaw, smiling, nobody going near him.

Because they had gone on to release three albums of new material
during the three-year layoff, the Stones had for this tour many songs
never performed in public. There was nothing in the set from *Their
Satanic Majesties Request*, an album done, as Jagger said, "under the
influence of bail." It was futuristic and introspective and, because Brian
was devastated by the events of his life, lacked guitar interplay. By
the time the Stones recorded the next album, *Beggar's Banquet*, Keith
had learned bottleneck. The band had stopped depending on Brian for
anything; if Keith could have played bottleneck and rhythm at the same
time onstage, they would never have needed another guitar player. The
current set consisted of four songs from *Banquet*, four from *Let It
Bleed*, two by Chuck Berry, two early Stones songs that featured Keith's
guitar, the last three singles, and "Satisfaction." As Stu said, "If Brian
Jones, Bill Wyman, Charlie Watts, and myself had never existed on
the face of this earth, Mick and Keith would still have had a group that
looked and sounded like the Rolling Stones."

"Sympathy" ended with the aisles packed, the air filled with shrill
cheers. As the Stones had changed from social misfits to satanic
majesties, the stupid girls grown up wrong had become stray cats.
"Bet y'mama don't know you can bite like that." Jagger took off the
black choker hung with gold coins, tossing it behind him, leaning
across the stage-front, shaking his ass at the stray cats, his red scarf
swirling.

Learning bottleneck had led Keith, and so the Stones, deep into
country blues. Mick sang the opening lines of "Love in Vain" in a
blue spot, and as Mick Taylor's bottleneck answered, the Stones
were caught by seven blue spots, two each on Mick and Keith. The
next two songs, "Prodigal Son" and "You Got to Move," had been too
intimate ("It's a wank") to rehearse. Keith and Mick did them alone,
perched on stools, the rock and roll audience listening intently, nobody sitting down, to the songs of old black men too poor to put glass
in their windows.

You may be high
You may be low

> You may be rich
> You may be po'
> But when the Lord gets ready
> You got to move

As the last note from Keith's National clanged into silence, Wyman started thumping heavy bass notes for "Under My Thumb." Many of the early Jagger/Richards songs (except the ones about Mick's mother) were about girls they met at debutante balls. This one seemed to be no longer in favor with Mick, but Keith liked his guitar part and didn't have to sing the words.

> Under my thumb's a squirming dog who's just had her day
> Under my thumb's a girl who has just changed her ways
> . . . It's down to me, the change has come, she's under my
>   thumb

Coming with a crash after the gospel truth, the song appeared to draw the audience toward the stage by levitation. Jon and Gary were driven backward, while Pete, incredibly, still ambled down front, bantering with girls in the aisle. Without pausing the Stones went into "I'm Free." Before the first chorus ended, Jon and Gary had been pulled onstage, Ronnie had run backstage with the crowd snapping at his heels, and even Pete had gotten out of the way.

The New York newspaper critics would judge this concert a failure, not as a musical performance but as a riot. "The biggest surprise at the Garden last night," the *Post* reporter wrote, "was that the Stones gave us a nice concert, no more and no less. Did Mick Jagger really think he was going to get busted for inciting to riot in a hall that was built for cigar smoke and the ringing echo of fight announcements?"

If Mick expected arrests and riots, he had said nothing about it; and if a little old riot were all anybody had wanted, things would have been simpler. But the Stones' last American tour had started with a riot on the East Coast, and there were more than enough sadistic elements floating around to confuse pudgy newspapermen. Sixteen thousand people listened to Mick sing

> We all free
>   if we want to be
> You know we all free

and the song ended with a surge of energy that seemed too strong for the Garden to contain. The Stones and their audience were following decent impulses toward a wilderness where are no laws, toward the rough beast that knows no gentle right, nor aught obeys but his foul appetite.

The lights went out, we heard a drum roll and soft, almost whimpering, harp sounds. Three spots, white-red-white, streaked through the arena's blackness to where Mick, crouched on the purple carpet, was asking, "Did you hear about the Midnight Rambler?" Mick made you feel all the madness and the terror as he purged the demons. The song was the soul of relentlessness: *Everybody got to go.*

"When suddenly the police move in, it's very disturbing and you begin to wonder just how much freedom you really have," Mick had said while awaiting his first trial. Mick talked of freedom, the newspapers talked of riots. Who was more correct? Stay tuned and hear the sad story. But is it freedom a man wants who sings

> I'm called the hit-and-run rape her in anger
> The knife-sharpened tippytoe

whirling, hands high on small of back, ribs and lips thrust out, then kneeling, swinging his metal-studded belt like a whip. What could he want—and what could they want, those who shriek in ecstasy at his song? And what did I want, watching them, taking notes? Whatever we wanted, it wasn't what we would get.

Hot orange lights seared the air. Mick, himself again, just having a romp, was saying, "Thank you, now we gonna do one that asks the question, Would you like to live with me?" To which Janis Joplin, backstage left, shouted her rude reply. In front of the stage, a blond girl in a gold vest, a redhead in a rose T-shirt and suspenders, and a brunette wearing a gypsy scarf looked on, gone with the wonder. Keith was shaking his head, lost in the music. Tony was crouching by the piano, alert to snatch Mick from the tidal wave of bodies. "We'd like to see you," Mick said, and the house lights came on as "Little Queenie" began. A boy by the stage, hands in air, was drumming on heaven's door. Jagger was grinding his hips, making eye contact with a girl in a petticoat dancing before the stage, his mouth open wide in a big orgasmic smile. Hendrix was smiling, as if saying to himself, This is it, the real rock and roll soup. I couldn't see anyone who wasn't smiling. Keith, his eyes closed, was controlling with nods and shakes the rhythm of the entire building—Charlie's rhythm and through him Bill's and so little Mick's and Mick's and all the way to the back of the Garden.

As "Satisfaction" began, Mick sat down holding a hand mike, one preaching finger waggling overhead. The audience began crashing onto the stage, two girls and a boy coming aboard at once, Sam, Tony, and one of Jaymes' men running to pick them up and set them gently down on the floor again. The loose women in the crowd helped on the high notes of "Honky Tonk Women," as Mick requested, and at the end of "Street Fighting Man," with Keith turning it up all the way and everybody in the place going mad, I started once again to hear over all a high singing sound like the Angel Choir, ringing up in the smoky, metal spines of Madison Square, a noise that much later, as I waited to be locked up, I could hear still ringing and ringing over the sounds of everything else. Down front a man was holding up a (stunned, it appeared) baby for a look. The audience was undulating like one giant creature.

Great red jugs of acid-laced Kool-Aid were being passed around, onto the stage and back into the crowd. The amplifiers were giving off heat and the smell of old-fashioned radios. Keith rested his guitar against his thigh, ripping it up and down like a gunfighter drawing faster and faster, over and over. Mick, by the edge of stage right, started moving backward in reverse-motion picture fashion and sailed the basket of red rose petals high out over the crowd where they hung for a moment, as the Stones unplugged and ran, and then started slowly to descend, floating on the high ringing howl.

We wheeled out of the Garden, stopping to honk at a saw horse somebody had left in front of the exit. A teenaged boy ran out with us, so fast that he kept up for three or four blocks. A few boys and girls followed in cars, not many, but we drove as if we had just robbed the Deadwood stage and, bouncing along, tore off our muffler so we really sounded terrible, racing through town in a limo full of bodyguards, wall-to-wall muscle, loving every second of it.

At the hotel we gathered in Keith's suite. Wyman went away with Astrid, and Mick went to a party at Jimi Hendrix's, where he would make off with the lady of the house and bring her to the Plaza for a few days to console him in his woman troubles. (Her name was Devon Wilson; Hendrix's closest female companion, she was reputed to have an appetite for all kinds of drugs and sex. She would die a few years later of an unexplained fall from a window of the Chelsea Hotel.) At the Plaza I had a stack of messages from Cynthia, but Keith, Charlie, little Mick, Sam, and I went to Slug's, a jazz club in the East Village that *The New Yorker* called "a frabjous sort of place, in a somewhat vorpal neighborhood."

On the way downtown I mentioned that Michael Lydon had told me about B. B. King going off by himself and getting drunk in Philadelphia because he thought he'd done a bad show.

"It's good that he still gets so upset," Keith said. "You got to be able to do it every night, and it ain't easy. Especially if you ain't done it in three years."

After driving around several wrong blocks we found Slug's. The neighborhood was dark, but inside the place was crowded and noisy with the sounds of the Tony Williams Lifetime—Williams on drums, John McLaughlin on guitar, and a white organ player. "Is there somebody who can get us a table?" Keith asked. I shoved up to the bar and said to the light-skinned, leading-man-style black bartender, "The Rolling Stones are here, could you have somebody get them a table—"

"Man," he said, drawing a beer, "we don't—"

"Cater to Rolling Stones?"

"That's right," he said—so hip and aloof that I was delighted— saying with a shrug that it may count for something uptown, all that popularity and screaming and money, but down here the only thing that counts is musicianship, mother.

"If you stay as straight as you are, you'll go to heaven," I said, and not looking up, still drawing beer, he smiled.

"Do you sell them drinks?" I asked.

"Sure, man," he said. I gave him an order and he said he'd send them to our table, there ought to be some space down front, and sure enough there were a couple of small tables. The Lifetime were starting another song, or whatever it was they played for half an hour at a time: sometimes melodies, sometimes noises, Williams sweating, doing things for sound effects—putting a mike inside his hi-hat cymbal and pulling it out as he closed it with an odd swipp! Lost chords strayed up from the organ, McLaughlin played weird noises on guitar. The music had little emotional appeal but they played with energy and enthusiasm, and it held your attention if only because it changed completely every couple of minutes. At one point Williams played a bopshoo*bop*! bopshoo*bop*! boogaloo pattern and Charlie said, "That's the only thing he's played all night that I play myself, actually."

Finally it was getting on toward dawn and the driver, who'd come in to listen with us, went out and brought the car around, and we went back to the hotel. "I'd never play anything like that," Keith said as we were driving along, "but it's good to go hear it."

At the Plaza Keith and I told Charlie, little Mick, and Sam good night and went to Jon Jaymes' room because Keith didn't have his key in his no-pockets pants. Jon came to the door in his white boxer shorts, hair rumpled, face rumpled. Keith told him to call a bellman while I went in and pissed in his—not his hat—his toilet, swaying a little, drunk and so tired, hadn't slept right since I didn't know when. We left Jon's and went down to sit on the rug in the corridor outside Keith's room. In a minute or two here came a little worried-looking Italian bellman. He let us in and I bribed him, because Keith had no cash, to go somewhere in the New York night—no room service at this hour—and fetch us back one cheeseburger, one hamburger, two Cokes, and one pot of tea.

"I've got something in here that might interest you," Keith said when the bellman left. Going into the bedroom, sitting down on the bed, he opened a drawer of the bedside table and took out a couple of capsules filled with white powder.

"No, not me," I said.

"Huh?" Keith said, looking up. "I've seen you do coke." Then he saw I was joking and opened the caps into two piles on a small tray.

"This is heroin," Keith said. "I don't do it very often, just take it when you get it—keep it around, you get hung up on it." He split each pile in two and sniffed two up, using the gold bamboo he wore on a gold chain around his neck, then handed me the tray and bamboo and headed for the living room. I inhaled the other two mounds of bitter powder and followed. Keith was in a corner threading a tape into his recorder, which was old and grey and looked like something John Garfield would use to call Dane Clark in a World War II jungle picture.

"Got something I want you to hear," he said. "Memphis Minnie— and some other things." The tape started, indecipherable. "Ah, it's not wound properly." Keith shook the recorder and it rattled as if it were about to fall apart. After a couple of shakes it was working fine, playing a tape of blues from the twenties and thirties—Minnie Douglas, Curley Weaver, Butterbeans and Susie. I went into my much-rehearsed speech about how the old bluesmen had been ripped off.

"This is a great song," Keith said.

"You can go to college, you can go to school," Washington Phillips sang, "but if you ain't got Jesus you's an educated fool—"

The bellman arrived with our food and I was so relaxed and vaguely nauseated from the heroin that I took one bite of my hamburger and put it down. Keith didn't eat either. Lucille Bogan sang "Shave 'Em Dry," which begins, "I got nipples on my titties big as the end of yo' thumb, I got somethin' 'tween my legs can make a dead man come—" and goes on from there to get dirty. We talked about the kids who came to the shows night after night, wondering how they really felt, a mystery to all of us. I thought of Mick onstage waving to the crowd with one hand in a V-sign, the other making a clenched fist. "I don't think they understand what we're trying to do," Keith said, "or what Mick's talking about, like on 'Street Fighting Man.' We're not saying we want to be in the streets, but we're a rock and roll band, just the reverse. Those kids at the press conferences want us to do their thing, not ours. Politics is what we were trying to get away from in the first place."

The tape ended and whipped around in the machine till the spinning ran down. Outside it was dawn, rose-gold light filtering through the long Plaza windows. We were both exhausted, eyes closing. "I think I'm gonna zonk, man," Keith said.

"Me too, if I can just make it to bed." I thanked Keith, went up to my room, undressed looking out at Central Park in the morning mist, lay down on the bed, manfully intending to make some notes, and fell asleep with my notebook on my chest, good night.

2 6

And when the curtains part, and you see a flailing mass of waving arms, it just does something to you. Right inside. There's a swaying and a roaring. Screams? I've heard some groups say they don't like them. Well, okay for them. But we like the screams. It's all part of it, the whole proceedings, do you see? That two-way thing all over again. Sometimes that atmosphere gets real tight. It feels as if it could snap.

BRIAN JONES

IN THE MIDDLE of June 1967 Brian Jones and Andrew Oldham —both of them drifting and being pushed out of the Stones' circle— were in California at the Monterey Pop Festival, hearing music by Otis Redding and Jimi Hendrix that was far better than any the Stones were then able to produce. Brian, dressed in layers of velvet and lace from the Chelsea Antique Market, stupefied with drugs, in films of the festival looks blurred, almost transparent. "Dying all the time/Lose your dreams and you will lose your mind," Mick had sung on the B side of the last single, "Ruby Tuesday," on which Brian had played ethereal, not to say haunting, flute. The last thing, Stu said, Brian ever did for the Stones.

In Chichester, on June 27, Keith and Mick appeared before Judge Leslie Block at the West Sussex Quarter Sessions, Mick in an apple-green jacket and olive trousers, Keith wearing a navy frock coat and a lace-collared shirt. Mick's case was considered first, with Malcolm Morris, Queen's Counsel, leading for the prosecution and Michael Havers, Q.C., for the defense. Chief Inspector Gordon Dinely, the first witness, testified that on February 12, at about eight o'clock in the evening, he and eighteen other police officers, three of them women, went to Redlands and found there one woman and eight men, among them Michael Philip Jagger.

Sergeant John Challen of the police party testified that in searching the premises, "I first went into the drawing-room and then went upstairs to a bedroom. There I found a green jacket, in the left-hand pocket of which I found a small phial containing four tablets. I took the jacket downstairs and Jagger admitted the jacket belonged to him and that his doctor prescribed them." Challen asked Mick who his doctor was, and Mick said, "Dr. Dixon Firth, but I can't remember if it was him." Asked what the tablets were for, Mick said, "To stay awake and work."

Called by the defense, Dr. Firth testified that the tablets, which were amphetamine, had not been prescribed by him, but that Mick had told him he had them and asked if they were all right to use. The doctor remembered this conversation as having taken place sometime before February and his having advised Mick that they were to be taken in an emergency but not regularly.

The doctor and the prosecutor exchanged opinions as to the propriety of telling Mick he could have the drugs and whether Mick's conversation with the doctor amounted to a prescription. Judge Block said he had no hesitation in saying that it did not, and that the only legitimate defense, a written prescription, was therefore not open to Michael Jagger. "I therefore direct you," he told the jury, "that there is no defense to this charge."

Within five minutes the jury came back with a guilty verdict. Judge Block granted Mick an appeal certificate and remanded him in custody at Lewes Prison. The London *Times* reported: "Mr. Jagger was driven from the building in a grey van with others prisoners on remand. Just before the van was driven out, about a dozen schoolgirls banged their fists on the closed yard gates, tried to scramble over them, and screamed, 'We want Mick.'"

On the second day of the trial, Keith, in a braid-trimmed black suit, met with the same judge and counsels before a new jury and pled not guilty to letting Redlands be used for smoking cannabis. The proceedings began with submissions concerning the relevance of certain evidence. Judge Block ruled that, within limits set by Mr. Morris, certain parties should not be named but the evidence should be submitted. Mr. Morris explained to the jury that it was necessary for him to prove that Keith had willfully and knowingly allowed cannabis to be smoked. The evidence would show, he said, that incense was being burned at Redlands to cover up the odor of cannabis. "That there was a strong, sweet smell of incense in these premises will be clear from the evidence," Morris said, "and you may well come to the conclusion that that smell could not fail to have been noticed by Keith Richards. There was ash—resulting from cannabis resin and smoking Indian hemp—actually found on the table in front of the fireplace in the drawing room where Keith Richards and his friends were. The behavior of one of the guests may suggest that she was under the influence of smoking cannabis resin in a way which Richards could not fail to notice."

The English newspapers, including *The Times,* ran photographs of Marianne Faithfull near the unnamed female guest part of the story. Years later she would confirm that the green velvet jacket and the amphetamines Mick was jailed for having were hers. The trial ruined whatever shred of good repute she might have had.

Keith testified that he had driven down from London with Mick and Marianne for a weekend party attended by Michael Cooper, Christopher Gibbs, Robert Fraser, and Fraser's Moroccan servant, Mohamed. (Fraser, in possession of heroin during the raid, had been found guilty and jailed along with Mick.) George Harrison of the Beatles and his wife Patti came late and left before the police arrived. Two other guests, not friends of Mick or Keith, also came—David Schneidermann, a Canadian familiarly known as "Acid-King David," and a person described in *The Times* as "an exotic" from Chelsea, customarily seen in the King's Road in red silk trousers and shirt, bells around his neck, and flowers behind his ears. His only known occupation at the time of the party was "forever blowing bubbles through one of those wire wands." The group drove down more or less in convoy to Redlands, arriving there late Saturday night or early Sunday morning. The party finally broke up about five o'clock in the morning. The four bedrooms upstairs in the house were occupied, so Keith slept in a chair downstairs.

About eleven o'clock Keith awoke to find Schneidermann already up and Mohamed in the kitchen. Keith had a cup of tea and went into the garden for an hour or so. When he went back into the house he heard people discussing a trip to the beach. All but two guests, neither of them Schneidermann, went to the beach and were there between twenty minutes and half an hour. Keith walked the mile and a half back to the house; most of the others went by car, including Schneidermann, who had a minivan. Sometime during the morning the Harrisons left.

In the afternoon Mohamed drove the others in a minibus down to the house of Edward James, the father of English surrealist art, at West-dean, on the Downs, a house reputed to contain a sofa shaped like Mae West's lips. But they were unable to get in and returned to Keith's about five-thirty. Keith went upstairs, had a bath, changed his shirt and got back downstairs between six-fifteen and six-thirty. Mohamed was pre-paring a Moroccan meal. By seven-thirty the meal was finished and the guests had collected in the living room. The television was turned to a film called *Pete Kelly's Blues*, but the sound was off and records were playing. Incense was burning.

"It just so happened," Keith said a number of years later, "we all took acid and were in a completely freaked-out state when they arrived. They weren't ready for that. There's a big knock at the door. Eight o'clock. Everybody is just sort of gliding down slowly from the whole day of sort of freaking about. Everyone has managed to find their way back to the house. Strobe lights are flickering. Marianne Faithfull has just decided that she wanted a bath and has wrapped herself up in a rug and is watching the box.

" 'Bang, bang, bang,' this big knock at the door and I go to answer it. 'Oh, look, there's lots of little ladies and gentlemen outside. . . .'

"We were just gliding off from a twelve-hour trip. You know how that freaks people out when they walk in on you. The vibes are so funny for them. I told one of the women with them they brought to search the ladies, 'Would you mind stepping off that Moroccan cushion. Because you're ruining the tapestries. . . .' We were playin' it like that. They tried to get us to turn the record player off and we said, 'No. We won't turn it off but we'll turn it down.' As they went, as they started going out the door, somebody put on 'Rainy Day Women' really loud: 'Everybody must get stoned.' And that was it."

The police did not know about the acid, so it wasn't mentioned at the trial. But the immoral atmosphere, the sweet smell of incense, the naked girl. . . . "Would you agree," Mr. Morris asked Keith, "in the ordinary course of events, you would expect a young woman to be embarrassed if she had nothing on but a rug in the presence of eight men, two of whom were hangers-on and the third a Moroccan servant?"

Keith: "Not at all."

Mr. Morris, regarding Keith as if he were—in the words of that horror writer Poe—"a loathsome—a repulsive mass of putridity": "You regard that, do you, as quite normal?"

"Man, we're not old men," Keith said. "We don't have these petty morals." All the papers quoted that line, and the jurors, the justices and the judge would all remember that line.

Mr. Havers made the error of bringing the rug to court. It was about eight feet long and five feet wide, orange on one side, with a fur back. Havers surely intended to show the jury that the rug was

capacious, enough material there for three fur-and-orange dresses—
but Woman Detective Constable Rosemary Slade said that she was the
third officer through the door when the search party entered the
house. She looked left and saw on the sofa a young woman in the
nude. When she returned to the living room after searching the upstairs, the young woman was still there, but she was then wearing a
rug around her shoulders.

Sergeant John Challen testified that he was in an upstairs bedroom
and had just found on a small bedside table a pudding basin containing ash and cigaret ends when he saw the young woman come upstairs
with a policewoman. She let the rug drop. Challen: "She had her back
to me. She was naked. I heard a man in the bedroom, using the telephone, laugh."

Woman Detective Constable E. D. Fuller testified that she went upstairs with Marianne. "I followed her upstairs, and at the top of the
stairs there was a uniformed police officer, and in a bedroom there
was a man using the telephone. She allowed the rug to drop and said,
'Look, they want to search me.' There was laughter. The clothing in
the room appeared to be hers. I searched her as far as necessary and
we returned downstairs. She was still wearing only the rug. Her behavior generally was that she seemed unconcerned about what was
going on around her."

Mr. Havers deplored the testimony regarding the girl who was "not
on trial or able to make a defense." He said, "I am not going to
allow this girl into the witness box. I am not going to tear that blanket
of anonymity aside and let the world laugh or scorn as they will."
Everybody who cared knew who the girl was anyway, especially after
the Mars Bar rumor got around. When the police arrived, so the
story went, Mick had been eating a candy bar that Marianne was holding
without the use of her limbs—how do these things get started?

On the last day of the trial, Keith was the only witness. He accused
the News of the World (they'd taken credit for tipping off the police
after an anonymous caller told them about Keith's "drug party") of
having hired Schneidermann, who Keith said planted drugs in his
house to ruin Mick's libel suit against the paper. (Later Keith decided
he'd been turned in by someone who was working for him at the time,
but you seldom know for sure.) Keith said that no one to his knowledge was smoking cannabis and that Marianne had been preparing
for a bath and behaved in a perfectly normal and decorous fashion.

In his final instructions to the jury, Judge Block told them to put
out of their minds any prejudice they might feel about the way
Richards dressed or about his observation on "petty morals" and to
ignore everything they had read in the newspapers about two of the
house party admitting to or being convicted of possession of drugs. He

asked the jury also to disregard the evidence as to the lady who was alleged by the police to be in some condition of undress and not to let that prejudice their minds in any way.

After being out for an hour and five minutes the jury came back and pronounced Keith guilty. Mick and Robert Fraser, who had been taken between court and prison in handcuffs, were brought up to join Keith in the dock for sentence.

The judge gave Keith one year's imprisonment and ordered him to pay £500 toward prosecution costs. Fraser was sentenced to six months in jail and £200 costs. "I sentence you to three months and one hundred pounds costs," the judge said to Mick, who burst into tears. There were yelps of pain from the gallery, crowded with teenagers.

Mick was taken off to Brixton Prison, Keith and Fraser to Wormwood Scrubs. Of his experience there Keith said, "Now Wormwood Scrubs is a hundred and fifty years old, man. I wouldn't even want to play there, much less live there. They take me inside. They don't give you a knife and fork, they give you a spoon with very blunt edges so you can't do yourself in. They don't give you a belt, in case you hang yourself. It's that bad in there.

"They give you a little piece of paper and a pencil. Both Robert and I, the first thing we did is sit down and write. 'Dear Mum, don't worry, I'm in here and someone's workin' to get me out, da-da-da.' Then you're given your cell. And they start knockin' on the bars at six in the morning to wake you up. All the other prisoners started droppin' bits of tobacco through for me, 'cause in any jail tobacco is the currency. Some of them were really great. Some of them were in for life. Shovin' papers under the floor to roll it up with. The first thing you do automatically when you wake up is drag the chair to the window and look up to see what you can see out of the window. It's an automatic reaction. That one little square of sky, tryin' to reach it. It's amazing. I was going to have to make these little Christmas trees that go on cakes. And sewing up mailbags. Then there's the hour walk when you have to keep moving, round in a courtyard. Cats comin' up behind me, it's amazing, they can talk without moving their mouths, 'Want some hash? Want some acid?' Take acid? In here?

"Most of the prisoners were really great. 'What you doin' in here? Bastards. They just wanted to get you.' They filled me in. 'They been waitin' for you in here for ages,' they said. So I said, 'I ain't gonna be in here very long, baby, don't worry about that.'

"And that afternoon, they had the radio playing, this fucking Stones record comes on. And the whole prison started, 'Rayyy!' Goin' like mad. Bangin' on the bars. They knew I was in and they wanted to let me know.

"They took all the new prisoners to have their photographs taken

sitting on a swivel stool, looked like an execution chamber. Really
hard. Face and profile. Those are the sort of things they'll do automatically if they pick you up in America, you get fingerdabs and photographs. In England, it's a much heavier scene. You don't get photographs
and fingerprinted until you've been convicted.

"Then they take you down to the padre and the chapel and the
library, you're allowed one book and they show you where you're going
to work and that's it. That afternoon, I'm lyin' in my cell, wondering
what the fuck was going on and suddenly someone yelled, 'You're out,
man, you're out. It's just been on the news.' So I started kickin' the
shit out of the door, I said, 'You let me out, you bastards, I got bail.' "

Mick was released from prison first, and *The Times* was watching:
"Mr. Jagger smiled and waved from his chauffeur-driven Bentley as he
left Brixton Prison yesterday at 4:20 P.M. As the car with darkened
windows drove along Jebb Avenue, which leads from the jail, and into
Brixton Road, Mr. Jagger sat in the back seat by himself, wearing a
beige sports coat and a yellow shirt. He smiled at photographers and
a small group of girls, most of them in school uniform, who were waiting to see him leave.

"The car then drove to West London to pick up Mr. Richards at
Wormwood Scrubs gaol, in Shepherd's Bush. When it arrived at 5:10
P.M. Mr. Jagger looked pale. After spending five minutes in the gaol
the car came out again with Mr. Jagger and Mr. Richards in it. It
stopped for half a minute as photographers thronged around. Mr.
Richards, wearing a dark blue Regency-style suit, gave photographers
a grin. The car drove off towards London." Their immediate destination was a meeting with their lawyers in King's Bench Walk, then on
to the Feathers, a Fleet Street pub where they talked to reporters.
They were freed on bail amounting to £7000 apiece.

Mick, wearing a button that said MICK IS SEX, drank an iced vodka
and lime and said, "There's not much difference between a cell and a
hotel room in Minnesota. And I do my best thinking in places without
distractions." Marianne later said that when she and Michael Cooper
visited Mick on his first night in Lewes Prison, he was almost in tears;
but there were no reporters in prison. Mick said that while in jail he
had written some poetry "connected a little with the circumstances"
and that he might write a song about it. "We don't bear a grudge
against anyone for what has happened," he said. "We just think the
sentences were rather harsh."

Keith said of being a criminal: "It's just like bein' Jimmy Cagney."

Handcuffs—"Jagger links"—went on sale in short but trendy Carnaby
Street.

The case was the occasion for much comment in the press. The
court action was approved by some newspapers and periodicals and dis-

approved by others, including the *New Law Journal* and *The Times*, whose editor, William Rees-Mogg, with his editorial "Who Breaks a Butterfly on a Wheel?" risked contempt charges for commenting on the case while it was under appeal. After an editorial in the *Sunday Mirror* asking why Mick and Keith's appeals were being put off, as they were, till October, before which time they could not travel out of the country, the Lord Chief Justice stepped in and the appeals were scheduled to be heard on July 31.

On the day the appeals date was changed, Brian was observed by devoted fans leaving his Courtfield Road flat with Suki Poitier, who had been the girlfriend of Brian's friend Tara Browne, the young Guinness heir who was killed the year before in an automobile accident. Suki looked like Anita (less hot in the eye and sharp in the tooth) and so looked very much like Brian, who was leaving the flat on his way to the Priory, a psychiatric hospital in Roehampton. Not even at such a posh zoo as the Priory were they prepared for a patient who arrived with chauffeur, entourage, and concubine, demanding (unsuccessfully) a double room. Brian had told his doctor, "I need treatment. I'm ill. I can't live any longer if life goes on like this."

One of the many things bothering Brian was that the raid on Keith's house and all its pursuant miseries—as well as Brian's own drug charges, on which he would stand trial in October—had come about because he had been babbling in Blaise's. A *News of the World* spy in the hip King's Road *boîte* observed Brian taking pills and showing some girls a chunk of hashish, inviting them to his flat for a smoke, talking about taking LSD. For some reason the resulting story identified Brian as Mick.

Brian was at the Priory twenty days. The day he left, one week before Mick and Keith were to appeal their sentences, a full-page advertisement appeared in *The Times*. It contained a petition of five suggestions to the Home Secretary, of which the key proposal was the last: "All persons now imprisoned for possession of cannabis or for allowing cannabis to be smoked on private premises should have their sentences commuted." Sixty-four people—including Ph.D.s, Nobel Prize winners, the Beatles (flashing their MBE's), and Graham Greene —signed it.

On July 31, Keith and Mick's appeals were considered by the Lord Chief Justice's court. Keith had the chicken pox and waited in another room where he wouldn't contaminate the Law. After two hours, with Havers and Morris arguing for and against the appeals, the court adjourned for five minutes and returned to quash Keith's conviction for lack of evidence. Since Mick had been clearly in possession of drugs without a prescription, his appeal against conviction was dismissed, but his appeal against sentence was successful, and the court granted him a conditional discharge, meaning that if he kept out of trouble with the law for the next twelve months, what had happened would not count as a conviction. If he committed another offense during that time, he would be sentenced for both offenses.

The experience of going to court and to jail had not been pleasant for Keith, but for Mick, who was not so much as Keith a natural outlaw, it was more difficult emotionally and more expensive. He had paid out several thousand pounds, an attempt to bribe police into dropping charges that failed to reach the right people. "Everybody has been burned before," the Byrds, at one time Gram Parson's group, had sung. "Everybody knows the score."

After the appeals and a hot, crowded press conference at Granada Television in Golden Square, Mick was flown by helicopter to a country house in Essex. Waiting in the garden for a televised interview with Mick were William Rees-Mogg, the editor of *The Times*; Father Corbishley, the Jesuit; Lord Stow Hill; and John Robinson, the Bishop of Woolwich. Their general desire was for Mick to admit that his case proved the healthy state of English justice, and the heavily tranquilized Mick, mush-mouthed, would not agree, but he was unable to mention anything specific to which he could object except persecution of homosexuals and capital punishment, both of which had already been legally brought to his position. The meeting's only conclusive note was Mick's: "I am very happy today."

Whatever the legal significance of the case, it came down in many people's minds to a battle between opposing ways of life. On August 14 the *Daily Mail* reported that Mick and Marianne had been publicly snubbed twice in three days, at a party at Kilkenny Castle and by taxi drivers at Heathrow Airport, who refused to carry them. "My kids have to ride in this cab," one driver said. The Stones were snubbed also by the BBC, which refused to show on one of its music programs a film the Stones had made to introduce their new single, "We Love You." Conceived by Mick in his cell, the record began with the actual sound of a prison guard's footsteps and the slamming of a cell door. It was going to prove not very commercial in England, but in the United States it would go to number one faster than any of the Stones' previous records. The film parodied the trial of Oscar Wilde, with Mick as Wilde, wearing a green carnation; Keith as the Judge with a wig made of pound notes; and Wilde's lover "Bosie" played by Marianne Faithfull in a miniwig.

One or two of the Beatles appeared as background singers on "We Love You." Keith and Mick had sung backing vocals and Brian had played tenor saxophone on the Beatles' recent single, "All You Need Is Love." Back in April, while the Stones were floundering in a sea of heartbreaking and lawbreaking (even Bill Wyman had been in the news; Diane, his wife, had left him in February, telling the press, "I'm not prepared to share him with thousands of strange women"), the Beatles released a lavish album, *Sgt. Pepper's Lonely Hearts Club Band*, on the cover of which they appeared, dressed as Sgt. P.'s L.H.C.B. in colorful satin uniforms, among a crowd that included Mae West, Karl Marx, Sonny Liston, William Burroughs, and a doll wearing a pullover knitted to read "WMPS Good Guys Welcome the Rolling Stones," around a grave that represented and, as it turned out, did signify the death of the Beatles. "The era of playing on each other's records" may have been, as Mick would say, a joke, but at the time the Beatles might have been, as John Lennon had recently said, more popular than Jesus. Lennon's statements resulted in much outrage, an extreme example of which was the burning of Beatles records sponsored by radio station WAYX in Waycross, Georgia, where Gram and I used to live. In a public apology, Lennon said he meant that the Beatles were "having more influence on kids and things than anything else, including Jesus." They were certainly an enormous influence; everywhere you began to see boys with long hair, flashing the V-sign for some undefined victory that would come someplace besides Vietnam.

The biggest and richest and best educated generation in history knew no better than previous and later tiny, deprived generations what life was about. Prudent people cultivated their gardens. Early in September, Charlie and Shirley Watts moved from the Old Brewery House at Southover into Peckham's, a thirteenth-century farmhouse at Halland, eight miles from Lewes, where Mick and Keith had been tried. A forty-acre farm went with the house, but Charlie said he intended to lease all the land except the garden to a farmer.

On September 14, four of the Stones left Heathrow for America— Brian and Suki being photographed by English *paparazzi*—to work on the $25,000 cover (a 3-D photograph with images that moved) for their new album, *Satanic Majesties*. On their arrival the Stones were delayed while immigration officers questioned Keith for more than half an hour before allowing him "deferred entry." When Mick and Marianne arrived from Paris on a later flight, Mick was also questioned and his luggage thoroughly searched.

After a seven-minute interview with the Stones the next morning, the director of immigrations said that they were being allowed to stay pending the arrival of court records. As Mick left, one of the immigration officers asked for an autograph for his daughter. The Stones stayed at the Warwick Hotel, where a war correspondent named Martin Gorshen, back from his third trip to Vietnam, where U.S. forces had increased in five years from five thousand to five hundred thousand, saw them and wrote a newspaper piece to complain: "We've got kids dying out there without a sound and we've got punks here who dress up like girls and make millions of dollars doing it."

The Stones had made millions—their Decca records had earned around a hundred million dollars—but they were having trouble getting at the money. While in New York they met with Allen Klein, who had taken the $1.4 million advance from Decca and deposited it not into the Stones' business account, Nanker Phelge Music Ltd. in London, but the U.S.-based N.P.M. Inc., Klein's own creation. It would take the Stones years to learn that Klein had spent all the money on General Motors stock, which produced little of the ready vital to being nigger rich. Their contract with Klein, he would point out when the time came, obliged him only to pay them the advance within twenty years.

Money was a big problem, but the Stones had bigger ones. Their major effort of the last two years had been, apart from staying out of prison, trying to learn to make Rolling Stones records without Brian. For most of the *Satanic* sessions Brian had been absent, spending a lot of time in Spain with Suki. Brian's trial took place on October 30 at Inner London Sessions. He was charged with possession of cannabis, methedrine, and cocaine, smoking and allowing his flat to be used for smoking cannabis. He pleaded guilty to possessing and smoking cannabis, otherwise not guilty.

The prosecutor, Robin Simpson, said that on May 10, at four o'clock in the afternoon, the police searched Brian's flat. Asked if he had any drugs, Brian had said, "I suffer from asthma, the only drugs I have are for that." Eleven objects were found in different places, in different rooms, to contain or to bear traces of drugs: two canisters, two wallets, two pipes, two cigaret ends, a box of cigaret papers, a jar, a chair caster used as an ashtray. The total number of grains of cannabis found was thirty-five and a quarter, enough to make from seven to ten cigarets. The police had shown Brian a tin containing some of the material now in evidence and a phial that appeared to have traces of cocaine. "Yes, it is hash," Brian had said. "We do smoke. But not cocaine, man. That's not my scene."

The defending attorney, James Comyn, Q.C., said that Brian had suffered a breakdown and had been under strict medical care. He had been very ill but had at last responded to treatment. Comyn said that Brian was a highly intelligent (IQ 133) and versatile musician and composer, with tremendous writing talent. The defense called Dr. Leonard Henry, a psychiatrist from Northolt, Middlesex, who said that Brian had been agitated, depressed, incoherent, and had to be treated with tranquilizers and antidepressants. He was very sick and got worse. He didn't respond to treatment and was recommended for treatment in Roehampton Priory in July. Brian was now less depressed and less anxious, but the doctor said, "If he is put in prison, it would be disastrous to his health. He would have a complete mental collapse, a breakdown, and he couldn't stand the stigma. He might injure himself."

Another psychiatrist, Anthony Flood, of Harley Street, testified that Brian was "deeply distressed, anxious, and a potential suicide."

Then Brian took the stand. He was wearing a navy suit with flared jacket and bell-bottom trousers, a polka dot cravat, and shoes with Cuban heels. Judge Reginald Ethelbert Seaton said that he'd been told Brian intended cutting out drugs completely. "That is precisely my intention," Brian said. He told the judge that drugs had brought him only trouble and disrupted his career: "I hope that will be an example to others."

"I am very moved by what I have heard," the judge said, "but under the circumstances nothing less than a prison sentence would be correct. I sentence you to nine months imprisonment for being the occupier of premises, allowing them to be used for the smoking of drugs, and three months for being in possession of cannabis resin, the sentences to run concurrently."

The judge also ordered Brian to pay £250 costs and refused to grant him bail pending an appeal. Brian was led away to jail as teenaged girls, some of whom were Brian's friends and loved him, left the courtroom in tears. The next day, Brian's appeal was set for December 12, and he was released on bail.

The other Stones were digging their trenches. Mick bought a country estate near Newbury, Berkshire, called Stargroves, with a twelve-bedroom mansion that had no running water. Keith had built a nine-foot wooden fence, like a fort in a Western movie, around Redlands, and further fortified the place with two guard dogs, a Labrador named Bernard and a Great Dane named Winston.

Andrew Oldham was fast fading from the Stones picture, and the Beatles' manager, Brian Epstein, had recently died. Mick and Paul McCartney began to talk about the possibility of the two groups' purchasing a recording studio and forming a joint production company to be called Mother Earth. Neither group was happy with its record company. After the effort of making what sounded like a difficult album and creating the elaborate cover art, the Stones were infuriated by a delay in the release of *Satanic Majesties* because Decca, so they said, were out of cardboard. The album finally reached the shops at about the time of Brian's appeal.

Brian appeared before a panel of four judges. Dr. Leonard Neustatter, a court-appointed psychiatrist who had interviewed Brian four times, said that he was intelligent but "emotionally unstable, with neurotic tendencies." In a report prepared for the appeals court, Dr. Neustatter wrote, "He vacillates between a passive, dependent child with a confused image of an adult on the one hand, and an idol of pop culture on the other."

Dr. Leonard Henry, again testifying for Brian, said that, faced with an intolerable situation, Brian "might well make an attempt on his life."

In the light of these opinions and the fact that Brian had never before been convicted of anything worse than peeing in a garage—though he had been guilty of worse things many times—the court substituted a £1000 fine and three years probation for Brian's prison term, telling him: "The court has shown a degree of mercy, but you cannot go and boast, saying you've been let off. If you commit another offence of any sort—you will be brought back and punished afresh. And you know what sort of sentence you will get."

Two days later, Brian was taken to St. George's Hospital in London after being found unconscious on the floor of a flat in Chelsea, rented in the name of his chauffeur, John Coray. Doctors in the hospital's emergency department wanted Brian to stay, but he left after an hour, saying he was only exhausted and wanted to go home.

Mick and Marianne were in Brazil for the holidays, staying at a remote beach where the people thought that Marianne was the Virgin Mary, the unshaven Mick was Joseph, and Nicholas, Marianne's two-year-old son, was the baby Jesus. Keith and Anita were in Italy, Bill and Astrid were in Sweden. Charlie was at home with Shirley, who was going to have a baby.

As the new year began, Jo Bergman, who had come to work for the Stones in September, made an analysis of their situation:

1. Rolling Stones personal working accounts overdrawn
2. Rolling Stones #3 account overdrawn
3. Telexes sent to Klein by us and Lawrence Myers
4. Promise of £2000 to be sent Thursday
5. Need £7000 to clear most pressing debts
6. Money needed for studio & offices
7. Summary
   (a) due to lack of funds in personal accounts, some bills paid out of Rolling Stones account #3
   (b) no funds for running of office
   (c) Rolling Stones accountant Mr. Trowbridge has been forced to find an alternative

The Stones started rehearsing in February and by mid-March were recording songs for a new album. Brian, who felt he could no longer play with the Stones, was participating very little. In March he was in the office and left a note for Jo, whom he feared, thinking that she was Jagger's enforcer.

> Dear Jo,
> I need the following dates for to do my recording thing in Morocco: 22nd→25th or 26th March. This is the only time I can get it done, and I honestly believe

I can get something really worthwhile from this venture
for us. If this means I have to miss a session or two, I
can dub my scenes on after, while vocals are being
done or whatever. Incidentally the Morocco thing is
only part of my venture. I am confident I can come up
with something really groovy. I will talk to you later
about financing the thing, if that be possible. I don't
need that much. Hope it happens!   Love Brian
                    Talk to you later—

Before Brian could get out of London, he was again in the news:
STONES GIRL NAKED IN DRUG DRAMA, the *News of the World* headline
said. Linda Keith, a disc jockey's daughter who had once been Keith's
girlfriend and was now, at least part of the time, Brian's, called her
doctor, told him where she was and that she was going to overdose
on drugs. The doctor called the police, who knocked down the door of
the Chesham Place flat, rented to Brian's chauffeur, where Brian
stayed in London. Linda was inside, right in style, naked and unconscious. After she had been taken to the hospital, Brian arrived at
the flat. "I had been at an all-night recording session," he told reporters,
"and when I came back just after twelve I found the police at the flat.
I was absolutely shattered when the landlord of the flat asked the
police to have me removed. He said, 'It's because you are trespassing.
We don't want your kind in this place.' I explained to him that I rented
the flat for my chauffeur and only lived here when I was in town. But
he wouldn't listen to me. I have paid six months rent in advance, but
it didn't make any difference to him. I can't understand it."
    The next day, Linda left the hospital and Brian moved to the Royal
Avenue House in the King's Road. And the day after that, Serafina
Watts was born.
    Brian went to Marrakech to record some musicians called the
G'naoua, Glyn Johns going along as engineer. Glyn and Brian didn't
get along, and the music was disappointing. Though he would return
to Morocco in the summer to record in Joujouka with Brion Gysin,
Brian was back in London by the end of April. The Stones had
finished a new single, "Jumpin' Jack Flash," with an optimistic chorus:

But it's all right now
In fact it's a gas

It was time. The *Daily Express* for May 9, in a story titled "Things
Look Bad for Rolling Stones," observed that the Stones had not had
a number one single since "Paint It, Black" over two years ago.
    But three days after that story appeared the Stones gave a surprise

performance at the *New Musical Express* Pollwinner's Concert at Wembley Stadium—they had been named the top rhythm & blues group. It was just like the old days, girls screaming, cops with linked arms holding back hysterical fans. The Stones did "Jumpin' Jack Flash" and "Satisfaction," and Mick threw his white shoes into the crowd.

Nine days later, four days before "Jumpin' Jack Flash" was released, Brian was again arrested for drugs. He had heard the screams for the last time.

2 7

Men have brought their powers of subduing the forces of nature to such a pitch that by using them they could now very easily exterminate one another to the last man. They know this—hence arises a great part of their current unrest, their dejection, their mood of apprehension. And now it may be expected that the other of the two *heavenly forces*, eternal Eros, will put forth his strength so as to maintain himself alongside of his equally immortal adversary.

SIGMUND FREUD: *Civilization and Its Discontents*

I S L E P T the sleep of the exhausted and overdosed but not for long because Gore called. Being like all speed freaks evangelistic, Gore wanted to take me to his doctor, and because I was crazy and going crazier I got up and dressed and went out to meet him on the corner in front of the shop Paranoia, I mean Paraphernalia. After about four hours' sleep I was still anesthetized by the heroin, didn't order any breakfast at the hotel, but arriving a few minutes early to meet Gore, I went into a small grocery, drank half a pint of milk and almost threw up on the spot.

To distract myself and kill time, I went across the street to a drug-store and called a girl I'd known slightly in Memphis, where she went to the Art Academy. She now lived in Manhattan and knew Ronnie

Schneider, whom she'd plied with an idea that had become all too common in the sixties; to film the old bluesmen with some of their rock and roll progeny, in this case the Rolling Stones. At least she didn't want to float the Band down the Mississippi, as another jerk had suggested, hauling Furry and Bukka out to the boat for a little bottle-neckin' and hambonin'. Ronnie had told me she wanted to talk to me. My reaction against him had been so violent that he was trying to soothe me, and his way of changing face, from considering me as carrion to accepting me at least for the moment as a fellow bird, was to say, Gee, we've got a mutual friend, she said she'd like to talk to you —so I called her and she told me that she had her plan all together, she just needed me to help her get one last detail, the Rolling Stones. I told her I'd see what I could do, knowing what that would be.

I crossed the street again and there was Gore, blond and tortoise-shelled and schoolboyish. He said his regular speed doctor was out of town, so we walked back over near the Plaza for a visit with one Adolf B. Wolfmann, M.D., D.D.S., D.M.D. He was not quite as bad as Peter Sellers in *The Wrong Box*, blotting his prescriptions with a kitten, but he gave you the feeling he had a lot to be surreptitious about. He let us in, a man with a grizzled red pompadour and a white hospital coat, throwing two bolts to open the street door, locking them again behind us, unlocking two more locks to let us into an inner office, opening another lock to let us into a small room with a padded examination table. Gore introduced us and said, "He wants to start taking the treatments."

"You want to start the treatments also? All right, wait here."

Maybe he went and pulled a tooth, but he came back with two horsecock needles full of I suppose Methedrine and egg yolk, Gore and I dropped our trousers, he shot us up, we paid him ten dollars American apiece, he threw the bolts to let us out, and we sailed away down Central Park South, hearing behind us the faint snapping of locks.

I had felt faint and limp-wristed, but with the charge in my ass I decided we didn't need a cab, we could walk across town to Madison Square Garden for the Stones' afternoon concert. Out of an earnest desire not to rob this account of its true interest, I will confess that I was carrying the red carnation from my bedside table at the Plaza; so there I went, boots, jeans, and leather jacket, sniffing a long-stemmed red carnation, looking like some insane faggot ought to be kilt with a shovel, as we walked briskly through the streets, fatigue gone, feeling ardent.

At the Garden Terry Reid was on. Not since "Bunch Up, Little Dogies" in Fort Collins had he seemed to be at one with an audience, but no other audience had seemed as gentle and peaceful as that one. I never heard him do that song again. Gore went out to make a phone call, checking on a delivery to his house for a party there tonight after the Stones' evening concert, and never came back. Pete and Nicole were at the show, and I went up and watched B. B. King and Ike and Tina Turner with them. Then I shouldered and slid and elbowed and threw my weight around with the guards and made it back to the stage, where the lights were going down and Sam was coming out, more mad-eyed than ever, to the mike: "The greatest rock and roll band in the world, the Rolling Stones." I kept wishing he would say, "The scaredest rock and roll band," but he never did, not even later, when there was no doubt about it.

The Stones came out, plugged in, the mushroom spines above began to reverberate with "Jumpin' Jack Flash." The traditional esthetic of popular songs required that the singer's life should be made desolate by the departure of his true love, who could make everything all right if only she would return. If such songs as Bob Dylan's "It Ain't Me, Babe" and the Stones' "Stupid Girl" and "Under My Thumb" defied that convention, they were not quite the same thing as songs about rape and murder. "Some of those early albums, like *Between the Buttons,* were so *light,*" Mick had said one day at the Oriole house while we were listening to an acetate of *Let It Bleed.* This tour would lighten his approach for good. He would go on singing about death and destruction, but he would cut out the Prince of Darkness business. He was about to have more darkness than he ever wanted.

The show was now tight, no flat spots. When Mick sang "I'm Free," all around the front of the stage were gum-chewing kids with glazed eyes, their arms held high, fingers in V-signs. One dark-haired girl, her large shapely bosom in a red and black gypsy blouse, was holding aloft her middle finger, considerably more appropriate. Kids were on the chairs, in the aisles, and in back people were yelling "Sit down."

"We'll all be standing soon," Mick told them, as Keith, hunching his back, lowering his shoulders, started "Live with Me" with peculiar whawhawha chords. By the time "Satisfaction" began, the room was once again a sea of bobbing bodies, one boy with his shirt off somehow hovering over the crowd, dancing. As "Street Fighting Man" neared its conclusion, Keith opened up his amps all the way and Mick, who'd been scampering along the edge of the stage waving with both hands, snatched up the basket filled with rose petals and scattered them—red rose petals flowing from his hands as if borne along on a breeze of guitar notes— then hurled the wicker basket out twenty yards in a graceful arc, petals drifting slowly down, clapped his Uncle Sam hat on his head and away we went, back to the hotel in limousines. This time I was the only person I knew in the car. For a mad moment I thought we were being kidnapped, but we went back to the hotel. I stretched out on my bed but couldn't get any rest because people kept coming in, editors and anthologists, literary flotsam, and Cynthia kept phoning, but I wouldn't take the calls. I lay in bed thinking about Nicole and how she had kissed me at the concert, and how I'd see her tonight at Gore's.

Then I was back at the Garden, sitting in section A, row 8, with Wexler's children, Lisa and Paul, and some of their friends. Michael Lydon and I took an early taxi because we wanted to see B.B., but the show was running late. The lights were still on and we waited, smoking grass. I put some mescaline tablets on my notebook and passed them around. I was taking them not to get high but to stay awake, the speed was running down. We sat through Terry Reid's loud and boring set, then a long delay, during which we smoked more dope, our silent vigil broken into once by Chip Monck, who said, "We're recording tonight as well, and it's complicated, please bear with us."

At last B. B. King came out in a blue suit, hands folded together on chest, making his little Afro-Oriental bow. He picked up his guitar Lucille, strapped her on, and sang "Every Day I Have the Blues." Everybody's fatigue seemed to fade away as B.B. played. I had seen him at a number of places the year before, among them the Fillmore in San Francisco, the day after Bobby Kennedy was assassinated, and the Club Paradise in Memphis, the city where Martin Luther King was assassinated earlier in the year. In the early fifties B.B. had created the archetypal electric blues guitar style. You could hear his life in his playing—the cows he'd milked, the fields he'd plowed, the streets he'd played on, the miles and years he'd had to travel to get to this night.

Alone, except for the drummer keeping time on the snare-rim, B.B. played a long ride that became a riff that started to shake as the band came in for "Little Bit of Love." B.B. played music that got all worried into tight note-cluster knots, then started to boogie and worked its way out of its trouble to ecstasy, perfectly expressive of human hopes, desires, fears, exhaustion, and beauty. Coming back for an encore, B.B. said, "This song is dedicated to you and to the stars of tonight's show, the Rolling Stones—because without them you wouldn't have heard B. B. King." He sang and played the same song he'd dedicated to Bobby Kennedy's ghost that night in San Francisco, the song that begins, "I don't even know your name, but I love you just the same—"

Jerry and Shirley Wexler showed up as B.B.'s set ended and I was headed backstage to speak with him. In the dressing room B.B. seemed tired and sad, and I went out to stand with Mick and watch Tina; this was our last chance to see her on this tour. By the time Mick slunk off to change we had been severely reminded that we were just two skinny white boys.

Wandering around backstage waiting for the Stones to go on, I noticed a great many heavyset security men. Now, in addition to the stop-sign buttons and the road-sign buttons and the GOD BLESS AMERICA buttons, there were red buttons and white buttons and green buttons. Jo, headed for the Stones' dressing room wearing all these buttons, said, giving me a green button, "Here, this is Italian power, it'll take care of you. Jon Jaymes says this is the only one that counts." Jon was fond of saying that the purpose of his organization was to make people aware that Columbus had discovered America. The Garden had lost the humane atmosphere it had possessed last night and was less freaky but no less tense than the Forum had been. The rear halls were full of strange beef and the audience was already down front, so I stayed behind the stage. When the Stones came out, Jo and Ronnie with them, I joined the tight little group moving on a raft of security men past the backdrop curtain, up the stairs to the stage. But as I climbed the stairs, two men I'd never seen before grabbed me and started to throw me off.

"Hey! Wait a minute!" I yelled, no time to reason with them. They were shoving me off the side of the stairs, I grabbed their arms, trying not to fall—and Ronnie and a couple of our familiar security men stopped them. "God, you people are rude," I told the gentlemen who'd been trying to break my neck.

"Buddy, this is my livelihood," one of them explained.

The big clock at the end of the hall said 12:01. It was the first thing everybody saw coming onstage. "I'll turn into a pumpkin," Mick said. "Sorry you had to wait—okay, babies."

"Jumpin' Jack Flash" began, and there was that feeling again—the tour was a drag, but when the music started it was all right now. The esthetic of this music—and its morality—demanded that when certain code-patterns of rhythm and melody were achieved, the only decent thing to do, in Joujouka or Congo Square or Madison Square, was to dance. Michael Lydon and I looked at each other, gave mad Indian war whoops and started to dance like medieval believers possessed by the spirit. Everybody was doing it; Mick was dancing like a demonic sprite. The very air was crazy; in spite of the icy smell of Mafia, the place seemed awfully hot. Mick was dripping wet when, at twenty past twelve, he said "Stray Cat." Sam, bent over like a graverobber, slipped onstage to put a Coke on the drum stand where Mick could reach it, sticking his head under Charlie's crash cymbal, and Charlie, seeing him, hit it harder. Mick and Keith did the blues songs devoutly, hunched over on their stools with a halo of light around their heads. From the rear of the stage I could see the audience, everybody listening, and the people backstage, nobody listening. "Under My Thumb" and "I'm Free" were very fast, Mick turning his back to the audience, lips curled, making faces at Charlie as if to say, Play harder. Jo, sitting on an amp stage right in an orange lace dress, looking like an eighteenth-century character, clapped time with "Midnight Rambler." As Mick said, "I'd like to ask you a question—would you like to live with me?", up the stairs came Leonard Bernstein with his wife, son, and daughter. Somehow Bernstein in his black turtleneck seemed to relax the atmosphere. Ronnie and one of our security men grabbed me—"Who's this? He's not with us! Let's throw him overboard!"—picked me up, both giggling madly, and rushed to the edge of the stage. I was laughing too, suddenly it was a huge party, not so threatening, just another show, the Stones were getting away with it again.

The lights went up for "Little Queenie," revealing thousands of lovely berserk kids. During "Satisfaction" somebody in the crowd was waving a crutch overhead. There was that sound again, the high keening wail over all the other sounds, a wild shrieking howl that seemed like the winds of change and joy—but things are seldom what they seem.

Mick, laughing, jumping straight up in the air, pointed to Charlie: "Charlie's good tonight, inne?" As "Honky Tonk Women" began, kids were washing onstage, Mick being attacked by a girl in a lavender crushed velvet dress, smiling as Sam and Tony rescued him. Right in front a tall black girl was looking at him, licking her lips. Behind the amps Leonard Bernstein and his family were listening, his son dancing. Keith, turning up his amps, saw me watching and started hitting his guitar strings harder, as Mick threw the rose-petal basket out into the rising wail.

Then back to the Plaza from the Garden in the limos for the last time. I went out again, to Gore's party. Nicole was waiting there for me. We went to her apartment and slept very little. In the morning I made it back to the Plaza in time to catch a plane to Boston with the Stones and the Maysles brothers.

There were news people with tape recorders and cameras waiting as we walked out of the terminal building at Logan Airport. One man, stepping close to Mick, thrusting out a microphone, asked, "Mick, will this be a *free* concert?"

"Ask the promoter," Mick said.

At the sidewalk, as we were getting into the limos, a large black woman came up and said, "I want yawlses autographs." Nobody paid any attention to her; everybody piled into the cars, and just before the doors closed she said, "I never will buy no mo' Rollin' Stones records."

We were driven to the Madison Hotel, which was attached to the Boston Garden, that night's venue. Up seventeen floors in a funky old elevator, down the badly vacuumed halls, we entered the Rolling Stones' quarters for the evening, three bedrooms and a suite. I lay down on the first bed I came to. The Maysles brothers were in the same room, dumping their equipment on the floor, talking about how much they loved Boston, their home town; they'd come up on Thanksgiving for two hours just to have breakfast here. Mick came in and sprawled across the bed.

"I'm sick," he said, "I ain't gonna do a whole show, I feel too bad.

I hurt in the head, stomach, crotch, and feet. We used to do twenty minutes, we'd do five songs in a show—take the money and run—we didn't know any better, didn't know at all what we were doing. We'd play like Savannah and there'd be two people diggin' it, so we thought what the fuck."

Sam came in to tell Mick, who'd asked for soup, that the hotel had no room service. It's grotesque, how you have to live once you've left home, but there it was, no room service. Mick asked Tony to go out to a restaurant for some soup. "Doesn't matter what kind as long as it's warm."

Tony exited stage right as from stage left, the sitting room door, in came Jon Jaymes, bringing news from the southern front. On the first page of notebook number nine I began writing about the battle of West Palm Beach, where the police had built stockades to contain hundreds of drug arrests. The governor was making arrests personally. Billy Graham had visited, disguised in a fake beard, talking to drug-crazed children in the crowd. The National Guard, on alert, was ready to move in—as were the Stones, ready to move in tomorrow, only now they weren't so sure they were going, if the things Jon had said were true.

"I have a friend there," I said. "He can tell us what's happening." I called Charlie Brown in Coconut Grove, left word at the bike shop where he worked, in five minutes the phone rang, Ronnie answered and gave it to me. I told Charlie that I was with the Stones and that we intended to go to the festival.

"Well, you can go down if you want to," Charlie said, "but I wouldn't advise it. I was down there, and I came back up here. It's all muddy down there and the cops are busting people."

"But the Stones got to play a gig down there tomorrow," I said.

"Oh, you have to. How are you going in? Are you going to fly to Miami and drive down?"

"No, we're going to fly into West Palm."

"He doesn't need to know that," Sam said, as Ronnie rasped, "He doesn't need to know that."

"Don't tell him," snarled Keith, who'd come in at the end of Jaymes' *caveat,* making fun of them both.

"Well, I wouldn't advise you to come in holding."

"That's not a problem," I said. "We're taken care of there."

"What is it?" Ronnie asked.

"He said not to come in holding," I said.

"We don't care about that," Sam and Ronnie said in unison. I was about to suggest they try for harmony.

"We're just worried about the kids," I told Charlie.

"Yeah," Keith said, taking long strides across the room, "if they're putting kids in a stockade, the kids are going to go wild, and the cops'll go wild, and then we can't help but go wild——"

"So what's happening to the kids down there?" I asked Charlie, as Keith went on: "The kids'll look to us for support, and if you can't give 'em that, what can you give them?"

"Look," Charlie said. "Call the sheriff's department of West Palm Beach County person-to-person, ask him what's going on, he's the local jurisdiction. Also you could call Governor Claude Kirk in Tallahassee, except he's in West Palm Beach at the moment, I don't know where he's staying. Call the *Miami Herald* city desk, maybe they could tell you that."

"How are you?" I asked.

"Fine. I've written a poem about Kerouac I'd like you to hear when we get the chance."

"Great. See you later."

I hung up. "We'll call down there," Keith said, "and if they're doing all that shit we'll tell them we're not coming. We don't want to start any trouble—but if that kind of thing is happening, we can't help but go berserk and start yelling things——"

"I'll call them," Ronnie said, going into the sitting room.

Mick was still lying on the bed, bottom lip stuck out, staring at the ceiling. "I'm not gonna change," he said. "I'm goin' on dressed like this——" He was wearing green slacks and a red wool sweater.

Sam, standing at the foot of the bed, leaning to one side, grey-faced, a constant three-day stubble like little insects over his jaws, mustache drooping, eyes worried and motherly, said gently, "Yes, you are, man."

"No I'm not," Mick said.

Sam took a drag of his cigaret and, hands on hips, peered at Mick through the smoke. "Now I know, man," he said softly, "that about five minutes before you go on you'll think, Right, better change——"

"No I won't," Mick said.

"Yes you will, man," Sam said, going out.

And in a few minutes Mick went into the bathroom and coming out asked Sam, who'd returned, "Where's the makeup?"

"Come in this bedroom," Sam said, leading him away.

Mick came back in uniform, and soon we went down on the antique elevator—its cables slipped, we fell several feet, the white-haired elevator operator looked up at the ceiling with a sad and droopy eye—and went into the Garden, to a small dressing room where the only refreshments were a few Cokes. While the guitars were being tuned, I checked out the arena, saw too many cops, didn't like the feel, and went back upstairs to take a nap. Just as I was going to sleep, Jo called, wanting to talk to Mick. Before I fell asleep again the doors burst open and in came the Rolling Stones and company, back from the wars. Ronnie was the first in and I told him about Jo's call as he passed, the steely glint of his sharkskin knifing the gloom. Mick hurled himself face-down onto the bed beside me.

"Was it a drag?" I asked with complete absence of tact.

"I couldn't care less," Mick mouthed into the pillow.

"Did you see that Re-elect Wyman to Congress sign?" David Maysles asked.

"What about that guy with no legs," Ronnie said. "He came onstage, Sam started to throw him back, lifted him up and from the waist down he wasn't there. He wanted Sam to set him up on the amplifiers."

Taking several sheets of accounting paper from his briefcase, Ronnie sat down on the bed between Mick and me. "This is for the first half of the tour," Ronnie said, pointing to a figure. $516,736.63. "That's just through Chicago. I figure you'll each take home a hundred Gs." He really said "Gs."

"More like ninety," Mick said.

"What were those reporters at the airport asking you?" David Maysles asked. "If this was going to be a free concert?"

"I wanted to do the whole tour free," Mick said, "till I talked to my bank manager. They tell you you're doing great, you've got all this money, until you want to buy something, some chairs or something, and then you discover you don't—you only give me your funny pay-pah." He sang the last line.

"We could take home what we're grossing if we'd had time to book it ourselves," Ronnie said. "We could have got eighty-twenty instead of sixty-forty."

"The accountant's dream," Mick said, waving his fist in a jerkoff gesture. He stretched back on the bed. "We could have done a lot of things, but we only had a week. If I hadn't gone to Australia we'd never have made it, the Bureau of Immigration took so long to approve us."

Tony came in with Chinese food, little paper cartons of bamboo shoots, peapods, beef, rice, but no plastic forks or spoons or chopsticks; instead, popsicle sticks, very tricky to eat with.

Mick was sitting up in bed, shoes off, socks in different shades of blue, trying to spoon up wonton soup with popsicle sticks.

"Why don't your socks match," Ronnie asked.

"It's lucky they're the same color," Mick said.

David Maysles, standing at the foot of the bed trying to eat Chinese chicken, began to swoon.

" 'Scuse my feet, man," Mick told him.

"Funky," David said. He moved away, blinking, threw me a glance (how pungent) and I started to laugh. At that moment Sam came in, stopped arms akimbo by the bed, took a deep breath and said, "Cor, your feet don't arf smell."

"I've been jumpin' about onstage for an hour and an arf, that's why," Mick growled.

"Well, man," Sam said in a conciliatory tone, "I'll tell you what you should do."

"I can't do anything," Mick said.

"Yes you can. At some time during the next two hours, right, wash your feet. Just give 'em a wash, right, it'll freshen you up. Always freshens you up to give your feet a wash."

Mick drew his feet up under him in defense and began talking to me about the future, where to live, what to do. "I made a ridiculous amount of money last year," he said. "I got paid for two films in the same fortnight. I don't know where to live. England is so small-town. They put me in jail in England. I've been arrested three times. They'll send me away eventually. And they tax you blind. I think I'd like to live in France and travel, live in different places different times. The south of France or Italy. That's the advantage of living in Europe, you don't have to live in one country. I never know what to put down on my passport for race—I always want to put English Gentleman. But I've got to find a place to live, got to think about the future, because obviously I can't do *this* forever." He rolled his eyes. "I mean, we're so *old*—we've been going on for eight years and we can't go on for another eight. I mean, if you can you will do, but I just can't, I mean we're so old—Bill's *thirty-three*."

"In eight years," I said, "he'll be——"

"Y'see wot oi mean?"

Time waits for no one, but we didn't know that then. Eight years sounded like a lifetime.

"Mick," Ronnie called from the front room, "Jo wants to talk to you." Mick limped away, and Michael Lydon and two young Boston girls came in. Sam let them in and right away took one of the girls back out. The other girl sat on the bed beside me. Michael introduced himself and the people in the room and began asking the girl, whose name was Georgy, about her neighborhood, whether she liked school, and so on. "I'm not a groupie," she said. "If you write about me, say I'm not a groupie." Meanwhile, Sam had told her friend, "You can meet the Stones, but you have to ball me first." They were in another bedroom, Sam was taking off his trousers, the girl was down to her bra and panties, and the door flew open. "All right, the jig's up, it's the cops," a voice yelled. It was Ronnie and Keith and Mick and little Mick.

"Aw, come on," Sam said.

"I didn't do anything," the bewildered girl said. "We didn't do anything."

"You ought to be ashamed, Sam," the boys told him.

Soon we went downstairs. It was late, I was tired, it was Saturday night in America, and I was over a day behind in my notes. While the Stones did their show, I did some catching up. I didn't expect the apocalypse to come in Boston.

After the show we went back upstairs, for no good reason, and when we came out the kids were waiting like in 1964, girls swarming over the cars, pressing against the windows. We drove slowly through them, stopping at times, then, as the crowd cleared, picking up steam. At the airport we parked among small dark planes and hiked across the asphalt to a twenty-seater. Once we boarded someone discovered that Tony had been left at the hotel, so a car was sent back for him. On the airplane were two plain groupies who had been in the dressing room by courtesy of Jon Jaymes. One of them, nineteen, from New Jersey, told me that she had been following the Stones on their American tours since she was thirteen, never before having gotten near them. At last Tony arrived and the doors were shut. I had a window seat behind the right wing, and I noticed something pouring out of the engine, some of it splattering on the ground and the rest spilling down inside where the spark plugs were igniting snorts of greasy blue smoke that burst into yellow shrieks of flame dancing over the wing in the chill New England night.

"It's on fire," Mick yelled. "We've got to get out of here. There's something dripping out of the engine, tell the pilot."

But the fire went out. "Just some excess oil burning off," the pilot said. By that time we were more or less in a line at the door. We sat down and the plane took off. Keith lit a joint and soon there were half a dozen going around the cabin. I was sitting next to Sam, who took out a 35-millimeter film can filled with cocaine and a small gold spoon. We passed them back and forth, the cocaine hitting the insides of our heads with little crystal explosions like buckshot hitting a chandelier. Sam, looking out the tiny porthole into the darkness, his eyes dark-circled, said in a low voice, almost a whistle, "Cor—tomorrow's the last day—the last day of the tour." There would be recording in Alabama and the free concert in California, but it was true, tomorrow would be the last official date of the Rolling Stones' 1969 tour. As if bringing himself back to reality, Sam said, observed for the record, "I've lost twenty-one pounds in America."

The groupie from New Jersey kept rolling joints out of her purse and passing them around. "This is my dream," she said, looking back at Mick. "I can't think about it. For years he's been my God. It's like I'm up in an airplane with—God."

We landed in cold, wet New York at the Marine Airport and I got into a limo with Jon Jaymes and his Columbus Day Marching Society, including Barbara the body-paint girl, Mike Scotty, and the two groupies. Jon was holding aloft the hand he'd hurt before the second show tonight in a skirmish with radical kids who'd been stopped by the cops from pulling down the U.S. flag. The kid Jon tried to hit had ducked, and Jon's fist had smashed into the wall. Eyes closed, looking like the great sleeping Buddha Kalinga, Jon held in midair the hand, wrapped in bulk, a hurt puppy's paw.

"It's really too bad for such a nice guy to get hurt," the New Jersey groupie said. "I want to thank him for bringing us along. I really hope I can thank him."

"I expect you'll get the chance," I told her.

The girl I found sleeping in my bed when I came back to the Plaza from Boston was wearing a purple silk dress and a sable coat. In the interest of privacy we changed rooms, walking through the corridors like in a scene from the Dodge House, a cowboy in a red shirt and a party lady in a purple gown, headed for heartbreak. I had loved her since I was sixteen and she was eleven. Ten years later she would nurse me back to life after I fell off the big rock in Georgia, receiving for her pains more heartbreak.

We could feel it coming in the morning when we said goodbye. I put her in a cab and went back upstairs for my suitcase. The immediate goal was to board a charter flight at twelve noon for West Palm Beach, where the Stones were scheduled to close the festival at sunset, so the Stones, the Maysles brothers, Michael, Ethan, Sam, Tony, all with baggage, were making a great pile in the lobby of the Plaza this Sunday morning. When I came down, I saw Jo standing by the elevators, weeping. Later she would tell me she'd been afraid she couldn't handle it, couldn't do her job. I walked to the other side of the lobby, where a bellman with somebody's bags, looming suddenly over me, said, Make room. A bit curt, I thought, especially since I wasn't in the man's way—we were both in the middle of a crowd and would have to turn sideways to move in any direction. I told the bellman that if he'd get out of my way I'd get out of his, which enraged him, his face turned red, he began to splutter. As he got himself under control and hauled away the bags, a girl in an army fatigue jacket came up and asked me if I'd vouch for her so she could go to Florida. I had never seen her before and told her I couldn't vouch for myself. Michael Lydon was standing nearby with his arm around Jo, who was still crying. The Maysles brothers and I decided to leave and took a taxi for the Marine Airport.

As we rode we talked about the Stones. David and Al seemed to know nothing about them and two months later, after their film was shot, would still be talking about Bill Watts. At the airport we walked out to the plane in the cold grey day, the rest of the group arriving as we were going up the stairs. We boarded the plane at about two-thirty Eastern Standard Time, all of us deploying for comfort. There were forty extra seats. Keith and Mick went to the back, and from Keith's tape recorder the sound of Chuck Berry soon filled the cabin. The Maysles brothers and I had taken seats at the front. The Butler Aviation stewardess brought beer and sandwiches in Saran Wrap, and after eating I fell asleep, waking up in about an hour to find us still sitting in the same spot, nothing happening, the world outside in the portholes darker and greyer.

Mick, in his red ruffled silk shirt and burgundy blazer, was standing in the aisle, talking to Ronnie. "What's wrong?" he asked. "We're sitting, sitting."

"I talked to the pilot," Ronnie said. "He says we missed our place in the lineup because we were late getting here, now we have to wait for some planes to land."

Outside we could see streaks of white in the failing light. It was beginning to snow. We sat in the maw of a great metal bird as if the machinery had us and we must wait on its pleasure. There was nothing else to do except eat sandwiches, drink beer, and talk.

"Did you see those kids last night?" Michael Lydon asked Mick, talking about the debutante ball at the Plaza as we had come in. "They were like something from a Scott Fitzgerald short story," Michael said. "I talked to a couple of the boys and a girl. I asked her, 'Do you know a lot of the Rolling Stones' songs have been written about you?' She said, 'Yes, and Bob Dylan's too, I think about it every time I hear the line, "with her fog, her amphetamine, and her pearls." ' She said she felt pretty good about it. They'd been doing grass and cocaine at the party. I said, 'Coke's good but expensive,' and they said, 'Yes, but it's good if you can afford it.' They must be really big debs. Not the best, but really good."

"Some of them asked me if I wanted to go to a deb ball," Mick said, "and I told them that there are no real debutantes in America."

"What do you mean, there are no—" Michael said.

"There aren't. There isn't," Mick said, "any American aristocracy, so there can't be any debutantes."

"But there isn't any anywhere, really," Michael said.

"Of course there is," Mick said. "There is in England."

"He thinks he'll be knighted," I said, "that's why he says that."

"Doesn't do you any good to be knighted," Mick said. "You have to be a baronet at least, that's the lowest—you're automatically a sir if you're a baronet. We used to play at those deb balls, that's where we met all our friends. That's not true, but I do have some dear friends I met there."

"How'd you get invited to play at those parties?" Michael asked. "Did the kids ask for you?"

"Yeah, they'd tell their parents to hire us. They paid very well, they've got the money. I just had an offer—fantastic, as much as we make at one concert here—to play at one of those parties."

"Just recently?"

"Yeah, like two weeks ago."

"Will you do it?"

"God knows I don't need that, they're horrible, people are always coming up with requests."

"But you really believe in the aristocracy," Michael said, missing Mick's irony.

"Well, nobody's about to do anything about that system. We have now a chance, since they gave the vote to eighteen-year-olds, to get three million new voters, make a change, destroy an irrelevant system. But England's so stagnant, the kids there are just like they've always been. Nobody's interested in doing anything except some people who are already into politics. You can't get anything together there. This is our only chance in the last fifty years to really change things, and nobody cares—"

"Change them to what?" Charlie asked. He and Sam Cutler were sitting nearby. "What are you going to put in place of the system we have now?".

"Nothing," Mick said. "Nothing would be better than a system that's irrelevant."

"That's *right*," Sam said. "We just need to stop the *cops*, right, from pushing people around. Eventually it comes down to that."

After spending weeks going from California, the Southwest, to Alabama, Chicago, the Eastern Seaboard, trying night after night to shake another bit of America loose, we sat waiting to fly to the last gig in Florida, helpless in an airplane that wasn't going anywhere, and began to discuss for the first time the question What Is To Be Done.

"The theme that keeps constantly recurring in your thoughts, man," Charlie told Sam, "is hitting a cop."

"My old man was a red, right," Sam said, "and I've seen what the cops do. I've seen them seize the subscription list of the *International Times*. There comes a time when you have to say, 'Right, this is it, I'm not moving.' "

"But everybody in politics is pushing you out into the street," Charlie said. "I don't like it."

"Wouldn't you go into the streets to fight the cops if it came to that?" Sam asked.

"No," Charlie said. "I wouldn't."

"Charlie's a true cockney," Mick said to me, as Sam went on trying to convince Charlie that hitting cops would solve the world's problems. "A real Londoner. But now he lives in the country and a lot of things I hate about country people I can see in Charlie. He'll join a preservation society and spend his time writing letters."

"I don't know about the societies," I said, "but preservation is what

I'd like to see, the preservation of life on the planet, there's not a stream in my home county that isn't polluted—"

"I don't know," Mick said, "maybe the natural thing is for the streams to be polluted, for it to die. Maybe that's what should happen."

"I hope not," I said.

We broke off talking because Keith came by, somehow showing just by walking past the idleness of our chatter: it's not what you say that counts. Keith had been snoozing in the back and was surprised, not surprisingly, to find us still in New York.

"If we're not gone soon we'll give up," Mick said.

Keith spoke to Ronnie, who went again to see the pilot, who told him that we'd be changing planes, there's something wrong with this one, but ours is here, on the ground, as soon as they have it ready we'll get on it and take off. Time stretched on, we ate more sandwiches. Outside it was nearly dark. "Let's forget it," Keith said. "It's too late. If we aren't gone in fifteen minutes let's not go." But the pilot told Ronnie that President Nixon had come in, Air Force One was landing, and no one could go in or out while that was happening. Air Force One was not landing, and most what of what we were told at the Marine Airport was untrue, but we didn't know it then, and so we sank a little further into acquiescence. "Fuck it," Keith said. "It's too late."

"But we made the guy that's promoting it—he's just an independent guy doing the whole festival himself," Ronnie said, "and we made him pay the whole guarantee in front, we've already got the bread."

"Well, we'll fly over and drop the money on the crowd," Keith said.

Mick and I were singing along with "Who Do You Love" on the Ronnie Hawkins tape Wexler had given me, doing the right words as Hawkins did the wrong ones. "Got a tombstone hand and a graveyard mind." At that moment the pilot came out of the cockpit and said, "Your plane just landed."

It was nearly seven o'clock. We went in the darkness across the wet asphalt to an identical but healthier plane, everyone taking the same seat he'd had before. Feeling a bit faint, I took out an amyl nitrite popper, broke it, inhaled it, passed it to the Maysles brothers, who inhaled without knowing what it was, and I enjoyed watching their surprise as their heads inflated.

We buckled up and zoomed off into the night sky, singing along with Keith's Chuck Berry tape, rushing from the amyl as the engines whined. The epic hiatus was over. "We're sorry for the delay," the stewardess said. "We hope we can make up for it during your trip." I had a vision of naked stewardess legs lying in the aisle as Sam (three times) and Tony helped her make up for the delay. A poker game was starting in the front of the plane and Mick went to join it. Ronnie came past, heading that way, and David stopped him to ask, "How do the Stones split their income? Does Mick get more than the others?"

"They split five ways, even," Ronnie said. "That's why I work for them." He went on up and joined the game. Joints were passing, and one of the security men, playing poker, asked, "Do you mind if we smoke?"

"Are you kidding?" Ronnie said.

Sam had been talking about fighting cops. We were going someplace where the cops and the kids seemed to be at war, and here the cops were getting high with us. I sat smoking with the Maysles brothers, trying to ease my mind. Mick came back and David told him, "I think you should direct this film."

"I'm not a director," Mick said. David kept insisting, but Mick didn't respond. David and I began to discuss films but soon began to differ, since I thought *Strike* and *Potemkin* were great films and he didn't.

I drifted back to the galley, Mick following. As he came closer he said, "I disagree," starting to giggle. "That's ridiculous," I told him. We leaned against the wall laughing, then got more beer and sandwiches and sat back down. Mick looked out one of the portholes. "If one does what he does for God, or the Good," he said, looking tired and pale, "then I haven't been able to find anybody doing anything better—certainly anybody in politics—than what I'm doing, or anybody better to do it with."

2 8

Interviewer: To get back to Buddy Bolden—

John Joseph: Uh-huh.

Interviewer: He lost his mind, I heard.

John Joseph: He lost his mind, yeah, he died in the bug house.

Interviewer: Yes, that's what I heard.

John Joseph: That's right, he died out there.

MICHAEL ONDAATJE: *Coming Through Slaughter*

"WHERE TO?"

"Inner London Sessions, Newington Causeway."

"In trouble, are you?"

"No, not really."

"With the law, then?"

"No, I'm a writer."

"Writing about a trial?"

"Yes, Brian Jones of the Rolling Stones is on trial today."

The taxi driver, a grey-faced old man with a nose shaped like a chicken's beak, turned to look at me over his shoulder, sniffed, and stared back through the rain-smeared windshield. We drove in silence along the oily Thames, past the Tate Gallery, then over Lambeth Bridge, past Lambeth Palace and the Imperial War Museum. I said, "It seems strange to me, as an American, but most English people appear to consider the Beatles a national asset, and the Stones a definite liability." The driver glanced at me again, very much like a rooster eyeing a shoelace. "Exactly. The Beatles have some funny ways, of course, meditation and all that, but at least as far as appearances go, they seem to be decent chaps. But the Stones—the look of them, and the way they carry on, with their drugs and young girls—the Stones are absolute dirt."

At Inner London Sessions, an old grey stone courthouse, I paid the driver and walked down the black cinder motorpath under a large, dripping oak. In the bare, high-ceilinged entrance hall, a guard directed me upstairs to the public gallery, there being so many reporters present that they occupied all the courtroom space reserved for the press, as well as a row of seats normally used by witnesses. On the public gallery's four long wooden pews sat about a dozen schoolgirls, aged anywhere from twelve to sixteen, and maybe two dozen old people, men and women who looked as if they might have had nowhere else to spend the day. I took one of several empty spaces in the back row.

A great light globe hung from the blue and white domed ceiling, but it did little to dispel the gloom that pervaded the deep brown walls, the courtroom chairs, with their dark red leather back-cushions and seats, and the sallow visage of the bewigged, black-robed Chairman, or Judge, Reginald Ethelbert Seaton. It was the same R. E. Seaton who, at Inner London Sessions on November 1, 1967, nearly a year before, had sentenced Brian Jones to nine months in prison.

To the right of Mr. Seaton were the ten men and two women of the jury; to his left, in the witness stand, was Detective Sergeant Robin Constable, a handsome, stocky young man, with dark hair and pink cheeks. He was telling the court what he had done on the morning of May 21, 1968. At about 7:20 A.M., he said, he had called at Brian Jones' flat in Royal Avenue House, King's Road, Chelsea, in the company of three other police officers, one of them a woman. For about ten minutes they knocked, rang the bell, one of them shouted "Police!" through the letter vent, but though they heard someone "moving about" inside, no one came to open the door. Finally Detective Sergeant Constable (who, earlier in his professional life, must have been simply Constable Constable) noticed an open refuse hatch, climbed through it into the flat, and unlocked the door for the other officers. They set about to search the living and sitting rooms, while DS Constable went into the bedroom. There he found Brian Jones sitting on the floor on the far side of the bed, wearing a caftan. "I could just see the top of his head." Jones extracted a telephone from beneath the folds of his caftan and placed it on the bedside table. "I was going to telephone my solicitor," he said. The DS showed Jones a search warrant and asked why he had not opened the door. "You know the scene, man," Jones said. "Why do I always get bugged?"

"What did you understand him to mean?" DS Constable was interrupted by Mr. Roger Frisby, counsel for the prosecution.

"I suppose, Why were we bothering him," the DS shrugged. He went

through Jones' bedroom, searching it carefully, and had just finished
when "Robin! Come here!" one of the other officers called. Taking
Jones with him, the DS went into the living room, where Temporary
Detective Constable Prentice was standing over a bureau, holding a
ball of blue wool. "I've just found this wool," said TDC Prentice. "Oh,
no," said Brian. "This can't happen again, just when we're getting on
our feet." TDC Prentice then opened the ball of wool, revealing a small
lump of cannabis resin, or hashish, inside.

"Jones spoke, then," said Mr. Frisby, whom the law required to prove
that Brian was *knowingly* in possession of the hashish, "before he had
seen what the wool contained."

"Yes, sir," the DS said. TDC Prentice had then passed the wool to
him, and he had asked Jones, "Is this your wool?" Jones' answer was,
"It could be." He merely shrugged in reply to all further questions. His
only other comments were, "Why do you have to pick on me? I have
been working all day and night, trying to promote our new record, and
now this has to happen," and, after being taken to Chelsea Police
Station, where he was charged with illegal possession of a substance
restricted by the Dangerous Drugs Act of 1964, "I never take the stuff,
it makes me so paranoid."

"No more questions," said Mr. Frisby, and retired to his high-backed
chair.

"Detective Sergeant Constable," said Mr. Michael Havers, Queen's
Counsel, rising to speak for the defense, "you remarked that Mr. Jones
was sitting, when you entered his room, on the floor beside the bed. Was
there anything sinister in that? A man may sit where he wishes, in his
own room, may he not?"

"There was nothing sinister," said the DS. He had testified fluently
with Mr. Frisby, looking rather proud in his grey check sport coat and
red tie; now he had a dogged, tight-lipped smile, and you could see him
stop and think before he spoke.

"When Temporary Detective Constable Prentice called 'Robin! Come
here!', what was his manner? Was he excited, would you say?"

"I suppose so."

"He was excited. When you and Mr. Jones came in, TDC Prentice
was standing over the bureau, holding the wool. Was there anything
else in the bureau?"

"There were a woman's stocking and a man's sock. In the top drawer
with the wool there was a Rolling Stones record."

"Do you know who lived in the flat before Mr. Jones?"

"Miss Joanna Pettet, the actress. She had lived there about six
months."

"Is she an American?"

"She is English, married to an American."

"Has she to your knowledge ever been involved with drugs?"

"No, sir. We investigated her at Scotland Yard, and at our request she was investigated in Los Angeles by the FBI. She has no drug record."

"Did she say the wool was hers?"

The corners of DS Constable's smile turned down. "She said it might be. She had no knowledge of the cannabis."

"Let's see," said Mr. Havers, touching his hand to his wig as if he were trying to remember. "When you came in, TDC Prentice was holding the wool?"

"He was."

"And he did not show what was inside it?"

"No, sir."

"What did you think it contained?"

"I . . . didn't know."

"Certainly you didn't, but what did you think? You had come to search for drugs. TDC Prentice called you excitedly. Surely you did not think it had nothing to do with drugs."

"No, sir."

"The point," said Chairman Seaton, seeing the point, "is that when TDC Prentice called, it was obvious to you that it had something to do with drugs. So it should have been obvious to the accused as well."

"No more questions," said Mr. Havers.

"Court will adjourn for a ten-minute recess," said Mr. Seaton.

About half the spectators left the public gallery for the recess. I moved to the low balcony wall and stood looking down into the courtroom. In the front pew, two old ladies who had been sitting next to a group of schoolgirls were talking. They looked like the kind of women who live alone, or with each other, in city apartments. ". . . spend a lot of their money on records. I don't think it's good."

"No, neither do I. Some of the words—"

"They say Frisby's a wonderful prosecutor."

A policeman wearing a blue uniform and black mustache was sitting in a chair by the gallery door. I asked him some questions, and he told me that English courts were not very different from those in America, except that a jury could bring in a verdict based on a majority, rather than a unanimous, decision. If this jury found Brian guilty, he could be fined £1000 and sentenced to ten years in prison. The policeman was not a betting man, but if he were, he told me, he would not bet on the defendant. "Second offense," he said, shaking his head. "They'll stick it to him."

As we were talking, people started coming back in. I sat down beside a pretty girl with long auburn hair. She looked about sixteen. "Are you a Stones fan?" I asked her.

"I'm not, actually," she said. "I happened to be here, so I decided to look in out of curiosity. I'm training to be a police youth counselor."

There was a door on the left of the courtroom leading to the jury chamber, and one on the right that led to a waiting room where the witnesses could not hear the testimony that preceded them. When court was once more in session, Mr. Frisby called Temporary Detective Constable Prentice to testify. He came out of the right-hand door, a small cop in a dark suit, took the stand, and repeated, almost word for word, the story we had heard from Robin Constable. He was followed by the last witness for the prosecution, who was wearing a white blouse and green plaid jumper. Woman Detective Wagstaff, looking as if she might have been a grammar school teacher, read the official police version from a little yellow pad. When she was dismissed, Mr. Havers addressed the jury.

In a moment, he said, Brian Jones would take the stand. They would have the opportunity to see and hear him, and to judge for themselves what sort of fellow he was. They certainly deserved this opportunity, and, indeed, Mr. Jones was eager to tell his side of the story. But they also deserved to be told fully and frankly all the facts relating to this case. It was a fact that Brian Jones had been arrested before on drug charges. He had appeared in the same court as today and before the same chairman. He was, on that occasion, guilty, and said so. He had been sentenced to prison, but the Court of Appeals, partly because of medical advice, decided that he should be fined and put on probation. Since that time he had been under the care of a court-approved physician. "I tell you all this," said Mr. Havers, "because it really is an important part of this case. To have spent months in all the worry and anxiety of court trials and litigation, with the threat of prison hanging over one—to have passed through all that and to be working and co-operating with the police and the parole board—and then suddenly to find oneself again, through no fault of one's own, in the same predicament—ladies and gentlemen of the jury, I ask that you listen with sympathy to the testimony of this young man—he has been under a great strain."

Then, as the girls in the front row of the gallery leaned forward, gripping the balcony rail, Brian came to the witness stand. He was dressed sedately, in a grey pinstripe suit, white shirt, and dark paisley tie; but there was no way to disguise the luxuriant, shoulder-length, blond mane.

There is a photograph, made a long time ago, before there were Rolling Stones in the world, which shows Brian as a thin, almost crew-cut boy in a sweater. He looks like a high school newspaper reporter, but his face is dominated by an expression of mad, wicked glee. Since then he had gained weight and hair, and his face had grown more wild. A few months before, in Joujouka, Morocco, Brian had recorded an album of music played by participants in the rites of Bou Jeloud, the name under which Pan, "the little goat god," there survives. Brion

Gysin had written a text to accompany the music. Watching the faces of the jury as they looked at Brian, I thought of a passage: "Who is Bou Jeloud? Who is he? The shivering boy who was chosen to be stripped naked in a cave and sewn into the bloody warm skins and masked with an old straw hat tied over his face, HE is Bou Jeloud, when he dances and runs. Not Ali, not Mohamed, then he *is* Bou Jeloud. He will be somewhat *taboo* in his village the rest of his life."

Brian's face was a sick white, and his voice trembled; three times he was asked to speak louder as, in answer to Mr. Havers' first questions, he admitted to being Lewis Brian Jones, aged twenty-six, a professional musician since 1963, when he joined the Rolling Stones. He had been arrested before, pleaded guilty, been sentenced to prison, appealed, and he was now on probation, seeing a doctor regularly. He had not used cannabis since the first arrest, eighteen months ago. He had used it rarely and experimentally and its effect—he had been having personal difficulties at the time—was to make him more unhappy. Inclining his head slightly to the right, with a small pale hand he brushed away the yellow hair that fell into his eyes. He had been staying in the flat at King's Road while a house he had bought was being decorated. He had taken over the flat a couple of hours after Joanna Pettet had left. Taking a first look round, he had seen a stocking, a sock, and a bottle of ink in the bureau. He did not recall seeing the wool, though the prolonged shock of this experience may have caused a mental blank. The Stones had been recording at this time, working at night when there was less disturbance, sleeping during the day. He had been in the flat eighteen days, but had spent about half the time at a friend's house. The night before the police raid he had taken a sleeping tablet prescribed by his doctor and had gone to sleep at about half-past one.

Up there, in Joujouka, you sleep all day—if the flies let you, Brion Gysin wrote. *Breakfast is goat-cheese and honey on gold bread from the outdoor oven. Musicians loll about sipping mint tea, their kif pipes and flutes. They never work in their lives so they lie about easy. The last priests of Pan cop a tithe on the crops in the lush valley below. Late in August each musician slips away up to the borders of Rif country to take his pick of the great, grassy meadows of cannabis sativa—enough to last him the year. Blue kif smoke drops in veils from Joujouka at nightfall. The music picks up like a current turned on. The children are singing,* "Ha, Bou Jeloud!"

"The first thing I heard was a loud banging at the door. I did not immediately become aware of what it was. A minute might have passed before I knew it was somebody very intent on entering the flat. I put on a caftan—kimono sort of thing—went to the door and looked through the spy hole."

"What did you see?"

No one who has seen the heat poised on the other side of his door can ever forget it. Brian closed his eyes and, as if he were at a seance, summoned up the picture, progressing from fear to a kind of fey amusement: "I remember seeing . . . three large gentlemen . . . of a sort I don't usually *see* . . . through the spy hole of my door."

"Who did you think they were?"

"Police, perhaps, or," he added mysteriously, "agents. I was afraid—"

"Of the police?"

"Yes, since last year I seem to have had an inborn fear of the police."

"If it please the court," Mr. Frisby interjected drily, "*inborn* means you've had it all your life."

"Ah, an acquired fear," Brian amended his statement. "I went back to the bedroom on tiptoe. I couldn't make up my mind whether to call my secretary or my solicitor. I was very worried."

"The police have said that ten minutes passed before they came into the flat. Do you agree with this estimate?"

"I can't agree or disagree. Some time passed. Certainly long enough to dispose of anything I shouldn't have had."

The gallery door opened and Suki Poitier, Brian's girl, came in with Tom Keylock. Suki, a blond model, very lovely in a frail, wasted sort of way, was wearing a black pantsuit and white silk blouse. A few people turned to see her. She looked back at them evenly. Tom, who had extricated the Stones from many tight places with hotel managers and other figures of authority in countries all over the world, could do nothing now to help Brian. They sat down together and listened.

Brian was saying that DS Constable had come into his bedroom and shown him a warrant to search for dangerous drugs. When TDC Prentice called, the DS had said, "Come along, Jones." Brian thought he saw the cannabis right away, but he knew they had come to search for drugs. He had been told.

"How did you feel when they showed you the resin?"

"I couldn't believe it," Brian said, his voice dramatically soft. "I was absolutely shattered."

"When DS Constable asked if the wool were yours, did you say, 'It might be'?"

"I might have said anything."

"Was the wool yours?"

"I never had a ball of wool in me life." Brian seemed to become more expansive when talking about his innocence. "I don't darn socks," he went on. "I don't have a girlfriend who darns socks."

"Later, when you were at the police station, you said that you never take cannabis because it makes you so paranoid. What did you mean?"

"That refers back to the events of last year. The effect of the drug for me was a heightening of experience that I found most unpleasant. That made me very frightened of it."

"Were you advised what would be the consequences of breaking your probation by using drugs?"

"Yes, sir. I have taken no chances."

"Had you the slightest knowledge that the resin was in that wool?"

"No," Brian said, "absolutely not."

Mr. Havers dismissed him, and court was adjourned for lunch.

David Sandison, from the public relations office that handled the Stones' affairs, came in as we started out. "What's it look like?" he asked.

"Hard to tell," I said. "The police have Brian's looks and reputation on their side. Seaton seems remarkably open-minded."

Sandison looked skeptical. "He was a bastard last year."

We went downstairs with Tom and Suki. Brian and Havers were waiting. The rain had stopped, but the sky was still a dull grey. We all walked down the street to a pub called the Ship. No one ate very much, but there was some drinking done. Entering the working-class pub, Brian fluttered a hand and gasped for "Brandy!" A swarm of photographers descended. Brian threw them brave little smiles.

A shabbily dressed man and woman, who must have been in their seventies, were sitting at the corner of the bar. "Who's 'at?" the woman asked.

" 'Im—that Rolling Stone."

"He don't look so smart now, do 'e?"

"He's got worries," the man said.

None of us talked much during lunch. Finally somebody paid the bill, and we went out. The Ship was on a corner, and as we passed the narrow old cobblestone cross street I noticed its name: Stones End. While I stood there looking at the sign, the photographers passed me, walking backwards, snapping shots of Woman Detective Sergeant Wagstaff, Temporary Detective Constable Prentice, and Detective Sergeant Robin Constable as they strolled back to the courthouse, trying to look modest.

In session once more, Mr. Frisby cross-examined Brian: "Mr. Jones, you have said that when the police arrived at the flat your conscience was clear—"

"Yes, entirely."

"—so why did you not open the door?"

"Because," Brian said, "I saw the . . . three large gentlemen, as I mentioned before. I was afraid."

"*Why* were you afraid?" Mr. Frisby asked, his tone implying how very strange it was that any citizen should fear the police.

"Well, the events of last year," Brian said, "and there had been so many drug raids in the Chelsea area—I was just worried, I wanted advice."

"Surely you knew what that would be. You would have to let the police in eventually. If you were innocent, there was nothing to fear. Yet you deliberately kept them out for as long as you could. And it's no good, you know, saying you could have got rid of anything in that time—for do not the windows of the flat open onto the King's Road, where there might have been police stationed outside, watching?"

"I expect," Brian said, "there might be other ways to dispose of it—"

"Could one way," Mr. Frisby asked, "have been to hide it in the wool?"

Brian shrugged. "It *could* have been."

Mr. Frisby walked over and touched the table where he had been sitting. Then he turned and asked Brian to tell the court who, if he had not done it, put the cannabis in the bureau?

Brian said that a lot of people had come in and out while he was living in the flat, but he had no reason to suspect any one person. He had no idea how the cannabis got there, and had denied it since the cannabis had been found.

"Denied what?"

"Knowing about the cannabis."

"You didn't say that."

"Of course I did."

"Your counsel has cross-examined the police officers, they said nothing about your denying it."

"I did deny it," Brian insisted. "I said, 'You can't do this to me again.' "

Mr. Frisby smiled, walked back, and touched the table. When he turned again, he asked whether Brian had ever used the bureau where the cannabis had been.

"No," Brian said.

"And you have no explanation for its being there. The whole thing, I take it, is a complete mystery to you?"

"Yes," Brian said thoughtfully. "A mystery."

"And so," said Mr. Frisby, turning a three-quarters profile toward the jury, "it must remain to us, unless we accept the only explanation that will accommodate the facts. What I am suggesting, you see, is that the cannabis was yours, that you knew it was there all along, and that you are now lying to us."

Brian's expression as he regarded Mr. Frisby seemed to imply that under different circumstances such an accusation would inevitably result in a duel. "I am not guilty, sir," he said quietly. "I believe that my whole conduct while the police were in the flat points to a denial."

The only other witness for the defense was Dr. Harvey Flood, Brian's psychiatrist. Dr. Flood told Mr. Havers that he had written a glowing report on Brian's character for the United States Department of Immigration. He repeated what he had said of Brian before the Court of

Appeals: "I believe that if you put a reefer cigarette down beside this young man, he would run a mile." But before being dismissed, he admitted to Mr. Frisby that there was no way he could be certain Brian was not still using cannabis.

Mr. Frisby touched the table once more and began his summation. He told the jury that it was impossible to look into a man's head and heart to see if he were innocent: he must be judged by his actions. And perhaps the only way to judge a man's actions would be to compare them with one's own. He doubted whether any member of the jury would be afraid to see the police at the door. Even a person with a record of arrests would have no reason to be afraid—if only he were innocent. Indeed, such a person should be particularly glad to see the police, and would say to them, "Come in, gentlemen," and "Have a look round," gloating a little, perhaps, because he knew that *this time* he was innocent. Is this what Brian Jones did? Quite the contrary. "He behaved like a man," Mr. Frisby said, "caught red-handed."

Mr. Havers, in his closing statement, contended that the cannabis the police found was not evidence of Brian's guilt, but of his innocence. It did not matter where the windows of the flat opened; Mr. Havers had not seen the flat, but he felt safe in assuming that it was equipped with a bathroom, and that in the bathroom there was a toilet. It would not have taken ten minutes, or even one, for a person to flush away a small lump of cannabis. Nobody could object to one's going to the lavatory on getting up in the morning. If Brian had known about the cannabis, he would surely have got rid of it.

Then Mr. Havers discussed the emotional complications of the case. Brian Jones, he said, was a member of a group which had met with tremendous success among teenagers, and tremendous prejudice from older people. Many of us, he continued, find pop music and the antics of pop musicians irritating and even maddening. Our own sons are wearing their hair long and down their faces, and are sporting fanciful shirts, which we sometimes find objectionable. But we must put these things out of our minds and look on the defendant as, say, Bill Jones— an ordinary young man. And we must attempt to put ourselves in a situation similar to his: What if one of our sons brought home a friend who left cannabis in the house, and later the police came and found it? What could anyone say except, "I did not know it was there." That is what Brian Jones had said. He can do nothing more.

Mr. Havers had just completed his summation when Mick Jagger and Keith Richards came into the gallery. Everyone—spectators, counsel, jury—turned to look: it was as if the outlaws Cole and Jim Younger had walked into a court where Judge Roy Bean was trying their brother Bob. Keith was dressed in a tan suede jacket, white T-shirt, and brown leather pants with, clearly, no underwear. Mick was wearing a long green velvet coat, a yellow scarf, and a wide-brimmed black hat. They sat down front with the schoolgirls. The one sitting next to Mick, a thin girl with a grey cloth coat and no makeup, turned to the others and her lips formed the words, "I can't *stand* it."

Chairman Seaton watched them until Mick removed his hat, and then he began the final address to the jury. He said that the burden of proof rested not on Brian but on the police, and that their case was entirely circumstantial. No evidence of using cannabis had been found—no ashes, no cigarette ends. There was only the cannabis itself, and the jury could decide for themselves whether it might have been disposed of before the police entered. "If you think the prosecution has proved without a doubt that the defendant knew the cannabis was in his flat, you must find him guilty. Otherwise, he is innocent."

Almost incredulous, David Sandison whispered: "Brian's going to get off."

Mr. Seaton's summation made it very hard to expect anything else. He concluded by saying that only a person completely ignorant of the qualities of an English jury could think that a man's style of dress or hair would prevent his receiving an impartial hearing.

The court recessed while the jury went out to make its decision. Mick stood up, clapped his hat on his head, and said, "Here come de judge."

Downstairs, Tom Keylock said, "Well, 'e just fuckin' told 'em what to do, dinne?"

"Sounded like it," Keith said. We were all lounging around the entrance hall, Mick was surrounded by schoolgirls, and for the first time that day, no one looked worried. Since Brian's arrest, a cloud of doubt had hung over the Stones' future. Now it looked as if all the worry had been unnecessary. Everyone was confident of winning. Somebody remarked that the jury was staying out a long time. Forty-five minutes had passed before the jury came back and we went to the gallery to hear the good news. It was not long coming. The foreman was asked if the jury had arrived at a verdict. "Yes, we have, Your Honour," he said. "We find the defendant guilty."

The London newspapers reported that "There were gasps from the public gallery when the foreman announced the verdict." Suki started to cry. Keith's shoulders were trembling. Brian slumped to his seat in the dock, his head in his hands.

Later, Tom Keylock said: "I've known Brian for years, and I love him. He's cheated me, he's lied to me. And the one time in his life the little bastard tells the truth, he gets done for it."

Mr. Seaton rapped with his gavel for silence. He looked very stern as a guard raised Brian to his feet. Last year he was a bastard. And at that time, Brian had not broken probation. "Mr. Jones," the Chairman said, "you have been found guilty. I am going to treat you as I would any other young man before this court." But last year Mr. Seaton had thought Brian guilty. "I am going to fine you, and I will fine you relatively, according to your means. Fifty pounds, and one hundred guineas court costs. You will have," the Chairman added in delicious irony, "one week to get up the money. Your probation order will not be changed. But you really must watch your step, and stay clear of this stuff."

A reporter who had covered trials in London for many years said, down in the entrance hall a few minutes later, that he had never seen a magistrate show so clearly his contempt for a jury. Brian came out, Suki on his arm, and grinned lewdly at the schoolgirls. *The children are singing,* "Ha, Bou Jeloud!" At the street they posed for the photographers, Brian, Suki, Keith, Mick, and the little girl who had been sitting next to Mick and who was now clinging to his arm.

Two men in working clothes stopped on their way down the sidewalk. One of them, who had red hair, asked what sentence Brian had got. Told that Brian had been fined, he said to the other man, "Crikey, you or I'd have got thirty years."

In a minute the Stones' cars were brought round. Brian and Suki were in Brian's Rolls-Royce. Mick and Keith got into the back seat of Keith's blue Bentley. "Give him some bird," yelled the red-haired man. ("Bird," in cockney rhyming slang, is short for birdlime, and stands for time.) "And a bath as well," his friend added, as the Stones drove away, the rebel flag of the Confederate States of America on the Bentley hood flapping gently in the breeze.

2 9

By the blazing creosote logs   feverish men lie down to dream
of a Savior riding on a great white Catholic mule
and freeze.
. . .
The rain gently lays its head
Across the rail,
It is almost a lifetime
Before the six o'clock flyer.
CHARLIE BROWN: "John Jack Kerouac 1922–1969"

"I HOPE we made up for it." The stewardess, who had done little and nothing special, sounded as if this were a permanent part of her routine. When we got off the plane, it was near the end of the day, the month, the decade, our youth. We were standing on the cold blown concrete of the dark deserted West Palm Beach Airport, where there was no snow, but the wind sought you out and chattered your jaws.

Stu, who'd flown down earlier, emerged out of the night with the news that two helicopters were coming to pick us up. While we waited, Stu said to me, "A friend of yours was down here looking for you, Charlie Brown, very helpful guy. The equipment came in on the plane and we had no way to take it to the gig, so I asked him where we could rent a truck, and he just happened to be driving one. Very helpful guy. You must thank him for us, 'cause we might not have made it otherwise."

"Where is he?" I asked.

"He went back to Miami."

When the helicopters arrived, we crept out to them, bent over, hunchbacked under the whipping blades. They took us up and down again a bit soon, hitting hard on the beach. We slogged through soft sand, crossed a lawn, climbed a spiral staircase, and entered the swank Colonnades' swankest suite, the Bob Hope, caves of ice glittering with crystal chandeliers, polished marble, gilt-laced mirrors. It was as tasteful as anything Las Vegas had to offer, and its mirrors had never reflected anything that looked like the group coming in with the Rolling Stones. Past velvet couches, a piano, a bar with drinks and food, we found waiting for us in a big bedroom, seeming rather out of place themselves, the festival promoters, Dave and Sheila Rupp, a compact, sunburned man in a khaki jumpsuit and a small, shapely brunette in a splendidly whorish red vinyl raincoat.

Dave owned a fast-car shop and Sheila was a schoolteacher. They couldn't have been more gracious, especially considering that the Stones were by now about eight hours late. The Stones were the least of the problems that the festival had brought into the Rupps' lives. "Since the festival my business has been firebombed and burned down," Dave said. "My fire insurance has been cancelled, the John Birch Society have been calling me and saying they're going to kill my wife and child."

The Maysles brothers' lights were going on as Dave went out to see about the rest of the group. I sat on the bed beside Sheila, whose lipstick matched her raincoat. "The parents call and say that the kids are like they are today because they have teachers like me," she said.

"They're right about that," Michael Lydon said.

"That was a compliment," I said.

"Where have you all been?" she asked.

I started telling her about the crippled plane and Air Force One as Mick, wandering into the room, heard what I was saying and in a glance communicated the hopelessness of explaining or even knowing where we had been or what we had been doing. He collapsed beside me on the bed as we laughed with determined impotence and indecision. The next question to which nobody knew the answer was whether the Stones should go on now in the dead vast and middle of the night or wait for sunrise. We amused ourselves the best we could while whatever combination of energies that propelled the Rolling Stones took its time deciding.

At Tony's request ("I got some other things to do") I rolled some joints for the gig, sitting in a black marble bathtub. The scene was filmed by David and Al, which alarmed Tony. You couldn't blame anybody for being confused about what was permitted. Then, finding a quiet bedroom, I called Charlie Brown, who came to the telephone from his little Coconut Grove snake-trapper's hut and read me his Kerouac poem. I told him I'd talk to him later and went out to the bar, where a waiter was heating soup and pouring drinks. As I approached, Mick and Charlie Watts were exchanging mutters. Charlie strolled away, and Mick turned to me. "Charlie's such a bitch," he said. He was naked to the waist, wearing a wooden cross on a leather thong around his neck.

"I've never thought of Charlie as a bitch," I said.

"You don't know him as I do." We ate soup and drank Scotch, standing at the bar, the Maysles brothers filming. Mick went behind the bar to get closer to the cold cuts, and in my dim awareness I remembered to ask Dave Rupp why he was doing this thing that was hurting him in so many ways. He started by telling me that as a teenager he had won nineteen world championship drag races. Later he had owned a nightclub in his hometown, Wichita, Kansas, where B. B. King and Bo Diddley worked and the Kingsmen (who recorded "Louie Louie," one of the all-time great brainless rock and roll songs) were the house band. "But this festival is the biggest thing we've ever done. The cops are pigs and the kids are great," Dave said, not loud enough for any of the cops in the Stones' entourage to hear. "I learned that when I was thirteen and outrunning the cops in a hot rod. We've lost our business, we've lost probably altogether a quarter of a million dollars, but it's been worth it because of the kids, the kids are great."

We broke off as the sound of a helicopter descending onto the lawn just outside the big windows drowned all talk. Dawn might never come, and it was time to go see these young people who for the last three days, in the mud, had been skirmishing with the authorities. Ethan, Michael, the Maysles brothers, and I went down the spiral stairs, out of the building's shadow into the yellow glare of the landing lights, and got on board. The Stones would follow in another helicopter. Palm trees thrashed in our wake as we lifted off for a ride above beach motels, each with its green-glowing chlorined pool, and away from city lights, over darkness, moonscape, empty marshes, until we saw a tiny clump of lights twinkling in the distance.

We were over the lights and then coming down to land on the dirt at the Palm Beach International Raceway, the Rupps' little drag strip. The surrounding countryside seemed only barren fields with standing mud puddles. A path toward the stage area had been made by laying planks and pieces of plywood across the puddles. We walked on the boards till we came to a dirt road where Bill Belmont was waiting in a blue Chevrolet. He drove us up behind the stage, which looked out over the Raceway. Inside a backstage trailer a suntanned, blond, waterskiing kind of girl named Rhonda was serving excellent tea with cream and sugar. Inside the cyclone fence a few yards away were thirty thousand people. Rupp had told them to use the fence's wooden supports for firewood. As the Stones came in and were being wrapped in blankets, I went out and walked beside the very tall stage down to the fence, where I told a security guard that I was going into the crowd and coming back.

"You can't do that," he said. I pushed past him, but the kids were pressing up to the fence, and as soon as I was among them a boy came up to me and said, "Don't I know you from Oklahoma?"

"Not me," I told him.

"Yeah, I know I've seen you down in Oklahoma, New Mexico, someplace—"

"I'm sorry."

People were chanting "Wavy Gravy! Wavy Gravy!" and incomprehensible shouts came from the public address system. The place had the desperate atmosphere of a refugee camp. Some people were standing, some were sitting, some were sleeping, wrapped in sleeping bags and blankets. The ones sleeping looked helpless, like corpses, lying on the wet dirt. Onstage there was a great whaling of drums and a fireworks rocket went off, streaking high above the dismal mud, purple, yellow, blue. Then Sam's voice, amplified, was saying, "Sorry for the delay, sorry for the hangups. We're here—will you give a warm welcome to the Rolling Stones?"

The crowd were on their feet, yelling. I went back past the guard and the fence and up the long sloping stairs. Michael was standing on the rear stage. "They better work hard to be as good as those kids," he said.

The Stones, wearing jackets, were starting "Jumpin' Jack Flash" and were working hard just being there. It was cold and the strings wouldn't stay in tune and the wind whipped the music around. As the song ended, Mick said, "Mornin'—West Palm Beach—wish I was down there—'cause I bet it's warmer down there with ya—"

By the time "Carol" ended, Keith was warmed up. He took off his black velvet jacket and started "Sympathy for the Devil," bare-midriffed in his red rhinestoned Nudie shirt. Working as hard as they could to overcome the circumstances, the Stones through a miracle of effort had everyone I could see dancing. "Fuckin' limeys," David Maysles said. "Let's beat up on 'em." In the distance at times I thought I heard screams, but I couldn't be sure.

"Sorry you had to wait," Mick said when the song ended. "May we be forgiven?"

Keith cut him off with the opening chords of "Stray Cat." They didn't do the blues songs—too cold to sit still. Before "Midnight Rambler," Mick said, "Now we're gonna slow it down a bit—for those people who're trying to get some rest and some nooky." There was a cheer whose weakness moved Mick to ask, "Have you been havin' a good time in Miami? Has it been muddy, has it been cold—"

Again Keith stopped Mick's talking by starting the song. After "Gimme Shelter," Mick tried again. "I think it's pretty amazing," he said, "because you're here. Everybody is amazing to get it together after all the hassles. It's important and you know it's important because you're here." He was vague as hell but all we had to go on was some vague sense of purpose drawing us together. Michael Lydon would write of this audience that "Their yearning to come together (where does it come from?), to experience that love-in, festival feeling they've heard so much about, floods up to the stage in waves of expectation so trusting and naive as to be at once absurd and deeply moving." Chip threw the spotlights' beams onto the crowd, and as "Live with Me" started, the people were writhing in the circling blue lights, underwater creatures disturbed in the deep.

The opening notes of "Satisfaction" hung out into the night like an automobile going over a cliff, drums crashing, bass notes rumbling out of tune, Mick Taylor's E-string breaking. All the music was being played by frozen fingers. After "Honky Tonk Women," Mick said, as he'd started doing in Boston, "Before we go we'd like to say a special hello to all the minority groups in the audience—all the fags, all the junkies—hi, junkies—all the straight people, cops—"

"They went home hours ago," a boy backstage said.

The Stones did "Street Fighting Man" splendidly and terribly in the awful cold. Near the end Chip pointed the spotlights into the sky, where at nearly five o'clock there was still no glimmer of dawn. The high-flung basket of rose petals turned, spilling in the moving lights, blood-red drops falling as we turned to leave.

We crowded into the backstage trailer. I told Keith how fine the effort had been, and he said, "The sound was pretty bad, I'm afraid. We were all out of tune, no way to stay in tune in that temperature."

"A lot of things could have been better," I said, "but—"

"Ah!" Sam said, shushing me as he bustled over. "We don't need to hear that."

"You didn't hear me right," I said, making a mental note that Sam was rounding the bend.

We went back, walking the planks, across the puddles to the helicopters and up into the coming dawn. Now that the show was over the color of the sky was at last changing, purple, mauve, lavender, rose, orange, red. The Stones were going to eat breakfast at the Colonnades, fly to Muscle Shoals, go to the Holiday Inn, and sleep. Such were their general intentions. We landed on the grass and walked down to the beach. On the ground it was darker and still cold, and the colors were not so vivid. Most of the group turned back toward the Colonnades. Keith and I stood sharing a joint and watching one bright blue-white point in a blue-grey corner of sky. "The morning star," Keith said, "and when she's gone we'll have the sun."

A goldfish-colored line shimmered on the black Atlantic as I turned to go inside.

We were all together in the Bob Hope suite, Stones, press, management, security, pilots. Behind the bar a black-tied, white-haired waiter was preparing breakfast. He took obvious pleasure in his work, piling steaming eggs, sausages, and rolls on gleaming plates. Sam, sitting with Keith and Charlie on a couch near the bar, asked for a pot of tea, and the waiter said, "Certainly, sir. I'll have to go down to the kitchen." He was still earnestly dishing it up five minutes later when Sam said, *"Please, man, could we have our tea, I asked you about twenty minutes ago."*

"Sir," the waiter said, as if he were speaking to a blind man, "I'm still serving these—"

"Just *leave* it," Sam said, "and go get the tea. *These* are the musicians, man, they've been up all night working, they're tired, they need their tea. These other people understand, they don't mind—even if you said Fuck 'em, they wouldn't mind."

"Sir, we don't need that kind of talk," the waiter said. Tony walked from the bar to stand in front of Sam, the sun that was brightening the suite shading the mounds and hollows of hard black muscle, making him look bigger than ever. "Wouldn't they, Sam?" he asked, so quietly that everyone in the room paused, listening. "I know at least one person who would." Tony stood over Sam, breathing lightly but a bit faster than normal, while Sam, who glanced up just once, swallowed, looked side to side and said nothing.

I was standing beside the bar. "I don't like the way he spoke to me, sir," the waiter said.

"I don't think he'll have anything else to say for a while," I told him.

He took my word for it and brought the tea, placing the tray beside Keith's boots on a low table in front of the couch. Keith was inhaling heaping spoons of cocaine from a film can, smearing his nose and upper lip with the white powder.

Jon Jaymes came over to the couch with a Dodge catalogue and told the Stones to pick out the cars they wanted, one per Stone, free from Dodge, to be delivered soon in England and replaced each year as long as Dodge felt like it. Charlie and Keith ordered aluminum-finish Chargers, Jagger wanted a Charger in purple, Bill also wanted a Charger, Mick Taylor wanted a station wagon, and they wanted another wagon for Stu and the office. Jon wrote all this down. There was something suspicious about a big fat mama's boy giving away free cars in the early morning light. As Jon walked away Mick looked at his wide back and said, "Christ, I can't stand that man—"

Keith went to the piano, began to play clunky rocking chords, and Mick, who'd showered and dressed in his black-and-white checkered suit, red shirt, and burgundy newsboy cap, leaning against a marble column, clapping on the afterbeat, sang "Lawdy Miss Clawdy." The performance worked on its own and as a parody of Elvis Presley. It was magic; even at this point of exhaustion it made you want to dance.

Downstairs, another kind of magic was going on. Jon and Mike Scotty were with the hotel manager, settling the bill.

"Give him a check from Teenage Enterprises," Jon said to Mike.

"Should I give him the Broadway address?" Mike asked.

"That'll be fine," Jon said. Something about the way he said it made you think that the Broadway address might be a parking lot.

It was nearly nine-thirty when we left, passing through the dining room where Johnny Winter and Janis Joplin and other musicians who had played at the festival were eating. They stopped, watching the Stones walk past. We went out to the front lawn, waited for a second helicopter, and flew to the West Palm Beach Airport. Jon Jaymes, Mike Scotty, the Maysles brothers, and Ronnie were going to New York. Sam was going to San Francisco to help Jo start setting up the free concert, and Michael Lydon was going home to Southern California while the Stones were recording in Alabama. We stood around the airport until everyone had left but the Stones, Stu, Astrid, Tony, and me. As he left, Jon had told me that he was holding me responsible for the Stones' welfare. He gave me his New York telephone numbers and said, "If anything happens, call me immediately." I was staggering-tired and left the others in the Butler Aviation office to go sit on the plane, a Constellation propeller aircraft that looked like a converted school bus. I sat down in a small rear cabin and went to sleep, waking up as Mick and Charlie joined me in the back and the rest took seats in the front. The engines started and the plane taxied to the middle of the runway, sat for a few minutes with the engines racing, rolled another few feet forward, turned right again, then forward and right once more, and we were back where we started. The engines stopped, and one of the pilots opened the door and got off the plane. Mick and I followed him. A mechanic standing on a ladder was working on one of the engines.

"What's the trouble?" Mick asked.

"Bad plugs from an oil drip," the pilot said. "We'll have it as good as, uh, ready to go in a couple minutes."

Mick and I walked across the landing field to a patch of rough grass forty or fifty yards away and lay down in the sunlight. Lying on his back, eyes closed, Mick said, "I don't feel very good about that plane."

"Neither do I," I said.

Bill and Astrid were coming towards us across the concrete.

"You should listen to your instincts," Mick said.

"How d'you feel about about that plane?" Bill asked.

"Don't like it," Mick and I said in unison.

"Neither do we," Astrid said.

"Let's see what everybody else thinks," Mick said, getting up.

Keith and Charlie were asleep, which counted as two votes for staying aboard, but Mick Taylor was awake and didn't like the plane either. Jagger decided to keep Tony with us, sleep somewhere close by, and fly to Alabama on another plane. Charlie woke up, and we asked if he'd like to come with us. "How about Keith?" he asked.

Keith was, as we pointed out, asleep. Charlie woke him up, but he wasn't interested. Charlie decided to stay aboard. Those of us who were staying in Florida got some of our bags out of the luggage compartment —couldn't find mine, but I was too tired to care—and walked back to the airport. In a few minutes Charlie followed, having correctly assumed that we had taken his bags. We had Stu's bags too. They retrieved them and headed back to the plane.

"We'll get a place to sleep," Mick said, "and see you in the morning."

"Be wistful," Charlie said.

I telephoned the Colonnades, where there were no rooms, and the West Palm Beach Holiday Inn ditto. "Next time don't tell them it's us," Mick said, and that worked. I made reservations for six people at the Holiday Inn in Palm Beach, a few miles away, all in my name.

We took taxis there, but when I asked at the front desk about the reservations the grim-faced manager, looking past me at the long-haired foreigners, said, "There must be some mistake, there's no record of that reservation."

"But I just made it," I said.

He went into conference with two women in an office behind the counter, came back and said, "Sorry, no rooms."

"Come on," Mick said. "If we're not wanted, we'll go someplace else."

"Just a minute," the manager said. He went back to talk to the women again, then returned to say, "We do have room for you, but if thousands of kids show up here, we'll get the National Guard in here to throw them out and you too."

"All we want is some rest," Mick said wearily.

"If thousands of kids show up it'll be because *you* told them we're here," I said to the manager.

We ate and got some rest. I invited Charlie Brown to come down from Miami for the evening, and the next morning he drove us to the Miami airport. None of us talked as we drove along in the cool early morning. About an hour earlier I had wandered into Mick's room, finding his door open and him lying in bed, talking earnestly on the telephone. "I can only say how I really feel, what's in my heart," he was saying. Then Tony had come in and asked me, while Mick was in the bathroom, whether I had heard Bill and Astrid fighting last night.

"I think he slapped her or something," Tony said. "She went down to Mick's room for a while afterwards." We had paid the bill and started to leave when the manager came out with a bill for another two hundred dollar's worth of phone calls. "I've been on the phone to Europe for hours this morning," Mick said, "trying to get a house in the south of France."

"Glad we got that in time," the manager said, friendly enough once we were leaving.

At the airport we told Charlie thanks and goodbye and boarded a flight to Atlanta. In Atlanta we had an hour and a half to wait, and Mick and I prowled the airport, leaving Tony with little Mick, Bill, and Astrid. We played pinball machines, bought GEORGIA STATE PRISON shirts, went out on the observation deck, and sat looking at the cold cloudy day. We talked about old Chuck Berry and Little Richard songs, and Mick said that Keith had written about three hundred unrecorded songs. "I've got a new one meself," he said. "No words yet, just a few words in my head—called 'Brown Sugar'—about a woman who screws one of her black servants. I started to call it 'Black Pussy' but I decided that was too direct, too nitty-gritty."

I asked Mick whether he took pills as a teenager like my friends and me in Georgia, and he said, "No, I didn't, I thought it was wrong. I was so—sort of suburban. I still think it's wrong."

Just before we went back inside, Mick said, "When I got off the plane yesterday I forgot about the angels Richard sent to protect me. I should have remembered and I would've known it was gonna be all right. He said, 'Remember, the angels are watching over you.' "

On the plane to Muscle Shoals, Mick and I talked about movies and acting, which didn't interest him much. "*Ned Kelly* cost two million dollars and I spent three months being cold and muddy. I don't want to be an actor, pretending to be a thief—if you wanted to be a thief you'd either really do it or let it alone. I'd like to direct movies, but I have to learn a lot more."

I pressed on, telling him an idea I'd had for doing Georgette Heyer's *The Black Moth* with the Stones, and other crackpot ideas, but he changed the subject. "Are there any vocal backing groups in Muscle Shoals?"

"Depends," I said. "What d'you need them for, what kind of thing?"

"Certainly not to sing, man," Mick said.

"Oh."

"Whoo," Mick laughed. "I don't like y'singin', honey, but I love the way you move."

At the Muscle Shoals airport there was a small terminal building with a large window through which, it seemed, most of the local population and the people from the surrounding cities of Florence, Sheffield, and

Tuscumbia were looking out at the landing field. Keith was slouching against a post in front of the window, wearing an antique Hungarian gypsy jacket (that would also be left behind at Altamont), and just to start things off right in Alabama, Mick walked up in full view of the watching rednecks and kissed Keith sweetly on the cheek. "How are you, babe?"

"All right," Keith said. "We been drivin' around lookin' at the woods this mornin', it's beautiful around here."

Stu drove us to the Sheffield Holiday Inn, where I was relieved to find my suitcase in my room. I made some phone calls, took a nap, woke up after dark, and went downstairs to have dinner with the Stones; fresh fish from the Tennessee River, red slices of country ham, grits, butter, hush puppies. They were discussing what to do with the tour money.

"We could get an American to bring it in for us," Bill said.

"We can't put it in the bank in America," Mick said, "but we can in Switzerland."

"We could," Bill said, "buy a 1909 Lincoln penny for ten thousand pounds and sell it for fifteen thousand."

The Muscle Shoals Sounds Studio, 3614 Jackson Highway, is a con-crete-block building every bit as glamorous as an automotive parts ware-house. Inside under the green, yellow, and magenta lights and orange and black acoustical ceiling panels, were Jimmy Johnson, a rhythm guitar player and recording engineer; Jim Dickinson; and Ahmet Erte-gun. In the middle of the recording room, the studio itself, there was a toilet filled with microphones and amplifiers, a blue plastic horseshoe over the door. The Stones began positioning themselves, preparing their instruments.

"What's the bass player's name?" Ahmet, bald, vandyked, Turkish, blasé, whispered to me.

"Perks," I said.

The Stones began the process of recording "You Got to Move." In-stead of doing it as it had been performed onstage, by Mick and Keith alone, they were all trying to play it. They made awful noises tuning, then looked for riffs, sorting themselves out within the music in the only way they knew to work.

"They really hard to play with," Charlie said.

"I'm hip," I said. He was a man trained in the styles of modern jazz and Chicago rhythm & blues who was attempting to play a song most often performed on Fred McDowell's front porch outside Como, Mississippi, not far from where we were. They could have got Fred to produce. It progressed so badly, with Mick making a couple of em-barrassing efforts to add to the classic lyrics, that Charlie told him, "I think you should do it with just you and Keith."

"Do you want to do it with just you and me and Mick?" Mick asked Keith.

"Nah," Keith said, because he had something in mind that he wanted to hear but couldn't explain to the others; they just had to strike out and keep stumbling forward till they tripped across it.

"Is this mike all right for doing it properly?" Mick asked portly, red-headed, good-ole-boy Jimmy.

After about ten unsuccessful takes they took a break. "You agreed with me, didn't you?" Charlie asked me.

"They should do it like they do it onstage or change it completely," I said, as if I knew.

On take twelve, with the song still sounding bad, Dickinson and I went to the Holiday Inn. I filled Dickinson in on what had been happening, called the girl in New York, and we drove back to the studio, coming in for the playback of take nineteen or twenty, the master take. "The new album's underway," Keith told me. "Listen to this. Play it for him."

Something had happened while we were gone, a Rolling Stones record had been created out of chaos, each of them had found his own way to the song. Keith, unsatisfied with the terrible raspy sound of playing the steel National with a bottleneck, had chosen instead a twelve-string guitar that sounded much worse. Charlie and Mick Taylor had worked out patterns that emphasized the stark melody line, and so had Bill, though he'd had to leave the bass for the electric piano, where he could take cover in the jangling overtones. Listening to Mick singing, "When the Lord gets ready, you got to move," I thought of the playback of "Midnight Rambler" when the Stones were mixing the album back in Los Angeles (what seemed a very long time ago) and I felt that my question about the Stones had been answered. They were not good or evil, they were for better or for worse artists, and all they wanted was to do their work; for this reason they were now working through the middle of the night in northern Alabama, after their tour was over, their money made. They never wanted to stop me or anybody else from doing his best. Mick and Keith were sitting in the middle of the studio on folding chairs, Mick playing "Brown Sugar" on the guitar, teaching it to Keith as he wrote the lyrics, not stopping till he had its three verses finished.

The next night around eight o'clock the Stones were back in the studio, getting ready to record. Just before leaving the Holiday Inn I had received a phone call from Ahmet, who was at the studio, worrying about the police. "I think there may be a bust," he said. "A couple of the musicians from the studio have been busted twice. We just flushed a quarter pound of shit."

"Sorry to hear that," I told him, knowing that nothing would make Keith change his ways. I didn't mention the call to anyone, and when we got to the studio the first thing Keith did was light a joint and walk past Ahmet to hand it to Mick. Ahmet didn't lose his composure, but his eyes rolled up, the slightest flicker in the direction of a faint.

Mick was sitting at the piano, playing and singing "Loving Cup," a song that was never to sound as good again. "We got a good track of this one in the can," he said to me as I stood nearby listening. "We might try to put voice on it—oh, we don't have the tapes."

Jimmy Johnson was putting Keith's amplifier into the mid-studio toilet, setting it next to the john. "This gives you a real shitty sound," he said.

"Pardon?" said Keith, who hadn't heard him.

"This," Jimmy said, indicating with a nod the toilet, "gives your guitar a real shitty sound—y'know? Get it?"

"That's the way I like it," Keith said, smiling.

During the day, Ahmet had produced a recording session with R. B. Greaves, an Atlantic rhythm & blues singer, and some of the regular studio musicians and a couple of their wives were lingering, trying to appear as if they didn't care about getting a good look at the Rolling Stones.

Inside the control room, Mick was asking the bass player's Southern belle wife, who was dressed as if she were going to church, where he could get some sleeping pills.

"I have some tranquilizers and muscle relaxers, they'll put you to sleep," she said.

"Can't I just get some sleepers?"

"You could see the doctor tom—"

"Or can't you get them in Muscle Shoals, aren't you supposed to sleep?"

"He'll fix you up tomorrow."

"I can call him. If you give me the name of a couple doctors, I can do it, it's very simple. . . ." Then he decided to forget it and went out to begin rehearsing "Brown Sugar" with the band. It sounded bad. "No, no, the tempo's all wrong," Mick said. "It's not—not so bouncy. It should sound fucking *dirty*."

Stu, playing piano, was complaining: "I do wish Keith knew something about chords. I'm tone deaf, I couldn't tune a guitar if I had to. I can hear changes but not what they are. Bill pulls a lot of things together because he has a good ear and knows chords. So I wait for him to get the tune together and get the chords from him. Keith gets upset if you ask him about chords because he plays three notes of a chord and doesn't know what it is."

When they managed to get a provisional track and came into the control room to hear it, Mick said to Jimmy Johnson, "We might need some background singers on this one, some black chicks."

"We use Southern Comfort, three girls from down here," Jimmy said.

"I don't care how they sing long as they wear those silver shoes," Mick said. After listening to the track, he said, "That's the way the song goes but it's much too jangly and simple. Everybody needs to bring his part out to make it a good record."

Mick Taylor, standing beside Mick, looking well pleased with what he'd heard, said, "That's what makes a good rock and roll record, simplicity."

Jagger glanced at the ceiling and didn't answer. He and Keith went back into the studio. Bill was already there, sitting holding his bass. In the control room, Charlie stood up to leave.

"Can't you do something about the drums?" Stu asked. The tom-tom was out of tune with the bass drum, and Stu was exasperated, not to say disgusted, that no one, not even the drummer, seemed to notice.

"What can I do?"

"You could *tune* it, couldn't you?"

"I never tune my drums," Charlie said, starting out of the room.

"Wait a minute. What do you *mean,* you never tune your drums?"

"Why should I tune something I'm gonna go out and beat on? After I hit it a few times it'll change."

He knew what he was talking about. Several hours and many repetitions later, the song was getting better. Ruining takes had earned Stu the Golden Pullover, Charlie a Pullover and a Dingleberry, and another Dingleberry for Bill. While the Stones were working, the studio phone rang and Ahmet answered. "Hello? Mick who? Who is this?" It was Jo, calling from San Francisco. She had been shopping at Saks and I. Magnin's and was now a bit cheered up. Sam, Chip, Rock Scully, and Emmett Grogan had been looking for sites for the festival. Sears Point Raceway was still under consideration, and Ronnie would soon be in town. This was just the sort of information Mick needed when he was trying to make a record. After the call the Stones listened to another playback, and Mick said, "Somehow it's not . . . relentless enough."

While they played the song some more, I stood in the hall talking about the size of recent music festivals with Ahmet, who mentioned, as if it were a curious biological fact, which perhaps it was, that "Black music is the most popular music of all time—and has been since it got started good, about 1921."

In the control room, Jimmy was rolling back the tapes. The Stones had at last made the take they wanted. "When you got a good groove," Jimmy said, "it's lak hittin' a ball over a fence."

They had the band track, but Mick was too tired to sing any more tonight. "All right," he said, "bring Lemon in, see if he can sing it."

One of the studio musicians, still hanging around, said, "Who?"

" 'At's Blind Lemon Jefferson, y'know," Charlie said.

. . .

When we woke up it was Thursday, our last day in Muscle Shoals. The Maysles brothers, who had been in San Francisco filming the negotiations for the free concert, were now with us, and so was Jerry Wexler, who had flown in from Los Angeles to see the Stones and to talk to Dickinson about coming to work for Atlantic with his band, the Dixie Flyers. Wexler and I drove to the studio together, packing a load of bootleg whiskey through the dry county.

Keith opened bottles of beer and Jack Daniel's and poured them together in a paper cup. "Mix it up," he said, "saves ya the trouble."

Ahmet opened a beer and passed it to Mick, who said, "It's great to drink illegally, it's a completely new buzz for me."

A minute later Mick was on the telephone with Tony: "You were? Followed you all the way? What do his feet look like? You can tell over here by their shoes—come back out here and see what happens."

Keith, Charlie, and Dickinson were swapping stories about playing on the same bill with Bo Diddley and his maracas player, Jerome Green. "Jerome could play a fucking waltz, couldn't he, Charlie," Keith said.

"Sure," Charlie said. He and Stu, great admirers of a Joe Turner album Wexler had produced, asked for tapes of outtakes, and Wexler promised they'd get them. Including Mick in the compliment, because he knew who made the deals, Wexler told the Stones he'd enjoyed seeing the last Madison Square Garden show. Earlier he'd told me that he and his wife had left early because the crowd was too rough.

"Leonard Bernstein was there," Mick said. "He came to the hotel, all flash in a black cloak, and he said—pushin' back his hair—'These people have asked me to write a symphony and they want me to do it with the Association, but I want to do it with the Rolling Stones.' I asked him, 'What's the matter, have you run out of melodies? Anyone can write a three-chord melody, why don't you ask Paul McCartney?' Which he probably has and's been turned down. But he really had been listening to our records. He knows ones I'd forgotten, awful ones, twelve-bar things. But why should they play our music? We can play better rock and roll than the New York Philharmonic. They shouldn't play our music and we shouldn't play theirs. 'Im an' 'is cloak—I've got a better cloak meself."

Ahmet, who was considered by some the greatest living proponent in high and low society of the perfect gesture, touched Mick's shoulder lightly to tell him that he had finished talking and said: "The last time I heard Billie Holiday was at the Hollywood Bowl, a jazz thing, she had a nice group backing her, and Lenny was there. She sang a lot of old things like 'Billie's Blues,' and afterwards Lenny went up to Shelly Manne and said, 'You wasn't playing blues drums on that blues,' and Shelly says, 'Man, lissen, you stick to Bach and I'll stick to boogie-woogie.'"

Having the floor, Ahmet went on, talking as he and Wexler liked to do about smoking marijuana before it was illegal. Well-known as a jazz lover when he was still a boy, Ahmet said that one day Lionel Hampton, seeing him talking to Mezz Mezzrow, had said, "What are you doing with that cat, he's a drug pusher."

"But he used to play with your band," Ahmet had said, and Hampton had told him, "We had to hire him or we couldn't get the real good shit."

"They used to call it mezz," Wexler said, adding a footnote.

It was getting a bit too historical in the control room for Keith, who took the Jack Daniel's out to the piano and began singing country songs, "Your Angel Steps Out of Heaven" and "Say It's Not You." Dickinson sang "Amelia Earhart," after which Mick, who had joined the group around the piano, said, "Right! Let's go on, Keith."

"What do you want to do?" Keith asked.

"You must have hundreds," Mick said.

"Yeah, I got some."

"Tell us about it."

"I'll have to get it together, just need some solitude for a few minutes."

"Go in that office up front," Mick said, "and holler when you're ready."

While Keith worked on his song, Ahmet, in another office, worked on Mick. Wexler and Dickinson and I went out to get a hamburger. We talked about doing a series of blues records that never happened, and Wexler and Dickinson agreed to meet in Memphis in January to talk further about the Dixie Flyers. I had bought a Nashville *Tennessean* out of a vending machine, and I looked at it while we waited for our hamburgers. On the front page there was a picture of a man the police said they considered responsible for the murders of Sharon Tate and her houseguests and the LaBianca family. His name was Charles Manson, he had long hair and a beard, and my first impulse was to think that he was probably innocent.

Back at the studio, we learned that Jo had called with bad news about the free concert. Ronnie had met at the Fairmont Hotel with three men from Filmways, the company that owned the Sears Point Raceway, and in twenty minutes the price had gone from five thousand to four hundred and fifty thousand dollars. "But it's for charity, Vietnamese war orphans," Ronnie had said, and the head man from Filmways had said, "I don't give a shit." Filmways also wanted film and sound rights to the show. Ronnie had called in Melvin Belli, one of the most flamboyant American lawyers, and now they were all—Ronnie, Jon, Sam, Jo, Rock Scully, Emmett Grogan, Chip Monck—trying to find a place for the party. "They can't stop us," Keith said. "We'll have it in a parking lot. They can't get as many people as we can because they ain't as popular as we are."

In the control room, Mick said, "We'll need a keyboard player on this one."

Wexler suggested calling one of the studio musicians, and Mick made a face. "I'm a keyboard player," Dickinson said.

"You'll do," Mick said. He turned to Jimmy Johnson, asked if the studio had an autoharp or a dulcimer, and said, "But we lost our dulcimer player, don't have nobody to play that anymore."

They went into the studio, where Dickinson discovered that the piano was out of tune, not with itself but with the present tuning of the Rolling Stones.

"There's a tack piano in the back," Jimmy Johnson said. Dickinson nodded but didn't move. His chance to play with the Rolling Stones had come and the piano didn't work. I pressed a few keys on the tack piano, hearing the clinky ragtime sound tacks give an old upright.

"I think this one's in tune," I said.

"But it's got tacks in it," Dickinson said.

"I *know* it," I said.

Dickinson went to the tack piano, sat down and began to play.

"Lights out," Keith said.

"Lights out, mouths shut," Mick said.

"Lights out in the boys' dorm," Keith said, "two in a bed."

Later, in the control room, listening to the last playback of "Wild Horses," Keith would tell Dickinson, who'd asked, that he had written the chorus and Mick had written the verses. "That's usually the way it works," he said. "I have a phrase that fits what I'm playin'—like 'Satisfaction'—I had that phrase and Mick did the rest. I wrote this song because I was doin' good at home with my old lady, and I wrote it like a love song. I just had this, 'Wild horses couldn't drag me away,' and I gave it to Mick, and Marianne just ran off with this guy and he changed it all round but it's still beautiful."

They played the song over and over, punctuating the repetitions with artistic encouragements to each other: "We want a soft warm lovely sound from you, Wyman," Keith said, "stop donkeyin' about."

Dickinson had written out the chords in numbers the way Nashville studio players did.

"Where'd you get that?" Wyman asked, looking at the chord sheet.

"From Keith," Dickinson said. He had taken Keith's first chord as the "one" chord, putting him in a different key from the one the song was in.

"Don't pay any attention to Keith, he doesn't know what he's doing," Bill said. He wrote a chord sheet that left out the passing chords and gave it to Dickinson, who put it up on the piano's music stand, from which Mick Taylor took it away. Dickinson went on playing.

"What do you think about the piano?" Jagger asked Keith.

"It's the only thing I like so far."

After listening to the first playback we spent some time standing in the hall smoking grass and sniffing cocaine. "You all right?" Charlie asked Dickinson. "It's hard work."

"It's better than if I was in Memphis," Dickinson said, "making sixty-five dollars for a three-hour session that lasts twelve hours. Shows what a strong union we have."

"Unions ain't no good," Tony said. He had not been arrested after all and was standing by holding the dope.

"He says he can't play, and he's standin' here, a piano player," Charlie said. "Ridiculous. We can't play either, legally."

"Why not just *ignore* the union rules?" Tony asked.

"Disc jockeys won't play nonunion records," Dickinson said.

"But we're doin' it," Charlie said. "We're here playing."

Mick said to start again. "All right, Grimblewick," Charlie said to himself. "Back to your percussion."

At four in the morning, the Maysles brothers, Tony, and Stu were asleep on couches at the studio, Jerry and Ahmet were asleep at the Holiday Inn, Mick was in a vocal booth under a blue-green light, Bill was sitting beside Charlie, Dickinson was at the piano, Mick Taylor and Keith were sitting on facing chairs. After another good take, Keith woke up Tony to give us more cocaine.

"That shit'll burn your nose out," Tony said.

"Won't hurt you for long," Dickinson said.

"Just burns out a few connections in the brain," I said.

"You never seem to miss them," Keith said. He inhaled deeply and shook his head. "Gram Parsons gets better coke than the Mafia. From some Black Panther dentist in Watts."

The take, on second hearing, was not good enough. "Doesn't seem the rhythm's coming in the right place," Keith said. Back in the studio, he said, "Tony, let's have some muggles."

"Yeah," Charlie said. "Some mezz."

The song began again, but Keith hit a wrong note. "Shit," Mick said.

"That was going good, too," Mick Taylor said.

"I accept the Golden Prune," Keith said.

Bill went into the john, nothing unusual. When he came back, Mick said, "All right? Everybody in the booth?" But instead of saying "booth," he said my first name, and he and Keith kept that up for the rest of the night. They were trying to be friendly.

"Yeah," Keith said. "Now, Bill, get it into your Hampton that this is it."

The song started well and went on until someone said, "No."

"Who said no?" Charlie asked.

"Jimmy said no," Dickinson said.

"Did you say no?" Mick asked.

"Tape's running out," Jimmy said. He reloaded the eight-track recorder.

"Everybody ready?" Mick asked. "Ready?"

"Yeah, all ready," Keith said.

"That's a moot point," Mick said.

"All right," Jimmy said. "Take eleven. This is the money take."

It wasn't, but the next one was.

By daylight the Jack Daniel's was gone and Keith and Mick were deeply into the J&B, overdubbing vocals on "Brown Sugar," lurching across the studio to the control room to listen to playbacks. Mick had forgotten the words and Dickinson had reminded him to sing the line, "Hear him whip the women just around midnight."

Talking in the control room to Mick Taylor, Charlie, and Bill, Mick said, smiling, looking collegiate, "We can make next year sort of get-out-the-way year if we really push it. We usually wind up at the end of the year all wasted, no ideas, no songs—but this year we're still pushing." Mick wanted to put out "Brown Sugar" and "Wild Horses" as a single right away, like next week. Anything seemed possible that morning in Muscle Shoals.

Keith was sitting on the control room couch, holding a Coke in his left hand and the Scotch bottle in his right. Dickinson was sitting beside him, wearing a black plastic shirt, looking greasy, as if he were about to go out and rip a tire off a semi. There was a gaping hole in the toe of Keith's python boot. Jimmy Johnson, who had been engineering the regular studio sessions in the day and the Rolling Stones undercover work at night, was still at the board, playing back tapes.

"How do you keep going, man?" Keith asked him.

"Courage," Jimmy said. He had taken, to my knowledge, no drugs. "Just thinkin' about how Glyn Johns is always flakin' out."

We were listening to "You Got to Move."

"Put the voices back with the guitars," Mick told Jimmy.

"Bring the drums up when they come in after the solo," Keith said.

"That vocal makes Brownie and Sonny sound like a coupla nowhere white boys," Dickinson said to Keith.

"Just 'cause they been playin' to all them white people," Keith said. "Have you heard Fred McDowell's wife or sister sing with him—I don't know what she is—"

"Wife from time to time," Dickinson said.

"She's great," Keith said. "She sings for herself."

Mick had told Dickinson that he needed to lose some weight, and Dickinson on the couch made a self-deprecating remark about being old—at twenty-nine—and fat.

"Doesn't matter if you're sixty-eight and bald," Keith said. "If you can do it, there's somebody who can dig it, but if you're a rock and roller you've got to be on the stage. A rock and roller doesn't exist unless he's on the stage."

Charlie had left the control room and now, at seven o'clock in the morning, was sitting alone in the studio playing the drums, pounding away. "*There*'s a rock and roller," Keith said.

Jimmy seemed to take forever to get the tapes ready. Mick played piano, Keith played piano, Mick played guitar, waiting. "Fuckin' 'ell, Shuscle Moals," Mick said. "Come on—even Astrid's gone 'ome." Astrid had almost always been present at the studio, but like a ghost, I'd never noticed her. Finally we heard the playbacks. Dickinson asked Mick if he'd mind his having a copy of "Wild Horses."

"No," Mick said, "but we don't want to hear it on the radio."

"I'm shocked you'd suggest it," Charlie said.

Mick had at the end of each night's work erased or destroyed all the outtakes. The Stones would leave not a trace behind them at the Muscle Shoals studio, nor would they pay anyone for anything.

"Too bad," Keith said as the tapes wound their last. "We didn't get to go to a juke joint."

We wobbled out into the early morning light. "Like to come back for two weeks or so," Keith said, "if we could rent a house and not stay at the Squaliday Inn."

There were a couple of carloads of friendly and relaxed Alabama teenagers outside. They took pictures and followed us back to the motel. We went to our rooms, cleaned up, Dickinson and I smoked my last joint—the Stones were out of grass and I'd mentioned that I had one joint left—and went down to the dining room for breakfast. Keith soon joined us. He had shaved and was dressed with his usual quiet good taste: white tennis shoes, raveled beige nylon socks, red velvet pants with long strings hanging from their hemless cuffs, black velvet jacket, brown cap, long yellow and black wool scarf. "Tea, please," he said to the waitress.

Behind me a woman was saying, "Ah thank ah'll give 'im a chemistry set," reminding me that Christmas was coming. Charlie and Mick Taylor, then Ahmet, then Mick, joined us. Mick was wearing his white velvet suit and red ruffled silk shirt, red muffler, burgundy maxicoat and cord cap. He sat down with us and ordered some corned beef.

Bill and Astrid sat at a nearby table. "Are you all with some group?" their waitress asked.

"Martha and the Vandellas," Bill said.

"Oh," the waitress said.

"You still got that joint?" Keith asked, wanting to smoke it at the table and give Ahmet a heart attack.

"Gone," I said.

"When's the plane?" Keith asked.

"We'll wait till we're called," Mick said, eating corned beef.

When we finished breakfast we went up to Keith's room to listen again to the new Stones recordings.

"Got some nice tracks," Wexler said. He had come to breakfast late. "Taking them back to London to add the sweetening?"

"Not very much," Keith said. "I like them just the way they are."

"I sent a song to Aretha once," Mick said—"Sympathy for the Devil," the one Wexler had described to me as being suitable for Sonny Bono or Burl Ives. "And she didn't do it. I was very disappointed. Very *hurt*."

"Well, man, ah," Wexler said, "there's still time—"

Soon we were at the airport, the little girls following us, snapping photos as we walked out to the plane. "Your daddy's gonna kill you," Tony told a girl who was posing beside him. We were going to Atlanta— Wexler would stay there for a record-awards banquet—and on to San Francisco by way of Dallas. Wexler sat beside me talking but I was too sleepy to hear him. Across the aisle Mick and Keith were sprawled, Mick's head on Keith's shoulder, asleep.

I passed out for about twenty minutes and we were in Atlanta, then aboard a crowded plane where we had to split up, Keith sitting with some soldiers in the tourist section. I sat next to a well-dressed middle-aged woman who was reading John Cheever's *Bullet Park,* a new book that season.

"That's a beautiful book," I said. We became involved in an odd, intimate conversation brought on by fatigue and romance and bourbon. We talked about Cheever's characters, how sad they were, how acutely they felt the limits of their lives. "No matter what, we're not in control, we don't plan any of the things that happen to us, they just happen and our hearts are broken by it all—"

I went back to speak to Keith, who gave me the cocaine and the gold bamboo and said, "Take this."

"Why, thanks." I went into the toilet and came back refreshed to find Keith, now in the first-class compartment, engaged in conversation with an advertising executive in a business suit.

"You're not free, man, you've got to do what they say," Keith said.

"You have to play what people want," the man said. "What's the difference?"

"No, we don't," Keith said. "We don't have to do anything we don't want to do. I threw my favorite guitar off the stage in San Francisco."

"You can't do that every night," the man said.

"I can do it as often as I feel like it. Not always but sometimes."

The man turned to me: "Do you believe this guy?"

"I believe him," I said.

"Ah, you know what my scene is," Keith said to me.

"Well," the man said, "what I do isn't bad, I've never hurt anybody."

"How can you be sure?" Keith asked, and then went on as if he didn't want to think about that one too long himself. "The problem is when you're talking you think you're arguing with Spiro Agnew, and you're not, you're talking to a perfectly reasonable man. But I really think it's true that you can't do what you want to do. So many people aren't doing what they want to do."

"Most of us do both," the man said. "We like what we do but we have to make money. It's a compromise."

"But that's so sort of sad," Keith said.

"But the world is not perfect," the man said.

"No," Keith said. "The world *is* perfect."

At that I had to reach over and kiss Keith on top of the head, a gesture of blessing that did not even bring a pause in the conversation. "You guys work so hard," he said to the man. "We work hard in concentrated periods but then we stop and it's four months of doing nothing—"

"It's a different schedule," the man said.

"Yeah," Keith said, "but most people don't dig their work. Americans are into a very freaky scene—like Spiro trying to speak for the people and he can't because most of the people are under twenty-five and into a very different sort of scene—"

"Are you sure they disagree with Spiro?" the man asked.

"I've just been talkin' to those guys, those kids who're goin' into the army at Fort Bliss—strange name for an army camp—they don't want to do anything but go to Juárez and score some marijuana."

"Don't they care about girls anymore?" the man said.

"Yeah, they all want to go to Juárez and screw some broads and smoke some dope. They signed up for four years so they won't have to go to Nam and fight in a war they don't believe in, for this idea of America as the policeman of the world."

"It's not a matter of being a policeman, it's a matter of protecting your interests," the man said.

"What interests, you got half a million soldiers in Vietnam which is certainly not yours. The North Vietnamese are right and they're gonna win."

"You know that?"

"Yeah, because I've seen films and read about it and talked to people who've been there."

"Yeah, but you don't know, you might have to fight yourself someday," the man said darkly.

"I do, all the time," Keith said, and then he seemed to despair of being able to get his point of view across to the man. "You don't know what it's like."

"What what's like?"

"Being a Rolling Stone, the attacks people have put on us, the violence—"

"You mean people try to beat you up?"

"They try to kill me, man, that's what I mean by violence, cops have pulled guns on me and offered to shoot me with them."

"Where?"

"Backstage in dressing rooms, for nothing, for the slightest pretext. The five members of this band have had to go through so much bullshit—"

The seat belt light went on and I went back to my seat, passing Mick and Charlie. "But in a love affair," Mick was saying, very earnest. I knew which five members Keith had meant. The Stones were so funky that one of them was a dead man.

When we got off the plane our peaceful interlude was over. The people who had been comic voices on the phone were all around us. Ronnie grabbed Mick, sideburning him along. "Don't worry about a thing, everything's being taken care of, we have a site, we can go out there tonight if you want to, Chip's out there, and Sam—"

As we walked out to the limousines a small boy asked me, "Are you a Beatle?"

"Yes," I said.

"What's your name?"

"Philo Vance."

"They'll believe anything," Keith said. "Philo Vance, the well-known Beatle."

Keith and I got into a limousine and Jon Jaymes followed us, talking about the free concert. "I'm insuring the whole thing," he said.

"What does that mean?" Keith asked.

"That means if there are ten murders, *I* go to jail."

30

His heart was achin', head was thumpin'
Little Jesse went to hell bouncin' and jumpin'
Folks, don't be standin' around little Jesse cryin'
He wants everybody to do the Charleston whilst he's dyin'
One foot up, a toenail draggin'
Throw my buddy Jesse in the hoodoo wagon
Come here, mama, with that can of booze
It's the dying crapshooter's—leavin' this world—
With the dying crapshooter's—goin' down slow—
With the dying crapshooter's blues.

WILLIE McTELL: "The Dying Crapshooter's Blues"

WHEN, IN 1968, I went to England for the first time to meet the Stones, wearing a trenchcoat in unconscious self-parody, I didn't know what I was getting into. Four weeks later when I returned to America to write what I could about the Stones, I knew that something was going on with them under the surface, and that I hadn't been able to get to the bottom of it.

In the summer "Jumpin' Jack Flash" had carried them back to the top of the pop charts. Their new album, *Beggar's Banquet*, was released in November after a long dispute over the Stones' proposed cover photograph of the graffiti on a toilet wall in a Mexican automobile body shop in Los Angeles. Decca refused to release the album with that cover. "The record company is not there to tell us what we can make," Mick had said. "If that's the way they feel about it, then they should make the records and we'll distribute them." At last the record was released with a white cover designed as an invitation. "We copped out," Keith said, "but we did it for money, so it was all right."

Also released in November was *One + One*, a film by Jean-Luc Godard that was in part about the recording of "Sympathy for the Devil." Filming had been completed for a movie called *Performance*, starring Mick and Anita. In December the Stones produced a filmed entertainment called "The Rolling Stones Rock and Roll Circus." It presented circus acts—tigers, acrobats, clowns, a fire eater—and rock and roll from the Stones, Taj Mahal, John Lennon, Eric Clapton, Jethro Tull, the Who. The Stones intended selling it to BBC-TV, but it was never finished.

At the end of the year, Keith, Mick, Anita, and Marianne went to Peru and Brazil. Seeing the black cowboys on the *pampas* inspired Keith to write a Jimmie Rodgers type of song called "Honky Tonk Women." Brian, who had moved into Cotchford Farm in November, spent the holidays with Suki in Ceylon. John Lewis, a young English friend of Brian's, would tell me sometime later that while in Ceylon Brian consulted an astrologer—supposedly, at one time, Hitler's astrologer—who told Brian to be careful swimming in the coming year, not to go into the water without friends.

On January 13, Brian was back in London to appear before a court that denied his appeal to set aside his guilty verdict. That left him with two drug convictions on his record, two strikes against him. At the end of January Mick and Keith came back to England and started months of work on the tracks for *Let It Bleed*. In March the Stones were asked to play at the Memphis Blues Festival and considered doing it with Eric Clapton because of the problems they would have getting Brian into the country.

Brian had used his upset over his impending trial as an excuse for missing sessions and had even avoided England, telling the London newspapers from Morocco, "I have the feeling my presence is not required." With his trial over and months of dental work finished ("What a waste," Jo said), Brian—though he had completed his Moroccan album, having spent £23,000 of his own money—was still not able to do his part, whatever that was now, with the Stones. "After the trial was over and Brian didn't get it together," Jo said, "the handwriting was on the wall." Early in April, Jo wrote a letter to Mick. "What's happening with the group?" she asked, and offered "a short report on what's really happening:"

> A few first thoughts—the office is completely loyal— also relatively free of intrigue and politics. No one is ambitious or on ego trips. It's a nice place to work.

Lately there hasn't been enough to keep minds together, and that leads us to the basic crunch: it's your
office.

1. What's happening to the group? Is there any real
interest in doing public appearances? Or do you want
to just record and make movies?

2. Aside from the Rolling Stones, any other projects?
Record company?

The Klein problem is more than a drag. We're pup-
pets. How can you work, or the office, if we have to
spend so much time pleading for bread or whatever.
It's never going to be efficient till that is straightened
out.

1. Klein—some way of finance—agony over
   money & contracts
2. Mick's personal plans
3. Records—you should just worry about the
   product.
4. Rolling Stones
5. Record company or studio
6. If the load is too heavy, fuck it. You really
   only should do what makes you happy. If you
   knew there wouldn't be any hangups.

On February 3, Allen Klein announced that he had taken over the
Beatles' management. The Stones, feeling neglected and resentful,
kept working on *Let It Bleed*, using the sixty voices (double-tracked)
of the London Bach Choir on "You Can't Always Get What You
Want" and a young mandolin player named Ry Cooder on Robert
Johnson's "Love in Vain," finding ways to add the exotic textures and
accents Brian had once provided. Brian would still come to some
recording sessions. At one he asked Mick, "What can I play?"

"I don't know," Mick said, "What *can* you play?"

The hand Brian had broken on Anita's head had not healed properly,
and Brian had trouble playing guitar. He tried playing harmonica, but
finally Mick told him, "You can't play anymore, why don't you go
home?"

Mick and Keith were looking for someone to replace Brian. In May
they invited Mick Taylor to some sessions. On May 25 they over-
dubbed saxophonist Bobby Keys on the rock and roll version of
"Honky Tonk Women." Sometime in the next week, Mick had a talk
with Mick Taylor.

At this time Mick was learning dialogue for his appearance with
Marianne in a film about the bandit *Ned Kelly*, scheduled to start pro-

duction in Australia early in July. The day the newspapers carried the story announcing the film, Mick and Marianne were arrested for possessing illegal drugs in the house Mick had bought the year before at 48 Cheyne Walk.

On June 8, with "Honky Tonk Women" ready for release, Keith, Mick, and Charlie went to Cotchford Farm to talk to Brian. Years later Charlie would say, "It was the worst thing so far that I've ever had to do." But he also said that when they told Brian what they wanted to do, he seemed relieved. "It was as if a whole weight had been lifted from his shoulders, and he said, 'Yeah, I want to leave.' "

Brian announced to the press that he had left the Stones. He called his father to say that it was only temporary, they wanted to play America, he would tour Europe with them next year.

In London's Hyde Park, starting in September 1968, a man named Peter Jenner, from the pop production firm Blackhill Enterprises, had been giving free concerts like the ones he had seen in California. "Honky Tonk Women" was scheduled for release on July 4, and the Stones planned a free concert in Hyde Park for July 5. Another letter from Jo Bergman:

The Rolling Stones

Telephone 01-629 5856   46a Maddox Street

Telex 266934   London W1

Dear People,

Here is a rough guide-plan for this week's events:

TUES. 1st July

    1 o'clock. Granada Theatre, Wandsworth Road The evening is theoretically free, unless anyone feels able to do interviews for FM stations in America at that time—i.e. 5-6 o'clock. I will ask you about this later.

WED. 2nd July

    12-2 o'clock. Music Scene introductions. These will be at the TRL Studio, 44/46 Whitfield Street W.1., and will be very quick. It is very important however that everyone make it by 12 o'clock because they must be finished in the studio by 2 o'clock.

    7 o'clock. Olympic-recording.

THURS. 3rd July

    1.30/2 o'clock. Photo session with an American photographer to do pictures for posters in America and photograph for the September album cover. This should take, at most, two

hours, probably less. Rest of the afternoon could
be rehearsals.

8-9.30 Top of the Pops taping at Studio G. Lime
Grove.

FRI. 4th July.

Rehearsals all day I presume. (Mick only—
meeting with Jane Nicholson and *Rolling Stone*
staff. Meeting with Jo to be arranged before rehearsals)

SAT. 5th July.

The Battle of the Field of the Cloth of Gold.

3.45 Albert Hall Car Park

After Altamont, when I was living in London, I talked many times
with Shirley Arnold, who was still running the fan club. She was one
of the most decent people I had ever met, English in the best sense of
the word. A few years later, when the Stones were living abroad and
she never saw them anymore, she stopped working for them. She would
spend a few years working for Rod Stewart and then one day she would
call Jo Bergman in California, where Jo was working for Warner Bros.
Records, and say, "I've left the business." It was to her credit that
she had never been in the business.

"Brian was in a terrible state for ages after Anita," Shirley said
one day in her gentle but frank blue-eyed manner, "but then Brian
was always in a terrible state, wasn't he? He was always losin' out,
every way. He so wanted to be—not that they're not normal, but he
so wanted to have a normal happy life, every way, wivvout any hangups.
But it never worked out. And he would never reach out for what he
wanted. He was so easily led. I went round very early one morning in
late 'sixty-seven. He rang up, he'd had a bad night. Maybe he'd taken
lots of things and hadn't slept for days. He said, 'I'm starvin'. Get
ten pounds from the accountant, get lots of food and bring it round.
I'm starvin. He wanted a big ham on the bone and that costs about five.
So I get round to the flat, which was in Courtfield Road, and there was
Brian and two other girls, couple of other fellows, all hangers-on who
weren't really interested in Brian. The food arrived and everyone sort
of dived in. There were eggs and bacon, and he'd asked for instant
mashed potatoes. He said, 'How do I cook sausages?' I said, 'Would you
like me to cook it for you, Brian?' He said, 'Oh, yes, please.' I was
cookin' his breakfast—and I was engaged then, I was engaged to be
married—and he was sayin', 'You're so normal, you're gettin' it all
together.' It was so easy, I mean anyone can cook a breakfast, and
Brian was sayin', 'You're so clever,' and I could imagine Brian tryin'
to cook eggs and bacon. I'll never forget, we had these big sausages,

and I put the fork in them—lots of people do, you know, put the fork in a sausage to stop it from explodin'—and he was sayin', 'Aw, I never knew that.' He said, 'I'm really gonna get it together with a nice chick, it's great to see you workin' in the kitchen.'

"By the time the breakfast was finished he was asleep. I woke him up and he ate his breakfast. He was so determined that morning to pull himself together and have a nice flat, and he was goin' on about havin' food in the fridge and havin' milk delivered. Nothing was normal in Brian's life, but he would never reach out and make it normal.

"Then he was with Suki. She made him happy, I think. Maybe she was the next best thing to Anita, I think that's what he was after. She looked like Anita in the earlier days. They looked like sisters. In the office we would see photographs of Suki and think that it was Anita. Suki was goin' with Tara Browne, the Guinness heir, and she was in a car crash and Tara died, and he died in her arms. She was in a terrible state. Brian was a friend of Tara's, and they went to the funeral together, and Brian had just lost Anita, so they started living together. Maybe it was because Suki really loved Tara and Brian really loved Anita that it never worked out for them. She was a nice girl to him. She looked after him. They seemed happy. But I think that was the thing with Brian, losin' Anita.

"Suki told me once that she went back to the flat and Brian was with Linda. I mean, that was wicked for a start, to do that, that was really terrible. She said he kicked her out of the flat. She was covered in bruises. And he also kicked the dog. So, you can't understand Brian, because he loved the dog so much, and he even took it out on the dog that night. I don't think anyone understands—understood him at all. I don't think anyone could begin to understand him.

"I remember when he lived in Windsor—I told you about the goat—they went away for a few days, someone looked after it, and it caught pneumonia and died. I told him on the telephone and it just broke his heart. There was Brian cryin' and there was me cryin' because he was cryin'. He was sayin', 'I want it stuffed, I've got to have it stuffed.' I found out from the taxidermist's how much it was gonna cost and rang Brian back and said, 'They'll do it. It's gonna cost four hundred quid.' He said, 'No, I can't do it, I can't have its insides pulled out.' I think they buried it in the garden at Redlands.

"He loved animals. Sometimes he was so sweet and gentle. He had the face that beamed out. When he smiled everything was great, the sun was shining. I always loved him. I've always loved all the boys, but when the fans send me letters and say Please tell me what he was like, I can type four pages without thinkin' at all about Brian. But then I think, I'm so lucky, at least I knew him, and it's all there, no one else can have it. I'm glad I knew him. But I always used to worry about Brian. I never thought he'd make it. He didn't think he'd make it himself. Mrs. Jones has got a tape, an interview with Brian saying, 'I don't think I'll be around when I'm thirty.' And he was always sayin' to Suki about makin' a will, and Suki used to say, 'When we're old and grey,' and he'd say, 'No, I'll never make it.' He could never see a future for himself. The boys knew it as well, he used to say to everyone that he'd never live to be old.

"It's been so great workin' for them, all the years I've been there, and I always knew that one day one of them would die, and I used to think that was the worst thing I could go through, but I knew it would be Brian. I could have expected it anytime, 'cause he went through so many changes, I knew it was comin'. But then when he left the group—I think Fred the accountant and I were the only two that spoke to him every day. He used to ring the office, and he was so happy. I don't know, maybe he was tryin' to convince us, or in tryin' to convince us that he was goin' to get it together he was tryin' to convince himself. We were talkin' about the Hyde Park concert the day before he died. He died on the Wednesday, I was talkin' to him on the Monday. I'd already met Mick Taylor—the week before—and Brian said, 'Have you met him?' I said, 'Yeah.' He said, 'What's he like?' I said, 'Oh, I don't think I like him.' He said, 'Oh, you will,' and he was ever so nice about it. He said, 'I think I'll come to the Hyde Park concert on Saturday, what do you think people would think about that, if I came?' I said, 'It would be a great idea, for you to go along and wish Mick Taylor luck.'

"Then on the Tuesday I spoke to him. He rang up and said, 'Can you send me down some photographs?' So I said, 'Yeah, and I'm still answering the letters for you.' He said, 'Oh, are you sure you don't mind?' He'd always put you in that position, are you sure you don't mind doin' it. I said, 'No, I'll answer the letters, I'll always work for you, don't be silly.'

"Suki was in Morocco, they'd just split u'. I knew Brian was livin' with a girl, Anna, I'd never seen her. I was lookin' after Matilda, Suki's dog. Brian thought the world of that dog. I went home on this Tuesday evening, and I'd just had the telephone put on at home, it had just been installed. One person knew the number. I rang Tom Keylock's wife, 'cause the boys were recording that night. Tom had gone down to Redlands. I rang Joan Keylock and gave her the number. So when the phone rang at one o'clock in the morning it could only have been Joan. That was the first time my phone at home had ever rung. I ran downstairs—Matilda was following me—picked up the phone. She said, 'Are you awake?' I said, 'Yeah, I'm downstairs, what's wrong?' She said, 'I've got some bad news.' I said, 'Brian.' She said, 'He's dead.'

"She was in a state, she'd only just heard, she heard before anyone else. Frank Thorogood, who was down there with Brian, was a friend of Tom's. As they pulled Brian from the pool, they realized he was dead. The first thing Frank did was to ring Joan and say, 'Brian's dead, quick, someone get Tom down,' because Tom was great at getting everything sorted out. She rang me before she even rang the studio to tell Stu to tell the boys. She said, 'Frank and Brian went for a swim, and Brian didn't come out.' I put the phone down, started to walk upstairs to the bedroom, and went hysterical. My parents got up and they said, 'What's wrong?' I said, 'Brian's dead.' Matilda was sittin' on the bed howlin', lookin' out the window goin' *Owrr, owrr*—it was as if she knew.

"Joan rang the studio, and Stu answered. She said, 'Is Tom there? Tom's got to go down to Cotchford.' I think Stu said, 'Oh, what's the silly bugger done now?' She said, 'He's dead.' Then he told the boys. I pulled myself together. I rang Jo about half-past one. I'd been ringin' and ringin' and there was no reply. I thought, I'll keep ringin' because obviously she's not there so I'm not gonna wake her up, I'll ring every five minutes until she comes in. She must have rushed in and got into the bath. I rang and said, 'Jo? Were you asleep?' She said, 'No, I'm just having a bath.' I said, 'I've got some bad news. Brian's dead.' She said 'No.' Then she said, 'Now why did he have to do this, we've got so much to do on Saturday with the Hyde Park concert, there's the estate to take care of, and he never had a will, there's the funeral—'

"I'm sure all of us just sat up all night. I left home about half past six, got into a minicab. The driver was a young fellow, and it was on the six o'clock news that morning, he said, 'Uh—Brian Jones is dead.' I said, 'Yeah, I heard.' And there was me sittin' there, I'd loved him for so long and worked for him so long, and there was Brian's dog sitting next to me, and there was the minicab driver telling me he was dead. We got to the West End and all the newspaper clippings were up—Brian Jones Dies in Swimming Pool—and I was looking at all these newspaper things and thinking, 'He's really dead, he's front-page news again.' I got out of the minicab at the wrong place, so I had to walk down, and I hadn't slept anyway, so I was really weird, and the lady in the cigaret kiosk, she knows me well, and I walked past her, I sort of walked out into the middle of the road, and she came out and got me, and I walked up into the office and opened it up. It was seven o'clock in the morning, and you can imagine the office, it was so quiet, and I just sat there. The first phone call—I think at half past eight—was Alexis Korner. He was in a state of shock, and he said, 'Is anyone there, has anyone heard the news, who am I speakin' to?' I said, 'You're speakin' to Shirley,' and he said, 'Well, then, you know how I feel.' He was tryin' to say I'm so sorry for you, because I knew Alexis when we first started, and I start crying when I hear anyone cry, and he just broke down like a baby. I could hardly see by the end of the day.

"The boys all showed it in different ways, Charlie actually cried, whereas I think Mick was too shocked. Charlie came up early, Mick arrived, Keith came in and grabbed hold of me and said, 'Are you all right?' I don't think anyone knew what was happening, 'cause even if they all had expected Brian to die young, when it happens it's still a shock. Then they started saying about Hyde Park, and the first thing Mick said was, 'We'll cancel it,' and then they said, 'No, we'll do it, we'll do it for Brian.' "

Over and over that day the flimsy record player in the Stones' office played Tim Hardin's *Bird on a Wire*. The Stones cancelled the photo session scheduled for the afternoon, but they went to the *Top of the Pops* taping that night. They rehearsed the next day, although Mick, ill with at least a sore throat and hay fever, didn't sing. He was scheduled to start *Ned Kelly* in Australia on Monday, but he didn't feel like going. The film production company's lawyers said that if he was well enough to sing in Hyde Park on Saturday, he was well enough to fly to Australia on Sunday.

In Australia, Marianne took an overdose of Tuinal after seeing not her face but Brian's in the mirror and spent days in a coma, hovering between life and death. Later she would say that while unconscious, she was with Brian. They took a long walk, talking together, and then Marianne said, "I've got to go back."

"I've got to go on," Brian said.

Marianne was replaced in the film by another actress and went as soon as she was able into a Swiss hospital to recuperate.

On July 21, for the first time, a man walked on the moon. On August 10 Marlon Richards was born. On August 18 Mick was injured while filming when a defective pistol exploded in his hand. On September 12, Mick was back in London by way of Tahiti. On September 29 he appeared in court and had his hearing postponed till December. A week later he would go to Bali for a few days, but he would be back to fly to Los Angeles with the other Stones on October 17.

An audience of a quarter of a million had been expected for the Stones' free concert in Hyde Park, but there may have been twice that many. Sam Cutler, who worked for Blackhill, was master of ceremonies. The English Hell's Angels, younger and much gentler than their American counterparts, acted as security, as they had at other such concerts, receiving a note of thanks from Jo Bergman for the Stones: "You really did good on Saturday, you helped make it possible for us to do our thing and it really knocked us out to see your pretty smiling faces."

The Stones started playing at Hyde Park as five thousand butterflies were released, after Mick read two stanzas from Shelley's "Adonais":

> Peace, peace! he is not dead, he doth not sleep—
> He hath awakened from the dream of life—
> 'Tis we, who lost in stormy visions, keep
> With phantoms an unprofitable strife,
> And in mad trance, strike with our spirit's knife
> Invulnerable nothings.—*We* decay
> Like corpses in a charnel; fear and grief
> Convulse us and consume us day by day,
> And cold hopes swarm like worms within our living clay.
>   .   .   .
>
> The One remains, the many change and pass;
> Heaven's light forever shines, Earth's shadows fly;
> Life, like a dome of many-coloured glass,
> Stains the white radiance of Eternity,
> Until Death tramples it to fragments.—Die,
> If thou wouldst be with that which thou dost seek!
> Follow where all is fled!—Rome's azure sky,
> Flowers, ruins, statues, music, words, are weak
> The glory they transfuse with fitting truth to speak.

"Mick read the poem," Shirley Arnold told me, "and then the butterflies came off, and one landed on me. It was so pretty, and I was sitting with Shirley Watts, and when the boys came on, she said, 'I miss his face.' The butterfly that landed on my arm had a broken wing, so she said, 'Oh, it's got a broken wing,' and she started to cry. I said, 'Come on, we'll go.' We only listened to two numbers and went back and sat in the caravan. It was a strange day in the park, it was a great day if Brian had been there, if he had been watching. I'm sure he was. All you could see was thousands and thousands of people—quiet, calm, not moving. A couple got up and danced. But I think if Brian hadn't died, there would have been a riot, because the music was fantastic. But they'd lost a Stone, and they just wanted to listen to the music. I think lots of the people were there to pay their respects.

"Mick went off to Australia—he was in a really bad state—and Bill and Charlie and Astrid and Shirley went to the funeral. There were so many flowers from the fans. I ordered a spaniel, 'cause that was his favorite dog. It was fantastic, it looked just like a dog, all in flowers.

"On the morning, the Thursday after Hyde Park, Fred picked me up at the office, and we went down to the Londonderry for Bill and Astrid, they were going down with us, and Suki was coming with us as well, we had a big limousine. Charlie and Shirley were making their own way with Stu and his wife. We get to the Londonderry and Suki walked in with a sad face, but the sun was shining, it was a great day for a funeral. We had this long drive to Cheltenham, talkin' all the time, mostly about Brian, but happy things. When we got to Cheltenham, as we pulled up outside the house, there's a big lawn, and that was covered with flowers, and there were so many people around. We expected to stay in the cars, wait for the other cars to come and get in the funeral cars and go along, but there was Mr. Jones and Tom Keylock at the door. Mr. Jones wanted to meet everyone, and they had a room for us with cakes and sandwiches and tea, which you really appreciate after bein' in a car for hours.

"Bill and Astrid went in and shook hands, and Tom said, 'This is Shirley Arnold.' Mr. Jones got hold of me and cried, which started me off again. He got hold of me and he wouldn't let go. Mr. Jones said that Brian had told him about me.

"Charlie and Shirley arrived, then the cars arrived and we walked out. We saw the coffin—it was bronze, really a lovely coffin—and we got into the cars. Hatherly Road, where Brian lived, goes on for about two miles, and going slow down the road, there were what seemed to be lots and lots of people. When we went past the school, all the little boys and girls were standing there looking, their teachers had let them come out into the playground. Then we got down into the town itself. There were so many people—the whole of Cheltenham came out just to stand and watch, whether they were sincere about it or whether it was just a nice day and we'll go look at the flowers.

"We all started to walk in behind the coffin to go into the church. Shirley Watts was walking with me, and she was crying and I was crying 'cause where we were walking, we could've touched the coffin, and Brian was in there. They brought the coffin in and put it on an altar, and the priest—I heard some of the things he said, about how Brian used to sing in the choir in this church. It was nice, the choirboys were singing, you could imagine that Brian was once a choirboy as well. They did a long service. Then the priest said, 'Mr. Jones has asked me to read you this telegram.' It was a telegram that Brian had sent to his parents about three years before when he was on a drugs charge. The priest said, 'I think Brian sums up everything he wants to say in this telegram: "Please don't judge me too harshly." ' He could've written it the day before he died, to be read when he died.

"Then we came out of the church and had about a five-minute drive to the cemetery, and things got out of hand, because there were so many people there with their children, lickin' ice lollies. It wasn't very nice, all these people trying to push to look down the hole. We were sort of ushered along with the parents. There was Fred and me and Bill and Charlie and Suki and Brian's sister Barbara and Julian standin' there with Linda, the image of Brian. The priest did another sermon, ever such a long one, and then they started to lower the coffin. It was so pretty, the sun was shinin' on the coffin. Usually you're gonna go down in a hole that's dark, this was covered in imitation grass and it was a really deep hole. We all stood over the side to watch, you're supposed to watch the coffin go down. It was hot, cameras were clickin', it was so sick, takin' photographs. I remember seeing the coffin going down and it was going such a long way. I thought I was going down the hole—"

3 1

Jerry Lee Lewis: H-E-L-L!

Sam Phillips: I don't believe it.

Jack Clement: Great God Almighty, great balls of fire!

Billy Lee Riley: That's right!

SP: I don't believe it.

JLL: It says, "Make merry! with the joy of God! *only!*"
But when it comes to worldly music, rock and roll—

BLR: Rock it out!

JLL: —anything like that, you have done talked yourself
into the world, and you're in the world, and you hadn't
come from out of the world, and you're still a sinner.
You're a sinner and unless you be saved and borned
again and be made as a little chile and walk before
God and be holy—and, brother, I mean you got to be
so pure. No sin shall enter there—*no sin!* For it says *no
sin.* It don't say just a little bit; it says *no sin shall enter
there.* Brother, not one little bit. You got to *walk* and
talk with God to go to Heaven. You got to be *so* good
that it's pitiful. I'm tellin' you what I know.

BLR: Hallelujah!

SP: All right. Now look, Jerry, religious conviction doesn't
mean anything resembling extremism. All right. You
mean to tell me that you're gonna take the Bible, that
you're gonna take God's word, and that you're gonna
revolutionize the whole universe? Now, listen. Jesus
Christ was sent here by God Almighty—

JLL: **Right!**

SP: Did he convict, did he save all of the people in the world?

JLL: Naw, but he tried to!

SP: He sure did. Now, wait just a minute. Jesus Christ came into this world. He tolerated man. He didn't preach from one pulpit. He went around and did good for others.

JLL: That's right! He preached everywhere!

SP: Everywhere. That's right.

JLL: He preached on land!

SP: That's right.

JLL: He preached on the water!

SP: That's exactly right! Now—

JLL: Man, he done everything! He healed!

SP: Now, now, here's, here's the difference—

JLL: Are you followin' those that heal? Like Jesus Christ did?

SP: What d'you mean . . . you . . . what . . . I, I . . .

JLL: Well, it's happenin' every day!

SP: What d'you mean?

JLL: The *blind* had eyes opened.

SP: Jerry—

JLL: The *lame* were made to walk.

SP: Jesus Christ—

JLL: The crippled were made to walk.

SP: Jesus Christ, in my opinion, is just as real today as he was when he came into this world.

JLL: Right! Right! You're so right, you don't know what you're sayin'!

SP: Now, I will say, more so—

BLR: Aw, let's cut it! It'll sell!

JC: It'll never sell, man, it's not commercial.

SP: Wait, wait, wait just a minute. We can't, we got to— now, look, listen, I'm tellin' you outa my heart, and I have studied the Bible a little bit—

JLL: Well, I have too. I studied it through and through and through and through, and I know what I'm talkin' about.

SP: Listen, Jerry. If you think that you can't, can't do good if you're a rock and roll exponent—

JLL: You can do good, Mr. Phillips, don't get me wrong—

SP: Now, wait a minute, listen. When I say *do good*—

JLL: You can have a kind heart!

SP: I don't *mean*, I don't mean just—

JLL: You can help people!

SP: You can *save souls*!

JLL: *No! No! No! No!*

SP: *Yes!*

BLR: You'll never make it.

JLL: *How can the Devil save souls? What are you talkin' about?*

SP: Listen, listen—

JLL: Man, I got *the Devil* in me! If I didn't have, I'd be a Christian!

—Conversation at Sun Recording Studio, 1957

IN THE LOBBY of the Huntington Hotel, waiting for the elevators, we heard a noise from the staircase and looked up to see a woman of some years, with copper-colored hair, dressed in a bright green wrapper, screeching at us. "I wish you'd take 'em all and clear out of here," she said. A girl with a tape recorder and two young men with cameras, underground press people who had been waiting for us in the lobby, looked at the woman, then at us, none of whom gave any sign of having heard her, and the girl and one of the men said, "Wow. Far out."

The press and the Maysles brothers were filming as we left the elevators to invade the upstairs corridors. "Is my local groupie in?" Keith asked, opening the door of his suite, throwing in his suitcases. "Ah, hello, dahling."

We found our rooms, stowed our bags and soon were back with Keith, listening to the Alabama tapes, Mick and Keith and me dancing around the furniture. Jo and Ronnie and the West Coast Promo Man David Horowitz were sitting around the room, all of us together again, Horowitz filled as usual with prissy, uncomprehending concern. Keith turned off the tapes so we could hear a TV news report that made the concert sound like a fine charitable act. "Will you be going?" the announcer asked his partner, who said, "Not me. I hear there's a scarcity of toilets, about one to every thousand people—and it'd be just my luck to be number 999 in line."

Mick, talking on the telephone to a San Francisco radio station, was asked about the changing locations, is everything all right, is it gonna happen?

"We said we'll do it and we will," Mick said. "We're goin' out in a helicopter soon to look at it—let you know more from the scene of the havoc."

Bergman, Schneider, and Horowitz were leaving. "We'll let you know about the helicopter," Horowitz said.

"Thanks," Mick said. The door closed. "Silly queen."

While Mick went to take a bath, Keith and Charlie and I smoked our last wisps of grass in a little brass waterpipe Charlie Brown had given me, listening to blues tapes. Keith answered a knock at the door, letting in two boys and a girl, who appeared to have wandered in off the street. I asked them if they had any dope and they said no.

"Isn't there any grass in this town?" Keith asked.

One of the boys left, coming back a few minutes later with a plastic sandwich bag of marijuana. We smoked it, rolled into great cigars, listening to Elmore James. Mick returned, wearing green trousers, an orange tweed sweater, and a camouflage jacket.

"Have some of this grass these people have been nice enough to give us," Keith said. They sat and watched us and said nothing, except that after we heard Jimmy Reed sing "Can't Stand to See You Go," one of the boys asked, "Can you get this record here? In this country?"

The tape ended and for some reason Mick and I sang "Lonely Avenue," remarking that it was written by Doc Pomus. "Though I'm not a walking Ray Charles discography," Mick said. "That country and western album turned me off."

We waited, smoking, ashes falling on Mick's pants. Finally Ronnie came back and said there were no helicopters available, we'd have to ride out in a limousine, it would take over an hour to get there. We wavered—maybe we won't go—Mick went to get his long coat, Keith and I started down the stairs. At one point we were all separated, so uncertain was our resolve. We kept calling to each other: "Are you coming?" We stood on the sidewalk, thinking about no sleep last night and how late it would be when we got back, but still we piled into the car and set out, though the driver wasn't sure how to get there, for Altamont, to the dusty road and the Crystals ringing in our ears and the dogs and the people and the fires on the hillside and the sound of the pipes, it was like Morocco, but it was also like anything you wanted it to be like, an imaginary landscape in the dark night of the soul where strange signs might be seen. Keith chose to stay here, while Mick and I elected to return to the city for what was left of the night.

Back at the hotel we stopped by Keith's room. "I've got some grass if you want a bedtime joint," I said.

"Naw, I'm gonna crash," Mick said, taking a sheet of paper from the desk to write Charlie a note about how nice it was at the concert site. We said good night, went to our rooms, and just before light broke through my window I fell asleep.

Four hours later Ronnie called to say that the limousines would be leaving early. I showered to wake up and dressed in the same clothes I'd worn for warmth the night before, old blue jeans, denim cowboy shirt, leather jacket. Downstairs Ronnie was waiting on the sidewalk by the limousines. Mick came along wearing knee-high burgundy suede boots, yellow crushed-velvet pants, a red silk shirt, a brown suede vest with red piping, and a leather cape of Keith's with a collar of what appeared to be chicken feathers.

With Charlie and Mick Taylor—Wyman wasn't ready to leave and would join us later—we drove to a pier where a helicopter would meet us, Mick talking about Cecil Beaton, who'd photographed him in New York. " 'Could you *twirl* once more, oh, lovely, yass, once again closer to me.' I asked him about Nijinsky," Mick said, "and he said, 'Oh, Nijinsky, yass, I'll never forget when he and Diaghilev broke up.' "

"We all felt it," Charlie said. He regarded Mick's velvet and leather and feathers. "Never top Brian Jones at Monterey."

"I'd never try to top that," Mick said, tossing his hair. "So over-dressed."

"Brian at the London Palladium, then," Charlie said.

"That was the purity of that style," Mick said. "After that he lost all sense of simplicity."

"Have you noticed," Mick Taylor asked, "there's kind of an atmosphere over the whole city like a carnival?"

"Kind of festive, you mean?" I said.

"Yeah, it's great." He smiled, but no one else did.

Charlie was looking away, distracted, as if he weren't seeing the buildings rush past. "Brian had a whole trunk full of jewelry," he said. The contents of the trunk, like most of Brian's possessions, had disappeared after his death. "It was like pirate treasure, a whole trunk full of little trinkets."

While the luggage was shifted into the helicopter, Mick led the film crew around the pier. Among the people watching was a fat, blond, white-stockinged, cross-eyed groupie. "Charlie," Mick said, "get in the film, Charlie."

"Kiss the girl," the cameraman said.

"No," Charlie said.

"On the cheek."

"No," Charlie said, with his turned-down smile. "Love's much deeper than that, it's not something to be squandered on celluloid."

We climbed into the helicopter and cranked off over the bay. "Did we remember the brandy?" Charlie asked, wearing the pilot's olive-drab bill cap. "We get the food in?"

"Yes," Mick said, "the loaves and the fishes."

As we flew over the California countryside in the shaking helicopter, I scrawled in my notebook, "dun-colored contours of earth below laid out like the kids last night but like giants in khaki sleeping bags." Long before we reached Altamont we could see lines of cars backed up on the highway and parked cars and then great swarms of people. We descended at a crazy angle to a spot a long way up the hill behind the stage, coming down with a bump. The doors opened and we were out-side in the crowd. Mick and Ronnie got out first and a boy ran up to Mick and hit him in the face, saying, "I hate you! I hate you!" I couldn't see it, I just saw a scuffle and heard the words. I grabbed Charlie and held on to him, because I didn't want him to get lost, God knows what might happen to him.

I don't know how Mick and Ronnie and little Mick moved so fast, but they disappeared, leaving me with Jo and Charlie Watts, the world's politest man. I tried to move him through the sea of sleeping bags, wine bottles, dogs, bodies, and hair. Like a mule in quicksand, he didn't want to go forward, didn't want to go back. "Come on, Charlie," I would say. "Just step right on them, they don't mind, they can't feel a thing." The ones who were conscious and moving about said, "Hello, Charlie," and Charlie smiled hello.

As we moved along, heading down toward the stage, we heard the Burritos playing in the distance, "Lucille" and "To Love Somebody" driven to us on steel-guitar beams. It was chilly but the sun was shining, there were Frisbees in the air. We learned later that the Jefferson Airplane, who played just before the Burritos, had been disturbed by Hell's Angels punching a black man in front of the stage. Marty Balin, the Airplane's lead singer, intervened and was knocked unconscious. We were pushing through the crowd, stumbling, trying to avoid the big dogs. People were tossing us joints and things. Looking at a yellow-green LSD tab, Charlie asked, "D'you want it?"

"I ain't too sure about this street acid," I said.

"Maybe Keith will want it."

We were getting into the backstage area, trucks and trailers all around, the people there standing up, but it was still crowded. We moved quickly now, glimpsing faces painted with crescents and stars, one big naked fat boy whose nostrils were pouring blood. The trailer we were headed for was surrounded by little girls, people with cameras, and Hell's Angels. Once up the steps and inside, we were in the eye of a hurricane, peaceful and redolent of ozone.

The Burritos' set had ended, and Gram and Keith and I sprawled on a bed in a corner of the crowded trailer with a two-year-old girl who sat on my lap and told Keith, "I'm gonna beat you up."

"Don't beat me up," Keith said. He had been out here all night, taking LSD, smoking opium, and seemed clear-eyed and content.

"I'm gonna beat you up," she said again.

"Is that a promise?" I asked.

"I beat both of you up," she said.

This trailer was where we had eaten chocolate chip cookies and sniffed cocaine in the early morning hours, but now the air was so thick with marijuana smoke that Jo, sitting at the fold-out table with Ronnie, taking turns on the phone as they tried to get a helicopter to pick up Wyman, started hyperventilating, shaking and quaking. Some of the New York heavies were outside the trailer, and I took them drinks, beer and coffee. Tony was there, his right hand bandaged with splints. "I punched a couple of guys out," he said, taking with his left hand out of his pocket a big Buck knife. "I got this to compensate."

A thin, dark-haired girl, fifteen at most, asked me, "Would you tell Keith something for the girl who was crying?"

Keith had mentioned an acid-freaked girl peeking in the trailer windows, crying "Keith, Keith." Thinking this girl was a friend of hers, I said, "There's nothing to be done for her, he talked to her already, she shouldna took all that acid."

"I *did*n't," she said. "It's me, please tell him. . . ." She started crying.

"Did you see that child, little con artist?" I asked Keith when I was back inside on the bed.

"Yeah, she couldn't say anything, just 'Keith, Keith, is it you, are you real?' I couldn't do anything for her."

Mick and Gram were leaning out the door, talking to people. Gram was wearing brown suede pants and a rhinestoned Nudie shirt with Thunderbirds on the front, Indians on the deltoids, a dancing brave on the back. A little while later Mick and I tried to walk around and see some of the show—Crosby, Stills, Nash, and Young were playing— but there was no way, it was too crowded, you couldn't move in the crush and what you could see you didn't want to be close to. Michelle Phillips of the Mamas and the Papas came into the trailer bearing tales of how the Angels were fighting with civilians, women, and each other, bouncing full cans of beer off people's heads. Augustus Owsley Stanley III, the San Francisco psychedelic manufacturer, known as Owsley, was giving away LSD, the Angels eating it by handfuls, smearing the excess on their faces. It didn't sound good but there was no way to do anything about it, nothing to do in the center of a hurricane but ride it out.

Wyman's helicopter was late, so we waited. Gram and I sat on the bed, smoking and singing Hank Williams and Ernest Tubb songs, until he said, as I was attempting to remind him of the words to "Filipino Baby," that he thought I had given up music for writing some time ago.

In the last light of day Wyman and Astrid arrived with a girl who had done some office work for the Stones in Los Angeles.

"He's really very nice, you know," Charlie said to me, talking about Gram. "I've been talkin' to him about San Francisco, and the hippies and all that, and he's got standards, he goes just so far and no farther. And when that girl came in, he stood up just naturally without thinking about it."

Soon we went out to a large yellow canvas tent a few yards away where the guitarists would tune. Jo was still trembling and I walked with my arm around her. The Stones had planned to go on at sunset, but the light was gone. Hell's Angels were guarding the tent. Inside, on a cardboard table, were a box of Ritz crackers and a chunk of yellow cheese. Keith and Bill and little Mick started tuning. All around the tent, people were trying to peek in. A boy looked into a slit in the canvas and an Angel reached through and pushed his face back.

I sat on the grass in a corner of the tent with Gram, who was talking as if we were about to leave high school forever. "I really liked what you wrote about our album. Would you write me a letter sometime, I'd sure like to have a letter from you."

"Sure, soon as I get the chance," I told him. I never got the chance.

"The lines you quoted about not feeling at home anywhere—that was really good, it was really where I was at when we did that album."

Jon Jaymes waddled in, giving the Angel at the tent flap a sad look, and I eased over to hear his news. "There are four Highway Patrol cars," he told Mick. "Those are the only ones available to take you to the airport. We can have them right at the back of the stage, so when you come off—"

Mick was shaking his head. "Not with the cops," he said. "I ain't goin' out with the cops."

"I knew you'd say that," Jon said.

For some reason, as he stood surrounded by Hell's Angels in the world's end of freakdom denying the only safe way out, I was proud to know Mick Jagger, and I put my arm around his shoulder, on his orange and black satin batwinged outfit, nodding my head in agreement. We looked at each other and began to laugh.

"Where's the stage?" Mick asked. We went to the back of the tent and peered out between two folds of canvas at the hastily constructed wooden platform about thirty yards away.

"Would you mind taking this guitar out there for me?" Keith asked me.

"Pleasure," I said. I didn't mind, and it would give me a chance to get a good position onstage.

Keith handed me his twelve-string. As I started out, an Angel, very short, maybe five-five, Mexican-looking, oily black curls, straggly whiskers, drooping greasy mustache, said, "I'll take you there." I appreciated his help. Night was upon us, and I wouldn't have wanted to fight my way through the dense backstage crowd. Trucks were parked behind the stage, a narrow passway between two of them. People were everywhere, exhausted, bewildered, lost, expectant. I followed close behind the Angel to the stage, where I handed the guitar to Stu, who looked worried.

He put the guitar on its wire stand in front of one of Keith's amps. I stood behind the amps, looking around. People were all over the stage, most of them Angels and their women. The Angels were pushing off everybody who wasn't an Angel or part of the stage crew. I had seen Angels before, and *en masse* they were just as lovely as I'd expected, filthy boots and jeans or motorcycle leathers, one bearded specimen wearing a bear's head for a hat, looking as if he had two ferocious grizzly heads, one on top of the other.

On the PA system Sam was saying, "The reason we can't start is that the stage is loaded with people. I've done all I can do. The stage must be cleared or we can't start." His voice sounded dead tired and flat and beyond caring.

An Angel—President Sonny Barger of the Oakland chapter, I believe—took the mike and said, in a voice not unlike Howlin' Wolf's, "All right, everybody off the stage including the Hell's Angels," and people started to move. Angels were on top of the trucks, behind the stage, on the side of the stage, on the steps to the stage. I was holding my notebook, thinking, God, where to begin, when I was wheeled around—All *right, off* the *stage.* Looking to see what had me, I found his body to my left, dressed in greasy denim, but no head. Still, he picked me up by the biceps so quickly and brought me with such dispatch to his eye level that I couldn't complain about losing lots of time. His eyes were hidden under the lank rat-blond hair that fell over his grime-blackened face. There they were, glints in the gloom, but they were not looking at me or at anything, he was so high he was blind, eyeless in Gaza.

Eyeballs rolling like porcelain marbles in their sockets, jaws grinding, teeth gnashing saliva in anger, "*Off* the *stage,*" he repeated in mild admonition, gentle reproof. It was that ever fresh, ever new, ever magic moment when you are about to be beaten to a pulp or to whatever your assailant can manage. This one, unlike the old last of the Con-

federates cop at the Ed Sullivan show, could, at least with his comrades, pound me into tapioca. I was in midair, still holding my notebook,
thinking that I could reach up and thumb his eyes, I could put my hands
behind his head and bring my knee up fast, depriving him of his teeth,
or I could shove two fingers into his nostrils and rip his face off, but
a little bird on the hillside was telling me that the moment I did any
of these things, hundreds of Angels would start stomping. I don't
remember what I told him. My next clear memory is of being alone
again behind the amps. I wasn't even wearing any badges. Earlier
today, on the way to the helicopter, Ronnie had been talking about
newspapermen calling for press passes, not believing there weren't any.
It's free, he told them, just come. Free at last. Well, not exactly.

"I just talked to one of the Angels," Michael Lydon said, appearing
at my side.

"So did I."

"I asked him if he liked the Rolling Stones' music."

"Did he?"

"He said, 'Yeah, I dig them.' "

The Stones were coming up the four steps between the trucks onto
the stage, a brightly lit center in the black fold of hills. The crowd,
estimated by the news media at between two and five hundred thousand,
had been tightly packed when we struggled through them about five
hours ago. Now they were one solid mass jammed against the stage.
There were eager-eyed boys and girls down front, Angels all around,
tour guards trying to maintain positions between the Angels and the
Stones. A New York City detective at Altamont was a long way off his
beat. The expressions on the cops' faces said they didn't like this scene
at all, but they're not scared, just sorrowful-eyed like men who know
trouble and know that they are in the midst of a lot of people who are
asking for it. Against the stage, in the center of the crowd, a black cop
with a mustache watched, his expression mournful, his white canvas
golf-hat brim pulled down as if he were in a downpour.

Sam came to the singer's mike and in an infinitely weary voice said,
"One, two, testing," then with a glimmer of enthusiasm, "I'd like to
introduce to everybody—from Britain—the Rolling Stones."

There was a small cheer from the crowd—they seemed numb, not
vibrant like the audiences in the basketball gyms after Tina Turner—
whoops and yells and shrieks but not one great roar. Bass-thumps,
guitars tuning, drum diddles, Mick: "All right! Whooooh!"—rising
note— "Oww babe! Aw yeah! Aww, so good to see ya *all*! Whoo!"
Last tuning notes, then the opening chords of "Jumpin' Jack Flash."

> But it's all right, it's all right
> In fact it's a gas

Some people were dancing, Angels dancing with their dirty bouffant women. A pall of wariness and fear seemed to be upon the people who were not too stoned to be aware, but the music was pounding on and though the drums were not properly miked and the guitars seemed to separate and disappear in places and you couldn't really hear Wyman's bass, it was hanging together.

"Ooh, yah," Mick said as the song ended. He stopped dancing, looked into the distance, and his voice, which had been subdued, now began to sound pacific, as he glimpsed for the first time the enormity of what he had created. One surge forward and people would be crushed. Half a million people together, with neither rules nor regulations as to how they must conduct themselves, can through sheer physical weight create terrible destruction. "Oooh, babies——" low motherly tone "——there are so many of you—just be cool down front now, don't push around— just keep still." He laughed as if he were talking to a child, looking down at the pretty stoned faces before him. "Keep together—oh yah."

Keith tested the first three notes of "Carol," unleashed the riff, and Mick leaned back to sing

> Oh, Carol! Don't ever steal your heart away
> I'm gonna learn to dance if it takes me all night and day

The sound was better, drums and bass clearer, guitars stronger. At the end Mick said, "Whoo! Whoo! Aw, yes!" He hoisted a bottle of Jack Daniel's that was sitting in front of the drums. "I'd like to drink, ah, drink one to you all."

Keith set out on "Sympathy for the Devil." As Mick sang, "I was around when Jesus Christ had his moment of doubt and pain," there was a low explosive *thump!* in the crowd to the right of the stage, and oily blue-white smoke swirled up as if someone had thrown a toad into a witches' cauldron. People were pushing, falling, a great hole opening as they moved instantly away from the center of the trouble. I had no idea people in a crowd could move so fast. Mick stopped singing but the music chugged on, four bars, eight, then Mick shouted: "Hey! Heeey! Hey! Keith—Keith—*Keith!*" By now only Keith was playing, but he was playing as loud and hard as ever, the way the band is supposed to do until the audience tears down the chicken wire and comes onstage with chairs and broken bottles. "Will you cool it and I'll try and stop it," Mick said, so Keith stopped.

"Hey—hey, peo-ple," Mick said. "Sisters—brothers and sisters— *brothers* and *sisters*—come *on* now." He was offering the social contract to a twister of flailing dark shapes. "That means everybody just cool *out*—will ya cool out, everybody—"

"Somebody's bike blew up, man," Keith said.

"I know," Mick said. "I'm hip. Everybody be cool now, come on—all right? Can we still make it down in the front? Can we still collect ourselves, everybody? Can everybody just—I don't know what happened, I couldn't see, but I hope ya all right—are ya all right?" The trouble spot seemed still. Charlie was making eager drum flutters, Keith playing stray notes.

"Okay," Mick said. "Let's just give ourselves—we'll give ourselves another half a minute before we get our breath back, everyone just cool down and easy—is there anyone there who's hurt—huh?—everyone all right—okay—all right." The music was starting again. "Good, we can groove—summink very funny happens when we start that numbah—ah, ha!"

Keith and Charlie had the rhythm pattern going, tight and expert, and Mick asked again to be allowed to introduce himself, a man of wealth and taste, but not about to lay anybody's soul to waste. Keith's solo cut like a scream into the brain, as Mick chanted, "Everybody got to cool out—everybody has got to cool right out—yeah! Aw right!"

Sounding like one instrument, a wild whirling bagpipe, the Stones chugged to a halt. But the crowd didn't stop, we could see Hell's Angels spinning like madmen, swinging at people. By stage right a tall white boy with a black cloud of electric hair was dancing, shaking, infuriating the Angels by having too good a time. He was beside an Angel when I first saw him, and I wondered how he could be so loose, nearly touching one of those monsters. He went on dancing and the Angel pushed him and another Angel started laying into the crowd with a pool cue and then a number of Angels were grabbing people, hitting and kicking, the crowd falling back from the fury with fantastic speed, the dancer running away from the stage, the crowd parting before him like the Red Sea, the Angels catching him from behind, the heavy end of a pool cue in one long arc crashing into the side of his head, felling him like a sapling so that he lay straight and didn't move and I thought, My God, they've killed him. But they weren't through. When he went down they were all over him, pounding with fists and cues, and when he was just lying there they stood for a while kicking him like kicking the dead carcass of an animal, the meat shaking on the bones.

The song was over and Mick was saying, "Who—who—I mean like people, who's fighting and what for? Hey, peo-ple—I mean, who's fighting and what for? Why are we fighting? Why are we fighting?" His voice was strong, emphasizing each word. "We don't want to fight. Come on—do we want, who wants to fight? Hey—I—you know, I

mean like—every other scene has been cool. Like we've gotta stop
right now. We've gotta stop them right now. You know, we can't,
there's no point."

Sam took the microphone. "Could I suggest a compromise, please."
He was a bit more awake now and the soul of peace and reason. "Can
I ask please to speak to the—" He stopped then because the logical
conclusion was, "—to the Hell's Angels and ask them please to stop
performing mayhem on people."

"Either those cats cool it," Keith said, "or we don't play. I mean,
there's not that many of 'em."

It was a fine brave thing to say, but I had made up my mind about
fighting the Hell's Angels while one of them had me in the air, and
probably the rest of the people present had concluded some time ago
that the first man who touched an Angel would surely die. Even as
Keith spoke an Angel was ripping into someone in front of stage left.
"That guy there," Keith said, "if he doesn't stop it—"

There was a pause while another Angel did slowly stop him. Still
another Angel yelled to ask Keith what he wanted. "I just want him to
stop pushin' people around," Keith said.

An Angel came to the mike and bellowed into it. "Hey, if you don't
cool it you ain't gonna hear no more music! Now, you wanta all go
home, or what?" It was like blaming the pigs in a slaughterhouse for
bleeding on the floor.

Horowitz was leading some of the women in our group back to the
trailer. Michael Lydon asked me, "Can I use your notes later? My old
lady's had a bad acid trip and she cut her foot and I need to get her
out of here." Later Michael wrote of the Angels, "Their absolute soli-
darity mocks our fearful hope of community, their open appetite for
violence our unfocused love of peace." At the time I thought, Notes? He
thinks I'm taking notes?

Stu, in his blue windbreaker, was at the mike, saying in a cool but
unhappy voice, "We need doctors down here *now*, please. Can we have
a doctor down here now to the front?"

You felt that in the next seconds or minutes you could die, and there
was nothing you could do to prevent it, to improve the odds for survival.
A bad dream, but we were all in it.

I looked around, checking my position, which if not the worst was
not good, and saw David Maysles on top of a truck behind the stage.
Ethan Russell and Al Maysles were up there with their cameras, and
more people, including a couple of Hell's Angels sitting in front dangling
their legs over the side like little boys fishing at a creek in the nineteenth
century.

"Hey! David!" I said.

"You want to get up here?"

"Sure." I stuck my notebook behind my belt and swung aboard, being careful not to jostle the Angels. At least now I would be behind them, instead of having it the other way round, which had given me worse chills than the wind did up here. It was cold away from the warm amps but this was, I hoped, a safer place and better to see from.

Hunkered behind the Angels, I noticed that only one wore colors, the other one in his cowboy hat and motorcycle boots was just a sympathizer. Sam was saying, "The doctor is going through in a green jumper and he's just here—" pointing in front "wavin' his hand in the air, look." The mass, like a dumb aquatic beast, had closed up again except for a little space around the body. (The boy didn't die, to my— and probably his—surprise.) "Can you let the doctor go through please and let him get to the person who's hurt?" Someone in front spoke to Sam, who added wearily, "We have also—lost in the front here—a little girl who's five years old."

Charlie was playing soft rolls, Keith was playing a slow blues riff. "Let's play cool-out music," Keith said to Mick.

They played a repeating twelve-bar pattern that stopped in half a minute. "Keep going," Mick said, and it started again, a meditative walking-bass line, the Stones trying to orient themselves by playing an Elmore James/Jimmy Reed song they had played in damp London caverns. "The sun is shining on both sides of the street," Mick sang. "I got a smile on my face for every little girl I meet." The slow blues did seem to help things, a little. A huge Angel with long blond hair, brown suede vest, no shirt, blue jeans, was standing behind gentle Charlie, patting his foot, one giant hand resting on Charlie's white pullover. The song ended without event and Mick said, "We all dressed up, we got no place to go," which was all too true.

"Stray Cat," Keith said, but there was another flurry of fighting stage right, partly hidden from us by the PA scaffold, a tower of speakers.

"Hey—heyheyhey look," Mick said. Then to Keith or to no one he said, "Those *scenes* down there."

I leaned forward and spoke to the cowboy hat. "What's happening, man," I asked. "Why are they fighting?"

Over his shoulder, out of the corner of his mouth, he said, "Some smart asshole, man, some wise guy wants to start trouble—and these guys are tired, man, they been here all night, some wise guy starts something they don't like it—arhh, I can't tell you what happened." Taking a jug of acid-apple juice from his Angel friend, he drank till his eyes looked, as Wynonie Harris used to say, like two cherries in a glass of buttermilk. Me, I lay low.

"Stray Cat" started, Mick sounding perfunctory, forgetting the words here and there, Keith playing madly.

A girl down front was shaking with the music and crying as if her dream of life had ended. In the backstage aisle between the trucks, the Angels and their women were doing their stiff jerking dance. Most of the women were hard-looking tattooed types with shellacked hairdos, but one of them, no more than fourteen, with a dirty, pretty-baby face, wearing a black leather jacket, was moving the seat of her greasy jeans wildly, and I thought of the little guerrilla in Fort Collins and was glad she wasn't in this crowd.

The Angel standing with his hand on Charlie's shoulder was being asked to step down off the stage by one of the New York heavies, a red-faced, red-haired, beefy man dressed in the light golf-jacket uniform. You could follow what they were saying by their gestures. The cop told the Angel to step down, the Angel shook his head, the cop told him again and pushed him a little. The cop had a cigarette in his mouth and the Angel took it out, just plucked it from between the cop's lips like taking a rose from the mouth of the fair Carmen, causing the cop to regard the Angel with a sorrowful countenance. It was only when two more men in golf jackets turned around and faced the Angel with expressions equally dolorous that he went down the steps. He came back a minute later but stayed at the rear of the stage, dancing, twitching like a frog attached to electrodes.

As "Stray Cat" ended, Mick said, "Ooh baby," looking up as if for deliverance and finding a shapeless human mass reaching into the darkness as far as he could see. "Baby—all along a hillside—hey, everybody, ah—we gone do, we gone do, ah—what are we gonna do?"

"Love in Vain," Keith said. The slow elegant Robert Johnson line began, building slowly. "I followed her to the station with my suitcase in my hand—oh, it's hard to tell, when all your love's in vain." The Stones had not forgotten how to play, but nobody seemed to be enjoying the music, at least nobody who could be seen in the lights that made the stage the glowing center of a world of night. Too many people were still too close together and the Angels were still surly. At stage right an Angel with a skinful of acid was writhing and wringing his hands in a pantomime of twisting Mick's neck. At stage left Timothy Leary huddled with his wife and daughter, looking as if he'd taken better trips. The stage skirts were so crowded that Mick had only a limited area to work. He looked cramped, smaller than ever and cowed, frightened, but he kept on singing.

Things were quiet during "Love in Vain" except for some heavy jostling down front, the prevailing mood of impending death, and the fear and anguish you could see in the faces. "Aw yeah," Mick said as the song ended. "Hey, I think—I think, I think, that there was one good idea came out of that number, which was, that I really think the only way you're gonna keep yourselves cool is to *sit down*. If you can make it I think you'll find it's better. So when you're sitting comfortably—now, boys and girls—" withdrawing the social contract— "Are you sitting comfortably? When, when we get to really like the end and we all want to go absolutely crazy and like jump on each other then we'll stand up again, d'you know what I mean—but we can't seem to keep it together, standing up—okay?"

In the background Keith was tooling up the opening chords of "Under My Thumb." A few people in front of the stage were sitting, going along with Mick, who for the first time in his life had asked an audience to sit down. The anarchist was telling people what to do. Then, just before he began to sing, he said, "But it ain't a rule."

"Under My Thumb" started—"Hey! Hey! Under my thumb is a girl who once had me down—" and Mick had sung only the first line of the song when there was a sudden movement in the crowd at stage left. I looked away from Mick and saw, with that now-familiar instant space around him, bordered with falling bodies, a Beale Street nigger in a black hat, black shirt, iridescent blue-green suit, arms and legs stuck out at crazy angles, a nickle-plated revolver in his hand. The gun waved in the lights for a second, two, then he was hit, so hard, by so many Angels, that I didn't see the first one—short, Mexican-looking, the one who led me onstage?—as he jumped. I saw him as he came down, burying a long knife in the black man's back. Angels covered the black man like flies on a stinking carcass. The attack carried the victim behind the stack of speakers, and I never saw him again.

The black man, Meredith Hunter, nicknamed Murdock, was eighteen years old. He had come to Altamont with his girlfriend, Patty Bredehoft, a blond Berkeley High School student, and another couple. They had arrived in Hunter's car at about two o'clock in the afternoon, parked on the highway and walked over to hear the bands. Near the end of the day Patty Bredehoft and the other couple were back at the car when Hunter, who had been hanging around the stage area, came to get her to go hear the Rolling Stones. Later she told the Alameda County Grand Jury, "When we finally worked our way up to the front of the crowd and the Rolling Stones started playing, there was a lot of pushing and there were Angels on the stage. And Murdock kept trying to go farther up toward the front. I couldn't keep up with him because I wasn't strong so I sort of waited back, didn't try to get as far as he did. He was as close as he could get, where there were some boxes with people standing on the boxes. I'd say there was about five people in between me and him, estimating, because the crowd was moving around, but I could see the upper part of his body.

"I was getting pushed around, and as I glanced up there, I saw either he had hit Murdock or pushed him or something, but this Hell's Angel who was standing, pushed him or knocked him back. It didn't knock him down, but knocked him back over the stage, and as he started to come back forward towards the Hell's Angel, another Hell's Angel who was on the stage grabbed him around the neck. They were scuffling around. I'm not sure which Hell's Angel it was, but I just remember he was scuffling around and there was a couple of people blocking my view of him because he was down on the ground. I couldn't really see him. As the people backed away, Murdock came around by my side and pulled a gun out. Then they came toward—well, a group of Hell's Angels—I'm not sure they were all Hell's Angels, but I know most of them were—they came toward him and they reached for his arm and then they were all kicking and fighting and stuff, Murdock and the Hell's Angels, and the fight more or less moved around towards where the scaffold was on the edge of the stage.

"I followed them around and then I was standing there watching them fight, or watching whatever—I couldn't really tell what was going on underneath the scaffold, and the Hell's Angel—I thought he was, was a Hell's Angel, but I wasn't quite sure because he had the jeans jacket on, but I couldn't see the back to see if it had colors on. He was holding the gun in his hand, laying in the palm of his hand, to show it to me, and he said something like, 'This is what we took from him. He was going to kill innocent people, so he deserved to be dead.' "

A young man named Paul Cox, who had been standing beside Meredith Hunter before the violence started, talked to the grand jury and to *Rolling Stone*. "An Angel kept looking over at me and I tried to keep ignoring him and I didn't want to look at him at all, because I was very scared of them and seeing what they were doing all day and because he kept trying to cause a fight or something and kept staring at us. He kept on looking over, and the next thing I know he's hassling this Negro boy on the side of me. And I was trying not to look at him, and then he reached over and shook this boy by the side of the head, thinking it was fun, laughing, and I noticed something was going to happen so I kind of backed off.

"The boy yanked away, and when he yanked away, next thing I know he was flying in the air, right on the ground, just like all the other people it happened to. He scrambled to his feet, and he's backing up and he's trying to run from the Angels, and all these Angels are—a couple jumped off the stage and a couple was running alongside the stage, and his girlfriend was screaming to him not to shoot, because he pulled out his gun. And when he pulled it out, he held it in the air and his girlfriend is like climbing on him and pushing him back and he's trying to get away and these Angels are coming at him and he turns around and starts running. And then some Angel snuck up from right out of the crowd and leaped up and brought this knife down in his back. And then I saw him stab him again, and while he's stabbing him, he's running. This Negro boy is running into the crowd, and you could see him stiffen up when he's being stabbed.

"He came running toward me. I grabbed onto the scaffold, and he came running kind of toward me and fell down on his knees, and the Hell's Angel grabbed onto both of his shoulders and started kicking him in the face about five times or so and then he fell down on his face. He let go and he fell down on his face. And then one of them kicked him on the side and he rolled over, and he muttered some words. He said, 'I wasn't going to shoot you.' That was the last words he muttered.

"If some other people would have jumped in I would have jumped in. But nobody jumped in and after he said, 'I wasn't going to shoot you,' one of the Hell's Angels said, 'Why did you have a gun?' He didn't give him time to say anything. He grabbed one of those garbage cans, the cardboard ones with the metal rimming, and he smashed him over the head with it, and then he kicked the garbage can out of the way and started kicking his head in. Five of them started kicking his head in. Kicked him all over the place. And then the guy that started the whole thing stood on his head for a minute or so and then walked off. And then the one I was talking about, he wouldn't let us touch him for about two or three minutes. Like, 'Don't touch him, he's going to die anyway, let him die, he's going to die.'

"Chicks were just screaming. It was all confusion. I jumped down anyway to grab him and some other dude jumped down and grabbed him, and then the Hell's Angel just stood over him for a little bit and then walked away. We turned him over and ripped off his shirt. We rubbed his back up and down to get the blood off so we could see, and there was a big hole in his spine and a big hole on the side and there was a big hole in his temple. A big open slice. You could see all the way in. You could see inside. You could see at least an inch down. And then there was a big hole right where there's no ribs on his back—and then the side of his head was just sliced open—you couldn't see so far in—it was bleeding quite heavily—but his back wasn't bleeding too heavy after that—there—all of us were drenched in blood.

"I picked up his legs and someone else . . . this guy said he was a doctor or something . . . I don't know who he was . . . he picked up his arms and he said, 'Got to get him some help because he's going to die. We've got fifteen or twenty minutes, if we can get him some help. . . .' And so we tried to carry him on the stage. Tell Mick Jagger to stop playing so we could get him on the stage and get some attention for him. No one told Jagger that, but someone was trying to tell him to stop and he kept leaning over and looking out at the crowd like he was paying attention and trying to figure out what was happening. He kept leaning over with his ear trying to hear what somebody was telling him, but he couldn't hear. So they kept on playing and the Hell's Angels wouldn't let us through . . . get on the stage. They kept blocking us, saying go around, go through some other way. They knew he was going to die in a matter of minutes. They wanted him to die probably so he couldn't talk. And so we carried . . . we turned around and went the other way. It took about fifteen minutes to get him behind the stage. We went around that whole thing and got behind where there was a Red Cross truck, something like that. And someone brought out a metal stretcher and laid him on that. Well, first we laid him on the ground. And then we felt his pulse and it was just barely doing it . . . real slow and real weak. His whole mouth and stuff is bashed up into his nose and stuff and he couldn't breathe out of his nose. He was trying to breathe out of his mouth. There really wasn't anything you could do. We carried him over to some station wagon and then whoever owned the car hopped in and some other people hopped in and I stayed there. I went over and they had this thing of coffee and I had it . . . poured it all over to wipe off all the blood."

The doctor who helped to carry Hunter backstage was Robert Hiatt, a medical resident at the Public Health Hospital in San Francisco. "He was limp in my hands and unconscious," Hiatt said. "He was still breathing then, though quite shallowly, and he had a very weak pulse. It was obvious he wasn't going to make it, but if anything could be done, he would have to get to a hospital quickly. He had very serious wounds."

Dr. Richard Baldwin, a general practitioner from Point Reyes who saw Hunter backstage, said, "He got a bad injury in that they got him in the back and it went in between the ribs and the side of the spine, and there's nothing but big arteries in there, the aorta, the main artery in the body, and a couple kidney arteries. And if you hit one of those you're dead. You're dead in less than a minute and there's nothing anyone can do. In other words, if you're standing in front of the hospital or even if he was stabbed in an operating room, there's nothing they could have done to save him. That's one of those injuries that's just irreparable."

When the trouble with the boy in the green suit started, the Stones had stopped playing. "Okay, man," Keith said, "look, we're splitting, if those cats, if you can't—we're splitting, if those people don't stop beating everybody up in sight—I want 'em *out of the way*."

An Angel in front of the stage was trying to tell Keith something, but Keith wouldn't listen. "I don't like *you* to tell me—" he went on, but another Angel, onstage, stopped him. "Look, man," the Angel said, "a guy's got a gun out there, and he's shootin' at the stage—"

"Got a gun," someone else yelled.

Mike Lang, one of the organizers of Woodstock, who had been helping with this concert, took the microphone. "People—hey people— c'mon let's be cool—people, please—there's no reason to hassle anybody, please don't be mad at anybody—please relax and sit down. . . ."

Sam, who'd been standing by with his hands jammed in his pockets, took over. "If you move back and sit down," he said, "we can continue and we will continue. We need a doctor under the left-hand scaffold as soon as possible please." He was listening to shouts from the front of the crowd. He listened to a girl for a few seconds and went on: "There's a Red Cross building at the top of the stage and there's been lots of lost childing, children, under the scaffold—if you've lost a child go and collect him or her there please—it's a Red Cross van. . . ."

After another pause during which no one onstage did anything but look anxiously around, Mick said, "It seems to be stuck down to me— will you listen to me for a minute—please listen to me just for one second a'right? First of all, everyone is gonna get to the side of the stage who's on it now except for the Stones who are playing. Please, everyone—everyone, please, can you get to the side of the stage who's not playing. Right? That's a start. Now, the thing is, I can't see what's going on, who is doing wot, it's just a scuffle. All I can ask you, San Francisco, is like the whole thing—this could be the most beautiful evening we've had this winter. We really—y'know, why, why—don't let's fuck it up, man, come on—let's get it together—everyone—come *on* now—I can't see you up on the hillsides, you're probably very cool. Down here we're not so cool, we've got a lot of hassles goin' on. I just—every cat. . . ."

There were shouts from the darkness. Mick peered out blindly past the stage lights and answered, "Yeah, I know, we can't even see you but I know you're where—you're cool. We're just trying to keep it together. I can't do any more than ask you—beg you, just to keep it together. You can do it, it's within your power—everyone—Hell's Angels, everybody. Let's just keep ourselves together.

"You know," Mick said with a sudden burst of passion, "if we *are* all one, let's fucking well *show* we're all one. Now there's one thing we need—Sam, we need an ambulance—we need a doctor by that scaffold there, if there's a doctor can he get to there. Okay, we're gonna, we gonna do—I don't know what the fuck we gonna do. Everyone just sit down. Keep cool. Let's just *relax,* let's get into a groove. Come on, we can get it together. Come on."

"Under My Thumb" was starting to churn again. The band sounded amazingly sharp. The crowd was more still. Without knowing exactly what, we all felt that something bad had happened. I assumed, and I was not given to flights of horrible imaginings, that the Angels had killed several people. Gram told me later that he saw Meredith Hunter lifted up, with a great spreading ketchup-colored stain on the back of his suit. Ronnie was running to the First Aid tent, outdistancing the Hell's Angel who had been leading him. Hunter was there when Ronnie came up, calling for a doctor. A cop said, "You don't have to scream for a doctor for this guy, he's dead."

Over the last notes of "Under My Thumb," Mick sang, "It's all right
—I pray that it's all right—I pray that it's all right—it's all right—"
"Let's do 'Brown Sugar,' " Mick Taylor said.
" '*Brown Sugah*'?" Keith said.
" 'Brown Sugar'?" Bill said.
"What?" Charlie said.
"He wants to do 'Brown Sugar,' " Mick said.
"Wait, let me change guitars," Keith said.
"Thank you," Mick said to the crowd. Charlie was playing rolls.
"Thank you. Are we all, yeah, we're gettin' it together—we gonna do
one for you which we just ah—" pausing, remembering that making the
record was breaking the law "—we just ah—you've never heard it before
because we just written it—we've just written it for you—" as Keith was
tuning— "I dunno how good this is gonna be, baby—ah, this is the first
time we've played it—the very first time we've played it." Keith
finished tuning and played the song's first chords. Mick shouted, "*We
gonna do one f'you now which we did for you, which we haven't ever
played ever before, we gonna play it for you for the very first time, it's
called 'Brown Sugah.' *"
Stacked like cordwood at the sides of the stage were bouquets of
red and yellow long-stemmed roses. As the Stones played, Angels threw
the bouquets into the crowd as if pitching babies out of airplane
windows.

> Scarred old slaver knows he's doin' all right
> Hear him whip the women, just around midnight
>
> Oh—brown sugar—how come you taste so good
> Oh—brown sugar—just like a black girl should

It was a song of sadism, savagery, race hate/love, a song of redemp-
tion, a song that accepted the fear of night, blackness, chaos, the unknown—the fear that the mad-eyed Norsemen, transplanted from
Odin-drunk mead halls to California desert, were still seeking mad-eyed
to escape.
"Ahhh, one mo' time—whoo, baby. Yeah—'ang you—awww—"
Taking a harp from Stu, Mick played a few menacing riffs of "Midnight
Rambler." Keith had changed guitars and was tuning again. Mick played
soft harp notes that trailed off as, head bent over the mike, he began
singing lullaby phrases, trying to soothe and gentle the great beast. "Aw
now, baby baby—hush now, don't you cry." His voice was tender, a
tone of voice that Mick Jagger had never before used in public and
maybe never in his life. "Hush now, don't you cry—" A few more notes

on the harp, and then, as if he were coming out of a reverie, gaining strength with each word, Mick said, "We gonna do you one which we hope you'll *dig*—which is called 'The Midnight Rambler.' Wshoo!" (expostulation of a field hand stripping the sweat off his forehead with a dusty forefinger)

> Sighing down the wind so sadly—
> Listen and you'll hear him moan

The song had scared me when I first heard it, because it was true, as nobody at Altamont could deny, the dark is filled with terror, murder and evil ride the night air. "I'll stick my knife right down your throat, honey, and it hurts!"

Things seemed to be settling down, as if the killer-lover lament had worked some psychic release on the crowd.

"Aw yah! Aw yah! Stand up if you can stand up," Mick said. "Stand up if you can keep it cool." He raised the Jack Daniel's bottle. "One more drink to you all." He drank and spoke again in his lullaby tone, "Awww, babies." Then, as if he were coming to again, he said, "It's so—sssweet! It's really sssweet! Would you like to live with—each other? I mean, you're really close to each other." He stared into the crowd and seemed to drift away again. "Wow," he said.

"You ready?" Keith asked.

"Yeah, I'm ready," Mick said.

"One two three faw," Keith snarled, and they started "Live with Me."

Around the stage people were dancing, but in front of the stage, staring at Mick, one curly-haired boy in a watch cap was saying, Mick, Mick, no—I could read his lips. Behind the boy a fat black-haired girl, naked to the waist, was dancing, squeezing her enormous breasts, mouth open, eyes focused on a point somewhere north of her forehead. As the song ended, the girl, her skin rose-florid, blinking off and on like a pinball machine in orgasmic acid flashes, tried to take the stage like Grant took Richmond. Completely naked now, she was trying to climb over the crowd to get a foot onstage, where five Angels were at once between her and the Stones, kicking and punching her back, her smothering weight falling on the people behind her.

"Hold it," Mick said.

"Stop that one," Keith said.

"Hey—heyheyheyheyheyheyhey*hey*! One cat can control that chick, y'know wot oi mean. Hey fellows, hey fellows. One of you can control her, man," Mick said, speaking the last sentence to the Angel nearest him onstage.

"Yeah, we're gonna do it," the Angel said, in a world of his own, as were all the Angels looking down into the crowd, trying to reach the girl with fists or boots, wanting to get down there and smash her face, stomp her throat, kick her tits off and send them sailing over the heads of this dumb sheeplike crowd, and kick her in the pussy till she bleeds to death.

"Hey, come on, fellows," Mick was saying, getting a bit frantic, "like one of you can control one little girl—come on now, like—like—like—just sit down, honey," he said to the girl, who was still on her back, flashing her black-pelted pelvis, her eyes black whirlpools staring at the sky as if she were trying to get above the stage, above the lights. If she could come up to there and keep coming into the night, above the world, she would shed her grossness like a chrysalis and be reborn, airborne, an angel of God. The Hell's Angels leaned out over the stage to stop her, to grab her, to slap her teeth out and smash her goddamn gums, thumb her crazy eyes out, pop her eardrums, snatch her bald-headed, scalp the cheap cunt.

"Fellows," Mick said, trying gently to move the Angels away, "can you clear—uh—and she'll—let—let—let them deal with her—they can deal with her." The people down front were managing to crawl out from under the girl, the Angels wanting to stay and get their hands on her. "Fellows, come on, fellows," Mick said, "they're all right."

Keith started playing and Wyman and Charlie and Mick Taylor joined in, as the Angels slunk bloodlusty to the side. Mick was singing:

> Yeah, I see the storm is threatening
> My very life today
> If I don't get some shelter
> I'm gonna fade away
> War, children, it's just a shot away

The Angels were cracking their knuckles, looking around red-eyed for flesh to rip. How are we gonna get out of here? I wondered. *Will* we get out, or will we die here, is it going to snap and the Angels like dinosaurs kill themselves and all of us in a savage rage of nihilism, the plain to be found in the morning a bloody soup littered with teeth and bones, one last mad Angel, blinded by a comrade's boots and brass knuckles, gut sliced asunder by his partner's frogsticker, growling, tearing at the yawning slit under his filthy T-shirt, chomping on his own bloody blue-white entrails. *

"Rape—murder—it's just a shot away," Mick sang over and over. In the crowd by stage left, where the trouble with the black boy in the green suit had taken place, an Angel was punching someone, but the victim went down fast and it was over. Standing close by, looking on, was a girl with phosphorescent white hair, a chemical miracle. It was impossible to tell whether she was with the Angel or the victim. "Love, sister, it's just a kiss away," Mick sang as the song thundered to a stop.

"Yuhh," Mick said, very low, then "Yuhhh," again, lower, like a man making a terrible discovery. "Okay . . . are we okay, I know we are." He was looking into the crowd. As if he had waked up once again, he shouted, "Are y'havin' a good ti-i-ime? OOH-yeah!"

"Little Queenie" was starting; it was the moment in the show when the lights went on to reveal rapt fresh faces. But not tonight. Even the people who were dancing in spite of the danger looked unhappy. At times Mick's voice sounded light, as if he had lost the bottom part of it, but Keith was playing like a man ready to dance on his own grave.

The song ended to cheers from the crowd, some people perking up. "I—I—I thank you very much," Mick said. "Thank you very much." The opening notes of "Satisfaction" turned on like a current of electricity. It would probably never be played better. Charlie kept a straight boogaloo like the Otis Redding version and it went on and on, Mick chanting, "We got to find it—*got* to find it—got to *find* it—early in the mornin'—late in the evenin'—" He shouted the song to an end, gave three Indian-style war whoops, and as his voice died to a whisper, looked out at the multitude, hundreds of thousands of people who had come because he had asked them, and he could give them nothing better than this, mayhem and terror.

"Justliketosaaaayyy," Mick said, then paused and seemed to lose himself once more, wondering what it was he'd like to say. After a moment he went on briskly: "Well there's been a few hangups you know but I mean generally I mean ah you've been beau-ti-ful—" in a lower tone— "you have been so groovy—aw!" (brisk again) "All the loose women may stand and put their hands up—all the loose women put their hands up!" But the loose women were tired like everybody else. A few girls stood up, a few hands were raised into the murk. On this night no one would think of playing "I'm Free," though that had been the whole idea of the concert, to give some free glimmer to Ralph Gleason's rock-and-roll-starved proletariat and to get away from the violence of the system, the cops' clubs, Klein's mop handle. The biggest group of playmates in history was having recess, with no teachers to protect them from the bad boys, the bullies, who may have been mistreated children and worthy of understanding but would nevertheless kill you. The Stones' music was strong but it could not stop the terror. There was a look of disbelief on the people's faces, wondering how the Stones could go on playing and singing in the bowels of madness and violent death. Not many hands were in the air, and Mick said, "That's not enough, we haven't got many loose women, what're ya gonna do?"

The band started "Honky Tonk Women," playing as well as if they were in a studio, Keith's lovely horrible harmonies sailing out into the cool night air. Nobody, not even the guardians of public morality at *Rolling Stone* who pronounced that "Altamont was the product of diabolical egotism, hype, ineptitude, money manipulation, and, at base, a fundamental lack of concern for humanity," could say that the Rolling Stones couldn't play like the devil when the chips were down.

When "Honky Tonk Women" was over, the sound system stopped working, then started again. "Hello—I got it back," Mick said. "Yahh—come back to—ah—we gonna, ah, we gonna, ah—we gonna kiss you goodbye—and we leave you to kiss each other goodbye—and—you—we're gonna see ya, we're gonna see ya, we're gonna see ya—again. . . ." And with that sudden softness he asked "All right?" in a voice as small as a kitten's. "Kiss each other goodbye—sleep—good night—"

The last song, "Street Fighting Man," started. ". . . the time is right for fighting in the street," Mick sang, a leader with an international constituency, unable to save anyone.

> Ah, but what can a poor boy do
> But to sing with a rock 'n' roll band

The music pounded hard enough to drive even the naked fat girl to Heaven. "Bye bye bye bye," Mick sang. "Bye bye bye bye." Stu handed me Keith's twelve-string guitar and told me the station wagons to take us to the helicopters would be at the top of the hill, straight back and up to the left. I slipped off the truck, taking the guitar by the neck, and struck out into the night, trying to get the people in the passageway between the backstage trucks to move and let me out. "*Please let me through,*" I shouted.

A boy about seventeen walked backwards ahead of me, saying, "We're gonna build a superhighway, man, never built one before but we're gonna build one on our own to show we can do it without grown-ups—"

Behind me Mick was saying, "Bye—by-y-y-y-e—bye," as I plunged on among shouts from unknown voices, trying not to run into people. I heard the Stones coming and Gram and Michelle's voices and called to them, all of us stumbling through the fucking blackness. At last, with our lives, we were off the stage, struggling through the dark, trying not to lose anyone. "Regroup!" Ronnie's voice rasped, and then we had reached the hillside, a steep slope that we were scrambling up through dusty clay and dead grass, me on one hand, elbow, and knees, holding the guitar. At the top of the hill was a cyclone fence, but we passed through a hole in it, still running, to a car and an ambulance. I got into the back of the ambulance, followed by a half-dozen or so New York heavies. Blowing the horns, we drove through the crowd that swarmed around us, moving as fast as we could. When we stopped near a helicopter and got out, I gave the guitar to Sam. The Stones, Astrid, Jo,

Ronnie, Sam, Tony, David Horowitz, Jon Jaymes, Mike Scotty, Ethan Russell, among others, boarded the small aircraft. Gram, Michelle, and I stood just outside the spinning blades wondering what would happen if we were left, lost in the blackness in this crowd, but Sam called, "Come on!" Gram helped Michelle on and got on himself and I got on. The little bulbous capsule was packed with heads and knees and I gladly hopped onto the only place where there was room to sit, the lap of David Horowitz, silly queen or not. The helicopter was shaking and lifting like an ostrich waking up, its hums and rattles drowning out everything except shouts. Mick and I exchanged glances, his eyes wide, lowering, lips pursed to whistle. I looked up and away, indicating how I wasn't even ready for glances.

In a few minutes the overloaded helicopter descended at the Tracy or Livermore airport, dropping too fast, the ground rushing up at us, instead of settling down gently like a hummingbird we came in on the skids at an angle like an airplane. We hit sharply but kept upright and bounced flat. We climbed out and as Keith, walking under the blades, headed for the airport building, he was denouncing the Angels: "They're sick, man, they're worse than the cops. They're just not ready. I'm never going to have anything to do with them again." He sounded like an English public school boy whose fundamental decency and sense of fair play had been offended by the unsportsmanlike conduct at soccer of certain of his peers.

Mick sat on a wooden bench in the little airport, eyes still hurt and angry, bewildered and scared, not understanding who the Hell's Angels were or why they were killing people at his free peace-and-love show. "How could anybody think those people are good, think they're people you should have around," he said.

"Nobody in his right mind could," I said, "that's why—" I started to say, That's why I said last night that you believe too much of the hype, but I didn't. He had paid for his beliefs and nobody had the right to condemn him.

"Some people are just not ready," Keith was saying, but how ready was any of us to live in the real world, a world that would each year become more like Altamont?

"I'd rather have had cops," Mick said.

"The Angels are worse than cops," Gram said. "They're bozos, just a bunch of bozos. They're so dumb. Michelle and I were standing by the right-hand side of the stage not bothering anybody, just standing as far away as we could be and still see, and one Angel kept trying to push us back, every two minutes. Every two minutes I'd have to explain to him all over again just like the first time that we were supposed to be there."

"Some people are just not ready," Keith said again. He had taken off the red Nudie shirt he'd worn onstage and slung it over his shoulder, and he was starting to shiver. "Hey, where are my jackets? Hey, Sam! Sam! Did you get my jackets outa the caravan?"

"They're on the helicopter," Horowitz said, without any idea where in hell the jackets were.

"Don't let it take off," Keith said, "a black velvet jacket and a Hungarian sort of gypsy jacket," forgetting the moldy Nazi greatcoat. "They both cost a fortune, don't let the copter take off with them."

Horowitz looked in the helicopter and came back with an old sheep-skin jacket, saying, "They weren't there, they must be in the trailer, we'll get them, don't worry, please, we'll get them but for now will you just put this on just for the moment, please?"

Keith did finally deign to toss the jacket over his shoulders, where-upon Horowitz, ever desperate to do the wrong thing, said to Gram and Michelle, "There's limited seating on the plane"—which had just landed—"but there's already another one on the way. You won't mind staying, will you, it'll only be about ten minutes."

Hearing this, I said, "Just a minute," to Gram and walked over to Keith. "There's room for Gram and Michelle on the plane, isn't there?"

"Sure," Keith said.

We went out to the plane, a fifteen-seater. After so many, the names all blend together and it doesn't matter if they're red and white or white and gold or if the seats are brown or two-tone green. It was a short ride to San Francisco and a not so short ride in limousines back to the Huntington, safe and more or less sound. Gram was kissing Michelle, trying to make out with her, and she seemed to be enduring it like a high school senior making do with a sophomore boy on the way home from a church hayride. "We wouldn't even be here if it wasn't for you," Gram said to me. "Thanks a lot."

"It was nothing," I said. We grew quiet as we approached the hotel. It was beginning to dawn on us that we had survived.

By the elevators was an *Examiner* with the headline, 300,000 SAY IT WITH MUSIC. Say what?

Keith was walking around his suite like a whippet, saying, "If Rock Scully don't know any more about things than that, man, to think the Angels are—what did he say? Honor and dignity?"

"He does seem to take a romantic view of things," I said from my position on the floor.

"Yeah, man," Keith said, lighting a joint as he stepped over me, headed for the couch. "He's just a childish romantic, I have no time for such people."

We listened to television news reports of the killing, speculating on whether we'd have to stay and testify, wondering whether we should get out of town at once, but we were too hungry and summoned a

waiter with a menu. "Oh, God," Gram said, "it's in French." He handed
the menu to Keith. "Here, you read this stuff."

"Ah," Keith said, "this makes it so much more complicated."

Just before the waiter arrived, Keith had been talking about the
Angels. "They're homicidal maniacs, they should be thrown in jail."

Far out, I said to myself. Mick had said he'd rather have cops, and
now Keith like Colonel Blimp wanted to throw the bastards in jail. The
Rolling Stones had played their comeback tour, it had worked, they
would get worse publicity than ever, they were still alive, the world's
greatest rock and roll band—but what could you do for an encore to
human sacrifice?

Sitting on the floor smoking, we listened a couple more times to
television reports of the killing, then didn't listen anymore. Keith
played the Alabama tapes. Ronnie and Jo went to the airport and bought
the getaway tickets. "I'll let you know in the morning if I'm going to
make the plane for Geneva," Mick told Jo.

Sam had passed out on the couch and we told him to leave, so he got
up and made it to a chair where he passed out again, gaunt and bristly
in his white turtleneck, head thrown back, mouth open. "Hey, wake up,
man," Keith said. "Go to bed, you're a drag to have around, you're
unconscious."

Sam opened his eyes, looked around quickly, then collapsed again
into a coma. We were all in varying degrees of shock, feeling as if we'd
been tossed up on the beach out of an angry storm.

When the food came, we ate and went on sitting, more or less speechless. We were all dead sleepy, but none of us wanted to leave. We had
been through a shattering experience, in a way the experience we had
been looking for all our lives, and none of us knew what to say. Talking
on the phone to a radio station, Mick said, "I thought the scene here
was supposed to be so groovy. I don't know what happened, it was
terrible, if Jesus had been there he would have been crucified."

When he was off the phone, he said that he was down on the idea
of the movie. "I don't want to conceal anything," he said, "but I don't
want to show something that was just a drag."

At one point in the evening, Mick and I were sitting on the floor with
Emmaretta Marks, a black girl who had spent some time with Keith in
Los Angeles before the tour started. Janis Joplin's name came up, and
Mick said that she tried hard to be funky but she still wasn't black.
Thinking of Taj Mahal's equipment boy saying that you can have more
fun with niggers than anybody else, I said, to see how Mick would react,
"Well, that's the dream, we all want to be black, what we think black is."

"*I* don't," Mick said. "I'm not black and I'm proud of it." Emmaretta
laughed, and Mick smiled for the first time since going onstage that
night.

Tony went to bed but the hotel objected to his having two women in his room. "I told them it was my wife and sister," he said. "They said I was immoral. Honky bastards." I called the desk and ordered them one more room.

At four in the morning we were still sitting around. Charlie usually went to bed early, but tonight none of us wanted to be alone. A scratchy old blues record was playing on Keith's tape recorder. "Can you get that line there?" Mick asked me. "What's he saying?"

I listened, but there was too much surface noise, the message was lost. "I can't get it," I said. "Something about God and the Devil."

"I'll play it back," Mick said.

I listened again. "I still can't get it." I was so tired that my ears were not clear.

"But it's the point of the whole song."

Finally I said good night and told Mick if I didn't see him tomorrow I'd see him in England. I went to my room, didn't call anybody, didn't even think, just got into bed and fell asleep.

3 2

Tragedy absorbs the highest orgiastic music and in so doing consummates music. But then it puts beside it the tragic myth and the tragic hero. Like a mighty titan, the tragic hero shoulders the whole Dionysiac world and removes the burden from us. At the same time, tragic myth, through the figure of the hero, delivers us from our avid thirst for earthly satisfaction and reminds us of another existence and a higher delight. For this delight the hero readies himself, not through his victories but through his undoing. Tragedy interposes a noble parable, *myth*, between the universality of its music and the Dionysiac disposition of the spectator and in so doing creates the illusion that music is but a supreme instrument for bringing to life the plastic world of myth. By virtue of this noble deception it is now able to move its limbs freely in dithyrambic dance and to yield without reserve to an orgiastic abandon, an indulgence which, without this deception, it could not permit itself. Myth shields us from music while at the same time giving music its maximum freedom. In exchange, music endows the tragic myth with a convincing metaphysical significance, which the unsupported word and image could never achieve, and, moreover, assures the spectator of a supreme delight—though the way passes through annihilation and negation, so that he is made to feel that the very womb of things speaks audibly to him.

FRIEDRICH NIETZSCHE: *The Birth of Tragedy*

"I THOUGHT that I'd fallen down, on top," Shirley Arnold said, "but I fainted at the side. The next thing I can remember apart from seeing the coffin go down was being back in the car, and I was saying, 'How did you get me up?' Everyone was saying, 'Are you all right?' Then we went back to the house, had a quick cuppa tea, and made our way home.

"While we were driving down to the cemetery—at the cemetery gates there was a policeman. He saluted as Brian went past, and Charlie laughed. I was so tearful, and I said, 'What *you* laughin' at?' and he said, 'The policeman saluted. Brian's curlin' up somewhere, lookin' on and lovin' it.' "

I didn't want to outstay my small welcome at the Joneses', but Mrs. Jones sat with me and the cat as Mr. Jones talked, rambling from one time of Brian's life to another, putting together clues. "Very soon," he said, "the two together, Jagger-Richards, were getting very uptown. Louie and I went to the Colston Hall, Bristol, in the fall of '66 to see Brian, when he and the group were playing there, and Brian seemed very different. All of his spark seemed to be gone. He was very unhappy. We didn't stay. Brian was not friendly. An indefinable change had come over him.

"It was typical of Brian that he called later, after the tour was over, and apologized. He said, 'I wasn't very nice.' I said, 'That's all right.' He said he had been upset about Anita—who I understand said after his death that she did him wrong.

"Brian played 'Honky Tonk Women' for me down at Cotchford Farm. It was his arrangement—but I believe it was re-recorded without him. We were with Brian about five weeks before he left the Rolling Stones—and I'm convinced that he had no notion of leaving the Rolling Stones then—but there were moves afoot to get him out.

"When Brian became a Rolling Stone it seemed that he had found his soul, he had achieved what he wanted. The criticism troubled him very much for our sake—when there'd be an attack in the newspapers he'd call. Especially later with the drugs, he'd say he was 'very upset because he knew it would react on you.' I told him it didn't, of course it did.

"After he was arrested the second time he called us—he was in tears. 'I've been fixed,' he said. 'I give you my word, Dad, I had no idea that blasted stuff was there.' I said, 'I believe you, Son,' and I did. He never told me a lie. When I was upset with him, even as a child he'd always tell me the truth about what he'd done.

"I never went to court. Brian asked me not to, so we never did. After the trials he always would call his Mum and tell her that things would be all right. He'd say, 'Is that a bit better, Mum?'

"And he'd call other times, fairly regularly—every month or so. When he felt happy and secure and strong he didn't. And sometimes he'd come to see us, thought nothing of time, he'd blow in at four in the morning. He's rung me at all hours of the night, from Hollywood, Vienna, Paris, Melbourne. . . . He called from Melbourne once and we talked for the best part of an hour. He was homesick. He'd been listening to Winston Churchill's funeral on the radio.

"I was very foolish once. I trusted that chauffeur, Brian Palastanga. He came here after having taken Brian to the Priory Nursing Home. I told him people had been rude to Brian's mother—he told Brian and Brian was terribly upset. He called up, all in tears. The whole experience at the Priory was very bad for Brian, a lot of psychological rubbish which made him feel a freak.

"The famine in Biafra affected Brian terribly. He felt he should go with Mick to Biafra to try to do something to help the situation. 'People say it won't do any good,' he told me, and probably it wouldn't have. But he had great feelings for the sufferings of others—animals, other people.

"Down at Cotchford Farm that night, Brian had gone to bed with his sleeping tablet, a 'sleeper' as he called them. He knew this Frank Thorogood, who'd been down there working on the place, and this nurse were up in his flat—a flat in the garage, away from the house. Brian had said that Frank could stay in the flat. Then when Frank brought the nurse out Brian was not happy with that. It was a small town, and Brian knew it might cause trouble. He got up from the bed and tried, so Anna told us later, to get Frank to leave, couldn't, then they had what was referred to as a 'party' which I interpret to mean that they had a few drinks together, and Brian was sleepy, he'd taken a sleeping pill after all. He got up, tried to get them to leave, and then after a few drinks decided to have a swim. With the pills and the drink and the warmth of the pool—Brian kept it at about ninety degrees or better—he simply went to sleep in the bath.

"I could never understand that statement the papers supposedly got from Anna about a 'party.' If one were planning to have a party, would he take sleeping pills first? Why? At the inquest, Anna never got to testify—she was so upset. I was horrified by people's knowing that a doctor had prescribed the drugs Brian had taken and their saying nothing at all about it. Nobody asked any questions. I wrote the police a letter telling them the drugs were prescribed, so they could investigate and have that cleared up at any rate, that the drugs were in fact prescribed for Brian by a doctor. I sent the letter on Friday, by Monday the doctor was out of the country. I have no idea what it means."

Jaws clenched, Mr. Jones peered at the cold fire, unable, though

Brian lay buried in Cheltenham Cemetery, to stop wanting to make things right. "I think," Mr. Jones said, "that when Brian was in the sixth form the school made a mistake. They wanted him to study science and technology. I said, 'The boy has an artistic temperament—shouldn't that be taken into account?' The school said, 'No, that's not practical. Science, technology's where it's at today.' Brian wasn't interested in that sort of thing at all. I remember buying him a hammer when he was just a little chap. He wasn't interested in it at all. Most boys love hammers—not Brian."

Asking about Linda Lawrence, I offended Mr. Jones. "You can't expect me to be proud of that side of my son's life. I felt that Brian never cared for Linda, that the only girl he ever really loved was Anita."

"But he—Julian—is your grandson," I said, fatuous and foolish, and until my own daughter, named after Billie Holiday, was safe with my parents, I would never know what the Joneses had been through. Once, yes, a family might withstand once, but Brian had done it and done it and done it. He was a menace. He was madness. He was out of control. "It was Brian's fanaticism that put the Rolling Stones on the map," Mr. Jones had said.

Had I done these things—everything Brian did, I did—had I done them on purpose to research the part? If so, how awful. And if they were accidents, how awful.

Soon it was late and I called a taxi. Mr. Jones, shaking my hand, said, "We've had no cards at Christmas, nothing from the boys. If you see them, remember me to them—tell them that if they want to write or call, I'd be happy to hear from them."

On the way to the hotel I told the driver, who noticed my accent, that I was a tourist, I'd heard about Cheltenham Spa.

"You're a bit late, you know. The waters spoiled about eight years ago."

Eight years—about the time Brian left Cheltenham.

The driver said he was thirty-two, a Jim Reeves fan. I told him that I wrote about music. "I liked the fifties rock," he said. "Jerry Lee Lewis, Buddy Holly. The Americans seem to have more feel for it. Now the Beatles and the Rolling Stones and all this nonsense—one of 'em's from here, actually."

"Really, who's that?"

"One who died. In fact he lived just five or six doors down from where you were tonight. His mother and father still do live there. We have 'em, fans like, who go to see his grave. We had two German girls, didn't speak a word of English, they came at Christmastime—a crazy sick business. Well, good night."

· · ·

Next morning I checked out of the hotel, leaving my bags at the desk, and took a taxi to the cemetery, on Priory Road. It had been cloudy, then raining, then the sun started to shine, bright and warm, and as we came to the cemetery it was starting to rain again, a few drops falling. We drove part way in, but a man trimming the flowers beside the motorpath stopped us, and I told the driver to wait. Down a path to the left, turn right, and there, on a corner south of the church, was Brian's grave, with its little metal marker. No stone yet; it takes at least a year for the ground to settle after being disturbed by gravediggers.

It looked so small, like Brian's old house, that once again I had the feeling this must be wrong—but it was right; this small man, never more than a boy really, from that small house, now in this small grave.

Standing before the grave, in the little cemetery on the edge of Cheltenham, you could see the Cotswolds in the distance, not too far away, not too tall, perfectly decent green English hills. The graveyard church was nearby, a small medieval building of dun and grey stones, decorated and protected by snarling, scaly gryphons, its spire reaching up into the grey sky. The rain was steady now, though lacy fir trees sheltered the graves. The number of Brian's grave is V11393, a single plot on a little turning of a lane in the cemetery, next to Albert "Bert" Trigg, beloved husband of Ethel.

Three sprays of flowers were on the grave, and a poem written in a schoolgirl's insecure tiny round hand on a white sheet of paper, folded and wrapped round with cellophane to protect it from the rain, but already fading with each day's condensation of dew.

> Only the living die
> By the hand of life
> Privileged, Branded
> Spoken to when alone
> By the voice of earth—
> Marked through multiplying nights
> Of sorrow and defeat, eaten by
> Victory.

And then, at the bottom of the page, in the same hand: "But it will never be the same without the boy we used to adore."

I replaced the note, standing over the grave, with the rain coming down all around, and looked up to where the sunlight was shining on the hills.

33

Who speaks of victory?
Survival is everything.
RAINER MARIA RILKE:
"Requiem for Count Wolf von Kalckreuth"

WHEN I WOKE it was bright Sunday morning in San Francisco, Pearl Harbor Day. I dressed and went down to Keith's suite. Charlie, Mick Taylor, Gram, Michelle, and Emmaretta were there. Mick had caught the nine o'clock plane to Geneva, taking with him the money the Stones had made in America. He and Jo flew together, Bill and Astrid taking the same plane to New York, then going to Sweden for a vacation.

In Keith's sitting room we had cocaine and Old Charter for breakfast, swapped addresses, and suddenly it was over. We went downstairs and took the last limousines of the engagement to the airport in the morning light. On the radio Buster Brown was singing, "Well, I want somebody to tell me what's wrong with me / I ain't in trouble, so much as misery."

At the airport we embraced and walked away. Gram and Michelle were going to Los Angeles. I was going to Memphis and then to London. Keith, Charlie, and Mick Taylor were going to England, Charlie to Shirley and Serafina, Keith to Anita and Marlon. Brian was staying in the churchyard near the hillside.

At Geneva the first customs official who saw Mick at once called the police. Mick and Jo were searched as they say in the body, but the only questionable items the police found were in Jo's luggage, herbal tablets from a Los Angeles naturopath, so they were allowed to enter the country. They opened a bank account, then took a Learjet with a German pilot to Nice, where Marsha Hunt joined them and they spent a day looking at houses in the south of France. The next day they flew to Gatwick with a French pilot. Over the Alps Mick and Jo discussed plans for the coming year. After Mick's drug trial there was the new single, "Brown Sugar," to finish for release in early February. Mick thought the Stones should spend February recording and arranging a tour to include all major European capitals and Moscow. The recording should go on through March and April. The tour should start with a May Day concert somewhere in the middle of Europe and end in Moscow in June. (The Stones knew people who knew people who knew a woman who'd been Khrushchev's mistress and was now Minister of Culture and was considered fairly hip and so there seemed a reasonable possibility.) There had also been an offer for Rolling Stones concerts in Japan. In July, Immigration willing, the Stones would appear at festivals in the United States. They would spend August on vacation, September and October recording, November on the road, and December was too far away even to think about. Not much of this happened, and none of it as anybody expected.

Keith and Charlie and Mick reached England early in the morning of a new day, tired, jet-lagged, still in Altamont shock, ready for anything, Moscow, Japan, the world, whatever it takes, but there were a crowd of newspaper reporters and photographers at Heathrow, and Anita was there with Marlon. The big story was that Anita might not be allowed to stay in the country unless she and Keith married to remove her alien status. "Keith, they're throwing me out of the country," she said, playing the scene to the hilt, holding aloft the baby she had feared would be Brian.

"Keith, what do you have to say about it? What are you gonna do about it?" the reporters asked, crowding around Keith as they had a thousand times before.

"We'll get it straightened out later," Keith said, heading for the exit, "but first I've got to get some rest."

C O D A

MUCH REMAINS untold, but at least you got to hear the band play. Following the tour that ended with Altamont, I went to live in England and stayed until, after a certain weekend at Redlands, I decided that if Keith and I kept dipping into the same bag, there would be no book and we would both be dead.

I spent time with the Stones on later tours, and they were always good, but there never seemed to be so much at stake. There was, though, just as much at stake, but it was harder to see. For one thing, we were never again in the desert, beyond all laws. At later Stones concerts I gave my seats to people like Sir John Gielgud and once to a candidate for vice president of the United States. Guitar players, producers, and women—except for Shirley Watts—came and went, terrible and wonderful things happened, in concert halls, outdoor arenas, nightclubs, jailhouses, courtrooms, bedrooms, as we persisted in our folly.

> Hump yo'se'f ter de load en fergit de distress,
>   En dem w'at stan's by ter scoff,
> Fer de harder de pullin', de longer de res',
>   En de bigger de feed in de troff.
> JOEL CHANDLER HARRIS:
> "Time Goes by Turns," *Uncle Remus,*
> *His Songs and His Sayings*

AFTERWORD: ONE HALF OF FOREVER

Writing this book seemed, at the time, like such a good idea. And it was, in the sense that the hunch I spoke of in Chapter 7 was justified, something was indeed about to happen, and I didn't miss it. But the book brought none of the benefits I'd hoped for, financial or otherwise, and hasn't to this day on the eve of the year 2000. I'd envisioned writing a book containing sex, drugs, rock and roll, violence, murder, mayhem, comedy, tragedy— a book that would make it possible for me to go back to my home country of South Georgia and write the stories I felt I was born to tell.

Well, *The True Adventures* contained all those elements, but it failed to prove commercial. I continue, perhaps stubbornly, to believe that this was through no fault of its own. The fault was partly mine, I suppose, for taking nearly fifteen years to write the book. By the time it appeared, in late 1984, the atmosphere in the United States was radically different from what it had been at the end of the sixties. Ronald Reagan was president, and the forces of greed had triumphed. Militarism, laissez-faire capitalism, indifference to the sufferings of the poor were upheld as positive virtues. The hippies and yippies had been replaced by yuppies, young urban professionals, and though some people put bumper stickers on their cars saying Die Yuppie Scum, they didn't die but reproduced. You can see their children at the nearest mall, wearing baggies and nose rings.

Why did it take so long to write the book? I had to wait for the statute of limitations to expire, I've said, but that wasn't the main reason. I had to become a different person from the narrator in order to tell the story. This was necessary because of the heartbreak, the disappointment, the chagrin, the regret, the remorse. We had all, Stones, fans, hangers-on, parasites, observers, been filled with optimism there in the autumn of 1969, optimism that the following years proved completely unjustified. In our private lives as in the public life of our time, we were disappointed, by others and by ourselves. This is I expect the experience of all generations, but we believed that we were different, that we were somehow chosen, or anointed, for success, for love and happiness. We were wrong.

My problem in writing the story was expressed in a Bob Dylan song: "if you can't bring some good news, don't bring any." What good news did I have to bring? Day and night for years I sought the answer to that question. The action in the book was not so disheartening as the action that followed and seemed to deny everything that had gone before. The significance of Altamont can be exaggerated but afterward things were different, and not just for the Rolling Stones. It was as if, in response to that event, the young men of the time got into their vans with their big ugly dogs and stringy-haired female companions and, reeking of patchouli, headed for the hills.

I did a version of this myself, going to an Arkansas Ozark cabin for the better part of a decade. Like my contemporaries, I tried to forget about saving the world. But I had this story, this burden to carry, and I couldn't let it go. I believed it was, in spite of everything, a story of lasting value, but telling it, in the face of clinical depression, drug addiction, domestic upheaval, nearly killed me. So torn was I that at times I begged for death and for years tempted death almost constantly, at last throwing myself off a North Georgia mountain waterfall onto the granite boulders below, smashing my face, breaking my back. It was an accident. I think.

The *I Ching* tells us that the superior man is like a gentle breeze that never stops blowing in the direction of his fate. (Desperate for guidance in those years, sometimes I consulted the *I Ching* so often that I would get the reading that says, in effect, Stop bothering me.) No matter how many times I lost my bearings, I came back to my story. At times, when hardly anything else did, it seemed to make a kind of sense.

The French film director François Truffaut once uttered a kind of zen koan by saying that films should not say anything and replying, when asked whether it was possible for a film to say nothing, that it was not. He meant, of course, that films should show, not tell. This is also the task of rendering in prose—to show, not tell. There also it is impossible. A number of readers complained about the epigraphs to the chapters, of which I remain rather fond. I intended the epigraphs to present or at least indicate a companion story, the exemplary tale of legendary jazz trumpeter Buddy Bolden, among others, to show that the Stones had precursors, they were part of a tradition. I also tried with the quotes from Brown, Freud, Lovell, Nietzsche, and so on to place this tradition within Western religious and intellectual history. No wonder people complained. But I felt, and still feel, the use of the quotes was justified. On the one hand the story was about a few people traveling around playing for kids to dance, as the noted philosopher Shirley Watts observed. On the other hand it seemed, if nothing else because of the numbers involved—millions of people cared about the Stones to some degree, at least enough to pay them money—that there was a larger meaning.

The war in Vietnam, the assassinations, the riots, the demonstrations, the drug war, were all part of the fabric of the period, the background against which the narcissism of rock and roll played out its (ultimately petty, perhaps) dramas. But the contrasts were so strong—characters like Brian Jones, Gram Parsons, and John Lennon, coexisting with Nixon and his cronies Spiro Agnew and John Mitchell. The bad guys were so easy to identify.
Then everything seemed to change around. The war, an obvious and ugly mistake, went on for more than another half decade. President Carter at least recognized the malaise of American life in the second half of the seventies, but could do little to change it. Who changed it was Reagan, giving the country what it craved, namely denial. *Death Valley Days* rerun as *Morning in America*. Meanwhile many of us kept on taking drugs to numb the pain of loss. We had lost loves, friends, goals, faith. That we survived is a miracle.

Part of the reason the book remains to this day little more than a rumor is the way it was published, as a sort of cross between a fan rag and serious cultural history. If it's well written, let people find out later, I advised, not being optimistic enough to believe that many readers, certainly the ones who had any interest in the Rolling Stones, purchased books based on the quality of the writing. I have read that in my happy native land three percent of the people buy hardback books. What minute part of that three percent reads for style? There were actually a couple of print ads for the book, its publisher making an enormous investment of faith. The ads appeared in the *Times* of New York and Los Angeles, newspapers read daily by all Stones fans, I don't think. Not even a classified in *Rolling Stone*. For the price of the ads in those two prestigious bicoastal papers, you could have bought at least a modest-size ad that someone who cared about rock and roll might have seen. But the book's editor, who'd been a high school sophomore when Jimi Hendrix died, had for whatever variety of reasons a disdainful attitude toward *Rolling Stone*'s founder, Jann Wenner, and proudly rejected the idea of buying ad space from him. This did the book little good with music fans.

My idea had been to have signings in convenience stores, 7/Elevens, airports. A concept greeted with a total lack of comprehension on the part of the publisher. The Stones were a mass phenomenon, so why not go where their fans were? Once again I was oversimplifying what smart folk had complicated for their own ends. Here's what I learned: the mass-market paperback racks are a quarter inch too small to accommodate trade paperbacks, even small ones. You are assigned a fate.

In England, where the business was not quite so perverse, the book was promoted ably and intelligently—by Susan Boyd, wife of novelist William Boyd—and appeared on the *London Times* bestseller list. From the beginning—even before it was finished—the book was a critical success. That is, people who write good books themselves, such as Mikal Gilmore, Harold Brodkey, and Robert Stone, read it and praised it highly, making me feel as if my time wasn't completely wasted.

I tried as consciously as I was able to write a book about famous people as if they were completely unknown to the reader, so that a hundred years later, say, someone could pick up the book and read it simply for the story, the working out of the characters' destinies. Naturally, I did not succeed entirely, but I have to admit I'm not ashamed of the attempt.

"This book tells you far more about Stanley Booth than you ever wanted to know," a reviewer in Chicago wrote. He was not alone in that opinion. In fact, the German translation left out an entire chapter, I'm sure because it wasn't about the Stones. But my objective was to write something more complex than a traditional biography.

The book possesses, as few have remarked, a highly deliberate form. Its three sections are preceded by scenes of Altamont, the location of the story's climax. That climax comes just after we topple (mentally) with Shirley Arnold into Brian Jones' open grave. From the outset I had the sense that telling Brian's story and the story of the 1969 tour in alternating sequence would make for a powerfully emotional ending. After Altamont we find ourselves back again where we were thirty chapters previous, in Chapter 2, Brian's parents' living room with Jinx the cat. The poem on Brian's grave was a gift to the writer from God, along with the rain and the sunlight shining on the hills. Nothing left to do after that but go home and rest.

The book was written in various media. First on the midget legal pads I'd jam into the front of my jeans before swinging up onto the stage to seek refuge behind Keith's amps. Later on regular legal pads used three or four at a time, rewriting passages on first one and then another, arriving finally at an acceptable version. The body of the book was created on a Royal upright typewriter using legal-size paper in much the same way that Kerouac, one of the book's principal style guides, used teletype paper. (The book's other stylistic heroes are Vladimir Nabokov, Evelyn Waugh, and—

most of all—Raymond Chandler. I tried to make every sentence one that could be spoken by Chandler's detective narrator Philip Marlowe.) Ultimately I typed the pages on an Adler, which I understand is the kind of typewriter Hitler had, a very good one.

The draft on legal pages was single-spaced, without capitalization or punctuation except for dashes here and there, as impenetrable as I could make it. There was a reason for my doing this. The book's original contract called for an advance of $51,000, a goodly sum in the sixties. On signing, I was paid $10,000. But soon afterward, a previous Stones book, a paperback, basically a clippings job by a British newspaper reporter, was republished with new photos and an updating through Altamont. The publisher for what became *The True Adventures* took umbrage, saying they expected an exclusive, and proposed cutting the advance to $26,000. By that time I'd spent the first ten and needed money to live on. My agent suggested I accept the lowered advance. In a lifetime he might do hundreds of books with the publisher, a few or maybe even only one with me. I, desperate, went along, handing over half the manuscript and receiving another eight grand—and that was pretty much the extent of my fiduciary compensation for telling this tale.

After the betrayal by my agent and some trouble with the law, I faded into the Boston Mountains of the Ozark Plateau. Back at my house in Memphis for a visit some years later, I received a letter from the agency informing me that the publisher had formally requested delivery of the manuscript, a preliminary to demanding return of the advance. My response was to go into the kitchen for a butcher knife, get a pillow from the bedroom, slice it open, take a handful of feathers, fold them into a sheet of typing paper, stuff it into an envelope, and send it to the agency. Then I went back to the hills, where I made the manuscript as close to unreadable as I could out of paranoia—maybe—because I would rather have died than let go of it before it, not I, was ready. I thought it might be the last thing I ever did, if I ever managed to do it, and I wanted it to be right, or as close as I could make it.

When at last the book was done, I wound up publishing it elsewhere and paying back the original would-be publisher. The advance, $20,000, enabled me to do that and pay my new agent—with nothing left over. But hey, I got to hear the band play.

A note on the title of the first hardback edition—I'd called the book *The True Adventures of the Rolling Stones* all the (considerable) time I'd been writing it. Some genius at the publisher's got the inspired notion of calling the first hardback edition *Dance with the Devil*. (Editors don't generally give a damn what writers think their books should be called, and in any case are without exception frustrated writers themselves, desperate to demonstrate what they sincerely believe to be their superior creativity. Young, unpublished writers should consider yourselves warned.)

Well, that edition came and, owing to the publisher's marketing skills, disappeared *muy pronto*. Because the book did quite well in the U.K. under its real title, the American paperback was called *The True Adventures*. The funny part is, a few years later the same publisher put out a novel by the actor Kirk Douglas, and it was called *Dance with the Devil*. Somebody at that publishing house really likes that title and may keep on calling books that until one is a big success.

In spite of everything, the book won the Deems Taylor award from the American Society of Composers, Authors, and Publishers. (Deems Taylor was the Second World War Leonard Bernstein. Leonard Bernstein was— never mind.) With that came other problems. A friend gave me a party at the St. Regis, attended by Harold Brodkey and a lot of other people, including Jerry Wexler, the only one with sufficient manners to call the next day and thank me for inviting him. "Jerry," I said, "I need to talk to you."

"Baby," he said, "Let's have brunch at the Friars on Saturday. They have all the latest lox and bagels."

When we met (the Friars was swell, great food, Buddy Hackett was there) I told Wexler about being booked on a global TV show that repeated four times over four days, seen by millions internationally. They'd called me around noon one recent Monday, told me they wanted me to do the show, and I'd asked them to call my publisher and set it up. "Please call me back," I said. After that the phone didn't ring for hours. Around five, I started calling the publisher's publicity office. No answer. At nearly seven, I called my editor's assistant, the one man in the building I knew I could trust. "Mark," I said, "would you please walk down the hall and get somebody in Publicity to pick up the phone?" He said he would.

"Hello?" a publicist answered, moments later.

I introduced myself. "Have you heard from the interview show?"

"Yes."

"Oh, good. Did you work everything out?"

"We told them there was a conflict in schedule."

"You told them what?"

"They want you to do the show, they'll do it whenever you want to."

"Call them back. Apologize, and say we'll do it whenever they want."

"You haven't done anything to apologize for."

"*I know that.*"

Writers can't get on television. That's the rule. At that point, 1985, only Truman Capote and, rarely, Norman Mailer and Gore Vidal could wangle airtime. William Styron, Philip Roth, James Jones, Kurt Vonnegut, everybody else could forget it. I had been offered a literally golden opportunity that my publisher's publicity people had simply tossed into the wastebasket. I told all this to Wexler.

"You're fighting," he said, "what I call the battle of the building."

"But Jerry," I said, full of my ignorant self as usual, "if these people promoted this book, it might make some money. Why wouldn't they want to make money?"

"What you're saying does not obviate the truth of my contention," Wexler went on placidly. "Somewhere in that building there is a man. And the man has not done *this*." He demonstrated with a mighty nod. "If that man should make that gesture, these people who you think are so incompetent would amaze you with their ability to take care of business."

That did it. I knew I was sunk for the length of that contract. Nothing to do but go home and write another book.

Fourteen years later the publisher let the book go out of print, making this new edition possible. In all that time they paid me not a dollar of royalties. I made no royalties on the paperback edition because the hardback had been published so unsuccessfully. The book sold many thousands of copies and generated a great deal of income, but not for me. Children, beware.

Five years after the book's initial publication, I did a *Playboy* magazine interview with Keith Richards. The Stones had, at that time, broken up. Keith and Mick were speaking only to disagree and were touring with different bands as solo acts. Keith had married the model Patti Hansen and had two little blond daughters, Theodora and Alexandra. He sat around throwing cigarettes up the air and catching them in his mouth. We'd both slowed down considerably. "It now costs Keith and me one one-hundredth of what it used to to get through an evening," I said in the introduction.

Around this time, I saw Keith and his band the X-pensive Winos on his birthday. Sarah Dash, the black singer who'd appeared on the Winos album, sang onstage with Keith. Later I asked the four-year-old Theodora, who'd seen her father perform that night for the first time, if she enjoyed the show.

"I wanna be a black girl," she said. Something inevitable about that, I thought.

The last time I heard the Stones, I went in like a civilian, with a ticket. Inside the entrance just past the ticket-taker a girl was passing out applications for Rolling Stones Visa and MasterCards with the tongue logo. I had a vision of NATO leasing the tongue to put on helicopters, tanks, bombs. In the sixties we believed in a myth—that music had the power to change people's lives. Today people believe in a myth—that music is just entertainment. The sixties myth was, need I say, much more interesting—but not so effective as a merchandising tool. Since it seems to have lost the final shred of moral or social significance, so that it is by no means any longer countercultural, rock and roll may turn out to be the Open Sesame to a nirvana of corporate sponsorship—catering recreational beverages, designer clothing, accessories, and weapons to centers of conflict for the greater glory of God and man.

The descendants of the Stones, those who consciously believe the Stones were part of a valuable tradition, such as the Black Crowes, operate in a cultural ambience where everything is déjà vu. It is as if their enterprise has been trapped within quote marks. I have seen the Black Crowes, joined by members of the Dirty Dozen, when they were better than the Stones have been in over twenty years, but what surrounds them has changed. Under the present dispensation, we're all good capitalists together. There are bands with social programs, from rappers to Kevorkian Death Cycle. But the entire business of music is so fragmented that protest is irrelevant, completely contained within a packaging and distribution system that changes nothing except the income of people in the system. Meanwhile children starve, governments kill prisoners, wars continue to rage, trillions of dollars are wasted on insane self-endangering weapons. Do I think music can stop these things? No. Do I think it should try? Perhaps not directly. But consider this line that I used to hear Furry Lewis sing: "My ole mistress promised me, when she died, she'd set me free; she lived so long till her head got bald, and God had to kill her with a white oak maul." Can't you hear the protest in that? Elvis Presley used to call "Hound Dog" ("You told me you was high-class—well, that was just a lie") his protest song. There is at the heart of this music a deep strain of mysterious insurrection, and the music dies without it.

Mark Twain said that if you wrote well enough your work would last "forever—and by forever I mean thirty years." *The True Adventures*, first published in the United States in 1984, has lasted slightly more than one half of forever. Whatever they are now, or may be in the future, the Rolling Stones, when they were young, put themselves in jeopardy many times because of who they were, what they were, how they lived, what they believed. During portions of those years, I was with them. Some people survived that era and some didn't. *The True Adventures* is the story of those days, when the world was younger, and meanings were, or seemed for a time to be, clearer. Almost forever ago.